a special gift

presented to:

from:

date:

The Women's Devotional Series

Among Friends
The Listening Heart
A Gift of Love
A Moment of Peace
Close to Home
From the Heart
This Quiet Place
In God's Garden
Fabric of Faith
Alone With God
Bouquets of Hope
Colors of Grace
Beautiful in God's Eyes
A Word From Home
Morning Praise
Heaven's Whisper
Grace Notes
Sanctuary
Love Out Loud
Renew
Blessed
Breathe
Altogether Lovely
Living His Love
Love You More
Notes of Joy
In His Presence
I Am Loved
Color My World With Love
Covered and Carried

NEW EVERY
morning

Tamyra Horst
EDITOR

Nampa, Idaho | www.pacificpress.com

Cover design: Erika Miike
Cover image: Dreamstime.com | Sara Winter
Interior design: Aaron Troia

The authors assume full responsibility for the accuracy of all facts and quotations as cited in this book.

You can obtain additional copies of this book by calling toll-free 1-800-765-6955 or by visiting AdventistBook Center.com.

Library of Congress Cataloging-in-Publication Data
Names: Horst, Tamyra, 1961– editor.
Title: New every morning / Tamyra Horst, editor.
Description: Nampa, Idaho : Pacific Press Publishing Association, [2022] |Summary: "A collection of devotional thoughts for women to encourage and strengthen faith"— Provided by publisher.
Identifiers: LCCN 2022002954 | ISBN 9780816368327 (paperback) | ISBN 9780816368334 (ebook)
Subjects: LCSH: Seventh-Day Adventist women—Prayers and devotions. | Devotional calendars—Seventh-Day Adventists.
Classification: LCC BV4844 .N475 2022 | DDC 242/.843—dc23/eng/20220217
LC record available at https://lccn.loc.gov/2022002954

May 2022

About the Editor

Tamyra Horst is passionate about encouraging, equipping, and challenging women to deepen their relationship with God and to serve Him with the gifts and passions He's given them. In addition to editing this devotional, she serves as the Women's Ministries director for both the Columbia Union and the Pennsylvania Conference and also serves as Communication director, Family Ministries director, and Prayer Ministries coordinator for the latter.

Dear Reader,

The North American Division (NAD) Women's Ministries team welcomes you to the 2023 edition of the women's devotional book. We are pleased and grateful that all proceeds from the sale of the book in the NAD will be used exclusively for scholarships in our territory.

We are praying that you will be blessed this year as you read devotionals from women like you—real women with real stories of God's love and providence in their lives. We look forward to hearing from you, and we hope that you will be inspired to submit your own stories to share with others.

DeeAnn Bragaw joined the Women's Ministries Department in July 2021. She previously served as the Women's Ministries director and Prayer Ministries coordinator for the Rocky Mountain Conference. She is passionate about showing the world the love of Jesus as beautifully expressed through His women!

Erica Jones joined the Women's Ministries Department in 2014. Her background in youth ministry has given her a heart for teens and their struggles. Combined with her media experience, it was easy for her to find her ministry niche in our department—teen girls and social media. Erica lives with her four-legged children: Boots the cat and Maisy the miniature shepherd mix.

Women Helping Women

There is an aspect of this book that is unique

None of the contributors have been paid—each has shared freely so that all profits may go to scholarships for women. Recipients of the Women's Ministries scholarships are talented women who are committed to serving the mission of the Seventh-day Adventist Church.

General Conference Women's Ministries scholarship fund in the North American Division

All profits from sales of the Women's Ministries devotional book in the North American Division support women's higher education in Seventh-day Adventist colleges and universities in the United States and Canada.

Purpose of the women's devotional book

Among Friends, published in 1992, was the first annual women's devotional book. Since then, the proceeds from these devotional books have funded scholarships for Adventist women seeking to obtain higher education. But as tuition costs have soared in North America and more women have applied for assistance, funding has not kept pace with the need. Many worthy women who apply must be turned down.

Recognizing the importance of educating women—to build stronger families, stronger communities, and a stronger church—each of us can help. Together we can change lives!

There are many ways to support our sisters

- Pray for women worldwide who are struggling to get an education.
- Tell others about the Women's Ministries scholarship program.
- Write for the women's devotional book (guidelines are available).
- Support women's education with a financial gift or a pledge.

To make a gift or receive materials, send us the following information:

Name ______________________________

Street ______________________________

City ______________________ State/Province ____________

Postal Code __________________ Country __________________

Email ______________________________

To contact us:

Women's Ministries Department
9705 Patuxent Woods Drive
Columbia, MD 21046

Phone: 443-391-7265
Email: ericajones@nadadventist.org
Website: https://www.nadwm.org/

The scholarship application and devotional book writers' guidelines are available at our website.

A New Song for a New Year

He has put a new song in my mouth—
Praise to our God;
Many will see it and fear,
And will trust in the LORD.
—Psalm 40:3, NKJV

I opened my eyes and literally jumped out of bed! The first day of school had finally come, and I couldn't wait! I pulled the new, cute dress my grandma had made over my head, singing a happy little made-up song. A whole new world was before me, with a new teacher, new friends, and new adventures! Of course, I was in first grade.

I didn't have quite the same reaction in seventh grade. When the alarm went off, I definitely didn't jump out of bed with a song. Now I'd have several teachers, the friend dynamics of preteen girls were challenging, and I was not at all confident about the clothes I wore that first day of junior high.

New. Sometimes we love it; sometimes we don't. Sometimes new is exciting; other times, frightening. Today, I'm so glad God's Word gives us a way to make this year one filled with hope and promise in the "new." No matter what has come before this day or what will happen in the days ahead, He invites us to sing! Psalm 98:1 says, "Sing to the LORD a *new* song, for He has done marvelous things!" (NKJV, emphasis added) Other versions invite us to sing to the Lord because He has done wonderful, amazing, miraculous, awesome, mighty things! Throughout the Psalms, we're invited to "sing to the LORD!"

But what if I'm struggling to find that song, and what if I can't sing? His Word has the solution: He'll *give* me the song! Psalm 40:3 says, "*He has put* a new song in my mouth." And in Ezekiel 36:26, He says, "*I will give you* a new heart and put a new spirit within you" (NKJV). Whatever the landscape of the year ahead, He's already there, sis! And the beautiful thing about singing a new song of praise to our God? We're told our song will create a song in the hearts of others! The rest of Psalm 40:3 tells us, "Now many will hear of the glorious things he did for me, and stand in awe before the Lord, and put their trust in him" (TLB). So He *gives* me the new song and then causes my song to bring others to Him. *Wow*! Who will hear your song today?

DeeAnn Bragaw

January 2

One Simple Thing

The one who calls you is faithful, and he will do it.
—1 Thessalonians 5:24, NIV

How long is your list of changes you need in your life? Mine used to be pretty long.

Every New Year's Day, I knew that the list was long, yet I hoped to achieve all the necessary changes. As the years rolled on, I noticed that nothing changed. Even the resolve to try changing something became less and less strong. Why bother?

Then, one day, I decided I would not write a list. I would not have a list at all.

Instead, I wrote a letter to God.

I told Him, "I am done trying to change, as I'm constantly failing. I give up."

I also gave Him permission to do whatever it took to change me into the person He wants me to be.

To show that I was really serious about that, I would change one small, simple thing in my life. I could do that. One small, simple thing. I could change that. The rest—the big list—God could deal with that.

My choice of one small, simple thing still required quite a bit of will and determination. It was going to be a lifelong change. I opted for something I had heard was very beneficial for a person's health. It boosts the work of white blood cells, invigorates, and helps you get out of the shower into a cold bathroom.

I was going to finish my warm showers with cold water.

I remember that first time. *Ooo! Ayyy! Brrr! Grrr!*

Well, nothing has changed since that first time. Cold water after my warm shower still doesn't feel nice. But I still do it—for almost thirty years now.

I cannot begin to tell you how many things in my life changed after that. I am amazed to see what God performed in my life. I opened the door and kept it open by continuing to do this one small, simple change in my life, and God did the rest.

I invite you to do the same. No, not the cold shower! But find one small, simple thing you can change in your life and continue doing it daily.

Let God do the rest!

Danijela Schubert

"What Would Jesus Do?"

Be kind and compassionate to one another, forgiving each other, just as God also forgave you in Christ.
—Ephesians 4:32, CSB

My friends and I had gone out to dinner to celebrate the New Year. We were not having a good experience with the waitress, but we chose to stay anyway. It was already getting late, and not many restaurants were open; it would be hard to find a table anywhere else. Besides, we had made a reservation, and it was raining and cold.

Our waitress was very rude. She informed us that we needed to order our food because the restaurant would be closing at ten o'clock. It was already nine o'clock. We quickly placed our order and asked for hot tea.

She forgot to give us utensils when she brought the tea, so we asked for spoons. She seemed very annoyed with this request. Twenty minutes later, she returned with one spoon, placed it very hard on the table, and walked away. My friends and I couldn't understand why she was so rude. Finally, the floor manager changed our waitress. I explained that all we wanted was spoons for our tea.

When she reappeared at the end of our meal, the young lady seemed to have a different attitude. She gave us our check. Since I was paying for the meal, my guests wanted to leave a tip. I objected—she didn't deserve it after the way she treated us. "No way!" I exclaimed.

Moments later, I heard a small voice in my subconscious mind asking, "What would Jesus do?" The words seemed so foreign to me. My guests insisted that they pick up the tip, and I finally agreed to let them. But there was a problem. I was paying for the check with my credit card, and they would need to put the tip on theirs. As we were discussing this, the waitress reappeared. When we asked her how to handle this procedure since the tip would be coming from another credit card, she gave us a condemning look. I then agreed to add the tip to my credit card and not cause any extra work for her.

I am reminded of our Lord and Savior as we stand before Him. We don't deserve all that His mercy and grace give us, yet He died that we might live. May we forever be so reminded when dealing with others.

Avis Floyd Jackson

January 4

Loving God

"And you shall love the Lord your God with all your heart, with all your soul, with all your mind, and with all your strength."
—Mark 12:30, NKJV

Jesus spoke the words recorded in Mark 12:30 to the scribe who had asked Him which was the first commandment. Jesus' response is an expanded version of Moses' words found in Deuteronomy 6:5. In expressing those words, Jesus gave a holistic approach to religion. To love God with the whole heart focuses on the emotional aspect of our lives. We feel more deeply with our hearts because our emotional expressions are rooted there. The soul addresses the spiritual dimension. While we emote through our hearts, we experience that spiritual transformation through our souls. The mind accommodates the intellectual facet of our lives. We may love with our hearts, but we need the involvement of the other parts of our lives to really love fully. Finally, strength is the physical aspect. It reminds us that we are God's creation. When we love God as Jesus requests, with all our heart, our soul, our mind, and our strength, we will be fully surrendered to Him. Fully surrendering our lives to God means that we love Him so much—emotionally, spiritually, intellectually, and physically—that we are willing to give Him everything, our all. When we love Jesus with our whole being, He will teach us how to truly love, and we will love others as we love ourselves.

The first year that I did not make any New Year's resolutions was 2021. It wasn't because I had grown cynical or discouraged by my failure to follow through with past resolutions. It was simply because I did not need New Year's resolutions to improve my life or my relationships. During my Bible study in 2020, I revisited those words of Jesus, and they made a very strong impression on me. I also realized that if I want a closer relationship with my Savior, I need to surrender all to Him, and what better way to do so than to love Him with my whole heart, soul, mind, and strength?

I, therefore, resolved in the middle of 2020 that I would love God holistically. My daily prayer, as a result, is to love God with my whole heart, my soul, my mind, and my strength. It's a work in progress, and as the Holy Spirit guides me, I realize that I not only love the Lord, my God, but I love my neighbor as well.

Valerie Knowles Combie

Heal the Wounds

Because the Sovereign LORD helps me,
I will not be disgraced.
Therefore have I set my face like flint,
and I know I will not be put to shame.

Let the one . . . ,
who has no light,
trust in the name of the LORD
and rely on their God.
—Isaiah 50:7, 10, NIV

Through the years, maybe, just maybe, you have come to be like me. A happy person—a person who loves God and who trusts in His providence, power, and provision. However, at the same time, you have become a person who has scars that linger in the background. Wounds from people in our lives or from situations. These wounds effectively remind us that there is still room for growth and pain that needs to be lifted from our hearts.

Some fears do not let you be completely free to trust God in a perfect way, fears that plant seeds of doubt. My verse for 2020 was Isaiah 61:1, 2, specifically where it says, "He has sent me to bind up the brokenhearted" (NIV).

By March 2020, a lot had happened in my country. After a heated political atmosphere and regional elections, we were quarantined by COVID-19. But even in the middle of all of this and without knowing what would happen tomorrow or even in the rest of the year, I knew that no matter what, God is with us, and He will use every situation to heal our wounds and free us of fear and doubt—if we let Him work in us.

Our hearts need to be bandaged and cared for in a way that only God can work out. We each need personalized attention and care because each person has their own set of needs and each person feels pain differently. Our emotions and bodies need rest from the chaos of living and daily routine. Our families need time to slow down. As women, we need someone to take care of us because we are too busy taking care of everyone else.

Yes, my sisters, 2023 is also a year to let God heal us—be restored and complete in Him. God wants us to be happy, and only He can give us perfect happiness. Let us ask Him to heal our wounds today.

Yvita Antonette Villalona Bacchus

January 6

God Loves Me!

And so we know and rely on the love God has for us.
God is love. Whoever lives in love lives in God, and God in them.
—1 John 4:16, NIV

I sat at a kidney-shaped table with four third-grade girls, playing multiplication bingo. I would draw a card and call out the multiplication fact, and they would put a plastic marker on the answer on their cards, trying to get five in a row. One of the girls proclaimed exactly how she would win the game and which column contained the winning combination. I called a few more math facts, but things just weren't going as this young lady predicted. Another math fact, and the lower lip came out as she moaned, "God hates me!"

That announcement surprised me. I pondered how I might respond. I called out another math fact, and again this child repeated the mournful words, "God hates me!"

"I doubt that!" I said.

One of the other girls chimed in, "I don't really think that God hates anybody." I was encouraged that she perceived God as loving.

I continued calling math facts, and with the next one, my student placed her marker on a spot that made her happy. Now she called out, "No, He doesn't!" and raising her hand to heaven, she exclaimed, "Thank You, God!"

Even though this girl's fickle pronouncements amused me, I was also aware that I had seen a truth played out before my eyes. When life is difficult, how often are we tempted to blame God or fear He doesn't love us? And our circumstances must sometimes seem as trivial to God as this child's situation seemed to me.

Recently, I sat with a woman who had more grief than it seemed possible to bear. Her pain was real, but she laughed as I told her this story. I reminded her that it is easy to question God's love for us in times of extreme grief and pain. But in those times, it is necessary to immerse ourselves in reminders of His loving character: Scripture passages, prayer, time in nature, and being with supportive Christian friends.

Today, dear sister, take a few minutes to remind yourself how much God loves you. May you be constantly aware of that great love, and may it fill your heart.

Marsha Hammond-Brummel

January 7

Loving Forgiveness

Let us therefore come boldly unto the throne of grace, that we may obtain mercy, and find grace to help in time of need.
—Hebrews 4:16, KJV

We were deep in conversation as Steve shined his motorcycle. Our granddaughter, Charlotte, and her mama came into the garage. This little one carries the energy of her four years. She chattered and literally ran circles around the motorcycle and the adults. Then she got thirsty. Knowing that her pop-pop keeps child-sized water bottles in his garage fridge for just such a need, she opened the door and helped herself. I helped her open the cap, and she drank deeply. Then she talked some more, cradling the bottle in the crook of her arm.

Suddenly, the water bottle slipped, landing on its side on the floor. She stared incredulously as the liquid darkened the concrete. I snatched it up and handed it back to her. Her eyes nervously searched our faces. "It's OK," I said, "no one is mad at you." She relaxed. Her mother and I smiled.

Then she realized that Steve had not reacted to her mishap at all. "I have to tell Pop-pop," she whispered. Walking to where he wiped his bike, she pointed to the puddle. "Look, Pop-pop, I did that."

He smiled at her and said, "It will dry."

"Yes," she replied and smiled back.

How beautiful! What if when we make a mistake, we react like Charlotte? She knew that her mom and I were not upset, but she had to check with the one in charge of the garage. She pointed out her spill without fear or excuse. She could accept responsibility because of confidence in her pop-pop to love and forgive her anyway.

This is the confidence we have in our Savior. It's inevitable; we mess up. We try to make things right with those around us, to seek forgiveness. Ultimately, we go to the One in charge, God Himself, and confess to what we have done: "I did that."

Herein is the grace of the Lord. He is not waiting to scold and punish. He has forgiven us. He reassures us that all is well between us. We have not lost our place in His heart, not even for a moment. Confession simply gives us the peace of mind to stay near to Him.

Ann Trout

January 8

When I Remind Myself

But Christ has shown me that what I once thought was valuable is worthless. Nothing is as wonderful as knowing Christ Jesus my Lord. I have given up everything else and count it all as garbage. All I want is Christ and to know that I belong to him. I could not make myself acceptable to God by obeying the Law of Moses. God accepted me simply because of my faith in Christ. All I want is to know Christ and the power that raised him to life. I want to suffer and die as he did, so that somehow I also may be raised to life.
—Philippians 3:7–11, CEV

I wish I could forgive the way that God forgives. Instead, I rehash my faults and flaws over and over again. It's sometimes easier for me to forgive others than to forgive myself. I get to a point when I just say, "Really? Are we here again?" I long to be more like Jesus. He chooses to let go . . . never look back. He makes the choice *not* to go there again (revisit the sin that I have repented for), and I trust that He is all He says that He is. Those sins that I have asked God forgiveness for have been cast into the deepest depths of the sea. Gone. Wiped clean.

We are told that Satan is the "accuser of the brethren," meaning that Satan will try to convince us that God could never love us. We need to recognize those thoughts as lies and instead believe what God says. What God says about us in His Word (the Bible) is truer than anything we could think or feel. Jesus said that those who build their lives on His Word are those whose lives stand strong and secure, able to weather anything in life (see Matthew 7:24–27).

One of my favorite stories is when Jesus is in the boat with the disciples while the storm is raging all around them. When I'm feeling doubt, that's the storm raging. Praise God that He *never* leaves my side. He is there when I doubt. He holds me even closer and desires to reveal Himself to me more and more.

If you've asked God to forgive you and to come into your life—you are forgiven! His Word says so. *He* says so. Thank Him for His forgiveness and begin to rejoice in your secure relationship with Him. He can change areas of your life that don't line up with His desire for you. First Corinthians 1:9 says, "God is faithful, through whom you were called into fellowship with His Son, Jesus Christ our Lord" (NASB).

Joey Norwood Tolbert

For Your Sake

"For if you forgive other people when they sin against you, your heavenly Father will also forgive you."
—Matthew 6:14, NIV

There's not a whole lot I remember about my childhood, but one lesson has remained with me for life. It happened when I was about eleven or twelve years old. I was always quite shy and didn't make friends readily at school. So it was quite a surprise when I was invited to the birthday party of one of my classmates. Since she lived only a few blocks from my home, my older brother walked with me to my classmate's house. I was so thrilled to be escorted by my older brother that I spent the entire time engrossed in our conversation.

I don't recall much about the party, but I do remember that when I was ready to leave, I couldn't recall which direction to turn when I reached the sidewalk. So I asked one of the girls at the party. She told me to turn left. I headed off. After turning left, I walked a short distance. But something didn't feel right. I turned and headed in the opposite direction. As I passed the sidewalk leading up to the house where the classmate lived, I noticed that two girls were standing in the doorway watching me. One of them had told me to turn left. The girls were pointing and laughing. Then I realized that the misdirection wasn't accidental but intentional.

My first reaction was to feel hurt that they would play that kind of trick on me. As I continued walking, I heard a soft voice say, "Forgive them. Not for their sake but for yours."

I chose to forgive them.

Over the decades since that incident, there have been multiple times when someone has done or said something that negatively impacted my life. Each time, I would hear that same soft voice, "Forgive them. Not for their sake but for yours." Always, I choose forgiveness.

Forgiveness isn't always easy. Forgiveness doesn't negate or excuse what the other person did. But forgiveness of others is critical in our relationship with Christ. Many times, in my experience, what was intended for harm, God turned around and made into something good (Genesis 50:20). No matter what happens, forgiveness is always the right choice. I am glad I listened to that still, small voice all those years ago. And I pray each one of us will listen to it today and every day.

Sharon Clark

January 10

Be More Mature

Brothers, do not be children in your thinking.
Be infants in evil, but in your thinking be mature.
—1 Corinthians 14:20, ESV

My nine-year-old granddaughter and I were having one of our frequent conversations. On that particular day, she wanted to talk about maturity—her maturity. Now that she was nine, she shared with me, she had new decisions to make. New choices about the different colors she should wear, colors in her room, and even colors for her crafts. She emphasized that there are some things that she would normally do as a younger girl that she would not do anymore.

Needless to say, I enjoyed our time together and mused at her intelligence and maturity. Was it not a few days ago I lovingly cradled this precious bundle of joy in my arms? Now I am amazed by her maturity and the fluency of her thoughts.

Klarissa was thinking about petty things—girlish things that she wanted to let go of simply because she was older. But there are spiritual lessons to learn from her experience.

When you were a spiritual babe, you were expected to behave like a babe, but now you are mature. You have put away childish behaviors. What does it mean to be a more mature person when a difficult decision has to be made? How does a more mature person behave in a hostile situation where forgiveness is the only way forward?

Whatever it is today that requires a more mature person, I invite you to pause and ask God to help you consider the areas where you need to mature and change your behaviors. Is it time to have the conversations and discuss the difficult matters you have been hiding from? Is it now time to be the mature person and reach out to that individual you have been at odds with for so long? Is it time to tackle the difficult decisions about how to care for your older parents—where it would be best for them to live, where they will receive the best care, and what you are just not able to handle right now?

Whatever the situation, I pray that today you would be the more mature person, recognizing that the earlier immature actions will not serve you to move forward. I pray a blessing on your decision, and I pray that the mature action you take today will benefit others, and you will be able to glorify God today and always.

Gloria Barnes-Gregory

It Is Paid

For by grace you have been saved through faith. And this is not your own doing; it is the gift of God, not a result of works, so that no one may boast.
—Ephesians 2:8, 9, ESV

The restaurant was packed, but we decided to stay despite the lack of privacy between tables. This was an opportunity for our son and his wife to have a good meal and a relaxing time while we tried to keep the kids entertained. My husband and I did our best—singing, talking, telling stories, playing—never aware that someone watched from a distant table. As we prepared to pay the bill, the waitress told us the meal was already paid for.

"What?" I replied in astonishment. Then she said with a smile that the man who had just left paid our entire check.

I was speechless! I ran outside, thinking that we did not deserve this unexpected gift. I needed to see this generous man. He saw me coming and smiled. I said, "Thank you for your amazing kindness to us. We don't deserve it."

With a bigger smile, he replied, "You are such wonderful grandparents!"

Have you ever lived in a culture or family where you had to do something to deserve something? Or have you ever felt that your best was never enough or that nobody sees what you do? This distorted and crooked feeling often leads us to devalue ourselves in God's eyes. It also creates in our minds a wrong picture of God—who He is, how He sees us as His children.

Talking to women in many parts of the world, I have found so much grief, guilt, and sorrow because of this wrong thinking. Praise God—He has a different message for you and me today. He did not say, "Do more; this is not enough; you do not deserve anything." No. Scripture says the Lord "knows how we are formed," and He remembers that we are made of dust (Psalm 103:14, NIV). To Him, we are precious "dust."

As you start the day, do not listen when the enemy says you don't deserve anything. Instead, listen to what Jesus says. He made you worthy because salvation is a gift, not a result of your works. Your redemption is paid.

Dear Jesus, although my mind cannot fully understand all that You went through to pay for my salvation, I thank You for paying the price—the full price—to set me free! Amen.

Raquel Queiroz da Costa Arrais

January 12

God's Timing, Not Ours!

Many are the plans in the mind of a man,
but it is the purpose of the LORD that will stand.
—Proverbs 19:21, ESV

Two weeks following the 2010 devastating earthquake that shook the island of Haiti, my colleagues and I were packing medical supplies and basic personal care items that we were taking with us to the island. We were going as volunteer nurses for two weeks. As we packed, we realized that we wouldn't be able to take all the boxes.

There was one box that I wanted to take along, a big box of Pedialyte. As I struggled to tape the box, my sisters kept telling me to leave it behind. With determination, I told them I would not. All the way to Haiti, I struggled with that box of Pedialyte. At one point, I wished I had left it, but by the grace of God, the box made it to Haiti.

One day, after working in the clinic for twelve long hours, we were ready for our tents and something to eat. As we entered the hospital compound, Lil suggested we go by the Mother-Baby Unit. As we entered the building, it was eerily quiet; you could hear a pin drop. No staff, doctors, or nurses were in attendance. As we walked around and looked at the babies, we realized they were motionless and were severely dehydrated. My colleagues excitedly said, "Jannett, the Pedialyte!" We got the box of Pedialyte, found some syringes, and started feeding the babies. Doctors and nurses eventually took over the care of the babies, and they slowly recovered.

As we left the building, no one spoke! We turned our hearts to God, thanking Him for how He led us that evening. God knew the Pedialyte would be needed, orchestrated us to take it with us, and then directed us to the Mother-Baby Unit!

My sisters, God has a plan for our lives. For His divine will to be carried out, we must walk in His footsteps. Whatever challenges you face today, you are not alone—God is with you and will always be with you.

Jesus, my Savior, thank You for Your love and Your leading in our lives. Help us to always be obedient to the prompting of the Holy Spirit. Keep our hearts pure, make us worthy of Your unconditional love. We love You, Jesus!

Jannett Maurine Myrie

A Faithful Provider

"For every beast of the forest is Mine,
And the cattle on a thousand hills.

"For the world is Mine, and all its fullness."
—Psalm 50:10, 12, NKJV

There have been times in my life when I was, or thought I was, in dire straits and complained to the Lord that if He owned the cattle on a thousand hills, couldn't He please sell off a few head and help me out! But do you know what? I have never been without what I needed, and more often than not, I've had much more.*

In 1973, after my husband lost his job on a ranch north of Denver, we rolled back into town, broke and homeless. A blizzard was in full swing. Not wanting to spend another night in the back of a '56 Chevy station wagon in subfreezing temperatures, we found a small studio apartment for US$100 a month. With some hesitation, I wrote a check for that amount, knowing there was nothing in the bank to cover it. But we would be gone early the next morning before the apartment owner would deposit the check. I didn't know what else to do. Would God provide? How would we cover the check? At least we would have one night in a warm place.

That evening, I brought a stack of clothes into the room for some reason, but I don't know why I did. The next morning, while gathering up things to leave, I put my hand into the pocket of a pair of jeans in the stack and felt a piece of paper. I pulled it out and, much to my surprise, saw I was holding a US$100 bill! I have no idea how it got into that pocket. I don't remember putting it there, but I promptly went and deposited it in the bank, giving us a whole month to regroup and plan our next move. Despite my imperfect plan to provide for our needs, God, in His perfect love, showed me He had a much better plan. He always does.

Many of you are experiencing uncertain times right now, maybe through no fault of your own. If you are, I want to challenge you to surrender any problem that seems bigger than yourself—and your ability to manage it—to the Lord. He has a thousand ways to get you through. He wants to be your Provider. He wants to reveal His love and care for you. And He wants a relationship with you because you are His beloved child.

Sylvia Sioux Stark

* This devotional was previously published on the author's Facebook page on April 30, 2020.

January 14

Simple Faith

Then you will call upon Me and go and pray to Me, and I will listen to you.
—Jeremiah 29:12, NKJV

During my sermon prep this week, I was reminded of a special faith-building experience I had with my son. It happened shortly after we were baptized . . . many years ago!

It was a beautiful day, so my husband and I decided it was time to fly our kite! It was an expensive one, a wedding gift, and we hadn't flown it much for fear it would be lost or damaged! But our five-year-old son, Matthew, was persistent in his desire to fly this kite. It was fun to see the joy on his face as we took it off the wall. It was about as tall as he was and certainly wider! Even so, we gathered the string and the tail and headed out to our new subdivision that was surrounded by several acres of woods.

My husband was very patient while teaching Matthew how to cast the kite into the air properly and let out the string. There was a good breeze, so the kite took off easily! We were all very joyful watching that kite soar into the blue sky! But then, the big question came: "Daddy, can I fly the kite?"

Dave did all the right things in teaching, and he was standing right there, so he invested great faith in Matthew and let him have the spool. The wind was strong, and the kite was high, and the gust surprised everyone! There went our big, beautiful, expensive kite right over all those trees! *Lost, lost for good!* we thought.

Our little guy came to me and said, "Mommy, we need to pray to Jesus!"

"You're right, buddy; we do!" I responded, but inside I thought, *Oh Jesus, please answer this boy's prayer!* We prayed. Then Matthew and his dad trudged into the woods.

They walked in a straight line to where they assumed the kite would be hanging in some tree. Then, I saw them heading back with big smiles and the kite! I shouted, "No way! Already?"

Jesus answered that little boy's prayer! Jesus says you only need a mustard seed of faith—and that is not much! Best yet, our faith will get stronger if it's practiced day after day in the ordinary circumstances of life—just like our little boy praying that Jesus would help him find his kite!

Cheri Gatton

Nothing Is Too Small for God

Take delight in the LORD,
and he will give you the desires of your heart.
—Psalm 37:4, NIV

During the annual meetings at the office where I work, two very special books were distributed to committee members. One was given on a Friday, and another one on Saturday. These two books meant a lot to me, and I was very eager to get a copy of each. I asked one of our administrative assistants if there were any extra copies left over, and she informed me that there were none.

I prayed about this matter, and I had the idea to go to the auditorium where they were having the meetings to see whether anyone might have left their copy at the material distribution center. It was the last day of the meetings. I went to the auditorium and asked the person at the distribution center to save me a copy of the books if they found copies left behind anywhere in the auditorium.

After I talked to the person, I went and sat in the center of the last row to listen to some of the presentations. After I sat down, I noticed right in front of me on the floor was a pile of handout materials that someone had left. No one was sitting in front of me. They appeared to be left behind and unwanted. A thought came to me to check the pile, and I did. And guess what! Both the books that I was longing to have were in the pile! I just couldn't believe it since these two books were distributed four days earlier. What were the odds of my finding them together right in front of me after all these days? I was so excited that I could not even believe my eyes! I immediately thanked God for hearing my simple prayer and giving me the two books that I desired to have! After the meetings were over, two ladies went through the auditorium and picked up all the materials that were left behind and found not a single copy of either of these books.

My God placed these two books right in front of me in answer to my prayer! We serve and worship an awesome God, and yes, there's nothing that our Almighty God cannot do, and He will do the same for you!

Stella Thomas

January 16

Miracle in Cuba

Now faith is confidence in what we hope for and assurance about what we do not see.
—Hebrews 11:1, NIV

Myrna Clark was born in a small town in Cuba. Her father was a businessman, and they lived comfortably for her first fifteen years. Then in 1955, Fidel Castro started a revolution, promising to overtake the dictator and start a democracy. In December, the war started. Hearing and feeling bombs dropping near their house, they prayed day and night for their safety.

In 1959, a new government took over. Life was back to normal, or so they thought. A year later, a Communist government was established. Life changed drastically. The first change involved how much land a person could own. All Mr. Clark's businesses were taken from him. A person could own five acres maximum, and the rest belonged to the government.

The Christian high school Myrna attended owned many acres of farmland. The government confiscated half of the acreage. The corn on the school's side of the fence grew tall and beautiful. The government's corn was straggly looking. God blessed the school with a large harvest, but the government's yield was small. During the following year's drought, people wondered whether they would lose all the vegetables needed for survival. The principal called a special chapel service, where he explained to the students the urgent need for rain. "If it doesn't rain, we will lose all our crops. We won't have food to feed you, and the school will have to close. We must trust God, but we must also do our part." Then he explained his plan. "We will have an all-night session of prayer, asking God to send the rain we so badly need. You will go back to your dorms, and we will pray. Those in the first room will pray. When they are finished, they will knock on the door of the next room, and those students will pray. We will pray until morning." And so they did.

The next morning, everyone looked anxiously at the sky. By afternoon, clouds had gathered, and rain poured down! But it only rained on the school's farm. Rain fell all summer—but only on the school's farm. Many people drove by the school that year to see the miracle God was working for the school. The harvest was so plentiful that it fed the students and there was enough left over to sell. God will work mightily for us when we trust in Him with our needs.

Dalores Broome Winget

Burning Bed

I will extol the Lord *at all times;*
his praise will always be on my lips.
—Psalm 34:1, NIV

It had been a cold day (for Alabama), and now it was a crispy, cold night as I prepared to go to bed. It was Friday night, and I felt especially tired from a week of being the chauffeur, chef, and maid while still working my full-time job teaching. Since it was so chilly, I turned on the electric blanket on my side of the bed. As I performed my nightly rituals, my mind reviewed the week, thought about Sabbath plans, and looked forward to climbing into a bed that would be toasty warm. However, my thoughts were interrupted by the smell of something burning. This odor confused me because the fireplace was not on.

I looked around the room, checked the electric blanket, and did not see any smoke or source for the smell. I reasoned it must be a leftover smell from the fireplace and climbed gratefully into my toasty warm bed. My husband joined me just as I climbed into bed. I mentioned the smell, and he, too, noted it. He looked all over the blanket, the bed, and the room but couldn't find a source for the smell. We chatted briefly, studied our Sabbath School lesson, prayed, and were soon fast asleep.

Suddenly, around two o'clock in the morning, my husband cried, "Fire! Fire!"

He quickly jumped out of bed. I groggily woke up and realized that, indeed, the foot of our bed was on fire. The flames were shooting up. We worked together to extinguish the fire quickly. The process of extinguishing the flames took less than five minutes. However, now we were wide awake. The electric blanket had initiated the fire. The earlier smell of something burning must have been a warning of the fire to come. Why did my husband wake up? What had caused his sleep to be disturbed? We talked about the dire consequences of not waking up—our children were upstairs sleeping blithely. What would have happened to them? Truly, "the angel of the Lord encamps around those who fear him, and he delivers them" (Psalm 34:7, NIV).

Although I am now a grandmother, I still praise God for His protective care for my family many years ago.

Edith C. Fraser

January 18

Count Your Blessings

I will not leave you comfortless: I will come to you.
—John 14:18, KJV

It was one of those terrible days in my college life that I didn't want to face. I was not happy at all. I hadn't fared well in my exams. I was sick and in pain as a result of kidney stones. My friends had let me down, and nothing was working quite right in my life. I started to grumble and ask God why He had created me with so many burdens to bear. Reluctantly, I got dressed to go to my clinical posting at a geriatric home.

As I entered the place, I could see the weary and worn-out faces of older adults who looked very dejected. But an older man sitting all alone and blissfully playing the flute caught my attention. I was attracted to the music and went over and sat near him. He was playing the song "Count Your Blessings," which encourages you to list your blessings. I started a casual conversation with him and was shocked to learn that he was blind. He told me that his children had rejected him. His wife had died, and he was alone. That was the reason he was there. Despite his trials, he bore a calm manner and a loving nature.

Thoughts flashed like lightning into my mind. If a blind older man who has lost his only wife, has been rejected by his children, and lives in a geriatric home has many reasons to count his blessings and thank the Lord, what do I have to complain about in life? That very moment, I changed my perspective about my life and started to thank God for His unmerited favor. I told God I was sorry for my whining and grumbling. "If we educated our souls to have more faith, more love, greater patience, a more perfect trust in our heavenly Father, we would have more peace and happiness as we pass through the conflicts of this life. The Lord is not pleased to have us fret and worry ourselves out of the arms of Jesus. He is the only source of every grace, the fulfilment of every promise, the realization of every blessing. . . . Our pilgrimage would indeed be lonely were it not for Jesus. [. . .] Let us cherish His words, believe His promises, repeat them by day and meditate upon them in the night season, and be happy."*

Father, open my eyes that I may see Your blessings, and show me how to be *a blessing to others today. Thank You! In Jesus' name, amen.*

Esther Synthia Murali

* Ellen G. White, *Our High Calling* (Washington, DC: Review and Herald®, 1961), 120. The bracketed ellipsis indicates this writer's omission; the unbracketed appears in the source.

January 19

Chasing the Sun

And ye shall seek me, and find me, when ye shall search for me with all your heart.
—Jeremiah 29:13, KJV

The workers had finished their tasks for the day. Renovations on my bathrooms were coming along to my satisfaction. I stepped outside to say goodbye and thank the men for the work completed thus far.

As they drove out of my driveway, I raised my head, and there, right before me, was a breathtaking sunset. I grabbed my smartphone and began clicking away. Wanting to get the right angle and position, I ran from the driveway to the left side of the lawn and then ran inside to the bedroom facing the road to get a higher and better view. Still not satisfied, I raced to the attic and got there just as the ball of fire slid gently beneath the branches of some trees. When I reviewed my captures, I was ecstatic that there were four spectacular shots.

The next morning, while on my daily walk, I reflected on my impromptu photoshoot the previous evening. Without any deliberation, I had sought optimal spots to get a specific view of the sun and thought nothing about running from place to place to facilitate getting great shots. There were no thoughts of my aching back or painful joints. No excuses for not pursuing what it took to get the best shots. My determined intent on capturing a spectacular sunset had propelled me in spite of everything else.

In my pondering, my Father spoke to me. "You see how you chased the sun? That's how I want you to pursue the Son! He can be everything to you, do everything for you, and give you everything you need."

Immediately, the trajectory of my thoughts changed. How many times had I rushed off for the day with just a quick prayer, neglecting precious time with my Savior? How often had I attended a business or work event rather than a prayer meeting? How frequently had I rushed past someone in need because I would be late for my appointment if I stopped to help?

As I agonized over my failures, a still, small voice reminded me that every day, I have an opportunity to edit my path with God's grace, that a better life is always waiting for me and for everyone who accepts the call and pursues the Son.

Florence E. Callender

January 20

Blessings of Blackouts

And you will seek Me and find Me, when you search for Me with all your heart.
—Jeremiah 29:13, NKJV

Eighteen-hour load shedding with no electricity from 4:00 A.M. to 11:00 P.M. every day. That was my new reality. The drought's effect on the dam producing most of the nation's electricity triggered a critical shortage, prompting the electricity provider to effect rolling blackouts.

This was not fun, but as days rolled by, I realized that my lifestyle had changed into something beautiful and blessed. I was studying God's Word and praying more. I had time to journal, write, and deep clean the rug in the living room.

I had often prayed and asked God to reveal ways that I could spend more time with Him. He had answered my prayer in a way that I had not anticipated—removing electricity from my life. Though I had to work harder to get through my daily chores, waking up in the middle of the night to iron and using LP gas for cooking and solar lamps for lighting, my soul was at peace because I was spending more time with my Savior.

Time opened up without twenty-four-hour satellite television beaming reality shows and no opportunity for binge-watching television series. Preserving my phone battery to last the day until I could charge it again limited my social media browsing. I had more time for the important things.

It dawned on me that such a simple thing as electricity can take precedence over time with God. It took a national electricity crisis to open my eyes to my spiritual famine, carve out time with God, and prioritize my writing.

It is God's wish that we spend time with Him. In those precious moments, we are renewed as we fellowship with Him. He intensely desires us to spend time with Him to deepen our appreciation of Him. Our characters are transformed to resemble His as we shun sin and worldliness. It is time we accepted His invitation, "Be still, and know that I am God" (Psalm 46:10, NKJV). I urge you to take time in Bible study, prayer, and ministry to others and allow God to reveal Himself to you.

Do not let the small things of this world hinder you from seeking Him today.

Shylet Chabata Dzvene

It Is Well

And the peace of God, which passeth all understanding,
shall keep your hearts and minds through Christ Jesus.
—Philippians 4:7, KJV

Although we live far apart, I talk to my mother often. Usually, the conversations reflect on something that happened that day. Sometimes we vent, and other times we laugh. I'm sure we have even cried a time or two. But this particular phone call was unexpected. On the other end, my mom's voice was strong and calm. "Your father is in the hospital," she shared along with a few other things that all seemed to blur after her opening statement. I blinked back tears as I listened, immediately thinking that I needed to be strong for her, trying hard not to panic.

My thoughts moved to my preteen son, who was visiting my parents for a month. Would he be in the way? How was he taking it? After getting a few more details about my father, we ended our call. I immediately called my son to see how he was doing. He picked up the phone quickly. His voice was also strong and calm, just like my mom's. I even asked him if he wanted me to come to get him. My angst immediately began to ease as I listened to him share that he was fine and that he wanted to stay a little longer to be with my mom to make sure she was OK.

After ending the call, I sat on my couch, baffled at the faith and trust in God of two individuals directly impacted by difficulty: First, my mother, who proved strong in her faith that God would work things out. Second, my son, who seemed to absorb her resolve and mirror her confidence that all would be well in the end.

Sometimes we worry from a distance about those who are close to us as they face unexpected difficulties. But at that moment, God reminded me that His arms move swiftly to gather His children closely and comfort them in time of need. Yes, God still uses His children to comfort each other, as my church family did for me upon learning that my father was in the hospital. Their prayers, calls, and cards were priceless. But I am a witness that God Himself is also present during challenging circumstances. My father recovered fully and returned to his normal activities within a few months. However, for me, the biggest recovery was that of my personal faith as I leaned onto the stalwart example of my mom and son.

LaKeisha Williams

January 22

Come and See

Jesus saw her weeping . . . and was troubled. And He said,
"Where have you laid him?"
They said to Him, "Lord, come and see."
Jesus wept.
—John 11:33–35, NKJV

Are you facing a crisis? Is life uncertain? Will you survive when options are exhausted? Are you watching helplessly as the situation quickly becomes a matter of life or death? This is how Mary and Martha feel when they send for their friend Jesus, who just happens to miraculously heal people. But Jesus doesn't come, and Lazarus dies. The funeral is held.

In this familiar story, we find four lessons. Our first lesson tells us to call for Jesus. He may not answer immediately, but we carry on believing He hears and is answering.

Jesus finally arrives, and each sister rebukes Him for being late—they know He could have healed their brother. When He asks where Lazarus is buried, they reply simply, "Lord, come and see." Our second lesson reminds us to let go of resentment and simply beckon Jesus to come to our stinking place and see our despair.

Our third lesson demonstrates that when Jesus looks, He truly sees our helplessness and vulnerability. His compassion moves Him to act—and to act gloriously. He sees a great multitude and acts gloriously by healing their sick; later, He acts gloriously by feeding them with five loaves and two fish. He sees a man lying beside the pool of Bethesda. He turns and sees a woman who touched the hem of His garment. He looks up and sees the faith of four men who lower their paralytic friend through the roof. As He passes by, He sees the man blind from birth. When Jesus sees, His compassionate acts bring forth glorious restoration.

And now Jesus sees two young women weeping for the loss of their beloved brother, for the guardian of their future. We expect Jesus to act gloriously. But not yet. Jesus wept. Our fourth lesson reveals that when our Lord is invited to come deep into our gritty lives and see the anguish of our broken hearts, He weeps with us. He feels our pain and sorrow; then He collects our tears in a bottle and mends our broken hearts because His compassions fail not.

Jesus may not arrive during our crisis, but He's on His way. He may not come when we expect, but He's never late. Mary and Martha, and you, too, are about to discover the day when our Savior enters our lives personally—that day is the glorious day of resurrection.

Rebecca Turner

God Winks

Take delight in the L*ORD,*
and He will give you the desires of your heart.
—Psalm 37:4, NIV

A friend of mine calls them "God winks." I call them "God hugs." They are the little things during your week when you recognize God did something for you because He cares and loves you. I believe God is winking at us all the time. If we paid attention, we could each look back on this week and share where we saw God reveal Himself to us.

In the small group I attend, we share the God winks we have observed. We call it "Word-of-Mouth Advertising for Christ," and it is a time of sharing that builds our faith in Him. If we believe God is alive and active, it is perfectly natural as His followers to attribute situations and circumstances to His providence. And this half hour in my small group has trained me to look for and recognize God winks.

An example of a God wink is Elaine, a single mom who lives near me. My husband made a connection with Elaine through his roofing business and invited her and her two grown boys to our house for a meal. As we ate and interacted with them, our conversation led to God. We found that Elaine wanted to connect with God, but she didn't understand the Bible. I told Elaine that I loved opening the Bible and reading it with others to understand better who God is. I invited Elaine to do that with me, and she said yes. For the last year, we have read through the Gospels of Matthew and Mark. We are currently in John. Each week, she comes with a thirsty heart to know more and more about Jesus.

What you may not know is that I had been praying for "thirsty" people for over a year. I desire to be a vessel to those who are seeking to know God. I desire so much for others to know Christ in all His glory and love and power! Before I met Elaine, I was at a discouraging point in my pastoral ministry and asked God, "Is there anyone who is truly seeking You?" And God winked and sent me Elaine. What a double blessing it has been to meet weekly and learn together how beautiful Christ is. And since then, God has provided my heart's desire in abundance; I am currently reading through the Gospels individually with six women every week. God has given me in abundance the desires of my heart. And I know He will for you too.

Lee Lee Dart

January 24

Overflowing Grace

And God will generously provide all you need. Then you will always have everything you need and plenty left over to share with others.
—2 Corinthians 9:8, NLT

What does God's grace look like to you? Do you picture a vessel being filled with water that represents God pouring His grace into your life? Or maybe you imagine God's grace as an ocean—never ending and plentiful. I see God's grace as a river. Water enters the river from the mountains, and the river flows to the sea. In the same way, I see God's grace flowing into my life and from me into the lives of those I meet.

God's grace flows out of His love for us. He loves us so much that He sent Jesus to die for our sins so that we could have eternal life. God's grace working in me changes my life, my mind, and my character. God's grace gives me life.

Let me ask you what may seem to be a strange question. Why is the Dead Sea in the country of Israel dead? Water flows into the sea but does not exit the sea. The Dead Sea is completely landlocked. Nothing lives in the Dead Sea—neither plants nor creatures. It is said to be ten times saltier than the other seas and oceans on the planet. The water that enters the Dead Sea is alive, but since no water flows from the sea, the life-giving property of the water dies.

When I think of my life and God's grace, I wonder, *Do I pour that grace into the lives of others, or do I keep God's grace to myself?* If I selfishly keep God's grace to myself, I become stagnant in my Christian growth.

How can we share God's grace with others?

Think of your daily life, and you will see how many people you meet each day who need God's grace. Someone says something hurtful or breaks a promise or breaks something we value. It may even be something big and life-changing, such as someone who lies about us, and as a result, we lose our job or are denied a promotion. Every day, we meet people who need God's grace and a touch of His love. I pray that our lives will be like a river that God's grace flows into and then flows out of us to bless others.

Heather-Dawn Small

A Song of David—Psalm 19

The heavens tell about the glory of God.
The skies announce what his hands have made.
Each new day tells more of the story,
and each night reveals more and more about God's power.
—Psalm 19:1, 2, ERV

I have been to many countries and lived in many places throughout my life. Every place on earth has its own beauty, like no other. There are unbelievably beautiful natural wonders across the world, from the pink lake in Australia and mystical peaks in China to the ice-blue terraces in Turkey and colorful caves in Chile. But it is always the elusive beauty found in the mellow hours of sundown and sunrise that, like nothing else, captivates my spirit in unique, profound ways.

It is no wonder David felt so fascinated by the trace of the sun in the firmament! To David, each new sunrise exemplified God's character. Each new sunset further revealed God's supremacy. Every morning, when David turned his head toward the far east, he was able to see God's hand clearly in the blissful display of gentle beauty brought by sunrise.

When light, shining down upon humanity in dots of pink and golden blessings, touched David's eyes, God's character became luminous and clear to him: God was a God of mercy and justice to all.

Each morning and evening, the heavens became a sort of "miracle box" for David. Its lid opened, exposing its inside to whoever wanted to see and reminding David that God's mercy toward His children is a continual ritual throughout their days and nights.

Heavens were indeed David's spiritual classroom. He drew strength in its beauty and comfort in its teachings. In the beauty and mysteries of the heavens, David uncovered the notion that "the LORD's teachings are perfect," that "they give strength" to the believer and "help even the foolish become wise" (Psalm 19:7, ERV).

This psalm, in my opinion, is indeed one of the most poetical and spiritual poems ever written. It is not only a literary work of art but also a door to God's secret sanctuary in the candidness of the heavens for all to see.

Olga Valdivia

January 26

A Song of David—Psalm 20

May the Lord *answer you in times of trouble.*
May the God of Jacob protect you.
May he send you help from his Holy Place.
May he support you from Zion.
—Psalm 20:1, 2, ERV

What a beautiful, profound, and heartwarming prayer Psalm 20:1, 2 is! Just the thought of the God of the universe focusing His commiserations on my infirmities by sending help from His Holy Place is more than my unpretentious mind can understand or even grasp.

Is this real? Can this really be real? David had no doubt whatsoever about it. From the deepest recesses of his heart came forth the words of his song.

There is a remarkable power in this prayer. But so that the blessing became fully understood and fully personal to the people of Israel, it also needed a visual component to it—especially in the context of the temple, where ritual actions were a focus.

Thus, the lifting of hands by the priest played an important part in the Hebrew worship when blessing the people. It particularly served as a reminder that the fullness of this blessing didn't precisely come from the human priest but, rather, from the God of heaven, who gives the victory. And I want to think that this practice may have taken its meaning from the battle of Rephidim against the Amalekites, when Aaron and Hur aided Moses by holding up his hands.

The lifting of hands by the priest made the worshiper conscious of their hopeless human condition, thus evoking true worship in the worshiper.

Our hands are tied up when it comes to our victory over sin and death, for we are completely and fully dependent on God's favor for our sustenance and our salvation. When we realize this truth, true worship takes place in our heart. Our understanding of our infirmities recedes in the fullness of God.

Psalm 20 is the paramount of all blessings. It encompasses every holy and precious gift God anxiously desires to bestow upon His earthly children, empathy, good health, benevolence, mercy, richness, forgiveness, and the needed requisites for a dignified life.

David is saying that in Christ, God has given us every spiritual blessing in heaven.

Olga Valdivia

The God Who Sees

Then she called the name of the Lord *who spoke to her, You-Are-the-God-Who-Sees; for she said, "Have I also here seen Him who sees me?"*
—Genesis 16:13, NKJV

Have you ever felt unseen or unheard? Invisible? Like no one cared about you except for what they could get from you?

Hagar did. When you read her story in Genesis 16, note that Abraham and Sarah never call her by name. Just "my maid" or "your maid." They did not ask her input or how she felt about their decision—was she willing to sleep with Abraham and become a surrogate for Sarah? Her thoughts or feelings didn't matter. Her hopes and dreams didn't matter. They didn't see her as a person but as a way to get what they wanted.

Life got harder for Hagar when she became pregnant, and Sarah's jealousy and anger flared. So Hagar fled. Ran. Hid. Just wanted to be out of Sarah's reach and done with the entire situation. Life alone had to be better than what she was experiencing. She had done what they wanted—met their expectations—and now was being treated "harshly" (verse 6).

God knew. He pursued her. The Angel of the Lord met her in the wilderness. He called her by name. He saw her. He heard her (verse 11). He cared. The Angel of the Lord asked her where she was coming from and where she was going. Note her answer when you read her story. She had no clue where she's going—she's just going. She could only tell Him where she's coming from. He sent her home with a promise of God's blessing for her and her son's future.

Hagar was the first woman to give God a new name: El Roi. The God who sees. She named her son "Ishmael," which means "God hears." She's able to return to an angry, wounded, jealous Sarah and die to self. The situation and Sarah's attitude had not changed, but Hagar had. Knowing God sees you, hears you, and has a plan for you brings peace and confidence that enables you to endure and persist despite your circumstances.

God sees you. He hears you. God promises He has a plan that brings a hopeful future. Rest in that truth. Let it bring you courage for the day and the challenges it brings. Remind yourself that no matter what anyone else says or sees in you, God delights in you. He loves you more than anyone ever has or ever will. He's crazy about you. And He. Sees. You.

Tamyra Horst

January 28

Those Women

How beautiful on the mountains
are the feet of those who bring good news.
—Isaiah 52:7, NIV

Have you ever thought about the women who followed Jesus and wondered exactly what it was that they did? Luke records, "After this, Jesus traveled about from one town and village to another, proclaiming the good news of the kingdom of God. The Twelve were with him and also some women who had been cured of evil spirits and diseases: Mary (called Magdalene) from whom seven demons had come out; Joanna the wife of Chuza, the manager of Herod's household; Susanna; and many others. These women were helping to support them out of their own means" (Luke 8:1–3, NIV). It is amazing enough—and could have been a bit shocking in that time—for a group of women to be traveling around with these men, but there is no hint of scandal.

Because of the culture, I imagine it was difficult for the women in the crowds who followed and listened to Jesus to come to Him or the disciples with their questions, but there were these women—Mary, Joanna, Susanna, and others—whom they could approach to ask their questions. Because these women had been traveling with Jesus and hearing Him so often, I am sure they could answer many questions. They certainly heard Him preaching in the synagogues and in the open fields. As they became more acquainted with Jesus and the disciples, maybe they dared to ask questions even for themselves—learning theology!

What stories they must have been able to tell! They had seen lepers healed, demons cast out, the teachers of the law and the Pharisees rebuked, and bread and fish multiplied. Even if they were not always with the group, they heard about the events. I wouldn't be surprised if these women brought many women, and even some men, to Jesus for healing and salvation.

These twelve men did not have any income while they were walking with Jesus from one end of the country to the other, so how did they pay for food, new sandals, and possibly even occasional lodging? Those women! They were financing the ministry out of their means!

It is no wonder that these same women were at the cross. It was women who were the first to know that He was resurrected. Those women! Women like you and me—if we so choose.

Ardis Dick Stenbakken

The Locked Door

Behold, I stand at the door, and knock: if any man hear my voice, and open the door, I will come in to him, and will sup with him, and he with me.
—Revelation 3:20, KJV

When my youngest brother was little, he accidentally locked himself in his bedroom. At first, it was fun, something that brought him a great amount of attention. But eventually, it was not so much fun. He couldn't get out, and no one else could get in. No attempts to convey to him the simple process of turning the doorknob to release the lock made sense to his inexperienced mind. Finally, the fire department was summoned to rescue Richard from his second-story predicament.

This episode reminds me of Jesus' invitation in Revelation 3:20, "Behold, I stand at the door, and knock: if any man hear my voice, and open the door, I will come in to him, and will sup with him, and he with me" (KJV). Our heavenly Parent desperately wants to enter our heart's room to bring peace, joy, assurance, and everything else we could ever need or want. But true gentleman that He is, He doesn't force access where He hasn't been invited. *Knock-knock.* Sometimes we hear him; sometimes we don't. *Knock-knock.* Sometimes we don't want to be bothered. *Knock-knock.* Sometimes we are in need but don't sense our need. *Knock-knock.* Sometimes we do sense our need yet don't understand how to open the door to the One who can help. We sense Him outside the door. We know He is there. He wants to come in, and we want Him to come in. *Knock-knock.* Where's the fire department? How do I open the door?

Perhaps that problematic door will open for you by one (or more) of four "handles." First, invite Jesus in, thus opening the door of Revelation 3:20. Second, believe Jesus wants to help you. "I have set before you life and death, blessing and cursing: therefore choose life, that both thou and thy seed may live" (Deuteronomy 30:19, KJV). Third, stick faith in the face of doubt. Tell Jesus, "I believe; help thou mine unbelief" (Mark 9:24, KJV). Last, trust Jesus to be true to His Word: "And this is the confidence that we have in him, that, if we ask any thing according to his will, he heareth us: and if we know that he hears us, whatsoever we ask, we know that we have the petitions that we desired of him" (1 John 5:14, 15, KJV).

Christine B. Nelson

Lost and Found—Part 1

"For my thoughts are not your thoughts,
neither are your ways my ways,"
declares the LORD.
—Isaiah 55:8, NIV

One of the last things he said to me as my marriage disintegrated was, "Who would have *you*?" Even sadder, I believed him! As a newly single mother, I felt so unwanted. *Will God abandon me too?* Still in shock, I struggled to help my two sons deal with their own pain. Then, unexpectedly, some church members strongly suggested we wouldn't be welcome to worship at church anymore because we were now a "broken home."

One late autumn afternoon, I opened an envelope from my supportive mother. Out fell a church paper clipping that advertised an upcoming singles "hobo party" in my area. It also provided contact information. "Go to this party!" Mom had written. My eldest son, a freshman at a boarding high school, said he would go with me to the party. I made the four-hour drive to visit him; then we drove to a hotel in San Jose to stay overnight since I'd brought Kitty, my gentle house cat. Kitty was one of the few who still seemed to love me. And how I loved her! When my son and I took a wrong turn after dark in this unfamiliar city, the party host came to find us and lead us to his home, the location of the get-together. He introduced himself as Russ.

Near the end of the evening, Russ said, "Tomorrow morning some from our group are going over to sightsee in San Francisco and Alcatraz. Would you and your son like to come with us?" We went and had a wonderful day riding cable cars and visiting Chinatown, among other sights. Back in San Jose, my son and I were about to get into our vehicle when Russ said, "Before you make the drive back to school and then home again, could I take you two to dinner? The Mexican restaurant opens in thirty minutes." We followed Russ to the restaurant, where my son had time to walk Kitty. Before going into the restaurant, I rolled down my window just enough to give her fresh air. After a wonderful meal, we returned to our car. Kitty was gone! A house cat on big city streets—no chance of survival! Another unspeakable loss!

My Christian walk has taught me that sometimes when we think we have lost our nearest and dearest, God is leading us toward one of the greatest "finds" of our life. Remember that.

Noni Weidemann

Lost and Found—Part 2

You, Lord, preserve both people and animals.
—Psalm 36:6, NIV

How had Kitty escaped through a mere three-inch opening at the top of my car window? We hadn't been in the restaurant that long! I was beside myself with grief! I'd already lost my marriage, my family as I'd known it, and my church fellowship. Now I'd lost Kitty, who had been a consistent comfort through the preceding absolutely horrendous months.

"Look," said our new friend Russ, "I'll go back into the restaurant and give them my telephone number. They can call me if they find your cat. I don't live too far away."

After a couple hours of driving, I dropped off my son at the boys' dormitory. He needed to get ready to help at a booth for the school's fall festival. While he did that, I went to the girls' dormitory to do his laundry. After starting the washing machine cycle, I sat down with a heavy heart to start a letter to my mother. I would tell her about my weekend, our new friend Russ, and the heartbreak of our missing Kitty. My heart was heavy and my stomach in a knot.

Suddenly I heard a soft-spoken male voice. "Here you are!" I looked up to see Russ standing in the doorway. He was holding Kitty! With relief and joy, I burst into tears. Jumping up, I reached out—for both of them. "Your cat came back to the restaurant after we left," he said. "The headwaiter phoned me. Surprisingly, your frightened Kitty let me pick her up and put her in my car. So here we are."

Indeed, there they were! The beloved cat—that I had lost, now found. Found, along with a kind new friend who had not only rescued my beloved Kitty but also would one day become the beloved of my heart. David once wrote that the Lord preserves "both people and animals" (Psalm 36:6, NIV). From experience, I know He does.

He also heals and preserves broken hearts and broken families. His plans unfold in ways we could never imagine. I'm sure God smiled every time He saw Russ and me writing letters to each other—every day—in the subsequent months. He and I got together as often as we could. Sometime later, surrounded by the children of our soon-to-be blended family and with God who had brought us together, we exchanged marriage vows. That was forty years ago.

No matter the loss, never give up on God—or His ability to preserve and heal your heart.

Noni Weidemann

February 1

Reminded by a Calendar

I have been young, and now am old;
yet have I not seen the righteous forsaken, nor his seed begging bread.
—Psalm 37:25, KJV

About eight years after I began to tithe, the Lord demonstrated, dramatically, how literally He fulfills His Word. Malachi 3:10, 11 proclaims to faithful tithers God's promise to pour from heaven's windows blessings beyond one's capacity to receive them. Here's how it happened in one of our family's most memorable encounters with God many years ago.

I had gone into town for our US$80 monthly allotment of food stamps, but before returning home, I stopped at the library to look at magazines. While hanging my coat and purse on a coat rack, an inner voice alerted me to think twice about what I was doing, but I ignored it and settled into a booth, quickly engrossing myself in the magazines. Later, when retrieving my coat and purse, I had a vague sensation that something wasn't right, but I grabbed them and hurried home. I then discovered what was wrong: I had been robbed! Our entire month's food allowance was gone. I had three people to feed and four weeks until more food stamps. A battle raged within—anger toward the robber and a struggle in realizing that, as a Christian, I must forgive. My husband reminded me of the Malachi promise, assuring me that God would provide for us. We agreed to tell no one what had happened. Then God began to work.

Three days after the incident, a woman handed me four dollars for some typing I had done as a favor. Four days later, a five-dollar bill was pressed into my hand just because the woman wanted me to have it. I thanked her, saying the Lord must have led her to do it, but was true to the agreement of not mentioning our loss.

Over the rest of the month, at about three-to-four-day intervals, the miracle continued to happen—small amounts of money given to us randomly. The end of the month had arrived with the tally: $80 stolen; $81.50 in blessings poured out of heaven's windows!

We still have the 1981 calendar where God's blessings were recorded on each day they arrived in February of that year. God supplied all our needs (and more!) according to His riches in glory by Christ Jesus (Philippians 4:19, my paraphrase).

Christine B. Nelson

The Best Place to Have a Heart Attack

"I will give you a new heart and put a new spirit within you; I will take the heart of stone out of your flesh and give you a heart of flesh."
—Ezekiel 36:26, NKJV

I had been busy with life, teaching Bible studies, serving as a chaplain, and doing many other things. One day, during story time with first graders, a pain suddenly shot up my left arm and into my chin. I silently prayed for protection. It went away.

On Tuesday, the strange pains returned. Sharp, piercing pains. They continued all day. My husband took me to the hospital. I was soon on a bed having various procedures, including blood work. Moments later, the doctor came into my cubicle. He said, "Try to relax, Pat. You are having a heart attack."

They would not let me go home. I spent many days on hospital bed rest. I wore a heart monitor. I didn't look sick. My friends were all teasing me.

An ambulance trip to the Kingston, Ontario, cardiac unit for an angiogram was not encouraging. Severe blockages to and from the heart created scary prospects in me. I had always thought that right living would overcome all the obstacles to good health. That is not always the case, as I was to learn. Genetic inheritance can be deadly.

I became part of the "Zipper Club" when I had a triple bypass.

The morning after my surgery, my surgeon came to visit me. He said, "I held your heart in my hand and watched it warm up, turn pink, and start beating. You will heal quickly because you are in such good health, otherwise."

Strict written instructions came home with me a few days later. Mostly, it was walk, walk, walk.

I send out a warning to other women. If it happened to me, it could happen to you. Signs of heart issues in women are not as dramatic as those in men. There was no outward sign that anything was wrong. I exercised every day and lived as healthfully as possible, but that was not enough.

Through it all, I kept thinking of the text where God promises to take out our stony hearts and replace them with hearts of flesh. My heart had been on a one-way trip to disaster. Now its plumbing is replaced, and I am on the way to many more years of usefulness.

Patricia Cove

February 3

Thoughts Are Powerful

For as he thinketh in his heart, so is he.
—Proverbs 23:7, KJV

Proverbs 23:7 is right on, and I have been experiencing this in a profound way. Part of my personality is melancholy, and it is quite easy for me to think negative thoughts. It comes second nature to me.

My husband drove our motorhome to fill with fuel and LP gas. He was gone from our house less than one minute when he called me, asking if I could find his wallet and bring it to him at the bottom of our subdivision's hill. My first thoughts paraded across the blackboard of my mind, *Oh, here we go again. Why did he forget his wallet? Now I will be delayed as well.*

But praise the Lord, He began to deal with my thoughts and reminded me of this most precious idea: "Why don't you think how blessed you are to be able to help your husband? You get the privilege to be of assistance to him."

Do you know, within seconds of thinking how blessed I was to be able to help my husband, joy began to grow in my mind, and it was exciting to carry out the request. When I showed up at the bottom of the hill where he waited patiently for me, I greeted him with a smile.

Isn't that amazing! Using the power of my thoughts, I could change my outlook on things. This reminds me of a testimony I heard on the radio. The woman speaker shared that she was ready to leave her marriage. She was frustrated about her husband and their relationship. She was ready to quit. Then the Lord suggested she greet her husband with the words "I love you" as he returned from work each day. Recoiling in horror, she boldly told God she couldn't do that. Could she just think the words but not say them?

So she began thinking the words. Each time her husband came home from work, she thought, *I love you.* And guess what? As the days and weeks passed, her feelings began to match her thoughts; then, she spoke the words and really meant them. Today she is very happily married and shares this story with others.

Is there someone in your life who bugs you? Maybe it's a coworker, a family member, or someone in the church. Ask Jesus to give you kind thoughts toward that person and see what happens. Are you up for the challenge?

Valerie Hamel Morikone

Strength for All Things

Do not be anxious about anything, but in everything by prayer and supplication with thanksgiving let your requests be made known to God. And the peace of God, which surpasses all understanding, will guard your hearts and your minds in Christ Jesus.
—Philippians 4:6, 7, ESV

Sometimes I think that we have two lives: the one we show the world and the one inside us. It doesn't mean that we are false or liars; it could just be that we don't feel comfortable showing what is going on inside of us.

Many times, we don't like the thoughts inside our heads because we lack the peace that can be given. We do things that we know are wrong. We grumble because we don't receive what we think we deserve. Paul tells us to present our requests to God in prayer, supplication, and thanksgiving because only God can guard our hearts and thoughts with peace.

Paul also gives us guidelines for taking care of our thoughts, "Finally, brothers, whatever is true, whatever is honorable, whatever is just, whatever is pure, whatever is lovely, whatever is commendable, if there is any excellence, if there is anything worthy of praise, think about these things" (Philippians 4:8, ESV). Does everything we think about meet these characteristics? How much time do we spend thinking these types of thoughts?

Paul invites us, "Rejoice in the Lord always; again I will say, rejoice. Let your reasonableness be known to everyone. The Lord is at hand" (verses 4, 5, ESV). He invites us not only to be happy but also to be good and have that goodness recognized everywhere.

I have often said or heard others say, "This is very difficult. It is more complicated than just deciding to rejoice or think good thoughts."

Paul knew it was hard but also knew where his strength came from. Even in prison, he said, "I can do all things through him who strengthens me" (verse 13, ESV).

Nothing is impossible for God. We just need to trust God and believe His promises. Every time life gets hard, we can remind ourselves of Paul's words in Philippians, then pray and give God our battles, ask Him to help us think good, honorable, lovely thoughts, and remember that we can do all things—including walk through hard things—because God will give us strength and walk with us.

Cecilia Nanni

Lunch With a Loved One

May the Lord make your love increase and overflow for each other.
—1 Thessalonians 3:12, NIV

"You can hang your jackets beside mine," Derion said excitedly. It was "Lunch With a Loved One" at my grandson's first grade class, a day I had eagerly anticipated, knowing that our family circle would grow even stronger.

"You want to see the tarantula? And here's the science corner with the shark jaw." Auntie Rochelle snapped a picture while baby Cherise smiled at everyone.

"Here's my desk," Derion exclaimed. "I'll get you chairs." Rochelle and I grinned as we settled in them, our knees close to our ears. As we ate our sandwiches, we thought about how mom, dad, and four-year-old sister had enjoyed being "loved ones" earlier in the month.

I gazed at adults sitting on the floor, surrounded by a huddle of children. People with white hair chatted to the teacher. "That's Mel's uncle who's sharing cookies," Derion explained, "and the lady with the cheese pizza is Shanna's babysitter."

"Lunch With a Loved One"—what a brilliant idea. Not "A Meal With Mom and Dad." Mom or dad might not be able to take time off work, but loved ones were present in abundance on that February day.

"Hey, Derion, have you showed them your stuff?" the boy in the adjoining desk asked. He, unlike the rest of the children, was sitting alone.

"Do you want to see my ruler?" Rochelle and I nodded enthusiastically. We admired his ruler and expected to see workbooks and pencils, too, but Derion was focused elsewhere.

"This is Harley," he explained. "He is my friend. Oh, here comes the lady with the camera!" I knew about the fundraiser and planned to purchase a photo so we could remember this special family day. I scooped up the baby, put my arm around Derion, and leaned close to Rochelle so that the four of us would easily fit into the picture.

"Hey, Harley," said Derion, "your grandma isn't here today. Come be in the picture with us!" We moved closer. The circle of love expanded: Derion, grandma, sister, aunt, and friend. This was definitely "Lunch With Loved Ones." I was blessed to participate that one day in February, but Derion, with his ability to include others, has lunch with loved ones every day.

Denise Dick Herr

Spiritual Life Insurance Policy

For God so loved the world, that he gave his only begotten Son, that whosoever believeth in him should not perish, but have everlasting life. For God sent not his Son into the world to condemn the world; but that the world through him might be saved.
—John 3:16, 17, KJV

I once read a folk story about a woman who borrowed her friend's priceless pearl necklace for a Valentine's Day ball. When she got home after the party, she realized the necklace was missing. She searched for it everywhere but couldn't find it. Terrified, shaken, guilty, ashamed, embarrassed, and confused, she decided not to confess it to her friend but instead stopped communicating with her. She looked for a similar necklace and found it was US$100,000. Mortified, she sold her house and paid a down payment toward the necklace. She moved out of state, far from her friend. Being a person of integrity, she worked multiple shifts and jobs, day and night—working over sixty-five hours a week for fifteen years and was able to finally pay off the necklace.

Nervously she visited her friend to return the necklace. The years of toil had taken a toll on her body, and her friend did not recognize her. In utter disbelief, her friend asked her why she had not communicated with her. She told her that the necklace had been insured, and the insurance had already paid her in full. All those years of hard work, guilt, shame, and distance were not needed. The debt had already been covered.

Sometimes when we make mistakes in our personal lives, we are terrified, shaken, guilty, ashamed, embarrassed, and confused. In our guilt and shame, we hide from God instead of communicating with Him in prayer and confession. God in all His goodness has already paid the price; His cross insures our lives. His gift is priceless and is paid in full. We just need to ask and claim our insurance, which is free of charge. We need to show faith in our policy.

The Bible is our life insurance policy contract, which we need to carefully study daily. We sign this contract in faith. And as we surrender ourselves daily in prayer and ask for forgiveness, in His mercy, He forgives us and redeems us from all unrighteousness, giving us the ultimate gift of life, a spiritual life insurance policy with eternal rewards.

Suhana Chikatla

February 7

Becoming Meek

"Blessed are the meek,
For they shall inherit the earth."
—Matthew 5:5, NKJV

In today's world, being sassy as a woman is admired. Being able to "clap back" and "read" someone, especially as an African American woman, seems to be admired. But is this true beauty?

In 1 Peter 3:4, Peter says that true beauty is having a quiet and humble spirit. This is what God admires the most.

This is an important teaching, especially if you are a single or divorced woman looking to be married. The wisest man who ever lived said that it is better to live in a corner on a housetop than with a brawling woman in a mansion. Wow! I can admit that one of the main offenses in my first marriage was emasculating my husband, constantly reminding him of my degrees and spiritual acumen with my attitude. This led him to seek honor in the arms of other women (not an excuse). Women need to understand that men *need* respect as much as women need to be loved and cherished. They need to be honored, which to them *is* love. I had been a fool who tore down my house (marriage) with my own hands and mouth through a toxic cycle of dishonor, unkindness, and unloving acts.

Now, this saying might be hard for some to hear. Many will take offense. The fear is that we will be taken advantage of and become a doormat. Remember that God is our Avenger, and He will take care of those who seek to abuse the meek. I, too, had a rebellious heart from childhood. I was naturally ambitious and had leadership qualities, which were good qualities that the devil wanted to skew. It was hard for me to accept authority figures because, deep down, I wanted to be the authority figure. But I realized that I needed temperance and meekness. I've learned that being meek does not diminish who we were born to be. Jesus is meek and lowly in heart, and we need to be like Him.

Let us learn from Christ how to be meek and lowly in heart. Let us take up our duties with cheerfulness, persistence, and dedication, seeing it as a great honor to serve others but, more important, to serve the God of the universe. Remember, the meek will inherit the whole earth!

Raschelle McLean-Jones

February 8

An Unexpected Gift

"Let your light so shine before men, that they may see your good works and glorify your Father in heaven."
—Matthew 5:16, NKJV

On July 18, 2019, I was at the dais to retrieve an item I needed in my chambers before the formal opening of court when an officer approached and asked if she could give me a gift for my garden. She excitedly told me of this beautiful but unusual desert flower that blooms only at night. I, too, became excited.

I looked at the tiny insignificant little weed in her hands and thought, *Another weed for my garden!* Her kindness was sincere. I decided I had nothing to lose in accepting her generous gift. After giving me detailed instructions on planting and caring for my gift, she assured me that a pleasant surprise awaited me.

As promised, my gift grew by leaps and bounds. Buds began to appear in the center of the plant. Its elongated leaves began to cover a wide expanse. One morning, I woke to a beautiful yellow flower, which faded with the warmth of the sun. So, this is it! My desert flower turned out to be an evening primrose, botanically named *Oenothera triloba*. A plant I've never heard of or seen before, although I planted many varieties of evening primrose over the years. The miracle of this is that today, February 8, 2021, in Southern Ontario, the temperature is hovering around nineteen degrees Celsius (sixty-six degrees Fahrenheit). Not exactly daytime desert temperature! My gift lies buried beneath a blanket of snow and ice but will burst through in the spring, to blossom again as a thing of beauty, to greet me at my front entrance.

One morning last summer, I looked out my upstairs window to what appeared to be a comical scene: a rabbit, a squirrel, and a bird were all trying desperately to get at my evening primrose through the wire mesh I installed around it. Although I have struggled to ensure my plant's survival, my furry and feathered friends all seemed bent on sharing my gift.

Nature assures me of a rebirth when spring arrives in a few weeks. This rebirth of nature serves to remind us of the gift of life that God has so graciously given each of us. As our faces differ, so do our talents and the beautiful, sweet spirit God has instilled in us. Let's not smother or bury it but let it shine for all to see and be blessed.

Avis Mae Rodney

February 9

O What Love!

Who shall separate us from the love of Christ? Shall trouble or hardship or persecution or famine or nakedness or danger or sword? . . . No, in all these things we are more than conquerors through him who loved us. For I am convinced that neither death nor life, neither angels nor demons, neither the present nor the future, nor any powers, neither height nor depth, nor anything else in all creation, will be able to separate us from the love of God that is in Christ Jesus our Lord.

—Romans 8:35–39, NIV

Wow! What incredibly powerful words! Have you ever read a specific scripture multiple times, but another time you read the words, they suddenly impact you so profoundly that you pause and reread them, slowly reflecting on the message?

Well, that happened to me recently. The scripture made such a deep impression on my heart that I read it over a few times. It was then that it took on a special significance. Maybe it was because I was going through challenging valley experiences, and I needed those words of assurance that no matter what may happen to me or what stormy times I may be going through, God has me covered, and nothing can separate me from His unfathomable love. How beautiful! Immediately, I felt a heavy burden lifted, and my countenance changed. I began to hum a favorite hymn.

I can tell you from experience that bad things can happen and cause your faith in God to be shaken. Sometimes it may be difficult to believe that this is true. Sometimes He may not come to our rescue immediately when life's hard blows knock us to the ground, and we begin to complain, to doubt, to despair, to become discouraged, to ask, "Why me?" and even to lose faith. Or He may use these challenging situations to test our faith or to give us a testimony to share that will encourage fellow travelers we meet along the road of life to let them know that God is real and that we can trust Him. He never fails.

I have been there, and God came through for me even when I stepped out of His will. It is no secret what He can do. I am thankful to God that I am more than a conqueror; I am a victor! I am a living testimony that He is real and loves us very much and always comes through for us. Nothing, no nothing, can separate us from His unfathomable love!

Shirley C. Iheanacho

The Love of God

"For God so loved the world that He gave His only begotten Son, that whoever believes in Him should not perish but have everlasting life."
—John 3:16, NKJV

A few years ago, I was impressed to study the love of God, which I did in two stages. In the first stage, I focused on six passages of scripture. In John 3:16, love may be defined as giving—God gave His Son. In Romans 5:8, love is equivalent to sacrifice. In Ephesians 2:4, 5, love is synonymous with mercy. In 2 Thessalonians 2:16, 17, love means comfort. In 1 John 4:9, 10, love is an active verb, and in Revelation 3:5, love means forgiveness.

Those six passages reinforced God's versatility; He loves us so very much that His love is translated into different meanings to meet our immediate and unique needs. His love also teaches me to be versatile and to love unconditionally. It teaches me that love is generous; it gives freely. Because I love, no sacrifice is too great, and my interactions should always be tempered with mercy. My love enables me to provide comfort for others, and because love is an active verb, it teaches me the importance of forgiveness. The first stage of my study propelled me into a deeper study of God's love.

The second stage was a four-year journey, during which time I studied God's love as manifested from Genesis to Revelation. During those years, I realized that some people's version of the God of the Old Testament is very different from the One I encountered. I've heard and read that the God of the Old Testament is an angry, vengeful, punitive warmonger who seemed to enjoy violence and destruction. That may be the reason why natural disasters are described as "acts of God." On the contrary, the God that I encountered in the Old Testament possesses the same consistent characteristics portrayed in the New Testament.

At the outset, in Genesis, God's love is manifested in His creative acts. Because He loved, He created a world with all the beauty and conveniences that people would need, and then He created Adam and Eve. That same image resonates throughout the Bible. The final text in Revelation 1:5, 6 portrays God's undying love embracing all the meanings as He cleanses us and elevates us to "kings and priests." Oh, what love! I pray that we could embrace God's love and daily study and grasp more of its depth for us.

Valerie Knowles Combie

He Will Lead Us

Commit your way to the L*ORD;*
Trust him, and he will act.
—Psalm 37:5, ISV

As I write this meditation, the world is in great distress. A pandemic is plaguing humanity; those who do not suffer from the disease face its consequences: social isolation, unemployment, and insecurity.

Churches were forced to close, as were some types of commerce and other activities considered nonessential and having a high rate of contagion. We lost physical contact, and many people found themselves in emotional isolation—a painful feeling that creates a huge void in the soul.

After four months of uncertainty, I felt saddened about not being able to attend church services, about being away from my brothers, family, and work colleagues. With a hushed voice, I cried out to God for help; I needed an answer to not panic.

That night when I slept, I dreamed that I was with other people in a city about to be destroyed by a terrible cyclone. The strong wind surrounded us, and the gusts brought fear and dread. All the houses were closed, and no one would let us in. I noticed that some houses were fragile and possibly would not withstand the storm, but the residents refused to leave them.

With nowhere to hide, wet and cold, we all entered a simple tent surrounded by canvas and wooden boards; inside it, we had only one chair to sit on. The cyclone came and destroyed the entire city, but our tent was intact—even though it was the most fragile dwelling there. The wind that howled outside did not even stir the hair of anyone inside the small hut; a lull surrounded us. Then someone said: "We are like the disciples in the rough Sea of Galilee; Jesus is here with us, so we are safe."

It thrills me to remember this dream. It made me realize how much God cares about my fears and problems. That night I realized that Jesus is with us all the time. We do not know when this pandemic will pass. But we believe that God will be inside our small, fragile tent. Nothing will shake us. What security in Christ we have!

Sueli da Silva Pereira

An Act of Love

"And when he saw him, he had compassion."
—Luke 10:33, NKJV

Many know the story of the good Samaritan. Jesus told this parable to illustrate that compassion and kindness should be shown toward all people. I have seen children's DVDs and storybooks illustrating the predicament of the man who was robbed, wounded, and left to die. This always left an impact on my grandson, Kyle, who learned very quickly that the kindness of the Samaritan was the way Jesus wanted him to be.

The road between Jerusalem and Jericho is about fifteen miles through some rugged country, providing hiding places for anyone intent on attacking and robbing the unsuspecting traveler. It would be a frightening experience to suddenly be struck, robbed, and left wounded on the side of the road.

We are told that a priest came along and, later, a Levite. Neither wanted to be involved with the wounded traveler. However, a Samaritan who came by stopped and had compassion on him. His kindness in helping this hurt man and getting him to safety saved him. This story came to my memory anew because I saw something the other day that I will never forget. A fire caused extensive damage to a family home in one of our suburbs. Emergency services were called, and fire units and an ambulance were in attendance.

The occupants were watching, utterly distressed, and to add to their grief, their beautiful husky dog was trapped inside. They weren't allowed to go near the house, but one of the firefighters broke a window where the fire had not reached and went to see whether the dog could be located. Not long after, he returned with the unconscious dog, which he had found under a bed. The medics, who were on hand, rushed to the dog, performed resuscitation, and gave oxygen. Then, to my amazement, the dog was lifted onto the stretcher, buckled up, oxygen secured, and placed into the ambulance to be rushed to the vet. The news later told the story, and the dog had survived. What an act of humanity toward this dog.

There are many stories of acts of kindness that occur around us. God bless them all. Are good Samaritans still around? Yes, and even working for God's creatures.

Lyn Welk-Sandy

February 13

Tissue Ministry

He will swallow up death forever,
And the Lord *God will wipe away tears from all faces;*
The rebuke of His people
He will take away from all the earth;
For the Lord *has spoken.*
—Isaiah 25:8, NKJV

I sat shivering with Susan on her lawn as our husbands talked to the firefighters preparing to leave. The water and smoke damage from the early morning chimney fire would take weeks to clean up. Tears had washed a clear path down Susan's smudged face.

As I answered the phone, I heard a sob. I had heard it enough to know to whom it belonged. Joan was having marital problems again. I listened and realized that this world has an ever-flowing river of tears.

On my bookcase sat a flowered box of tissues. Tissues. I had given so many away lately because of tears—tears of joy, tears of sorrow, tears of frustration, and tears from devastation.

People have all kinds of ministries: singing, TV, radio, and so on. *Could mine be a "tissue ministry"?* I wondered. The more I reflected on it, the more it fit.

Tears punctuate the Bible from cover to cover. Eve shed tears at the death of Abel. David wept over Absalom. Jesus wept over Jerusalem, and on and on. Every tribe, every culture, has tears. Obviously, our Creator designed us with the ability to cry. The emotional traumas of life would need a natural safety valve: tears.

A tissue ministry requires caring enough to listen, not only with the ears but with the heart. You need to be sensitive. Someone people can be trusted to keep confidences. It requires a willingness to be inconvenienced and have some of your plans interrupted. The bottom line is that Jesus did not tell us to change people but to love them by listening and caring. Sharing a tissue can be in person or virtually with a hug or phone call.

God will someday wipe away all sad tears forever. In the meantime, we can all consider being tissue ministers by lovingly listening to those in need of having their tears wiped on this side of heaven.

Marybeth Gessele

February 14

But the Greatest of These Is Love

And now these three remain: faith, hope and love. But the greatest of these is love.
—1 Corinthians 13:13, NIV

It was a muggy day in the clinic in Guatemala. My calves and feet were aching from standing. My brain was tired of interpreting. I felt that if I had to give the speech about having high blood pressure one more time, my brain would collapse. What kept me going was holding the precious little babies the mothers would bring in to see the doctor. This made the mission trip all worthwhile. I would make the babies laugh and giggle.

Then he came in. I smelled him before I saw him. I was reminded of why I had decided to be a teacher and not a health-care professional. Flies swarmed about his head. He was filthy, emaciated, and disoriented. A horrible stench emitted from his mouth. To make matters worse, while he was in the waiting area, he urinated on the chair in our clinic. When the time came for us to wait on him, I am ashamed to say that I backed away from him.

I felt terrible. What would Jesus have done? He would have greeted him warmly and asked him how he was doing. Seeing as he was more in need than many other people we had that day, Jesus might have even spent more time with him instead of rushing him off as I had.

We sent him away with several medications, and I forced a feeble, "Que Dios le bendiga (God bless you)." I felt like a phony. If I meant what I had just said, I could have at least conjured up a genuine smile. But I didn't. I was just glad that he was gone. I was not looking forward to cleaning up the mess he had left behind.

This experience got me thinking. The Bible tells us that we are not going the extra mile like Christ would have us do if we love only those who are easy to love. It is only in loving those who are difficult to love that we are fulfilling the command to love your neighbor as yourself. I pray that I will have more of the Holy Spirit in my life so that I can love everyone that I meet, no matter how hard they are to love.

Mary C. D. Johnson

February 15

Knowledge + Application = Harmony

Be kindly affectionate to one another.
—Romans 12:10, NKJV

"Can you come here and help me finish this jigsaw puzzle?" Melissa was enjoying a visit from her aunt, uncle, and slightly older cousin and used every excuse to do things with him.

"When I finish what I'm doing," he called back.

Stomping into the kitchen, fists shoved into jean's pockets, Melissa exclaimed, "I do not understand why he can't leave what he's doing and go back to it later!"

"What's he doing?" I asked, keeping my face straight when I really wanted to laugh.

"Oh, some egregious algebra project."

"Get used to it," I said smiling. "When you grow up, you'll likely marry someone just like him." Melissa grimaced. "The male brain is wired quite differently from ours," I went on. "It actually takes less energy to run too because if he's working in one hemisphere, the other side is idling. Think of their brain as having two rooms connected by a narrow hallway. To leave his algebra project in the left hemisphere, metaphorically he'd need to turn out the lights and lower the air conditioner, walk along a narrow hall, and then turn on lights and air in the right hemisphere. After that he'd be ready to work on the jigsaw puzzle, a right-brain activity. It can take several seconds to switch gears."

"Oh," said Melissa. "No wonder he wants to finish the algebra project first."

"Our brain hemispheres, yours and mine, function much more as one unit. If any part is on, it's all on. The hallway between the hemispheres is much wider, and we tend to run back and forth easily between the two sides."

"I do that all the time," said Melissa, laughing. "It's easy. I start one thing, work on it for a while, start something else, go back to the first project, move to yet another, and so on."

"Understanding more about gender brain-function differences can help you to be kindly affectionate to each other," I said. "The apostle Paul specifically admonishes that."

"OK," Melissa called to her cousin, laughing. "Let me know when you're ready to switch gears and move into your right brain. Meantime I'll work on something else."

It would be wonderful if we adults would learn as quickly as a child does, I thought.

Arlene R. Taylor

Impact—Part 1

Bear ye one another's burdens, and so fulfil the law of Christ.
—Galatians 6:2, KJV

Death affects us all, sometimes through illness, sometimes suddenly. The questions arise, "What am I going to do with the time that I have?" "How am I going to impact the lives of those around me?" "How can I be a blessing or a safety for those I meet or know intimately?"

I have been thinking about this a lot lately. Our school recently had our biannual school sports program. As teachers, my colleagues and I were busy. At one point, I interacted with one of the teachers as she moved around. I could tell that her mind was distant, and her eyes looked sad, a far cry from her normal demeanor. I longed to ask her if she was OK, but it was neither the time nor the place. I told myself that I would talk to her the next day.

But she wasn't at school the next day. We assumed she was exhausted. Two days later, I awakened at four thirty in the morning to find I had missed several phone calls. I returned the calls and received news that forever changed my view of the world. Our colleague had been found murdered, along with her eldest daughter and two others. Disbelief, shock, and sorrow all washed over me. Anger came next. Later, I would experience fear as a woman living in a world where women were seen as expendable. There were two more murders that same week; women killed in domestic violence disputes. But the death of our colleague tormented all of us in the staff room and haunted me because I will forever ask, "What could I have done? What if I had asked her if she was all right that day? Would it have made a difference today?"

As women, many of us live in unsafe situations. Some of us hide it so well that we fool those around us into thinking we are OK. God has given us eyes to see not just the immediate but also the hidden—if we would just look. We are to be our sisters' keeper. We cannot assume that everything is well just because we see a smile. We cannot be so wrapped up in our own woes that we miss the signs of distress. It takes so little to genuinely ask, "Are you OK?" It doesn't take much to reach out and show concern. These simple acts of caring and kindness can make all the difference.

Let us not experience the pain and regret of wondering, *What if I had . . . ?* Let us trust God when He prompts us to make sure a friend is OK.

Greta Michelle Joachim-Fox-Dyett

February 17

Impact—Part 2

Let your light so shine before men, that they may see your good works, and glorify your Father which is in heaven.
—Matthew 5:16, KJV

The walls are plastered with love messages; reflections shared about a woman who was thought of and missed profoundly. "We will always love you." "You always encouraged us to do our best." Written by little hands, these messages will never be seen by their teacher because she had died.

I hated being in that room because these messages remind me of the circumstances under which she was taken and that caused immeasurable sorrow for her and for other women like her whose lives ended violently. But another thought soon overpowered the dark and encouraged me to look at the sentiments expressed—not as a reminder of violence but as a testament of impact and a barometer of character.

For two terms, she had been with these young people and impacted their hearts and minds with positivity, principles, beauty. These marks were made not only on the students but also on her colleagues, church family, and friends. I wondered about my mark, my footprint, my impact. Would my family and friends have fond memories of our special moments together? Are my students better for having contact with me? What would God comment about my character? Is He happy that I am allowing Him to work in and through me to encourage positive change in those around me, or is He saddened by my attempts to do all in my power? What fragrance do I emit? What is the testimony that my life shares to cheer others along the way?

I will continue to seek answers to these questions—not out of any need for self-glory but to leave others the better for having met me even for a short while. God wants us to let our light shine so that it can be used to point others to Him, where they can find solace and love and acceptance. Like those students who wrote the messages about their teacher—her life and care for them revealed that they were loved and accepted and seen as beautiful in God's eyes.

Even in death, Abby's impact is felt. God continues to use her life as a lightning rod for change. We do not need to wait for death to allow God to impact others through us.

Greta Michelle Joachim-Fox-Dyett

Are You Listening?

Trust in the LORD with all your heart,
and do not lean on your own understanding.
In all your ways acknowledge him,
and he will make straight your paths.
—Proverbs 3:5, 6, ESV

I watched as my husband peered around the counter at the server who had been preparing my apple pecan salad. My husband and I had just finished explaining to two servers why it had to be topped with grilled chicken and nothing else. I have a severe gluten allergy, and even the slightest amount can make me seriously ill. Unfortunately, my son had gotten the last grilled chicken. We tried to explain that if his sandwich had not been made, they could have put the grilled chicken in the salad and given him another option. They indicated that they understood and went back to preparing our meals.

A few moments later, my husband once again got the server's attention. She had been in the process of removing the chicken from the sandwich to add it to the salad. Though we had explained that even the slightest contact with gluten would make me ill, they hadn't understood.

My husband later explained to me that the Holy Spirit had prompted him to take those few steps to the right to see how the salad was being prepared. For a few moments, he battled with his fear of confrontation. Then he remembered the message that he had received in his morning devotion that day: "Perfect love casts out fear" (1 John 4:18, ESV). Remembering that God had not given him a spirit of fear gave him the courage he needed to safeguard my health.

God is concerned with every aspect of our lives. Nothing is so insignificant that He doesn't want to be involved. But we must be willing to listen to Him. We must be willing to do what He tells us regardless of how we feel about it. The Holy Spirit speaks in a still, small voice. It may simply feel like a nudge of conscience, but obeying Him can have a significant impact.

Father, I'm thankful that You want to be a part of my life. Help me to be willing to listen and obey when You speak. In Jesus' name, I pray, amen.

Aminata Coote

February 19

Love Connection

And we have known and believed the love that God hath to us.
God is love; and he that dwelleth in love dwelleth in God, and God in him.
—1 John 4:16, KJV

Today, I am reminded of the TV game show that first aired in 1983, *Love Connection*, hosted by Chuck Woolery. A bachelor or bachelorette was introduced to three prospective dates with the hope of selecting the right one and making a love connection.

Shows promoting love connections are very popular these days. Last week, *The Celebrity Dating Game* debuted and is much like the original *Dating Game* except the chosen single wins a date with a celebrity. It would be a fantastic game if the singles could select to compete for their favorite celebrity. And there are *The Bachelor* and *The Bachelorette* shows that are filled with hopeful singles looking to receive the final rose, an engagement ring, and a proposal.

COVID-19 brought with it a stay-at-home order, and I have become obsessed with the Hallmark Channel. Each movie has a different story, but they all end the same: a perfect love connection with the couple living happily ever after. Really?

I recently heard a sermon at church about being connected with the vine. In John 15:5, Jesus tells us, "I am the vine" (KJV). By this statement, He was trying to help us understand the value of being connected to Him by faith. A deep and growing relationship with Him will result in peace in all circumstances, hope in trials, strength in adversity, and joy that cannot be taken from you. Relationship with Him is the ultimate love connection and true happily ever after.

John 15:7 tells us: "If ye abide in me, and my words abide in you, ye shall ask what ye will, and it shall be done unto you" (KJV). In other words, so long as we are connected to Jesus and His words abide in us, we can ask what we wish, and it will be done for us.

Have you made this ultimate love connection?

Sylvia A. Franklin

Where My Heart Is—Part 1

For we know that if the tent that is our earthly home is destroyed, we have a building from God, a house not made with hands, eternal in the heavens.
—2 Corinthians 5:1, ESV

As a young child, I never felt that I belonged. Listening to such radio programs as *One Man's Family*, I realized my life didn't compare in any way to the dramatizations that were portrayed via the air waves.

So what created my sense of not belonging?

My childhood began in 1931 with a mother, father, and child—me—during the throes at the end of the American Great Depression. A dark shroud hung over us, a lure for my daddy that possessed an odd name: The Bottle. That's what my mommy called this invader when my daddy came home drunk.

When I was five, my parents separated, and I became a ward of Family and Children's Services. It was like a foster home in a decent neighborhood, not an institution. The middle-aged matron cared lovingly for us children who were now a family of unrelated people—but all of us kids knew this wasn't the way most children lived. In the five years that I lived there, I wasn't unhappy—never a pouter or a pity-me kid—but inside me was the desire to be like the other children at school whose parents came to school programs.

Yet there was an aspect of living with this patchwork family that I loved: teamwork. I learned quickly to enjoy the work ethics we were taught. Best of all, we went to church and learned about Jesus, something I'd never known before. At church, happiness prevailed. I was given a document called a passport to heaven with a photo of me and a drawing of Jesus to verify my official travel status. Anticipation of a better home evolved for me.

Then at age ten, I went to live with mom again. Our first home was one room, then other temporary lodgings followed. The frequent uprooting wasn't explained. I continued yearning for that heavenly home. Belief for a better home was set in my heart, and I had a passport to go there! Today I continue to look forward to that heavenly home with our heavenly Father.

Betty Kossick

February 21

Where My Heart Is—Part 2

By faith he [Abraham] looked forward with confidence to a city with lasting foundations whose designer and builder is God.
—Hebrews 11:10, *The Clear Word**

At the age of twelve, I set out to search for God's home after discovering Bible words that changed my life: "And we know that all things work together for good" (Romans 8:28, NKJV).

In time, I learned that Jesus was born as a baby, died as a man upon a cross, and arose from a tomb that couldn't hold Him. I held questions in my mental quiver. I needed answers.

A six-year search finally led me to Bible studies, suggested by my boyfriend. Before then, none of the many churches I visited ever offered me in-depth study of God's Holy Word. The studies led me to understand why Jesus came willingly to die for me—and for every human who ever lived for that matter, though some choose not to accept His gift. I discovered that Jesus' Father is my Father, too, and that my yearning for a home in heaven is the Holy Spirit working on my heart. And I understood the rest of Romans 8:28, "to those who love God, to those who are the called according to His purpose" (NKJV).

By this time, the fellow who told me that Bible studies would answer my questions about God had asked me to marry him. We established our marriage with a plan of home and family—not only on this earth but also in heaven and in the earth made new. In the book *The Adventist Home*, Ellen White writes, "God would have our families symbols of the family in heaven."† With an eternal home in sight, I learned that home is God's idea not only for an earthly lifetime but also for eternity. I also learned that home means all the redeemed of the earth, the family of God, living together, worshiping God, caring for each other.

For me, home is where the heart is. That statement is more than lovely words. It's a journey with Jesus.

I look forward to entering the heavenly home where my heart is.

Betty Kossick

* Jack Blanco, *The Clear Word* (Hagerstown, MD: Review and Herald®, 2003), 1269.
† Ellen G. White, *The Adventist Home* (Hagerstown, MD: Review and Herald®, 1980), 17.

February 22

Family Heirlooms

I have learned the secret of living in every situation.
—Philippians 4:12, NLT

As a little girl, I looked forward to the time when I would inherit precious family heirlooms. As the eldest daughter, I knew the day would come when I would be given my grandmother's cut-glass bowls or my mom's anniversary vases or perhaps my great-grandmother's china. It was a rite of passage, and the age-old tradition meant that family pieces, usually obtained at some great sacrifice or expense, would be looked after from one generation to the next.

As expected, I did receive my share of those handed-down collectibles and enjoyed them fully for many years. But recently I discovered something disconcerting.

Nobody wants my precious things.

It seems styles have changed. The treasured cut glass bowls would just take up space, my children tell me, and what can you use them for anyway, since they're not microwavable? And you can't put Great-Grandma's china in the dishwasher. I was heartbroken.

So if my children do not want these things, what remembrances can I leave them from my generation and those before me? What keepsakes do I have that are not in the china cabinet?

What we must hand down to them is the open sharing of our life experiences, particularly how we have seen the hand of God in our lives—how we have been able to endure gut-wrenching trials through our trust in Jesus—things we probably never spoke about before. As adults, they can comprehend and better appreciate their parents' life journeys. They have grown-up trials of their own. And the knowledge of how we managed our own predicaments and sorrows, with God's help, can bring courage and strength for today, as well as the future.

Perhaps sharing our weak moments and, in some cases, grief or painful experiences can be of more value than a cut glass bowl, more timeless than a set of china—handing down a source of strength to our adult children.

Linda Nottingham

February 23

Stop Trying to Fit Into Things You've Outgrown

"For my thoughts are not your thoughts,
neither are your ways my ways,"
declares the L*ORD.*
"As the heavens are higher than the earth,
so are my ways higher than your ways
and my thoughts than your thoughts."
—Isaiah 55:8, 9, NIV

Have you ever bought an outfit that was just a size too small? I haven't done that (recently), but what I have found is that after the pandemic, my going-out outfits were just a size too small. (Friends, please make me feel better and tell me it's not just me!)

As the world opened back up and there were places to be that I needed to be dressed up for, I looked in my closet and realized that my dresses were just a bit too small. Yes, I could work toward my goal weight—but follow me, I'm going somewhere.

I tried to put them on, but they just didn't fit well, and I was uncomfortable in them. So I went and bought a few new dresses because I had only a few days before a speaking engagement.

As tempted as I was to buy the size I used to fit into, I knew that would not be wise. So I went ahead and reluctantly bought the next size up. They fit well, and I felt confident as I was dressed for both work and speaking publicly.

This was when the thought hit me, *Stop trying to fit into things you've outgrown!* Not just my outgrown outfits—but in any area of my life. Sometimes, I am trying to squeeze myself into situations that no matter how much I want to fit, I just don't. I need to realize that there are times that certain situations just will not fit—and that's OK.

There have been times when God has called me out of work situations, and it was time to move on. There have been times when God has called me out of friendships and types of conversations that no longer fit, and as difficult as it may have been, I had to go.

God knows exactly what He needs to strip from us so that He can take us on the journey that He wants us on. Is there any situation in your life that you are desperately trying to squeeze yourself into? It's OK to reassess where you are—and move into the next growth phase.

Kaysian C. Gordon

When We Want to Give Up

Our Lord, we belong to you.
We tell you what worries us,
and you won't let us fall.
—Psalm 55:22, CEV

The day I wrote this meditation, I was tired; I had not been out for two weeks. I was sick, and I was tired of being sick. I have a disease that doesn't kill but has no cure.

That day, I decided to read Psalm 55 (CEV), and it fit me like a glove because there you can see that David was also tired and sad: "Listen, God, to my prayer! Don't reject my request" (verse 1, CEV). Sometimes we feel that God doesn't listen to us, that He seems to be doing other, more important, things.

The psalmist continued: "My heart is racing fast, and I am afraid of dying. I am trembling with fear, completely terrified" (verses 4, 5, CEV). I don't know what worries you, what hurts you, or what scares you. We all go through situations where we feel insecure, weak, and exposed and just want to escape—just like David, who said, "I wish I had wings like a dove, so I could fly far away and be at peace. I would go and live in some distant desert" (verses 6, 7, CEV). Although if I could choose, I would flee to a beach or a warm forest.

But the truth is that we can't always escape from our reality, and that is why the best thing to do is face it. David knew this. "Morning, noon, and night you hear my concerns and my complaints" (verse 17, CEV).

This is the recipe that David shares with us: keep in touch with God, let our escape be with Him because He is the one who will save us, and at any time of the day when we speak to Him or sing to Him, He hears our voice.

And the chapter ends in a sublime way: "Our Lord, we belong to you. We tell you what worries us, and you won't let us fall" (verse 22, CEV). Bring everything that is hurting you, everything that is making you tired and sick, and give it to Him; He will take it and will accompany you, keeping you on your feet. I like to imagine that when you bring your problems, discomforts, or illnesses to Jesus, you give them to Him, He grabs them, puts them on His shoulder, and walks beside you.

Today, let's tell God, "Lord, I am tired; I leave *everything* at Your feet."

Cecilia Nanni

February 25

PUSH While Waiting

For the word of the LORD is right,
And all his works are done in truth.
—Psalm 33:4, KJV

Psalm 121 is one of my mother's favorite psalms. She would read it to me when I was in a disheartened mood. Now, it is one of my favorites:

"I will lift up mine eyes unto the hills, from whence cometh my help. My help cometh from the LORD, which made heaven and earth. He will not suffer thy foot to be moved: he that keepeth thee will not slumber. . . . The LORD is thy keeper: the LORD is thy shade upon thy right hand. . . . The LORD shall preserve thee from all evil: he shall preserve thy soul. The LORD shall preserve thy going out and thy coming in from this time forth, and even for evermore" (Psalm 121:1–8, KJV). God is my hiding place and strength in my time of need. As a child, I had to learn that God will allow negative events into my life so that I can grow and learn to wait on Him. The waiting time or season may be over today, tomorrow, or perhaps years from now. Until then, I must wait.

There is something I can do in the waiting season. I keep busy by praying! God's permissive will is—and always desires—what is best for me because I am His child, and He loves me. Not all my prayers are answered the first time or in the manner I desire, but I keep praying anyway—I pray until something happens (PUSH).

Along the way, I have learned to step into unexpected blessings, step over the mess life brings me, and not sweat the small stuff! Life is too short to be anxious! I am mindful that if God answered every prayer in the manner I first wished for, it might not have been best for me. Constantly praying renews my spiritual life and keeps me growing in my Christian faith. I know from experience that He may not come when I want Him; however, He is always right on time! I suggest that you, too, hold on and thank God for the many blessings He sends our way and for the waiting seasons when He is growing us to our best.

Yvonne E. Ealey

No Worries, No Doubt, Just Trust God

Fear thou not; for I am with thee: be not dismayed; for I am thy God: I will strengthen thee; yea, I will help thee; yea, I will uphold thee with the right hand of my righteousness.
—Isaiah 41:10, KJV

God, our Creator, knows that we are frail and easily frightened when faced with the vicissitudes of life. So, throughout the Bible, God reminds us, "Be careful for nothing; but in everything by prayer and supplication with thanksgiving let your requests be made known unto God. And the peace of God, which passeth all understanding, shall keep your hearts and minds through Christ Jesus" (Philippians 4:6, 7, KJV).

I think of the disciples who set the boat out to sail after a long day of Jesus teaching and healing the multitude. Jesus went to sleep, and all was at peace until "there arose a great storm of wind, and the waves beat into the ship, so that it was now full" (Mark 4:37, KJV). The disciples, forgetting that Jesus was in the boat—that there was no need to fear—found Jesus and cried, "Master, carest thou not that we perish? And he arose, and rebuked the wind, and said unto the sea, Peace, be still. And the wind ceased, and there was a great calm. And he said unto them, Why are ye so fearful? how is it that ye have no faith?" (verses 38, 39, KJV).

In another story, there was a famine in the land. God sent the prophet Elijah to the widow of Zarephath, saying, "I have commanded a widow woman there to sustain thee" (1 Kings 17:9, KJV). Elijah, upon meeting this widow, requested that she make a little cake for him first, and then cakes for her and her son. She hesitated because she had just enough flour and oil to make a cake for her and her son and feared that she and her son would die. Elijah assured her that if she did as he requested, God had promised to provide. The flour and oil would last as long as they needed it. They could trust Him and His promise.

So when our faith is being tested, our spiritual eyesight blinded, our stamina weakened, our emotions drained, we can stand on God's promise that He will never leave us nor forsake us. He is our strong and sure refuge . . . a very present help in time of trouble.

Cynthia Best-Goring

February 27

God Is Not Unfair

For God is not unjust. He will not forget how hard you have worked for him and how you have shown your love to him by caring for other believers, as you still do.
—Hebrews 6:10, NLT

In 2019, our health professionals team received an invitation to present a nursing conference in Kenya. The team coordinator provided a list of the requirements, which included a visa to enter the country. The mission trip was scheduled for late May. Since I was invited to attend my great niece's cotillion in Maryland during Easter weekend, I planned to make a personal visit to the Kenyan embassy in Washington, DC. I carefully assembled all the documents required for the visa application and eagerly awaited the day for our air travel.

After attending the cotillion and visiting with family and friends, it was time to visit the Kenyan embassy. We arrived very early and waited for the office to be opened. Once inside the door, we waited our turn and presented our documents. We had anticipated completing the process in the four business days left before returning home but were told that the visa application process would take ten business days.

The attendant also said we had two options: purchase a money order for the expedited fee to get the visas before leaving or provide a self-addressed priority envelope to have the visas mailed to us. He directed us to a post office three blocks away where we could obtain either option. Arriving at the post office, we found people waiting outside a locked door. We prayed and waited forty minutes, but no one showed up to let us in.

We walked back to the embassy and presented our dilemma to the attendant. I began explaining to him that we were going on a mission trip and that we had previously worked in Kenya for six years as missionaries. He listened carefully, told us to take a seat, and disappeared with our documents. I continued praying for divine intervention.

Before reaching my seat, I was called back to the desk. "Have a nice trip," the attendant said as he handed us our passports. I opened the passports and was pleasantly surprised to see the visas enclosed. When I asked about the fee, he just smiled.

This reminded me of God's promise, found in our text for today, that we can depend on Him. He keeps His promises. Let us put God to the test. He never fails.

Lydia D. Andrews

The Appointment

But now having been set free from sin, and having become slaves of God, you have your fruit to holiness, and the end, everlasting life. For the wages of sin is death, but the gift of God is eternal life in Christ Jesus our Lord.
—Romans 6:22, 23, NKJV

This morning I accepted an appointment from my optometrist's office. My acceptance was in the form of a website registration to get my name in the appointment book. It was the reservation for a much-coveted time slot with the physician. This schedule is golden. There are often no vacancies available in the appointment schedule. There are even days of the week when the doctors do not come in for appointments. Those appointments are valuable, and I did not want to miss mine. So after completing the registration, I hurriedly went to my computer calendar to enter the appointment to ensure that I would get in to see the optometrist. My fingers raced across the keys to get that appointment solidified. It was as though if I didn't do this, I would lose the appointment.

Interestingly, as my eyes finally fell on the appointment square on the calendar, I was surprised to find that the appointment had been entered already. It was entered automatically from the source when I accepted the invitation. There was no need for me to do anything other than accept the invitation for the appointment.

It took only a brief moment for me to reflect on the significance of this little scenario. Is it not just like us to feel that we have some task to complete to secure our appointment with Jesus even after He has reserved our place with Him on that special day? He extended the invitation. My reservation was confirmed and registered automatically in the book of life when I accepted His invitation. It is human nature to feel that if it is too good to be true, it cannot be true. But when it comes to the free gift of salvation, it really is that good, and there is nothing we can do to earn our salvation—our reservation for eternal life.

Ella Louise Smith Simmons

March 1

I'll See You Tomorrow!

For the Lord himself shall descend from heaven with a shout, with the voice of the archangel, and with the trump of God: and the dead in Christ shall rise first: then we which are alive and remain shall be caught up together with them in the clouds, to meet the Lord in the air: and so shall we ever be with the Lord.
—1 Thessalonians 4:16, 17, KJV

My heart was heavy. A young woman whom I loved was dying of breast cancer. She had been my foster daughter many years ago. I was flooded with memories of conversations we'd shared and the fun things we had done together. I remembered hugging her close and kissing the top of her curly blonde head. But now, she was many miles away.

As I drove home from work, I remembered that my husband had an appointment that evening. I would be home alone. He had encouraged me to buy supper somewhere so that I wouldn't have to cook for just myself. I remembered seeing a Facebook ad for a new place that advertised wholesome, homemade, takeout food. They had both vegetable and mushroom pot pies on their menu, so I stopped to try one. When I entered, a man ahead of me was telling the woman waiting on him that he always eats out in that area of town, and if the food was good, he would be back.

Without missing a beat, she replied, "Well then, I'll see you tomorrow!"

I chuckled to myself. I liked that she had such faith in her product.

Faith!

This brief exchange prompted me to consider my faith in Jesus. I know that His Word is sure, and that gives me faith that there is indeed a better "tomorrow" coming. The loved ones to whom we have said goodbye will be reunited with us. There will be no more tears. No more goodbyes. No more cancer. I will one day see this much-loved daughter again. I am confident that Jesus is Lord, and He is faithful. So I can find comfort and even joy by saying, "I'll see you tomorrow!"

Marsha Hammond-Brummel

Worship in the Pandemic

Remember your Creator
in the days of your youth,
before the days of trouble come
and the years approach when you will say,
"I find no pleasure in them."
—Ecclesiastes 12:1, NIV

I have always been fascinated by youth in my church. They surface as shy kindergartens, fidgeting nervously in front of the church saying their memory verses, then gradually metamorphose into confident youth displaying their various talents for the Lord.

I did not realize the wealth of talent that the youth in the churches here in Jamaica possessed until "face-to-face" worship was replaced by "online" worship during the pandemic. Amateurs in technology received on-the-job training and soon became experts. Musical talents exploded among young adults, teens, and amazingly uninhibited children who were a breath of fresh air. Sermons were preached with godly power and eloquence by young men and young women. Many of these young people were emboldened to declare to the world stories of the struggles they were having, which adults may not be as honest to admit to at church and even more so to the world. These testimonies no doubt helped many to deal with similar issues. My worship experience reached a new height, and all this resulted from a devastating pandemic, where some blamed God and stopped worshiping Him. But Satan was a defeated foe as it let our youth shine for our Protector!

One reassurance that I received from this experience is that God's church is alive, despite the many problems we may have in our midst. I am saddened when I hear numbers being quoted for the attrition of youth in our churches around the world. We do need them for the continuity of the work, so we all must seek, find, and unearth their hidden talents and encourage them to use these for the Lord before Satan uses them for his gain. I believe that if older members slowly step aside and systematically give young people responsible positions, along with guidance from our wealth of experience, empathy as we remember our imperfect past, and correction with love, the church will retain them and will remain alive and well!

Cecelia Grant

March 3

Alone, but Not Alone

Keep me as the apple of Your eye,
Hide me under the shadow of Your wings.
—Psalm 17:8, NKJV

When the world shut down because of COVID-19, I was very optimistic that it would not be a lengthy lockdown here in Canada and that, as a progressive country, we would have "all the answers" to take care of the situation rapidly. But as the days turned into weeks and the weeks into months, the infection rate and death rate in my province of Ontario remained at a level that prevented the leaders from reopening churches. I missed the physical touch.

I live alone, so I find great joy in fellowshiping with my church family. I especially look forward to prayer meeting and Sabbath worship. The singing, praying, and sharing together bring me great joy.

Sadly, within a week, I lost three family members and a few family friends. My mind stopped absorbing the loss. I accepted the offered calls of condolence, the prayers and promises. I prayed many prayers myself and read and reread the promises, and I found comfort in them. Later that day, someone asked me, "Sonia, how are you really doing?"

"I am coping," I replied. But was I really?

At bedtime, I couldn't settle; I felt alone; I needed a hug, a real human touch. I needed a face without a mask, I needed a hand without a glove, and I needed someone who would not back away because they were scared to breathe the exhaled air that came from me. I was not coping. *Dear God! I need a hug!*

Then I remembered the promise I had claimed that morning, "Keep me as the apple of Your eye; hide me under the shadow of Your wings" (Psalm 17:8, NKJV). I realized He had not lost sight of me. I am right in His focal point. I am hidden under His wings. I called out, "God, please hold me, squeeze me close to You." With a tear in my eye, I hugged and squeezed my own body, but I felt His squeeze and the comfort of His presence. I was not alone. Soon, I drifted off to sleep, and I awoke a few hours later with the reassurance of His presence.

Be assured that He will not leave you or forsake you, for under His wings we abide.

Sonia Kennedy-Brown

March 4

God Is My Shelter

Whoever dwells in the shelter of the Most High
will rest in the shadow of the Almighty.
I will say of the L*ORD*, *"He is my refuge and my fortress,*
my God, in whom I trust."
—Psalm 91:1, 2, NIV

I am fortunate to live in a country that still has lots of old buildings dating back hundreds of years. Many towns have historical centers with studwork houses, narrow alleys, and even city walls with gates. It is almost like taking a trip back into history. Strolling along the streets with beautiful old houses is an uplifting experience. Inscriptions show when the houses were built. These houses are not just buildings; they are monuments of history and human lives. They have sheltered many generations.

Then there are the impressive churches and cathedrals, built with high, vaulted ceilings and steeples and stained-glass windows intended to instill reverence for God's awesome majesty. Many date back to the thirteenth or fourteenth century. These buildings have seen people worshiping God in different ways throughout the centuries. They have inspired fear of a God who torments sinners in hell, and the gospel of a loving God has also been proclaimed within their walls. They have protected people who fled wars, pestilences, and persecution.

On the top of a cone-shaped mountain just outside the town where I live, I can see one of the many German castles. The Hohenzollern castle dates back to the thirteenth century, although the building I now see was rebuilt in the neo-Gothic style starting in 1850. With its many towers and fortifications, it is an acclaimed masterpiece of nineteenth-century military architecture.

Perched high up on the mountain, the castle is visible over long distances. Every time I approach my home, I see the fortress on the mountain and am reminded of Psalm 91. I, too, can dwell in the shelter of the Most High and rest in the shadow of the Almighty. I can say, the Lord "is my refuge and my fortress, my God, in whom I trust" (Psalm 91:2, NIV). But sometimes, the castle is hidden in foggy clouds and is invisible. And yet, I know that it is there, even though I can't see it. We may not always be able to see how God is sheltering us in our darkest moments. But He is there. Always. Trust Him.

Hannele Ottschofski

March 5

He Is in Charge

"For my thoughts are not your thoughts,
neither are your ways my ways,"
declares the LORD.
"As the heavens are higher than the earth,
so are my ways higher than your ways
and my thoughts than your thoughts."
—Isaiah 55:8, 9, NIV

As I write this, a significant portion of the world's population is under some sort of government-decreed restriction on activity and mandated physical isolation as a result of COVID-19.

The pandemic has led many people to question where God is in all this. Many say they know exactly why this is happening and make pronouncements about the end of the world. I understand all the talk. I have had moments when I wondered why God is allowing us to go through this—not just the physical restrictions but the impact this is having on so many people because businesses have had to close, and millions have lost their jobs and source of income.

I have prayed and asked God to stop this virus, as have others all over the planet, yet more people are infected every day, and people die. It is easy to think God is not interested in what is going on with us down here. When those thoughts enter my head, I must find a way to bring my thoughts back to where they need to be.

I try to count ways that God has shown clearly that He cares about what happens to me. Each of us can think of times when God has intervened in the small things in our lives, whether it is finding misplaced keys or someone calling just when you needed to hear what that person had to say. Someone I know was down to her last US$20 because she couldn't work due to coronavirus restrictions. She happened to see a neighbor, who told her from a safe distance that she had left a gift in her mailbox. Retrieving the envelope from her mailbox, my friend found US$1,000.

God works in mysterious ways. He does not always answer our prayers the way we expect. However, He is always looking out for us, and He is always in control.

Jean Arthur

Not Living Up to Your Name

"I will make you into a great nation
and I will bless you;
I will make your name great,
and you will be a blessing."
—Genesis 12:2, NIV

Jabez is a man whose story is told in the Old Testament. In 1 Chronicles, Jabez, a well-respected man, is hinted to be an ancestor in the lineage of the kings' tribe of Judah. His name is Hebrew for "he will cause pain." His mother stated, "I gave birth to him in pain" when she named him. What a way to describe your child! From birth, Jabez lived with this name and the knowledge that he had brought pain and sorrow to his mother. He cried out to God to change his legacy.

"Jabez was more honorable than his brothers. His mother had named him Jabez, saying, 'I gave birth to him in pain.' Jabez cried out to the God of Israel, 'Oh, that you would bless me and enlarge my territory! Let your hand be with me, and keep me from harm so that I will be free from pain.' And God granted his request" (1 Chronicles 4:9, 10, NIV).

Jabez's prayer to God was answered. His prayer nullified the label, and his life contradicted his name. He did not cause harm. Instead, the Bible tells us that he was more honorable than all his brothers. There is a town bearing his name mentioned in 1 Chronicles 2:55 where families of scribes lived—although it's not known if it was definitively named after this Jabez.

Sometimes we are given a label by others that can hold us back if we allow it to. We can let what others say what they believe about us cause us to feel shame or less than we are. People may call us names or say things that make us feel afraid or limit ourselves. Jabez is an example of what to do when others limit us. Turn to God. Cry out to Him. Pray and ask Him to make us a different person. God will grant us our requests and grow us to be the people He desires. He will enlarge our impact on this world when we trust Him and not what others say.

D. Renee' Mobley-Neal

March 7

Wholly, Holey, Holy

And no one was able to answer Him a word,
nor from that day on did anyone dare question Him anymore.
—Matthew 22:46, NKJV

They gathered there in the crowded temple courts—young men, ardent and zealous, arms locked across rich-robed chests—exchanging sly glances through half-closed eyes at the young Galilean looking unflinchingly back at them with the calm dignity of a king. They'd been bitter enemies once, these Pharisees and certain Herodians and Sadducees, but now they were one, allied under a shared enmity to Christ. Exuding a false sincerity, they questioned Him. "Is it lawful for us to give tribute unto Caesar, or no?" (Luke 20:22, KJV). "In the resurrection, whose wife of the seven will she be?"(Matthew 22:36, NKJV). "Teacher, which is the great commandment in the law?"(Matthew 22:28, NKJV).

It wasn't thirst for greater enlightenment that brought them here. They had despised and rejected His teachings, challenged Him mercilessly, and laid schemes to ensnare and condemn Him. No, it wasn't pure, bright truth they were thirsting for this day—they thirsted for His death. And that they would get. But not now, not on this day. On this day—this last day Christ would ever teach in the temple—His enemies must bide their time.

In a voice choked with anguish and a heart wrenched from sorrow, Christ turned to the awestruck crowd who witnessed this strange contest between the corrupt priests and this Teacher, whose knowledge and goodness only shone brighter after every assault. With amazed anxiety, they heard Him exclaim, "O Jerusalem, Jerusalem, . . . how often would I have gathered thy children together, as a hen doth gather her brood under her wings, and ye would not!" (Luke 13:34, KJV).

The young Galilean passed through the temple for the last time; with Him went God's presence, forever withdrawn from the temple built for His glory. It's true; not all received His grace that day, but a voice that has reached down the millennia declares, "A seed shall serve him; it shall be accounted to the Lord for a generation" (Psalm 22:30, KJV) and "the earth shall be full of the knowledge of the LORD, as the waters cover the sea" (Isaiah 11:9, KJV). Amen and amen!

Jeannette Busby Johnson

What's in Your Hand?

And the Lord said unto him, What is that in thine hand?
—Exodus 4:2, KJV

Fear is a weapon of paralysis. As recorded in Exodus chapter four, God called Moses to lead Israel's children out of bondage, and his experience is a classic example of using what one has. When God called Moses to be His spokesman in Pharaoh's court, he felt utterly empty-handed and unequipped physically. I can imagine his confusion and fear of inadequacy, both socially and politically. But God, who can fight any battle with the flimsiest of things, reminded him that even the rod in his hand would be a tool by which wonders would happen.

Like Moses, I knew I was no match for the plethora of challenges facing me while raising my children in a fast-paced city without a commensurate source of income. I had no paid job, so I resorted to selling secondhand clothing—a situation in which I was often overcome by fear and shame. One evening, I realized that if God didn't perform a miracle, the children would have no food for lunch to take to school the next day. It was sobering to look at them and not meet their most essential physical need—food! My husband was struggling to make ends meet in another city, and I had our old worn-out car. Suddenly, a thought flashed in my mind, *Use your parked car as a taxi.* I had never done taxi driving before; moreover, the environment was a very crazy and chaotic one for an old car, which might easily give out on me. Undaunted, I prayed and asked God for His protection.

With my teenage brother-in-law acting as my conductor and bodyguard, we set off from Okoba village to Ikeja, Lagos, and did not return home till after midnight, having made just enough for the next day, N50.00—less than US$1.00! This was a fair achievement. God protected us and the car from the rough roads and the insanity that floated all around us. He used an old worn-out, overlooked tool in my possession to perform a miracle of providing food for my six-member household. Sometimes we do not realize the value of what we have in our hands until we are in a gravely trying situation.

Indeed, "the angel of the Lord encampeth round about them that fear him, and delivereth them" (Psalm 34:7, KJV).

Ekele P. Ukegbu-Nwankwo

March 9

Five Loaves and Two Fishes

There is a lad here, which hath five barley loaves,
and two small fishes: but what are they among so many?
—John 6:9, KJV

"OK, J, stay in the line with this lady while I quickly go to get an item."

I looked around to see the protesting eyes of a little boy loudly declaring, "She's a stranger!" I, too, was ready to join the protest. However, before we could unite in a full protest, his mother was gone. We then fixed our gazes on each other, quickly concluding that we might as well make the best of the situation we had been thrust into.

We proceeded to order and collect our meals. J found a table for us, and we sat down. After finishing a beautiful grace, he declared, "I'm a Christian, you know!"

These words flowed from his tongue with such ease and profound pride yet with such innocence and humility. I asked him how long he had been a Christian, to which he promptly replied, "I am nine years old now, but I was baptized when I was eight. I have always loved God!"

Just as we were about to engage in a deeper conversation, J's mother returned. She politely interjected and indicated to J that he would have to complete his meal on the plane as they had to go. She thanked me, and J introduced her by name and gave me a personal invite to his city (all this now to her amazement . . . I had to smile). We wished each other a safe trip and said our goodbyes.

As I reflected on the experience, five words resonated with me . . . five precious loaves to feast on, "I have always loved God!" I was reminded of the little boy in the story recorded in John 6:9 who, like J, willingly shared what he had, no doubt motivated by love. May we all demonstrate that childlike faith and give our all to a Savior who promises to make us fishers of men, and the blessings will continue to multiply!

Simone E. Johnson

Love Written in Marker

The grass withereth, the flower fadeth:
but the word of our God shall stand for ever.
—Isaiah 40:8, KJV

Our granddaughter's birthday was coming soon. Her planned quilt, designed to match a pillow she'd received earlier from me, was not quite ready. I had done the piecing for the top (planning, placing, and sewing the blocks). Next, a long-arm quilter stitched all the parts together: the top, batting, and the backing. I also had someone embroider one of the blocks with a message from me. When it was finally completed, as I was admiringly looking over it and thanking God that it would at least get there in her birthday month, I realized I'd left out the word *love*. I always include the word *love* in those messages.

Oh no! In my haste to get it there within a certain time frame, I'd overlooked writing that word on the directions for the lady who embroidered it. I didn't want to be disappointed with myself, so I grabbed a permanent marker and wrote it on there with the marker. When I told our son what had happened, he sounded a little dubious—a marker? Yes, and it didn't bother me at all because love was in every effort made to get that quilted blanket together.

Unlike us, God has not left anything out of His messages that will cause us to doubt, question, or disbelieve His Word.

Our son probably thought that even a permanent marker might fade or completely wash out with repeated use and washings. Through the centuries, efforts have been made to destroy the Word, keep people from reading it, and minimize its value for our salvation. But even if those efforts had been successful, God's Word tells us that we can behold Him everywhere, so we are without excuse (Psalm 19:1–4; Romans 1:20).

We can know how much God loves us by reading His Word and beholding His works in nature. His outstretched arms on the cross prove it all and manifest love in action. God's plan of salvation is for everyone. We can't say God doesn't love us because of anything that He omitted to show, do, or have written for us. May God bless our desires to know Him better and better each day.

Sharon M. Thomas

March 11

Trusting God

But in the day that I'm afraid, I lay all my fears before you and trust in you with all my heart.
—Psalm 56:3, TPT

I believe that when I came out of my mother's womb, fear was there to welcome me into the world. I was a World War II baby. My dad came home with post-traumatic stress, and nine months later, a very beautiful but anxious child was born.

Research tells us that our environment plays a vital role in who we will ultimately become, and that environment starts in the womb. An eight-week course on emotional healing allowed me to investigate what my childhood environment was like. I discovered the spirit of fear was part of my womb experience. I was afraid of everything, always thinking and looking for the worst. It took the joy out of living and the excitement out of adventure. My imagination ran wild like your dreams after you watched a horror movie.

One incident that comes to mind is the night I had to speak at a camp meeting. Being the only woman among theologians who would speak that week was scary. The timing of my speaking did not help because it was well into the week on Thursday, which was Women's Emphasis Day. Yes, there was lots of time to rehearse my message and pray for clarity of speech, but there was also a lot of time to worry. There was the fear of wondering whether I was speaking what God wanted. There was the fear of messing up. Finally, kneeling in prayer and confessing my fears, I gave them to the Lord. After all, this was His ministry, and I am His servant. "Please allow Your Spirit to stand up in me and speak," was my prayer. And He did.

The spirit of fear is not from God but real, nonetheless. God gave us the Spirit of love, power, and a strong mind. Otherwise, we would lose our minds because fear torments us. The Word of God tells us repeatedly to "fear not." Why? Because He will never leave or forsake His children. *Never!* God is with us, and His perfect love casts out fear.

Whenever fear comes knocking, instead of paralyzing me and causing anxiety and stress, it motivates me to trust God. Trusting God is knowing Him and believing He will do what He promises. Always! So I can say with the psalmist that I lay all my fears before Him whenever I am afraid, trusting Him with all my heart.

Shirley P. Scott

When Angels Ride Harleys

For He shall give His angels charge over you,
To keep you in all your ways.
—Psalm 91:11, NKJV

I was nervous. I had never driven an RV before, but I found that whichever way I turned the wheel, the rest of the vehicle followed. I felt confident now, and we had to drive through only one large city on our trip from Hazelton, British Columbia, Canada, to Berrien Springs, Michigan, United States of America.

I stuck closely behind my husband, who was driving our pickup truck, pulling a trailer with my horse inside. "Whew! We made it!" I breathed a sigh of relief after we got past the last bit of construction and left Edmonton. On the open road now.

"We can do this," I exulted. Just then, my husband turned off onto a side road. *That is odd*, I thought, *it will be so hard to turn around*. I wasn't happy when he stopped, got out of the pickup, and walked to the RV.

"There is something wrong with the pickup," he said. "We need to drive back into town to Canadian Tire." I reluctantly agreed and followed him to the parking lot.

But the service at the desk was disappointing. "No, we can't get to your vehicle for another week."

"What? We have a horse out there and have an important appointment at Mayo Clinic. We can't stay here!" The man busily gave me a couple of other places to call and returned to his desk. The calls brought the same response. No one was available to look at the truck. As I ended the last call, I was wailing, "But I have a horse in there. We can't stay here a week!"

At that moment, a gray-haired man on a Harley Davidson motorcycle headed toward the store door instead stepped over to us. "I couldn't help hearing your conversation. I have a friend that can help." Another couple of phone calls, and we were now a parade led by a flashy Harley, followed by an old horse trailer and truck, and then the RV. Our kind rescuer led us to his mechanic friend, who quickly looked and pronounced he could fix it without even removing the horse from the trailer and told us there was a great Chinese restaurant around the corner where we could eat while we waited. Was our new Harley friend an angel? Maybe not, but the angels sent him.

Sherry Taujale Shrestha

March 13

Breath: God's Priceless Gift to Mankind

Then the Lord God formed a man from the dust of the ground and breathed into his nostrils the breath of life, and the man became a living being.
—Genesis 2:7, NIV

The outbreak of COVID-19 has given me cause to contemplate and evaluate much of what I hold dear. Two items that I have been contemplating for a few months now are the concepts of breath and life. Many mornings, as soon as I'm awake, my mind shifts into that contemplative mode. What is breath? What is life? Are these two one and the same?

Breath to me is a most amazing thing. Often these days, I sit quietly, breathe in, and hold it for as long as possible, then exhale slowly. This process has become so fascinating to me.

No one in this world can gather and store breath, this most valuable commodity. Each living being can take only one breath at a time, but before taking in that one breath, another breath must be let out—one in, one out. It's an exchange. You cannot take one in and not let one out. That ounce of breath at a time is what keeps all life-forms alive.

So then, what is life? Leviticus 17:11 says, "For the life of a creature is in the blood" (NIV). Hmmm. "For the life of a creature is in the blood"—what does this mean? I know that blood is the river of life that transports oxygen to every cell. It seems to me, then, that the blood without that one breath is dead.

Of all God's creation, humans alone can boast that they received life directly from God. Genesis 2:7 states, "Then the Lord God formed a man from the dust of the ground and breathed into his nostrils the breath of life, and the man became a living being" (NIV). How precious, how marvelous is that!

Yes, breath gives life. This most valuable commodity was given to man at Creation. God thought it so valuable that He took the time to personally breathe the breath of life into the newly formed man's nostrils, and the man became a living soul.

Jasmine E. Grant

Kitty!

"Let not your heart be troubled; you believe in God, believe also in Me. In My Father's house are many mansions; if it were not so, I would have told you. I go to prepare a place for you. And if I go and prepare a place for you, I will come again and receive you to Myself; that where I am, there you may be also."
—John 14:1–3, NKJV

Kitty was the name given to the weak-looking stray kitten that came into our yard. My two grandchildren, Demetrio and Alayna, fed and nursed Kitty until she became strong. This kitten soon became a part of our family. She was very playful and happy. About two weeks after living with us, a dreadful accident occurred: Kitty fell and died. There was not a dry eye in our house. We all wept as we said goodbye to Kitty. What an unwelcome interruption to our happy home. Everyone was now so very sad. Gloom was everywhere because our beloved Kitty had died.

It was never in God's plan for sadness and death to be the experience of His children. Our pets and all humanity were made to live forever in happiness. An enemy entered our great big, wonderful world and spoiled it. God made all things bright and beautiful; all the creatures were made for our happiness and joy. But our joy will return when Jesus puts an end to sin and death. After that, no one will die; we will have new pets, and they will never die. All our plants will live forever too; roses will bloom eternally, never to fade. Everything will be in perfect harmony. Animals that are now harmful will be nice to be near. No one will be unkind, no crime, no sickness, and no crying. Heaven will be perfect for everyone to enjoy, and best of all, we will see Jesus face-to-face.

The earth made new will be so beautiful; I can hardly wait to go there. The Bible describes it to us in such beautiful and magnificent descriptions: "But as it is written: 'Eye has not seen, nor ear heard, nor have entered into the heart of man the things which God has prepared for those who love Him' " (1 Corinthians 2:9).

Heaven is such a safe place that no kitten will fall and die and no humans will get sick anymore. Let's accept Jesus into our hearts now and look forward to when He comes again.

Jacqueline Hope HoShing-Clarke

March 15

Handing Over the Keys

For He shall give His angels charge over you,
To keep you in all your ways.
—Psalm 91:11, NKJV

My daughter and her friend had each been looking for the "perfect grad dress." Not finding what they considered to be the right one, they asked if we could go to Spokane, Washington, United States of America, on a shopping trip. It was the beginning of spring break; most snow had melted off the roads we would travel during the four-and-a-half-hour drive to Spokane. Always up for an adventure, I said we could go. We booked a hotel, and with a prayer for safety, we headed off. We shopped and ate out, and the girls' mission was accomplished by two o'clock the next afternoon!

My daughter asked if she could drive home. The day was beautiful. We asked God to travel with us and were on our way. About eighty kilometers (fifty miles) from home, she pulled over in the town of Beaverdell, British Columbia, Canada, for gas. She handed me the car keys and asked me to drive the rest of the way.

As we started on our last stretch, the sky quickly clouded over. We were suddenly buffeted by a strong wind and engulfed in a blanket of fog and blowing snow. Suddenly, a large tree branch was coming directly toward the car. Just as quickly, the tree disappeared and came down with a crunch on the back end of our Subaru wagon. I slowly pulled off to the side of the road to survey the rest of the damage. The girls, though shaken, were uninjured. The windshield was broken. The passenger side headlight was out, and that side of the hood was buckled up under the windshield. The sides of the car were not even scraped, but the back end showed that something heavy had hit and glanced off the roof—yet the rear window and taillights were still intact. Not far behind where we had stopped, a large tree now lay across the highway. The wind was still blowing, swirling the snow, and with no cell coverage, we proceeded on home.

This incident has come to mind many times since, particularly when driving on mountainous roads. I am so thankful for our heavenly Father's constant, watchful care. When we trust Him and ask for His companionship, He will "give His angels charge over [us] to keep [us] in all [our] ways" (Psalm 91:11, NKJV).

Beverly D. Hazzard

He Has Our Back

Sing, O heavens; and be joyful, O earth; and break forth into singing, O mountains: for the Lord hath comforted his people, and will have mercy upon his afflicted.
—Isaiah 49:13, KJV

For forty years, God provided food for the children of Israel. He didn't give them the manna for a week at a time. He gave it to them daily. If they collected more than a day's worth at a time, the unused manna rotted by morning. Why? Scripture said it was like coriander seeds, but coriander seeds can last much longer than a day. The fact that the manna melted when the sun "waxed hot" means that it was only one day's supply. God designed the manna to be good for only one day. He wanted His children to rely on Him for their daily sustenance. He wanted them to look forward to the next day. He wanted them to know that He was the One who brought them out of Egypt and was going to be the One who would feed them during the journey to Canaan. He wanted to remind them daily.

The Lord knows what our needs are. He will provide for us no matter what is on the horizon, if only we trust that He will do what He promised: put food on our table, provide water to quench our thirst, and give shelter from pestilence. We tend to think that we have to gather and hoard things to make sure that we are not lacking, forgetting that everything in the universe is God's, and He will never leave us nor forsake us (see Hebrews 13:5).

While Jesus was with His disciples, they, too, forgot that they were in the presence of a powerful Master who fed Israel in the desert as well as the five thousand and the four thousand. We have so many examples of the power of our Omnipotent God; still, we worry about our tomorrow. Sure, there is pestilence in the world, but He will protect us as He did the children of Israel from the plagues in the land of Egypt. He said that not a hair of our head would fall without His knowing. Sometimes I imagine God chuckling at all the solutions men think they have, not realizing that the answer is in His hands.

I pray that this precious promise will encourage your heart: "Who shall separate us from the love of Christ? Shall tribulation, or distress, or persecution, or famine, or nakedness, or peril, or sword?" "Nay, in all these things we are more than conquerors through *him* that loved us" (Romans 8:35, 37, KJV; emphasis added).

Flore Aubry-Hamilton

March 17

God Cares About Our Tears

Thou tellest my wanderings: put thou my tears into thy bottle:
are they not in thy book?
—Psalm 56:8, KJV

No matter how hard I tried, I couldn't contain the tears. I was on my way to a client's house. I decided to stop at a mall and sit down for a while until I could control myself.

When I saw a security guard watching me, I lowered my head and tried to hide my tears. He walked up and sat down next to me. I did not have the courage to look at him.

He told me that he noticed that I was very sad and then quoted some Bible promises. They were familiar verses. *I don't need someone telling me Bible promises,* I thought. I felt bad. I was proud of my knowledge of the Bible, and now here was a stranger reminding me of God's promises.

The security guard got up, apologized, and went to his post.

Suddenly I realized that all the anguish that I had been feeling was gone. Peace filled my heart. The tears that I couldn't control dried up. The reason for my crying had not been resolved, but I felt a strange peace, and this was all I needed. I went on my way in peace and no longer crying.

The next day I was again close to the mall and decided to go to the security guard to thank him for his words and let him know how he had helped me. Someone else was in his place with the same uniform. I asked him where the security guard from the previous day was and described him.

He told me that there was no other security guard. I was shocked. There had to be! I had seen him. He had talked to me. He had shared God's promises and encouraged me just when I needed it most.

Had the God who cares about every tear sent me an angel?

I believe that angels sometimes appear in human form to encourage, guide, and speak God's peace to us. And even when we can't see them or hear their advice, they'll certainly be by our side when we need it.

Isabel Cristina de Almeida

Purposeful Provision

But my God shall supply all your need according to his riches in glory by Christ Jesus.
—Philippians 4:19, KJV

Finally! I decided that the time had come for me to purchase a vehicle of my own. Though I had had my driver's license for some time, I was not very keen on purchasing a vehicle. I had a real fear of the reckless driving that I have seen on our roads from time to time. I also had very little interest in borrowing funds to purchase a vehicle. I chose to wait until I could purchase it with cash. I wanted a reliable vehicle that was in great condition with low mileage. I also wanted a hassle-free process.

And for years, I got by quite well with other modes of travel. But the time had come to have my own transportation.

I prayed for a vehicle over a week or so. Searching the newspaper one Sunday, I began calling a few numbers for vehicles I had an interest in. On about my fourth or fifth call, I found what I wanted. The Holy Spirit led me to the right person, who, coincidentally, was also a person of faith and who, after speaking with me on the phone, felt impressed to hold the vehicle for me despite having already talked to several people who were also interested in it. He assured me that he would tell any other interested person who called that the vehicle was already taken. He asked me to arrive early in the city so the transaction could be done on the same day if possible.

I thanked God for leading me to the right vehicle! We completed the necessary transaction, and I left with a vehicle that perfectly fit the description of what I wanted. And yes, God blessed me so I could purchase the vehicle with cash and no loans. God is so awesome! And I must confess that after two weeks of driving on the roads, my former fears about driving went away, and now I drive safely and confidently with God's help. And finally, the entire process took only two days and was hassle-free.

So today, my sisters, know that whatever your needs are, you can take them all to God. He has a plan to meet all your needs—way beyond your expectations. Trust Him to meet your deepest needs because only He can truly satisfy them.

Althea Y. Boxx

March 19

One Free Flight, Please

Ye have not, because ye ask not.
—James 4:2, KJV

Lord, please allow me to get a free plane ticket. You know how to do it. Thank You and amen." This was my prayer in December 2019. I had traveled from London, England, to Saint Maarten in the Caribbean twice that year, and my friend had just announced her wedding date for May 2020. I could not miss that wedding, which meant another expensive plane ticket (to the same destination) within a few months. So I prayed a bold prayer.

What confidence did I have to pray for a free plane ticket? Well, my first trip to Saint Maarten that year was free. I was traveling back to London in December 2018 when the airline announced that the flight was overweight and offered a few passengers a travel voucher in exchange for giving up their seats. I accepted the offer in a second.

A year later, I was asking God to do the same thing. I was not even traveling on that same airline, but I trusted Him to provide. On the day of my travel, I prayed and waited to hear whether the plane was overweight. I was excited (not even concerned) to hear that it was overweight, but instead of asking people to give up their seats, they would refuel in Antigua to make it easier for the plane to take off above Saint Maarten's hills with less fuel weight. What was supposed to be an hour-long stop in Antigua turned out to be an extended delay because a tire on the plane was damaged and required changing. Thank God for His providence! I finally landed in London four hours delayed after missing my connecting flight from Amsterdam.

Under European Union (EU) law, I was entitled to compensation of up to six hundred euros for a flight delayed more than three hours. I received a travel voucher for eight hundred euros! Thank God for answering my extraordinary prayer and exceeding my expectations!

When I told my friend about this, she laughed and said, "We have not because we ask not." There are so many things that God wants to give us, but we sometimes lack these blessings because we do not ask nor think He cares enough to grant them. I thank God for His past blessings that give me confidence and faith that He can do it again and again and even more than I can ask or think. What do you want Him to do for you, through you, in you? Would you just ask?

Kimasha P. Williams

Free Gift With Purchase

"For God so loved the world that He gave His only begotten Son, that whoever believes in Him should not perish but have everlasting life."
—John 3:16, NKJV

Oh, it is awesome to receive a gift when you have purchased something, isn't it? I love seeing the advertisements that say, "Free gift with purchase."

It can, of course, depend on the gift whether it is worth anything to us. Ever see that "free toaster" with your purchase of, say, US$1,000,000? Not exactly an even trade-off there. The value of the gift is decided by the person receiving it.

My daughter wanted to go to a couple of her favorite makeup stores for her birthday because they offer their perks members a birthday gift . . . *no* purchase necessary! Now you're talking! This was very valuable to her because, as a seventeen-year-old, she likes makeup. We hit all the stores that offered this whopper of a deal to pick up her gifts. I, in turn, went the next month to get my birthday freebies; however, it wasn't the same thrill for me as it was for her. I still love to get gifts though.

What type of gift holds value for you?

How about if someone gave their life so you could live? Wouldn't that be the ultimate gift? Jesus said, "Even as the Son of Man came not to be served but to serve, and to give his life as a ransom for many" (Matthew 20:28, ESV).

Friends, there is no more costly gift then someone's life. Our "free gift with purchase" is just waiting for us to receive. Jesus offers it to us each and every day. We need only to accept it. We did not have to make any purchase, but a purchase was involved. Jesus bought us with His very blood! He made the purchase, but we get the gift that comes with it. God values you and me so much that He gave His one and only Son so that we could live forever with Him. Now, that's value!

No gift can top that gift. God knew what it would take to redeem His people who willingly chose to sin against Him, but He did it anyway. I could never make a purchase as costly as Jesus made. But I am so eternally grateful that I get the free gift of His purchase. Aren't you? Collect your gift today.

Cyndi Woods

March 21

You Cannot Out Give the Lord

Bring ye all the tithes into the storehouse, that there may be meat in mine house, and prove me now herewith, saith the Lord of hosts, if I will not open you the windows of heaven, and pour you out a blessing, that there shall not be room enough to receive it.
—Malachi 3:10, KJV

One evening, my eighty-nine-year-old husband and I discussed the amount we should donate to one of our favorite Christian charities. We suddenly realized that we might soon face the possibility of moving into an assisted living facility and how expensive that could be. "Is it even wise to make this donation?" we wondered.

"God has never let us down," we reminded each other. We have always returned an honest tithe and been liberal with our donations. Even when times were difficult, we had everything we needed. Somehow, we always had enough to pay the tuition for our children to go to Christian schools through college. But as soon as they graduated, those funds were gone!

We decided on the amount to donate and were happy with our decision. We mailed our donation check the next day as it was the last opportunity before a long holiday weekend.

When our mail arrived the first day after the holiday, my husband called to me, "A check came in the mail today." We weren't expecting a check, and at first, I thought he was teasing, but he wasn't. Sure enough, there was a check, and it covered the amount we had given for our donation, plus a little over 10 percent more. The money came from a source that used to send a check once a month, although we had received nothing for almost a year.

We were amazed that this check was already coming to us when we mailed our donation. Not only did God "return" the amount of the offering we gave in faith, but He also thoughtfully added a little more! Again, we were amazed. We received enough extra to cover our tithe for the unexpected check and replenish the donation amount. Praise the Lord for His generosity!

We just cannot out give God. "Try me now in this," says the Lord of hosts. Have you tested Him yet on this promise? Have you watched Him pour out blessings?

When we generously give our tithes and offerings, He faithfully stretches our dollars. Our Creator God loves to create ingenious ways to provide for us.

Anna May Radke Waters

The Mercy of God—Part 1

The troubles of my heart have enlarged;
Bring me out of my distresses!
—Psalm 25:17, NKJV

I flipped over the church bulletin several times and reread the announcement about an outreach trip to the AIDS hospice. A recent addition to the Asia-Pacific International University faculty in Thailand, I wanted to join some missionary activity. The invitation appealed, but one serious consideration stood in the way.

Since childhood, I had an abnormal fear of anything related to death: coffins, the dead or dying, morgues, the sick, and even pictures of anything morbid. One look would plant the images vividly in my mind and could haunt me for years. Not wanting to turn down requests to sing at funerals, I reduced the fear by walking to the front with eyes glued to the floor. I held on to the arm of another singer to lead me to where we should stand; I raised the songbook close to my face to block the view. The fear was ridiculous, torturous, and real—persisting despite my parents' and friends' words of reproof and counsel.

The dilemma notwithstanding, the desire to do something worthwhile—visiting the AIDS hospice—prevailed, and I showed up at the designated time and place. I worried about my fear. Suppose I fainted in front of the sick? How would I sleep through the nights? Would my attitude hurt the patients I was supposed to cheer?

All too soon, the van parked near the building. I walked alongside the dozen students and teachers to the entrance. The pungent smell of disinfectant hit hard, but I could not turn back now. We donned masks and gloves. Surprisingly, I felt no dread as we entered and started giving massages, changing diapers, and feeding patients. On the ride home, I felt strangely happy as I pondered the transformation in me.

Not long after, on one of the subsequent bimonthly visits, a man died in the third-floor ward where we were massaging patients. That I could watch an attendant prepare the corpse for cremation was beyond me. I would have fled down the stairs in terror if this had happened before the hospice trips. That night, I slept untroubled by the scene, a confirmation that God had cured me of the phobia that had plagued me in the past.

Bienvisa Ladion Nebres

March 23

The Mercy of God—Part 2

You anoint my head with oil.
—Psalm 23:5, NKJV

On one of our twice-monthly visits to the AIDS hospice, I noticed an unfamiliar patient seated at the entrance. Sores covered this recent addition to the ward. He did not look as sick and thin as the other patients, but the scabs on his arms and legs made me shudder.

I will not give him a massage, I decided. *Let the others do it.* Thinking (and secretly glad) that twelve others could help him, I searched a section of the ward that would least likely be his quarters and started offering massages to the sick.

I finished with a patient and prepared for the next person to massage. As I turned around, I came face-to-face with the man I had noticed at the entrance. How long he had been standing there, I had no idea.

"I want massage," he addressed me. He spoke English! Hardly any of the sixty patients in that ward did. I could not mistake the message.

"You want a massage?" I echoed and smiled to hide my surprise and unbelief. Why me? Where were the others?

"Yes." He lay down on his bed four feet away.

Starting from his head, I dropped some oil on his scalp and massaged. But on his arms, back, and legs, I poured oil. The dry skin could not absorb enough. I added more oil and gently rubbed it in. Soon bits of scaly skin started to slough off. More oil. Dead skin accumulated on the bedsheet, so I scooped it up and dropped the pile in a bin close by. I worked silently, praying, while he watched my every move without a word.

On the next trip, I could hardly wait to see how the man was doing, but on his bed lay a different patient. I walked through the ward but found no trace of him. To this day, the question remains: Why, of the more than ten others in the group, did he ask me? Did he know my thoughts? I will never know. But those minutes that I gave him a massage spelled a day of victory for me. It taught me several lessons, one of which was, "I can do all things through Christ who strengthens me" (Philippians 4:13, NKJV), for the Lord had enabled me to do a deed I could not have done on my own, one which I detested.

Bienvisa Ladion Nebres

A Home for the Homeless Family

My people will live in peaceful dwelling places,
in secure homes,
in undisturbed places of rest.
—Isaiah 32:18, NIV

A tearful granddaughter called on me one day. "I am so sad," she said. As her story unfolded, I realized that her heart was broken over a homeless family that she passed that day on her way home from school. It was the second time that she had passed them, and the second time that she and her mom did not have enough money to give them.

By the end of our conversation, we decided on four approaches to raising funds for her project. These would ensure she would have a little money to give the next time she saw homeless persons, especially homeless families with children. First, she would put away a portion of her allowance and give from that. Second, she would ask family and friends to contribute to her Homeless Family Project Fund. Third, she and my other granddaughter would give their toys to the children or sell some of their toys to raise money for the families. Finally, maybe she would ask her mom to help her create a GoFundMe project for the homeless families. Our conversation ended on a happy note, and she left feeling better, eager to start planning her projects.

We are living in difficult times. As I write this, we are facing a global pandemic that has resulted in many families losing their homes, plunging them into despair. The presence of sin has also contributed to a spiritual homelessness. Yet God has promised that, one day, He will put an end to all this pain.

A comforting promise came to my mind as I thought about the incident that caused so much sadness. While there are homeless people now and children who are hungry and, yes, even without toys, Jesus tells us, "Do not let your hearts be troubled. You believe in God; believe also in me. My Father's house has many rooms; if that were not so, would I have told you that I am going there to prepare a place for you?" (John 14:1, 2, NIV). One day, all the pain and sadness will end. Even if we do not have homes of our own now, Jesus promises us one in heaven.

What a blessed hope for a positive future. I look forward to that day. How about you?

Gloria Barnes-Gregory

March 25

Death Sentence

For the wages of sin is death; but the gift of God is eternal life through Jesus Christ our Lord.
—Romans 6:23, KJV

Recently I have been experiencing a decline in health as a result of various diseases, some autoimmune, some neurological, and some genetic. I've also received new diagnoses for symptoms I've had since childhood, which brings a sense of relief even though the disease itself is incurable. At least there are answers. In researching each of the issues I struggle with daily, I found three commonalities among them: stroke, heart attack, and sudden death. It sounds like a death sentence! Especially since I've already had ministrokes and am experiencing heart issues.

I'm sure many readers can relate. Chronic pain, autoimmune disease, cancer, or any of a host of diseases that plague our modern society may be affecting you even as you read this. Some of these diseases can be cured, some can be treated or managed with improved diets and lifestyle or medications, and others simply progress with no known treatment or cure available. To those who are living in these realities, it may also feel like a death sentence, and that can be discouraging at times.

But did you know we are all under a death sentence? That's right! The difference between our earthly sicknesses and this particular death sentence is twofold: this death sentence is eternal, but there is also a cure! Romans 6:23 says, "For the wages of sin is death; but the gift of God is eternal life through Jesus Christ our Lord" (KJV). Thankfully, this text not only reminds us that we are under a death sentence because of our sins but also gives us hope! There is a treatment and a cure for this death sentence—and that cure is Jesus, our Lord and Savior!

No matter what you're going through, dear reader, the death sentence you face in this life is temporary. This world will pass away someday soon, and our earthly troubles and illnesses will end also. The challenges many face daily with health, finances, marriages, and more will all end when Jesus returns. Let's choose Jesus and allow Him to cleanse us from sin and remove the eternal death sentence from us.

Samantha Nelson

In Our Darkest Moments, the Son Shines

For God, who said, "Light shall shine out of darkness," is the One who has shone in our hearts to give the Light of the knowledge of the glory of God in the face of Christ.
—2 Corinthians 4:6, NASB

One night as I put my baby boy to sleep, I cried. I felt alone with no one to turn to. Even the God I served seemed far away. In my pain, I cried out to Him, "Lord, You know my heart and my desire. I know I have failed You. Please hear my cry and show me You still love me." The room I was in was so dark that I could not see my hands or the child on the bed.

Suddenly a bright light shone through the window. It shone directly on the Bible that my father had given me. A small voice said, "You need to read your Bible and turn around." In my darkest hour, He was still with me. That light affirmed His presence.

Twenty-nine years later, my husband and I decided that we would like to visit my parents in London. All my siblings were also going. It was great to see everyone after such a long time. It was a great family reunion, but it was soon time for me to return home.

Only two weeks after I came home, I received a call from my sister. My mom had a fall and was in the hospital. They assured me that she would be OK.

A few days later, my sister called again. The news was not good. Test results showed my mom had pancreatic cancer. The doctor gave her one week to live. My heart sank. I went home and told my family the bad news. This time, I was not alone in the darkness. In our Friday night worship, we asked God for a special airfare. God answered our prayer. I was able to go and see my mother.

Three weeks after my mother was diagnosed with pancreatic cancer, she went to sleep in Jesus. The day of the funeral was a wet, cloudy London day. Again I asked God to shine through. God came through for me again. As they lowered her into the ground, a bright ray of sunlight shone on my son's back. As I looked up to the sky, I knew it was the Son shining to assure me He was with us.

Sisters, even in your darkest moments, trust God; believe Him. He will shine in your darkest moments. Because of that Light, I'm holding on.

Dawn M. Phillips

March 27

Victory Over Sin

Fight the good fight of faith.
—1 Timothy 6:12, NKJV

The other morning, sitting on my porch enjoying some long-awaited sunshine after wintry days, I was aroused to full attention when a couple of fighting sparrows arrived in the yard. I can't remember ever seeing little birds fight so intensely and for so long. They chirped loudly and clung to each other, rolling on the ground, then rising and attacking again before falling to the ground. This happened over and over, and I wondered whether they would survive. Eventually, they stopped, and one flew off with the other in hot pursuit.

I've seen dogs fight and also cats in vicious fights. God never intended His created creatures to fight each other, nor did He intend that they attack humans. The sin of man and woman has destroyed the peace that God instilled in all His creation.

We have absolutely nothing to thank the devil for as we look at the condition our world is in, with the suffering of humankind and God's creatures. Right from the beginning, throughout Bible times, and down through the ages, all the atrocities with their results have been devastating. "Nevertheless we, according to His promise, look for new heavens and a new earth in which righteousness dwells" (2 Peter 3:13, NKJV).

It's encouraging to hold to God's promises and safely abide in His presence. The great controversy between good and evil besets us constantly. The evil one is out to destroy those who obey God. His holy Word constantly warns us of all things we face in life. Oh, how important it is to read His Word faithfully. Every day, our lives are challenged with decisions to do right or wrong. These fights in the mind can be conquered only by the truths of God. "However, when He, the Spirit of truth, has come, He will guide you into all truth" (John 16:13, NKJV).

The Bible warns us in Ephesians 6:12, "For we do not wrestle against flesh and blood, but against principalities, against powers, against the rulers of the darkness of this age, against spiritual hosts of wickedness in the heavenly places" (NKJV). So "put on the whole armor of God, that you may be able to stand against the wiles of the devil" (verse 11, NKJV).

I'm looking forward to the earth made new, where all the fights of this life will be over. We won't see little sparrows in conflict with one another again. What peace.

Lyn Welk-Sandy

The Fruit of *I*

For thou hast said in thine heart, I will ascend into heaven, I will exalt my throne above the stars of God: I will sit also upon the mount of the congregation, in the sides of the north: I will ascend above the heights of the clouds; I will be like the most High.
—Isaiah 14:13, 14, KJV

When the British and French were fighting in Canada in the 1750s, Admiral Phipps, the commander of the British navy, was asked to anchor outside Quebec to support the land forces when they arrived to attack the city. Phipps's fleet arrived early, and as the admiral waited impatiently, he grew weary of the statues surrounding a nearby cathedral and commanded his marines to shoot at them. He shot so many rounds at these statues that he was of no use when the land forces arrived and the signal was given to attack. Too many Christians today are like Admiral Phipps. They are so occupied with attacking other saints that they are of no use; they are only a hindrance to the cause of Christ.

The negative fruit of *I* are sin, pride, lie, partition, and die; all these have the letter *I* as their center. Coincidently, the letter *I* is also in the center of Lucifer, who reflects all these characteristics. Lucifer's pride created a partition for God and the angels. And his lies tempt people to sin and have a partition from God and eventually die.

God hates pride (Proverbs 8:13; 16:5, 18). Pride is a very serious sin; pride brings disgrace (Proverbs 11:2). God absolutely hates a proud heart, but He gives grace to the humble (James 4:6), and so we are to clothe ourselves with humility toward one another (1 Peter 5:5). For he who exalts himself will be humbled, and he who humbles himself will be exalted (Luke 14:11).

The positive fruit of *I* are unity, unite, win, His, and Him. When we unite and work in unity toward His cause, we will be able to win souls for Him.

What fruit would you like to sow in your churches, in your homes, in your heart? Do you want to sow the fruit of unity or the fruit of division? Today let's pledge to unite to win one from sin and into Him.

Suhana Chikatla

Muddy Waters

If any of you lacks wisdom, let him ask God, who gives generously to all without reproach, and it will be given him.
—James 1:5, ESV

A few weeks ago, I told my mom we had decided to put down our cat, Princess Margaret. I listed all the reasons why we thought it was time. She said, "Are you trying to convince me or yourself? Because Dad and I talked two months ago, and we thought it was time then." Princess Margaret's pain and discomfort were evident, but my emotions kept getting in the way of what I knew needed to happen. Since initially making this decision, I struggled with guilt because behind the sadness, I was kind of happy. I was happy because I wouldn't have to deal with her missing the litterbox anymore, and there would be no more stuffing a pill down her throat—which she and I both hated. I was happy we wouldn't have midnight howling sessions or need to take her when we moved because it would have been hard on her and us.

A woman I know lost her husband a few months ago. He had severe dementia, and she kept him home even though she had difficult medical problems. When he passed away, I remember her struggling with guilt and wondered why. Although a pet is nowhere near the same as a spouse, I now have some glimmer of the guilt she went through. Guilt about her own happiness and relief that someone she had taken care of for a long time, who made her life more difficult even though she loved him, was now gone. The relief, the freedom . . . the guilt.

"The heart is deceitful above all things" (Jeremiah 17:9, ESV). Our hearts muddy the waters regarding hard choices and emotions. If you have ever struggled with guilt over the barrage of feelings you have about a loved one passing away or a pet needing to be put down, let me reassure you that you are not alone! You loved that person or pet to the end, even if your thoughts were not always loving, even if you grieved the loss and felt relief. As humans, we have complex emotions. It is not wrong to have mixed feelings. Ask God to help you through troubled times, and He will. He may not change the situation, but He will walk with you and give you wisdom. All you need to do is ask!

Deidre A. Jones

March 30

Allow God to Fight Your Battles

The Lord shall fight for you, and ye shall hold your peace.
—Exodus 14:14, KJV

Many years ago, as a young woman married fewer than two years, I began to have medical issues that could not be ignored. I sought the medical attention that I needed and even got a second opinion. It was determined that the only solution to my problem was abdominal surgery. This news shook me to the very core of my being. I had never had any medical issues greater than the common cold. Although my husband was there, I felt he did not understand the extent of my anxiety and pain. I finally reached out to my best friend and coworker, who provided the support that helped me get through the crisis.

The surgery went well, and the recovery was uneventful. I gave praise and thanks to God for the successful outcome, knowing what the possibilities could have been. I wish that this was the end of the story, but the worst was yet to come.

One of the more mature women of the church, who should have been mentoring the younger women, decided to expound on my medical status without consulting me. She told others that I had had a hysterectomy and would never be able to have a child. That rumor spread like wildfire. My initial reaction was anger. I felt a need to refute that lie, but the Holy Spirit spoke to me and reminded me of how the Savior was misrepresented and even put to death.

I was immediately humbled, strengthened, and encouraged as I reflected on the path that Christ had trodden, which led to His death on the cross. I felt a sense of relief as the multiple negative thoughts that had flooded my mind were replaced with thoughts of what Christ had endured. The Lord, in His mercy, removed the hurt and anger and filled my heart with joy, peace, and love.

Two years later, I gave birth to an eight-pound, thirteen-ounce healthy baby boy! Indeed, the Lord will fight your battles if you trust Him.

"Trust in the Lord with all thine heart; and lean not unto thine own understanding. In all thy ways acknowledge him, and he shall direct thy paths" (Proverbs 3:5, 6, KJV).

Mary Head Brooks

March 31

Lesson From the Dandelions

For, lo, the winter is past, the rain is over and gone;
the flowers appear on the earth.
—Song of Solomon 2:11, 12, KJV

For many years, my husband raised sheep. The children and I picked dandelions and fed them to the sheep. Our animals had a great fondness for these very prolific little plants. We picked basketfuls and raced to the barnyard to see whose basket would be emptied first. The dandelions seemed to grow as fast as we harvested them.

I was a beekeeper, and the dandelions were treasured treats for my busy little bees. The bees produced a golden honey from these blossoms. I often stood in the middle of the activity and listened to the happy hum of the bees as they sipped the nectar and carried it off to the hives.

The common dandelion is a very complex plant. Few take time to give this plant a second look. The dandelion flower goes to bed before dark. It opens up early in the morning. The actual blossom has close to three hundred ray florets, which are surrounded by two rows of floral bracts. The bees thrust their proboscises deep into each floret to sip the nectar.

The dandelion was brought to North America from Europe and Asia. Because it has a long taproot, it survived the long trip and thrives even in subsoil. I am sure the first dandelion blooms must have cheered the lonely pioneers. The early settlers ate the leaves and ground up the roots for a beverage. It is usually the first blossom of spring and the last one in the autumn. I have eaten a dandelion salad, and it is passable—not my favorite, but it is definitely a spring tonic.

My neighbors have no dandelions in their lawns. They work very hard to keep their lawns a green carpet. My lawn is a yellow carpet. I do not cut the lawn as long as the yellow blooms abound. It is a super food for my friendly little bees and butterflies.

You can cut down all the dandelions in your yard. New ones will pop up tomorrow. I'm glad. They remind me that Jesus never gives up either. We can learn to be like the humble dandelion. Always be ready to pop up again and shine.

Patricia Cove

The Umbrella

My help comes from the Lord,
the Maker of heaven and earth.

He will not let your foot slip—
he who watches over you will not slumber;
indeed, he who watches over Israel
will neither slumber nor sleep.
—Psalm 121:2–4, NIV

Most summers when my children were young, we went to the local village fete with all sorts of fun activities, rides, and stalls. Here in the United Kingdom, the weather in June can be a shade unpredictable, and to say we are prone to the occasional heavy shower of rain can be a slight understatement.

One summer day, we had only just arrived at the fete when the heavens opened and it began to rain. My three children were still quite young, and I wondered how we would keep dry. Should we leave and return to the car? How sad they would be if we did.

My middle daughter, Verity, wanted to have a go on the tombola despite the rain that trickled down her face! As children sometimes are, she seemed oblivious to the rain and asked for the money to buy a ticket. With tombola, you pick from a bucket of folded tickets, and if you pick a ticket with a good number on it, you can choose a prize. To my thrill and amazement, she came running back within minutes, clutching a large umbrella. "Look, Mummy! Look what I've got us," she said as she passed me the umbrella.

She had chosen not only a winning ticket but also just the right prize.

I am sure God was looking over us, knowing we needed an umbrella, and this was His way of providing exactly what we needed through Verity on that June day.

There are many special memories of our summer days, but this one stands out as one of my favorites. Now, years later, whenever I think of the fetes, I smile and think of the umbrella and how special that was—the perfect provision and timing God made complete through my daughter. *Thank You, Father, for caring and meeting all our needs, both small and large, especially when it is in such a lovely way as through our children. Amen!*

Laura A. Canning

April 2

Showers of Blessing

"I will make them and the places all around My hill a blessing; and I will cause showers to come down in their season; there shall be showers of blessing."
—Ezekiel 34:26, NKJV

Recently I was rereading one of my favorite books, which, according to the Library of Congress, is the best book written on the life of Christ outside of the Bible. I had prayed previously about something appropriate to present to a group of women on the theme "Shower of Blessing," which was a couple of weeks away. As I read *The Desire of Ages*, two sentences jumped out at me. "From [Jesus'] earliest years He was possessed with one purpose; He lived to bless others."* And "The atmosphere of hope and courage that surrounded Him made Him a blessing in every home."†

Jesus came as a shower of blessing to us—to the leper, the ill, the widow, the depressed and possessed—He came as a blessing and example to all. Oh, that we might live to be a blessing to others each day.

A few days later, I was reading *The Desire of Ages* again, and I couldn't believe that "showers of blessings" was used twice in the chapter I was reading, chapter 14. "All who are consecrated to God will be channels of light. God makes them His agents to communicate to others the riches of His grace. His promise is, 'I will make them and the places round about My hill a blessing; and I will cause the shower to come down in his season; there shall be showers of blessing.' Ezekiel 34:26."‡ A few paragraphs down, I read, "And he who seeks to give light to others will himself be blessed. 'There shall be showers of blessing.' 'He that watereth shall be watered also himself.' Proverbs 11:25."§ So it looks like when we bless others, we will be blessed, and isn't that just like God. May we be a "shower of blessing" to someone today and every day.

Rita Kay Stevens

* Ellen G. White, *The Desire of Ages* (Nampa, ID: Pacific Press®, 2005), 70.
† White, 74.
‡ White, 141.
§ White, 142.

Healing Words

Like golden apples in silver settings,
so is a word spoken at the right time.
—Proverbs 25:11, NOG

People are very sensitive to the power of words. Everything we hear has a big impact on the mind. Words are not just details or letters thrown in the wind. They have the power to destroy or build lives. So it was with Telma, a passionate admirer of the arts. Telma loved drawing and painting from the time she was little. Her talent did not go unnoticed by her mother, who always encouraged her to grow her gift. Aware that she needed to become even more skilled in the arts, Telma decided to enroll in a course for designers and painters. She started well and was satisfied with the new knowledge acquired.

One day she came across an image that was difficult to execute. After several unsuccessful attempts, she asked for help from her teacher, who promptly said, "It seems that you don't have as much talent as you imagined. In fact, you don't have any talent; look for something else to learn." Those harsh words paralyzed Telma; what had given her so much pleasure seemed, after that, a great failure. The teacher's bitter and unnecessary words destroyed her self-esteem, causing her to abandon art classes forever.

Jesus' words are different. He offered encouraging words both to happy and excited people and to people hurt by the circumstances of life. Among so many emotional reports, we can remember the story of the suffering widow who had just lost her only son. She was on her way to the cemetery to bury him. Her soul was bleeding in pain; her tears reflected her broken and hopeless heart. But when Jesus saw her in such a sad moment, He was moved with compassion and said lovingly, "Don't cry" (Luke 7:13, NOG). Then He resurrected the young man and restored him to his mother. Tears were replaced by shouts of joy and words of gratitude.

In our time, good and kind words like those of Jesus are lacking. In a world powered by social networks without filters of kindness and purity, it is possible to make a difference. Words that bring life are more valuable than pure gold arranged in beautiful silver trays. They bring life and peace in the heart where they rest!

Sueli da Silva Pereira

April 4

He Notices

"So do not fear; you are more valuable than many sparrows."
—Matthew 10:31, NASB

Usually, a sparrow is a powerful little bird. To me, it is a symbol of joy, simplicity, creativity, and friendship. The sparrows quiet my soul as I sit on my chair, watching them from our porch as they feed at the bird feeder, making their little tweeting sounds.

Today, I saw a sparrow sitting by the side of our home, apparently unable to fly away. As I looked, I felt so sorry for it. Why was it just sitting there? "Get up, Nancy," I said to myself. "Go see what is wrong with the bird." As I walked toward it, the little bird didn't fly away. I reached down and gently picked it up in my hand. I feared that it would die. What could I do for this little dying bird?

I took it inside and tried to give it some water, but the sparrow would have nothing to do with the water. I sat with the little bird, trying to warm it in my hand and stroked this sweet, small head and spoke softly to it. Not much later, the little sparrow took its last breath and died in my hand. It brought tears to my eyes. Oh, how I wish I could have saved that little bird!

I was reminded of Matthew 10:29, "Yet not one sparrow falls to the ground without your Father's consent" (GNT). Another Bible version says it this way: "But not a single sparrow can fall to the ground without your Father knowing it" (NLT).

If our Father in heaven can see a tiny sparrow, how can He not see us when we fall? Have you ever thought about how often the Lord must hold us in His arms? Or how many times He cries with us? How many of us have been hurt, scared, betrayed, as the world around us seems to only want to hurt us?

I hope I gave a measure of comfort to the little sparrow as I sat with it, and I hope that in the future, as I notice people out in the world hurting, I will try to comfort them. I need to remember God has asked me to comfort and help others.

I would like to say to you, turn to our loving God. He's the One who loves us unconditionally even though we are not worthy. He not only notices us but also cares enough to want to save us. Only through His Son, Jesus, can we have eternal life.

Friends, do not fear because God not only notices—He is with us.

Nancy A. Mack

Crocuses

"I am the light of the world; he who follows me will not walk in darkness, but will have the light of life."
—John 8:12, RSV

In my childhood, spring in Maryland, United States of America, arrived exuberantly and radiantly. Above my head hung canopies of pink and white dogwood blossoms. At my shoulder cascaded sunny forsythia. Bright pink azaleas blazed near my waist. When I looked down, the blue fire of hyacinths shone near my ankles. And by my toes, thick, waxy petals of crocuses, brilliant gold and vivid purple, blazed proudly into the spring air. They seemed to laugh and joke as they brightened the world.

As an adult, I moved to the almost-prairie of Alberta, Canada. Here, spring is more reluctant. After five months of snow, she begins her timid advance. A few steps forward, then a rapid retreat when a blizzard chokes the air. Some warming days encourage her to try again. Another snowfall stops her progress. Some days, the returning geese walk on still-frozen lakes. There is no color, no greenery.

Then the days lengthen, the buds on the trees swell, and the lake ice begins to thaw. It's time to look for the first flowers of spring.

We won't find them in our neighbors' flower beds. Instead, we hike on muddy paths to find a sunny slope. There, from the still-brown grass of winter, peep the crocuses. They're not like the crocuses of my childhood. They're not gold and royal purple; they don't flaunt thick, waxy petals.

Our shy prairie crocuses are also called Pasque flowers. They bloom around Easter, the time Christ, the embodiment of the paschal lamb, the Light of the world, gave His life so that we might eschew darkness and live in His light.

I think of Him as I look at this harbinger of spring. The flowers are small. Their purple, almost white petals are thin and fragile. The light shines through them and illumines the stamens that create a crown in the center. I always feel that this flower radiates hope. It's not jolly like the crocuses of my childhood; instead, it conveys the solemn joy of renewal—the joy of resurrection. The light of life shines through this flower. I want Him to shine through me too.

Denise Dick Herr

God's Lilies

"For the vision is yet for an appointed time;
But at the end it will speak, and it will not lie.
Though it tarries, wait for it;
Because it will surely come,
It will not tarry."
—Habakkuk 2:3, NKJV

Years ago, I began counting the days I've spent waiting for Jesus to return. One year, as I counted the thousands of days, despair began to take root. Angry at how far the Promised Land still seemed, I asked, "How long are You going to take?"

Gently, He whispered, "Some lilies take a long time to bloom." Unaware that any lily can take years to bloom, I googled it. Among the search results was an article, "Ten of the Slowest Plants to Ever Bloom."* Scrolling through the article was an interesting worship time. At number nine was the Madagascar palm, which was only discovered in 2008. It made the list because it flowers so infrequently no one had noticed it wasn't a regular palm. As I thought about this palm, God reminded me that though it may seem that He is just taking years to do the same work for me that He has accomplished in days for others, the flowers aren't the same. At number six was the kurinji plant, which blooms so reliably every twelve years that some use it to track their age. He reminded me that long delays do not mean uncertain results. At number one was the Himalayan lily, which grows to a height of nearly ten feet (three meters) and blooms after five to seven years. He reminded me that His ways are mysterious but always for my good.

After long weekends parked in the sun, unopened for days, my car usually has a stale air smell, but that morning as I opened my car, I was greeted with the delicate smell of lilies. The smell faded faster than I wished, but the fact that God would freshen up my car with lilies just because He can etched the morning's lesson in love as I realized that God loves me deeply and spends an insane amount of time orchestrating meaningful-to-me ways to remind me to trust His plan. In His garden, every flower blooms in its time.

Melissa Martinez

* S. Grant, "10 of the Slowest Plants to Ever Bloom," ListVerse, August 11, 2013, https://listverse.com/2013/08/11/10-ridiculously-slow-to-bloom-plants/.

Promised Hope

For the Lord Himself will descend from heaven with a shout, with the voice of an archangel, and with the trumpet of God. And the dead in Christ will rise first. Then we who are alive and remain shall be caught up together with them in the clouds to meet the Lord in the air. And thus we shall always be with the Lord. Therefore comfort one another with these words.
—1 Thessalonians 4:16–18, NKJV

My husband of fifty-four-plus years is now asleep in Jesus. He entered into rest in Jesus on April 5, 2019. This date will be forever seared into my mind as a day of great sadness, yet a day of relief. Gone are his suffering, his pain, and his anxiety, replaced by that blessed sleep that comes to those who know and love Jesus.

Now, I have begun a new chapter of my life. Part of this newness of a changed life for me will be dealing with enormous loss. Instead of intensively caring for Melvin and his needs, I have time—and time is a great commodity. That I do not have Melvin to share it with is sadness beyond belief, but I have that blessed hope of renewal when Jesus comes to take all of us home to live with Him forever. This life is but a blink when compared to what waits for those who love Him and love His Word.

Today is called Good Friday. It is celebrated by most of Christendom as the day Jesus paid the supreme debt for all our sins. We will never understand this kind of love, the agony of crucifixion, and grace that is completely foreign to our carnal minds. Yet, we believe, and we trust, and we hope. Our thankfulness for His life is unmeasured. This grace is unlimited, incomprehensible, not understood, but it is available in sufficient measure to assure us that, one day, we will live in the earth made new.

With each passing day, we are given the strength to cope. We are given unlimited holy strength to live as Jesus wants us to live. We are given insight into this strength that comes from loving and sharing with those we love, their impact on our lives, and the shared desire to be together forever. I cling to that knowledge, that promise, the encouragement in God's Holy Word, and the sacrifice that Jesus made for all of us to rise above the cares of this world and live with Him forever when He comes again to redeem us as His own.

Grace A. Keene

April 8

The Cedar Tree

And he shall be like a tree planted by the rivers of water,
that bringeth forth his fruit in his season;
his leaf also shall not wither.
—Psalm 1:3, KJV

The giant cedar tree with its network of branches and verdant green leaves had stood by the roadside for years. Its foliage shaded all the passersby who needed rest and shelter from the burning sun.

Winter came, and it seemed odd to see it bare. For six months, I watched with great expectation. Then it dawned on me that someone had kindled a fire in the hollow trunk to kill it. Every day, I wondered why somebody wanted to deprive us of the shade for our car on the hot days. Time went by, and just before Easter, it rained for two weeks.

Good Friday passed, and on Easter Sunday, I was surprised to see tiny buds peeping out of the bare tree. Slowly, the tree was clothed in greenness and waved its leaves and branches in the air as if praising God. When I mentioned it to my husband, he exclaimed, "It's resurrection morning, and God has resurrected the tree to put to shame those who were trying to kill it."

In Psalm 1, David likens the righteous to a "tree planted by the rivers of waters" (verse 3). This was the case with our cedar tree.

In Mark 11:12–14, Jesus pronounces judgment on a barren fig tree. Instead of early mature figs in spring, it had only leaves. This tree was supposed to bear fruit in spring and summer, but the onlookers found only abundant leaves in spring. It was giving promise of fruit. But it was a hypocritical tree, so Jesus cursed it, and the disciples marveled to see how this large tree dried up from the root.

What type of tree are you? Are you like the one planted by the river that will bear fruit? Or are you like the barren fig tree, just spreading your leaves and unable to bear fruit? If you feel more like the cedar tree, with the fire of destruction burning at your root and your spiritual leaves falling, don't lose hope. Resurrection morning is coming, and you will receive new life to bring forth the fruit of Galatians 5. If you are cut down, may your influential light continue to shine so that others will come to know Christ as their Savior.

Bula Rose Haughton Thompson

What Is Your Stone?

The Sabbath day ended. Mary Magdalene, Mary the mother of James, and Salome bought spices. They were going to use them for Jesus' body. Very early on the first day of the week, they were on their way to the tomb. It was just after sunrise. They asked each other, "Who will roll the stone away from the entrance to the tomb?"
—Mark 16:1–3, NIrV

Jesus is dead. Joseph of Arimathea takes His body from the cross, places it in a tomb, and rolls a stone in front of it. The entrance is closed. Jesus is blocked in by a big stone.

The thoughts of the women who followed Jesus during His ministry revolve around this stone during the whole Sabbath. How can they move it? Who will roll it aside for them? Their hearts are as heavy as this stone. They are filled with grief and despair. Their hope is buried behind this huge stone.

Can you relate to this? Are you in a situation like this right now? What is your stone? What is so cold and hard in your life that it takes away your perspectives—that it fills your whole life so that you cannot think of anything else? Have dreams been shattered and hopes been destroyed in your life?

"Then they looked up and saw that the stone had been rolled away. The stone was very large" (Mark 16:4, NIrV).

When they arrived at the tomb, the stone was no longer there. What a sudden change! The obstacle they had been focusing on all this time was gone. The stone was rolled away, and Jesus was no longer hidden behind that stone.

The tomb could not contain Him. Death did not conquer Him, but He conquered death. He is risen and alive.

Jesus can move your stone, too, no matter how big it is, and give you a new, unobstructed view of Him.

May you experience this resurrection experience, not just this Easter but every day.*

Dagmar Dorn

* This devotional was previously published by Dagmar Dorn on the blog *Morning Manna Devotional*, "The Stone," April 1, 2021, at http://www.eudwomen.org/en/home/morning-manna/devotional/go/2021-04-01/the-stone.

April 10

Silent Sprouting

And the LORD shall guide thee continually, and satisfy thy soul in drought, and make fat thy bones: and thou shalt be like a watered garden, and like a spring of water, whose waters fail not.
—Isaiah 58:11, KJV

Life can be exciting growing up in the countryside of central Jamaica. In this place, you are encapsulated in nature, waking up to the majestic sounds of musical birds and radiant greenery that compels you to stand still and acknowledge God's beautiful creation. Here the air is fresh, unpolluted, and soft on your face. These nature scenes provide you with a brief journey into the Garden of Eden with lush succulent plants. It is, indeed, a sight to behold.

I am a great lover of plants, and I have kept a beautiful patio garden for quite a number of years. I grow a variety of plants, but I especially find great joy in seeing my orchids sprout. And when they are in full bloom—oh, so beautiful!

Since I also love photography, I use my garden as a ministry moment by taking photos of my plants and sending them to other women to light their day so that they, too, can sprout and appreciate a softer side of life with the unrivaled beauty of God's creation.

Recently, I was tempted to throw away some stalks of a particular variety of orchid, thinking they would not sprout again. However, this variety has been faithful and bloomed many times. The Holy Spirit impressed me to keep them and exercise some patience. I obeyed the Spirit, and a couple of weeks later, to my pleasant surprise, new sprouts began coming out of what I thought was dead. And yes, I could not wait for them to bloom. And when they did, it was something to behold! Beautiful, pink, and radiant.

As it is in the natural, so it is in the spiritual. Let us not count out the silent sprouts in our lives that are taking time to develop. We all have sprouts that we would like to bloom in our lives. These silent sprouts vary from woman to woman and differ through the various stages of life. But whatever your silent sprout is, remember that the ultimate sprouting happens when we allow God to guide us continually and satisfy our soul in drought. He promises that we will be like a well-watered garden, like a spring whose water never fails.

Happy sprouting!

Althea Y. Boxx

It's Not Dead

"You have granted me life and favor,
And Your care has preserved my spirit."
—Job 10:12, NKJV

A friend gave me an orchid for my birthday about four years ago. It had pink flowers and lasted for several months. When the flowers faded, I noticed that the leaves at the bottom of the plant were still green and thriving. I decided to water the plant even though the flowers were long gone. Then I had the bright idea to clip two dried long-stem roses on the sticks in the pot to bring "life" back to my plant. So the watering continued most Wednesdays.

The plant remained on the end table in front of the large window in the family room. In July 2021, I noticed a long, green shoot stretching toward the window. It looked creepy to me, so I removed the dried roses and clipped the stem to the stick. Before long, I noticed several tiny buds on the end of the orchid stem. I was so excited that my dead plant had come back to life four years later. I continued watering the plant with renewed enthusiasm and watched daily as the buds grew bigger and bigger.

A few weeks later, I was greeted by a beautiful light-pink flower with a deeper pink middle. That made my day. One flower after another opened until there were six. I could not help but think that God loves me so much that He made that plant blossom as a love letter to me.

Sometimes in life, we feel that we have been forgotten and dead to the world. The pandemic seemed to magnify things as we were in isolation. Many felt abandoned and forsaken, and some even died alone.

I thought of Lazarus, who died physically, and his sisters were upset with Jesus because He was four days late. Little did they know that God is always on time. Four days or four years is nothing for God, the Creator of time. No matter what state of mind we find ourselves in, God knows exactly what is going on with us. He promises to be with us and reminds us in Isaiah 49:15, "I will not forget you." How reassuring is that? Family and friends may forsake us, but God never will. Just as God did not forget my orchid, He has not forgotten me—or you. We are engraved in the palms of His hands (verse 16). I speak life into you today.

Sharon Long

April 12

Lessons From a Tree

"Every branch in Me that does not bear fruit He takes away;
and every branch that bears fruit He prunes, that it may bear more fruit."
—John 15:2, NKJV

In June 2006, I moved to Stone Mountain, Georgia, in the United States of America, started a new job, and bought a home. The new job and setting up house didn't allow for anything other than cursory glances at the cherry blossom tree on the front lawn. Fall and winter came and went, and spring reared its head with delightful tulips, delicious scents of hyacinths, budding trees, and numerous new plants pushing through the earth. How I love the spring season!

It was finally time to beautify the outside of my home. I looked forward with delight to seeing the frothy pink and white blossoms on the cherry blossom tree. I was in for such a disappointment! That first spring, half the tree produced blossoms that lacked luster and vibrancy. I wondered about the other nonproducing half of the tree but figured it would bloom the following year. The next spring, the results were the same—few blossoms. A friend advised against cutting the tree down and suggested pruning the nonproducing branches, which I did.

Surprise! The following year, there were new branches and more blossoms than the previous two years. And the next spring, I won the prize: more branches and lush blossoms that delighted my senses. A spectacular sight! The dead branches had effectively prevented the tree from reaching its full blossoming potential. Removing them restored its luster and vibrancy.

That year of full blooms, the Holy Spirit showed me that the same is true when we do not eliminate the last vestiges of sin from our lives. What dead branches are we still grasping? Could they be our propensity to judge others and disparage their characters for our gain? Our unwillingness to forgive, the books we read, the television shows we watch, the love of money, a lack of time with God? What's preventing the full surrender of our will to God? What is preventing us from taking possession of the "promised land"? Are we wandering in the wilderness, worshiping false gods?

Let's make it to the Promised Land. Don't miss out on eternal life by holding on to dead branches.

Terry Roselmond-Moore

Growing Into Maturity

But grow in the grace and knowledge of our Lord and Savior Jesus Christ. To Him be the glory both now and forever. Amen.
—2 Peter 3:18, NKJV

My coworker Roslyn has a green thumb. The plants around the office thrive as a result of her careful attention. One day, she received an African violet as a gift. Soon she noticed that it was not flourishing as expected. Many of the leaves slumped as if exhausted by the struggle of living or were yellow around their edges from malnourishment. She brought it to the office from home for a change of scenery, hoping it would "catch itself." She set it in a sunny spot next to another African violet whose purple flowers brought us daily joy.

"This one doesn't look as healthy as the others," I said, pointing to the sickly newcomer.

In an effort to save the struggling plant when it didn't improve, she took it to a nearby nursery for a diagnosis. When she returned, her grim expression told me the prognosis wasn't good.

"The woman at the plant nursery said it's dying. It has no roots," Roslyn said.

Although I have no talent with plants, especially a delicate African violet, I appreciate their beauty as evidence of God's creative power. It hurt to think it might not be saved. It had become a casualty of its environment. The pot was too big and deep to provide what its roots needed to grow into maturity. When the root system does not fill the pot, an African violet cannot absorb all the water that it needs. It cannot grow to its full potential.

However, Roslyn had returned from the plant nursery with advice on starting new growth from its healthy leaves. We became excited about the prospect of its future. It could be restored and eventually bloom, we hoped.

I tried to imagine the grief our heavenly Father must feel when one of His precious "flowers" withers in their faith before they have a chance to mature. We must maintain a firm connection to God to live. Our roots must be entrenched in Him from whom we receive our nutrients for growth. Just as the African violet was in the gentle hands of a true gardener, we also can thrive if we are rooted in the loving care of the Master. He is excited about the future He has planned for us and knows that He can restore us and cause us to "bloom" for Him.

Sherma Webbe Clarke

April 14

In God's Garden

"Many daughters have done well,
But you excel them all."
—Proverbs 31:29, NKJV

Most people prefer a well-designed garden with plants and flowers strategically placed to maximize space, sunshine, shade, and soil quality. However, when we examine our natural habitat, we find that the Master Gardener designed earth's garden in such a way that there is room for all to thrive in a beautiful and harmonious pattern. Each complements and benefits the other while sustaining our environment. So it is with each woman. We are created as a thing of beauty—a bouquet of humanity in God's eyes. We often don't view ourselves that way. But God does! He gave each of us specific gifts and talents that are unique to our personalities.

You may not be the chief executive officer (CEO) of your company, but you are certainly the CEO of your home. You may not be the chief surgeon of your local hospital, but you are the chief medical officer to your children. No one else can soothe the aching tummy, mend the scarred knee, dry the falling tears, or heal the bruised ego of a small child as quickly and as well as a loving mother. You may not be a professor at a prestigious university, but you are the first and best teacher your child will ever have. You may not be a dynamic preacher commanding huge audiences, but you are the best example of Christ's love your child will ever know.

In God's garden are women of every color, size, shape, height, talent, and beauty. There are plants in our gardens that are tall and sturdy, short and secure, dazzling in beauty and splendor. Each contributes to the total effect of a lovely garden. Women in society are brilliant leaders of countries, government, industry, research laboratories, medicine, politics, law, technology, and banking. All contribute their God-given talents, wisdom, and expertise to help make this world a better place.

We must do all we can to encourage and support girls and women in our home, our church, and our community to be the best they can be. Let's remind them that they are truly "a thing of beauty" in God's garden!

Avis Mae Rodney

Secrets of Our Green World

The LORD God planted a garden eastward in Eden,
and there He put the man whom He had formed.
—Genesis 2:8, NKJV

As I studied for my small group at church, I read a quote from author Ellen White on how Adam and Eve "held converse with leaf and flower and tree, gathering from each the secrets of its life."*

I enjoy the sights and smells of trees, especially the pine, which has such a healing scent. Working in my garden, picking flowers for a vase, or gathering red clover to give to our guinea pig, I see an abundance of activity among the plants. The praying mantises from the previous season have built egg cases on the azalea bushes. The nymphs have come out and are scattered all over the front yard greenery. I counted about six adults that have decided to stay in the same area. The bumblebees, wasps, and occasional honeybee come by to feed on the zinnias, as do the butterflies and hummingbirds. Maybe these creatures are not only gathering food but also in their own way communicating with the plants too.

I've noticed Lily, our pointer mix dog, does just that. On many occasions, she will walk gently around a tree or blueberry bush or dahlia plant. She walks in slow motion, with the plant gently caressing her. As she moves around it in circles, it almost appears as if she is receiving something from the plant, and she is obviously enjoying it. Are they "talking" to her? When I see this activity, I ask Lily, "Are you communing with the plants again?"

It makes me ponder what is happening here that I am missing out on.

Reading the quote from Ellen White reveals that, at one time, humans were able to commune with the plants. God designed something deeper for us to enjoy than just the incredible beauty, smells, and textures. He planned an intimate connectedness with our green world. Sin changed how we interact with creation. Oh, how I will enjoy this gift back in its fullness after Christ comes to take us home and we live eternally on the new earth, discovering all He created us to experience. But until then, let's ponder anew these wonders and glimpses of what He has planned for us one day!

Rosemarie Clardy

* Ellen G. White, *Patriarchs and Prophets* (Nampa, ID: Pacific Press®, 2005), 50.

April 16

What Is the Color of Your Hydrangeas?

He has made everything beautiful in its time.
—Ecclesiastes 3:11, NKJV

When I lived in New York, hydrangeas were my garden's colorful powder puffs. Their large round blooms appeared early in the spring. Many were pink, blue, or lilac. However, my hydrangeas did not remain one color. The blue would turn purple or violet as the weeks passed, adapting to the changing temperatures. One year, however, as the harvest of pumpkins and apples ripened, my hydrangeas that had been blue, then purple, were now berry-red. How well they had adapted to the changing temperatures! We, too, have our seasons of happiness and gloom, youth and aging. There is beauty in each season if we can only appreciate it.

As young moms, we may be so busy with obstetrician's visits, baby formula, and social media that we may not see the beauty of our season. Do we appreciate the blessing of robust health? What about the gift of opportunity, a past not yet full of mistakes, clear eyes, a clear mind, and hands and feet not afflicted with rheumatic pains? Enjoy your youthful blue hydrangeas. In the blossoming days of midlife, we may be exhausted with after-school activities for our little musicians and soccer players. We also may be trying to help pay the mortgage and insurance while building a career. But are we too busy to rejoice that God gave us the ability to work? Are we too tired to be thankful for a job that pays for the SUV or the compact, the apartment or the house on the hill? Pause for a minute. It's summer. Enjoy your lilac hydrangeas. Then fall comes in with its loneliness, empty nest, empty heart, and obituaries. Our fall creeps in with doctor's visits, MRIs, and CT scans. Fall limps in with its retirement homes and forgetfulness. Yes, our fall may be here, but we are still alive, albeit with more salt than pepper in our hair and with replaced knees. We may still have loving spouses, children, and grandchildren who willingly run our errands.

Blue, lilac, cranberry: what's the color of your hydrangeas? Whatever it is, enjoy the changes that time has wrought. Revel in the beauty of your hydrangeas, and remember that the God who loves us "has made all things beautiful in its time."

Annette Walwyn Michael

Eden: God's Classroom

And this is life eternal, that they might know thee the only true God, and Jesus Christ, whom thou hast sent.
—John 17:3, KJV

The "Education in the Garden of Eden"* Sabbath School lesson led me to realize that Eden was God's first classroom.

"The LORD God planted a garden eastward in Eden; and there he put the man whom he had formed. And out of the ground made the LORD God to grow every tree that is pleasant to the sight, and good for food; the tree of life also in the midst of the garden" (Genesis 2:8, 9, KJV). Here our first parents were to receive their education. Ellen White described it this way, "The system of education instituted at the beginning of the world was to be a model for man throughout all aftertime. As an illustration of its principles a model school was established in Eden, the home of our first parents. The Garden of Eden was the schoolroom, nature was the lesson book, the Creator Himself was the instructor, and the parents of the human family were the students."†

God gave Adam dominion over the work of His hands. He gave Adam the authority to name all the creatures God had made. Adam also gave Eve her name: "She shall be called Woman [*Isha*], because she was taken out of Man [*Ish*]" (Genesis 2:23, KJV).

Although we don't think of a garden as a schoolroom, it makes perfect sense, especially one like Eden, filled with the unspoiled riches of God's creation. From our perspective today, it is hard to imagine how much these unfallen beings—in an unfallen world and being directly taught by their Creator—must have been learning in their classroom.

Had Adam and Eve remained obedient to God, they would have received in their Eden classroom their "doctoral degree," which is eternal life. They could have continued to eat from the tree of life forever.

The highest "degree" anyone can receive is eternal life with our Lord and Savior Jesus Christ. Amen.

Moselle Slaten Blackwell

* "Education in the Garden of Eden," *Education*, Adult Sabbath School Bible Study Guide (Nampa, ID: Pacific Press®, 2020), 6–12.

† Ellen G. White, *Education* (Mountain View, CA: Pacific Press®, 1952), 20.

April 18

Persevere

Are not five sparrows sold for two farthings, and not one of them is forgotten before God? But even the very hairs of your head are all numbered. Fear not therefore: ye are of more value than many sparrows.
—Luke 12:6, 7, KJV

I had never grown vegetables before, so I decided to make a vegetable patch. I prepared the soil and sowed my seeds in trays. I watered them and waited patiently. Finally, I could see some shoots but not from all the seeds I had sown. I was disappointed and started to worry that these remaining seeds might not germinate. However, I continued to water all my trays, and eventually, the others started to grow. Soon it was time to transfer my plants to the vegetable patch. The ones that germinated last were a lot smaller than the others, but I planted them as well, wondering whether I might be wasting my time and effort. Nevertheless, I continued to tend to all my plants: feeding, watering, and weeding. Eventually, I could not tell the difference between the earlier and later plants because the smaller ones had caught up with the larger, producing vegetables.

My experience with the vegetable patch reminds me of our spiritual journey. We may not be as knowledgeable as others, and at times we may be disappointed with ourselves as I was with my smaller plants. I was not sure they would produce, but I continued to nurture them. And they persevered. Likewise, where we are lacking, we, too, must persevere and continue to feed on God's Word so we can bear the fruit of the Holy Spirit: "love, joy, peace, longsuffering, gentleness, goodness, faith, meekness, temperance" (Galatians 5:22, 23, KJV).

Just as I removed the weeds from my vegetable patch so that my plants could thrive, I must remove, with God's help, anything that would keep me from walking closer to Him. Let us be patient and nurture those around us who may not be as far along in their Christian walk.

Just as I persevered with my plants, God patiently works with us. He knows we are each different and will not grow at the same rate. Yet He knows us individually and said that the very hairs of our heads are numbered (Matthew 10:30). He's given us a wonderful promise as we continue to grow in Him: "For I know the thoughts that I think toward you, saith the LORD, thoughts of peace, and not of evil, to give you an expected end" (Jeremiah 29:11, KJV).

Jenetta Barker

A Beautiful Impact

Having then gifts differing according
to the grace given to us, let us use them.
—Romans 12:6, NKJV

Esther had many qualities that made her a great queen. She was humble and listened to her family and God. She had a loving, sincere heart for the welfare of her people. She believed in the power of fasting. She was willing to die for what she believed in, and she knew how to strategically execute a plan. Yet none of these fine qualities and more are why the king chose her to be queen.

He chose her because she was beautiful.

Now before you turn the page, hear me out. If she wasn't something good to look at, she never would have been able to use those other talents. The king was drawn to her beauty. People all around Esther noticed her for her beauty. But it wasn't just her outward beauty. She was gentle, helpful, and not demanding or mean. She was beautiful from the inside out.

I believe that all women are beautiful. A woman's beauty can be in her eyes or the way she throws her head back in laughter. God has given all women attractive qualities in some way, shape, or form. He created us in His image, and He is beautiful. We reflect some of His beauty to the world around us.

I think we forget that. We try so hard at times to fit into a man's world and think bringing beauty to our days and to others may lessen our ability to lead. Yet Esther's beauty enabled her to make a difference—not for herself but for those around her, her people, the Jewish nation. This reminds me that French women are taught that their femininity is an asset, not a liability. We can be just as hard-core as we are soft.

When Esther went before the king to save her people, she let her beauty open the door to the king—her outward beauty but also her gentle, servant heart that invited the king to dinner. The king was so impressed that he offered her up to half the kingdom. And when she asked for her people to be able to defend themselves, he granted her wish and had her enemy destroyed.

Ladies, let us reveal God's beauty to the world around us.

D. Renee' Mobley-Neal

The Provider

"For after all these things the Gentiles seek.
For your heavenly Father knows that you have need all these things."
—Matthew 6:32, NKJV

I have had three occasions when the Lord stepped in and provided outfits that I needed for three different church functions. When I lived in Charlotte, North Carolina, United States of America, the church choir was to sing in an Easter program. We were all to wear something purple. I had no purple in the closet, and I had no job. I did get a small monthly check for my personal use. But where would I find an inexpensive purple outfit?

While riding the bus one day, I saw a well-known thrift store. The next day I stopped at the store and went through the racks. I looked through rack after rack and saw no purple dresses. I had one more rack to go. I looked through the last rack, and halfway through, I saw a purple dress. It fit perfectly! I praised the Lord—and I received many compliments when I wore the dress that Easter. "I got this through the Lord," I told people.

The second time, I lived near Atlanta, Georgia, United States of America. I wanted to attend a women's retreat and needed something dark green to wear. I prayed and then went to a couple of thrift stores. Finally, at the last store, I was successful! I bought a dark green suit and went to that retreat, again praising God for providing.

The third time, I lived in Arizona, United States of America, and sang in the choir. For the special women's day service, everyone was to wear coral. I looked in my closet but did not have anything coral. I had seen coral but never bought items of that color. I looked at a thrift store on the corner and wondered if God would again provide. I prayed and went inside. The store was emptying because it was almost closing time. I quickly found a coral dress. Once again, there is a photo of me in that choir matching all the other members.

"So why do you worry about clothing? Consider the lilies of the field, how they grow: they neither toil nor spin; and yet I say to you that even Solomon in all his glory was not arrayed like one of these. Now if God so clothes the grass of the field, which today is, and tomorrow is thrown into the oven, will He not much more clothe you, O you of little faith?" (Matthew 6:28–30, NKJV). The Lord is good.

Sharon Denise Smith

Bank-Card Mystery

"For the eyes of the Lord run to and fro throughout the whole earth, to give strong support to those whose heart is blameless toward him."
—2 Chronicles 16:9, ESV

Early on the morning of a doctor's appointment, I sensed a very special urge to check through my handbag and purse—a task I had already done the day before. Reluctantly, I began to remove the unnecessary items and checked through my medical and business cards, organizing them as I went. To my surprise, my major debit card was missing.

I emptied both the handbag and purse again, this time slowly and laboriously checking item by item. Once everything was in order, I still had not found the card. I rushed to my dressing table and anxiously searched, but no card. I literally ran to my study desk and rummaged through papers and books—no card. Panicked, I suddenly remembered the car. *That must be where the card is because I usually use my card at the drive-through*, I thought. After a frantic search, still, the card was nowhere to be found.

"Where is my card? I need it for my medical appointment, and time is running out! O my God," I cried out, "help me; I cannot find my card." I decided the only thing to do was rush into the bank and get a new card before going to the doctor.

"Lord, why this delay? I don't understand why this has to be so frustrating," I prayed. But I headed to the bank, trusting that God knew and had a reason for everything—even the lost card and extra trip to the bank.

At the counter to be processed, I was required to provide my identification card. I easily handed my driver's license to the banker, feeling very pleased with how organized I was. The banker looked at the driver's license and asked, "Do you have another identification card because this one expired more than a month ago?"

"What?" I shouted. Then I remembered my prayer and realized God was leading. I didn't know I was driving illegally. God allowed this frustrating trip to the bank so I would learn about the driver's license and take care of it. I had other identification cards and so was able to get a new bank card, get to my doctor's appointment on time, and apply for a new driver's license, praising a God who guides and protects.

Jacqueline Hope HoShing-Clarke

April 22

Faith Over Feelings

Seek the Lord while He may be found,
Call upon Him while He is near.
—Isaiah 55:6, NKJV

One night as I lay in my bed, I silently prayed to God, asking Him, "Where are You? Why can't I feel Your Presence? Please don't abandon me!"

The Bible verse about seeking God while He can be found (Isaiah 55:6) resonates with me and scares me all at once because it means that there will come a time when God literally cannot be found.

The Bible says in Revelation 7 that God has His angels at the four corners of the earth, holding back the four winds of strife until all of God's people are sealed. But as the time approaches for God's Son (Jesus Christ) to return to earth and usher His faithful followers to heaven, God will release His angels from holding those four winds. This action will birth a time of trouble like never before that will affect every human who lives on earth. According to Amos 8:11, 12, people will be desperately "seeking the word of the Lord" but not find it (NKJV).

We need to be ready, and the only way that we as Christ's followers can be ready is if we seek God daily while He can be found. But in times when God still can be found, it is important to choose faith over feelings! Our feelings are fickle; we cannot rely on their whimsy forecasts. But we *can* rely on God's Word. Jesus Christ promises to be with us until the end of the world (Matthew 28:20).

When your feelings tell you that God has forsaken you, override your feelings with faith by focusing on scripture that says God will *never* leave you *nor* forsake you! While I still struggle with choosing faith over my feelings, resting on God's promises to always be there for me keeps me encouraged and reminds me that I need to trust Him, not how I feel.

The Bible says in Psalm 146:3, 4 not to put your trust in princes nor people because they are mere mortals who cannot save you. Only Jesus Christ can save your life!

Choosing faith over feelings makes all the difference! Won't you trust Him?

Alexis A. Goring

An Intimate Companion

Call unto me, and I will answer thee, and show thee great and mighty things, which thou knowest not.
—Jeremiah 33:3, KJV

As I lay on my bed, I felt lonely—again. Even though I have felt lonely many other times before, this time, it was heart-wrenching. The Easter holidays were hard. School was out, and my son was spending time with his grandparents. I felt alone. The longing desire to be with someone led me to contemplate my situation. I was thirty-two, single, with no boyfriend that I could call my own. I was lonely.

As I conversed with my small circle of single friends, Sherina, Teena, and Tiana, I told them that I wanted to start praying again for a companion. I started praying on my own and with my friends. They were definitely praying too. I prayed specifically for a loving, God-fearing companion, someone who would love me and accept and love my nine-year-old son.

At first, I was a bit hesitant. I thought to myself, *Do I have to ask God for this again? He's been silent. I think I'll just wait for Him to send someone.* Nevertheless, I relentlessly pursued God in my desire for Him to not just hear but to answer my prayer.

One morning, I called Tiana and expressed my discouragement. She prayed for me, and I felt a bit relieved. Afterward, I prayed and left it in God's hands. That was the best decision I made.

God heard our prayers and answered—but not with a man.

I was working from home, preparing my projections and plans for the next month's sales. After I completed my tasks for the day, I went to take an afternoon nap. I lay down on my bed and whispered a prayer in my mind. Truly the Lord answered me. Within that short time frame, I felt God's presence like I never have before. I no longer felt alone or discouraged. I knew that God was with me and loved me more than any man could.

If you are searching for a man, God is waiting to be the intimate companion that you need. He knows your need and loneliness and promises, "Delight yourself also in the Lord, and He shall give you the desires of your heart" (Psalm 37:4, NKJV).

Rosemary Kasandra Lucien

Jesus Is My Husband!

For thy Maker is thine husband; the L*ORD* *of hosts is his name; and thy Redeemer the Holy One of Israel; The God of the whole earth shall he be called.*
—Isaiah 54:5, KJV

As a therapist, I see many clients in a week. One Friday morning, I had a five-year-old client to test. He was struggling with attention problems, and his mother wanted him to be tested so he could get the help that he needed in the classroom. As we engaged with his ADHD testing, he kept talking and getting distracted. At one point, he asked me if I had a dad. I knew he meant a husband, and I told him, "No." He asked if I had children, and I told him, "Yes." Then he told me that he would pray for me to get married and have a dad. By this time, I was chuckling to myself, but I was also thinking about how God works through little children.

Well, he prayed in the name of Jesus that God would send me a dad. I told him thank you, and then he told me that my dad was waiting at my house. Jesus sent him there, but he was invisible. "You can't see him, but he's there." I was amazed at the faith of this five-year-old boy. He didn't understand about life, but he knew that whatever the problem, Jesus could fix it. I forgot about the prayer as I was busy working.

As I was having my evening devotionals, I was lamenting to God about how alone I was and that I wished I had someone who could be there and share my life with me and be with me. And then, I remembered that little boy's prayer. God is my Husband. He is right here, in my house and in my car as I travel. He provides the things I need and takes care of me. He is there to talk to whenever I am lonely. Then I remembered Isaiah 54. This is a tremendous scripture for a single woman in this world. Beginning at verse 4, we read, "Fear not; for thou shalt not be ashamed: neither be thou confounded; for thou shalt not be put to shame: for thou shalt forget the shame of thy youth, and shalt not remember the reproach of thy widowhood any more. For thy Maker is thine husband; the LORD of hosts is his name; and thy Redeemer the Holy One of Israel; The God of the whole earth shall he be called" (Isaiah 54:4, 5, KJV).

Praise God! We never have to be alone. God is always with us. He is our Maker and our Redeemer. He made us, and He saved us from a life of loneliness and shame.

Eva M. Starner

I Know the Backstory

"Be strong and of good courage, do not fear nor be afraid of them; for the Lord *your God, He is the One who goes with you. He will not leave you nor forsake you."*
—Deuteronomy 31:6, NKJV

The comic panel spoke volumes: grief unsurpassed. It showed a rear-view picture of two young people sitting on a park bench. The young lad sat with his arm loosely draped around a younger girl. They both wore sports jerseys. His was a green Broncos one. Hers, a yellow Toronto shirt. Sorrow flooded my soul at the beautiful image because I knew the backstory—the story behind the picture.

April 2018 heralded a horrific series of events in both of my favorite Canadian provinces—Saskatchewan and Ontario. In Saskatchewan, the lives of seventeen young-adult junior hockey players abruptly ended when a huge tractor trailer collided with their bus as they traveled to their game in Humboldt, Saskatchewan. The entire country reeled in silent shock at the news.

No sooner had we come to grips with our grief and started the slow healing process than we were hit with more devastating news. In a suburb of Toronto, Ontario, more than ten people were deliberately plowed down by a man driving a rented van on the sidewalk.

Amid the carnage, police uncovered baby carriages and wheelchairs. I bemoaned the lives of those innocent people, ages three to ninety-three. Rage spread across the land. Its contagion spread across me. "Bless the victims, their heartsick families, the perpetrator, and all our saddened souls," I found myself praying.

Still pondering the angst-laden events, I remembered my mother sharing that our precious Savior, Jesus Christ, had experienced even greater pain—spiritual, emotional, physical—more than two thousand years ago. But there is a glorious, unforgettable backstory. The scripture reveals that Jesus Christ allowed that agonizing experience because He had a redeeming purpose in mind. He planned to save every person who believed in Him. He endured the pain of the mocking scourges and the vicious blasphemy of the crowd at Calvary for each of us. And I know He would have done it just for wretched, sin-filled me.

Thank God for His redeeming backstory.

Glenda-mae Greene

April 26

Mess on the Road

And I will bring the third part through the fire, and will refine them as silver is refined, and will try them as gold is tried: they shall call on my name, and I will hear them: I will say, It is my people: and they shall say, The LORD is my God.
—Zechariah 13:9, KJV

I couldn't help but notice the bright orange construction blocks that lined both sides of a normally clear street as I drove home. The bold colors of the construction boulders hid the gentle hues of the flowers blooming in the background. I slowed down, making my way slowly through the narrow strip of road. Half of the normally smooth road was now a mess of rocks and dirt.

"Why would they be digging up the well laid road?" I thought aloud.

"They are going to lay cables for a superfast broadband service, Mum," my son responded. The internet service wasn't the best in the area and was causing a bit of frustration. Reliable connectivity would certainly be welcome. That meant, however, that the tarred road that looked smooth and neat had to be dug up, the pathway littered, and the generally quiet street filled with noisy machinery. The street was different from what I was accustomed to seeing it, and I didn't like it. But I knew that if I wanted a better solution to the internet connectivity issues, there was no way that could be done without digging up the dirt to make room for the cables.

It crossed my mind that I had a connection with Jesus that, on the surface, seemed smooth like the tarred road. There were a few communication challenges that were frustrating at times. However, I wasn't willing to let myself be opened and my sins be laid bare. Just like the road needed to be dug out and emptied first, my heart also needed to be opened up and emptied. I realized that unless I allowed God to dig out the clutter in my life, He couldn't establish a clearer connection for me to communicate with Him.

Is there some digging that needs to be done in your life too? It may be painful and shameful and may even disrupt your self-image, but it is only temporary. Once you have opened up and let your true self be made vulnerable to God, you will experience a renewed connection with Him.

Lord, may I be willing to be opened and cleaned out so that I can hear Your voice more clearly. Amen.

Grace Paulson

What Was I Thinking?

"And I will put enmity
between you and the woman,
and between your offspring and hers;
he will crush your head,
and you will strike his heel."
—Genesis 3:15, NIV

I should have known better. The way I behaved that long-ago morning surprised me and caught me off guard. Just recuperating from surgery, I picked up the welcome mat outside my door to shake it off. To my surprise, a little snake lay curled up in its place. Shocked, I began stomping on the creature until I felt sure it was dead.

Now with the deed done, I realized what could have happened. First, I was wearing only slippers with my heel exposed; I could have been bitten, and small and baby snakes can be poisonous. Second, I could have injured myself because the surgery involved stitches across my stomach. And third, sometimes animals pretend to be dead. I decided to leave the supposedly dead reptile there so my husband could dispose of it when he returned.

My mom warned me all my life that if I saw a snake, to be sure to kill it—even if I saw one in my dreams. But now, despite the warning, I felt faint, realizing I could have been bitten or could have lost my life by acting so foolishly. The Bible tells us in Genesis 3:15, "He [Eve's offspring] will crush your [the serpent's] head, and you will strike his heel" (NIV).

Why didn't I listen to that warning? The snake could have bitten me; instead, there I was crushing it with my heel.

We are living in the time of a global COVID-19 pandemic, political unrest, and racial rioting. Isn't it time for us to heed the warning signs of our soon-coming King?

Lord, help us not to act foolishly and lose sight of what is soon to come upon this earth but prepare ourselves for the blessings in store at the soon return of Jesus. Lord, please help us use our time to grow closer and build a stronger and lasting relationship with our Lord and Savior. Then and only then will his (Satan's) head be crushed.

Bessie Russell Haynes

April 28

The Cure for Venom

"And I will put enmity
between you and the woman,
and between your offspring and hers;
he will crush your head."
—Genesis 3:15, NIV

On February 14, 2014, the news broadcast the story of Jamie Coots, a snake handler and pastor of the Full Gospel Tabernacle Church in Middlesboro, Kentucky, United States of America. For four months, Pastor Coots had been traveling around with a rattlesnake and was bitten by it during a weekend church service. He refused to accept the cure for the deadly venom in his body and eventually died.

Snakes are elongated, legless, carnivorous reptiles. They are sly, slippery, and stealthy. Some snakes are venomous, but not all are. The venomous ones inject their deadly venom to kill their prey, while others wrap themselves around their prey and constrict and suffocate them.

After Creation, man's first encounter with a snake was in the Garden of Eden. God had warned Adam and Eve not to touch a certain tree, but Satan disguised himself as a beautiful serpent and hid in that very tree—the tree of the knowledge of good and evil. Eve was drawn to the tree, and Satan spread the venom of deception to her. Eve was beguiled, ate the fruit, shared it with Adam, and plunged the whole world into sin and eternal death. In Genesis 3:15, God instituted the cure to counteract the venom of sin. He would send His Son Jesus to rescue humanity and crush the head of the snake—Satan.

According to Numbers 21, when the children of Israel reached Edom, they had to detour around it. They grumbled and complained bitterly about God and Moses. God sent fiery serpents into the camp. Many Israelites were bitten and died from the venom. After the people cried out to God, He told Moses to make a bronze snake and put it upon a pole, and all who looked on it would be healed. This was their only cure.

In John 3, Jesus talked with the Jewish leader Nicodemus about the kingdom of God and spiritual rebirth. Jesus explained that just as the bronze serpent was lifted up in the wilderness, the Son of man must be lifted up that all who believe may have eternal life.

Bula Rose Haughton Thompson

April 29

So Let Us Give

So let each one give as he purposes in his heart,
not grudgingly or of necessity; for God loves a cheerful giver.
—2 Corinthians 9:7, NKJV

I'm quite familiar with today's text, as I've heard it quoted many times when someone is speaking about a money offering. Yet when I came across that same text just the other day and contemplated it again, my thoughts focused upon the words *cheerful* and *giver*. Just then, I wondered whether those words might hold a double meaning.

When we've been unjustly accused of something we didn't do or say, the human reaction is often anger and bitterness. Satan even encourages us to think about it, talk about it, and carry it around our necks for a while. For many, it might last a lifetime! Some who have been unfairly wronged never receive an apology or hear another person ask for their forgiveness. I have been in that position, and I've found that I have a decision to make at some point. Am I going to forgive? Or will I hold on to that bitterness?

A friend, family member, or coworker may do or say something to hurt us deeply, but in some instances, they had no intention of hurting us. Still, there we are, having to deal with wounded feelings.

When all is said and done, what do we do with the message in 2 Corinthians 9:7? The text uses the words "every man according as he purposeth," which means "as he chooses," to do in his heart. The text continues, "Let him give; not grudgingly, or of necessity." When someone apologizes to us or asks our forgiveness, we must choose to either keep hanging on to our bitterness or cheerfully assent to their request.

Just think how much better off our world would be if there were more "cheerful giving" of forgiveness!

Terry Wilson Robinson

April 30

The Dice

We may throw the dice,
but the Lord determines how they fall.
—Proverbs 16:33, NLT

My dear sister in Christ, do you struggle with wanting to be in control of almost every situation like I do? Whew! A bit of relief came with that confession. The desire to take matters into my own hands and arrange, direct, instruct, and in other words, control everything often stifles the joy out of many things. As often as I think I have learned to let go and allow God and other trustworthy persons in my life to take the lead, I still end up holding on tightly.

The book of Proverbs has been a source of refuge and strength for me in so many ways. I have read this book in the Bible again and again. And every time I read it, I learn something new and refreshing.

In one of my most recent readings, I came across Proverbs 16:33, which reminds us that when a die is thrown, we can't control the outcome—only God knows how it will fall. Now, let us be clear; this is by no means advocating gambling, and I chuckle at the thought. But it suggests that even though we work feverishly to direct how events in our lives turn out, the outcome is determined by God. Hallelujah! Thank You, Jesus! That is an awesome concept. So when that application is declined or that investment falls through or maybe that relationship ends, could it be that God decided that the outcome of those thrown dice was not what He desired for you at that particular time?

This idea does not preclude the fact that our actions and decisions contribute to how things happen in our lives, so we do have to keep that in mind. But as painful as some of the disappointments we face are, rest assured that God has control of the situation. He will allow the right outcomes so we can put our trust in Him. May God help us not fall prey to the idea that we should let our desire to control things get in the way of His leading in our lives.

May God bless you as you surrender your will to His divine leading and swiftly obey when He shows you where to go.

Taniesha K. Robertson-Brown

Nesting Grounds

Even the sparrow has found a home,
And the swallow a nest for herself,
Where she may lay her young—
Even Your altars, O Lord of hosts,
My King and my God.
—Psalm 84:3, NKJV

Lately, we've been sleeping with our bedroom window open,* so I can hear the twittering when it starts around five o'clock in the morning. I lie there enjoying camping, without actually camping—hearing the birds chatter while sleeping inside. And boy, do they have a lot to say: the dove's mourning cry, the mockingbird sharing a variety of dialects, and that one squawker reminding me not all bird sounds are pleasant. It is a rare thing nowadays to find a place free from the noises of humanity. Thankfully, at five o'clock in the morning, people in our neighborhood are kind enough not to start mowing their lawns.

We will move soon, and although our apartment will be backed by woods, a busy thoroughfare is not far away. And of course, in an apartment, we will be surrounded by people. I doubt I will be able to have the door open and hear the birds. Life will be considerably different. As I look around at all the stuff we've packed and the boxes littering every corner of our house, I can't help but be a little sad. Many things have changed for us in the past couple of months. Some things we had control over, and life threw some unexpected things at us. But Jesus says, "Are not two sparrows sold for a penny? And not one of them will fall to the ground apart from your Father. . . . Fear not, therefore; you are of more value than many sparrows" (Matthew 10:29–31, ESV). If God cares for the tiny birds so much that He knows what happens to each one, how much more does He care for you and me and for all people? The next time you listen to the birds sing, I pray you will think about the above scriptures and know that God is right beside you, should you choose to make His altar your home.

Deidre A. Jones

* This devotional was previously published on the Highland Seventh-day Adventist Church's blog. "Nesting Grounds," *Highland Seventh-day Adventist Church: Sabbath Thoughts* (blog), May 30, 2020, http://highlandcounty22.adventistchurchconnect.org/sabbath-thoughts-blog/nesting-grounds.

May 2

The Miracle—Part 1

Be anxious for nothing, but in everything by prayer and supplication, with thanksgiving, let your requests be made known to God; and the peace of God, which surpasses all understanding, will guard your hearts and minds through Christ Jesus.
—Philippians 4:6, 7, NKJV

My last child was my miracle. The pregnancy had been normal for the first four months, but on a routine check-up, the doctor noticed something like a black spot and that the baby's movement was not normal. He referred us to a specialist immediately. At that appointment, they told us news I will never forget—my unborn baby had incredible challenges. They offered us several choices, including terminating the pregnancy.

My heart was heavy. I remember the ride home was silent—tears streaming down our faces. God seemed silent. Our hearts were broken as we cared for our two little boys and wrestled with the decision before us.

We called our parents to tell them the news, and my mother responded with a strong voice, "We are going to pray." All I knew then was that I was tired and hurting so deeply. Everything around me seemed meaningless. But the unborn baby inside me was breathing life, and the bond I had with him was unspeakable—I couldn't explain it, but he was joy in the midst of the uncertainty.

One night as I attempted to sleep, I remembered my God and who He is—that He is love; He is the Comforter, the Protector, the Provider. I couldn't pray, but I started to sing a song of praise and made a covenant with God. I asked Him to save my son's life and take mine instead. God would answer, but this death would not be physical. It would be dying to the things of this world and focusing on the Author and the Finisher of my life, God.

The next day, our pastor came to pray with us. He taught me to touch my big belly and speak life as we prayed for God to pour out mercy and grace upon my unborn child's life. I cried again—but this time with joy and praise to God. I began praying scriptures and claiming them for my son. God's words began to fill my thinking. I began to trust Him and His Word more. God's peace began to fill my heart and mind as I declared God's Word over the life of my unborn child.

Unathi Jiya

The Miracle—Part 2

"For My thoughts are not your thoughts,
Nor are your ways My ways," says the LORD.
"For as the heavens are higher than the earth,
So are My ways higher than your ways,
And My thoughts than your thoughts."
—Isaiah 55:8, 9, NKJV

We were silent as we went to our next appointment with the specialist. The peace and trust continued. I knew that God was in control and accepted whatever God's decision and plan for my life and my unborn baby would be. I claimed His promise that His plan was not to harm us but to prosper us and give hope and a future (Jeremiah 29:11). I was meditating on the Word of God. The doctor waited for our decision. I finally told him we wanted to do the offered procedure; whereas I knew that it might not be the best decision, I trusted God. The procedure was easy and took only a few minutes. We didn't know whether this procedure would be able to save our baby, but our hope was in God.

The doctor suggested we go home to the Eastern Cape where our families could support and care for us. He knew that we were exhausted and in pain—that this had taken a toll on us both emotionally and physically. When we arrived in the Eastern Cape, my husband decided I should go straight home to my mother to get the love and comfort I needed. My mother and I continued to pray for positive results and, more than that, for God to prepare me for the worst if it came to that point.

Christmastime was drawing near, and I thought about the birth of Jesus Christ. I started to find comfort in the thought of our Savior's birth. It reminded me that death is not eternal. I enjoyed Christmas and focused on the love of God, who sent His only begotten Son to save my unborn child and me. I felt the heavy burden lifted from my shoulders.

Three days after Christmas, the doctor called us with the best news—our son was completely healthy! We were in awe of God. In May 2010, Milani (meaning "be rooted to God") was born—healthy and beautiful. God had heard my prayers and brought me peace and trust—and then blessed me with a healthy child. Praise God!

Unathi Jiya

May 4

Reflections

And I saw a new heaven and a new earth: for the first heaven and the first earth were passed away. . . . And God shall wipe away all tears from their eyes; and there shall be no more death, neither sorrow, nor crying, neither shall there be any more pain: for the former things are passed away.
—Revelation 21:1–4, KJV

On April 28, 2016, I was excitedly planning a road trip to South Carolina to see my mom, who was in the hospital. On May 1, I had no idea my visit would turn into planning a funeral service. To say the least, my siblings and I were painfully crushed and saddened. After the funeral services, I had days of driving alone in my vehicle when I was overcome with an array of emotions and sadness.

I often reflect upon my mom's love and kindness to my siblings and me. In this world so full of sin, I think about God's goodness and love toward us. He has given my family and me the fortitude to endure. I find comfort in the words the apostle John wrote in the book of Revelation centuries ago, "There shall be no more death," "and God shall wipe away all tears"! One day, I will see my mom and my brother (who passed away May 4, 2020) again when Jesus comes for His children. The statement of no more tears reminds me of the chorus from the joyous song, "When we all get to heaven, what a day of rejoicing that will be!"*

The enjoyment of no more sorrow, no more pain, and no more tears and the pleasure of no more sin will be a treasured gift. But seeing the face of Jesus and our loved ones is an even greater reward that awaits God's children. The Bible tells us that our minds cannot comprehend what is in store; it is far greater than anything we could imagine or think. "But as it is written, Eye hath not seen, nor ear heard, neither have entered into the heart of man, the things which God hath prepared for them that love him" (1 Corinthians 2:9, KJV).

May we remain faithful.

Barbara Stovall

* E. E. Hewitt, "When We All Get to Heaven," 1898, public domain.

Rejoicing in the Promise

And God shall wipe away all tears from their eyes; and there shall be no more death, neither sorrow, nor crying, neither shall there be any more pain: for the former things are passed away.
—Revelation 21:4, KJV

My mom passed away in 2013. It all happened so suddenly. I was the women's ministries leader at my church and was conducting the Sabbath-day senior citizen program entitled "Time on My Hands." The beautiful bulletin had a picture of aged hands on the front. It was a beautiful program. I had asked my mom to do the children's story. She did a phenomenal job. She finished the story and sat down next to me, placing her head on my shoulder, and said, "My head is hurting."

"Mom, just rest," I replied. After church, we felt she needed to go to the hospital. Little did I know, my mom was having a major stroke. I was devastated.

I had so many plans in the works for women's ministries: seminars, a women's retreat just for our ladies, new-mother nurturing classes, volunteering to give moms a night out each month with free babysitting service, and divorce and bereavement counseling. I was planning a workshop to teach teens how to cook, sew, and knit and provide mentors for them to have a haven to discuss anything. I was on a roll with wonderful spirit-filled plans for my ladies, and then suddenly, my life was in tatters. My sweet mom—my earthly rock, friend, and confidant—was gone in what seemed like an instant. I would no longer hear her voice whisper, "I love you, darling daughter." I was numb for months and eventually gave up my position.

Looking back, I see God's divine handling of this situation. He understood my pain—His only begotten Son had suffered a cruel, unjust, and painful death just for me, for mom, and for each of us.

On this side of life, I will never fully understand how my Father could give up His Son to die on the cross, but I do know it was His love for me that compelled Him to make such a sacrifice. My mom loved me, but no one has loved me more than Jesus. I will continue to rejoice in His promises.

Zandra LaMar Griffin-Willingham

May 6

Comfort for the Helpless

"Blessed are those who mourn,
For they shall be comforted."
—Matthew 5:4, NKJV

As I sat in my quiet place spending time with the Lord, I was mourning. Five days earlier, our dogs had run off and gotten lost. Though we looked everywhere we could, we could not find them. We live in the country surrounded by thousands of acres of ranch and farmland; they could have been anywhere. We prayed that the Lord would guide them home.

I had to accept the reality that they might never come home. I cried before the Lord in grief. I wasn't crying in anger or regret; I was crying in sadness and helplessness. I quoted Job 1:21 to myself several times: "The Lord gave, and the Lord has taken away; blessed be the name of the Lord" (NKJV).

Nothing is impossible for our God! He knows the end from the beginning. So, as difficult as it was, I needed to trust in His answer to our prayers and submit to His will, but still, my heart was heavy with grief.

Then I looked, and there was my cat, Pogo. He never comes to my quiet place. He sat right next to me, looking into my eyes. He rubbed his head against my arm. It was as if he were saying, "Don't be sad; I'm here with you; you are not alone." I felt the presence of God through our kitty. I often play a Christian instrumental station on my phone while I spend my quiet time with God, and just then, the song "Abide with Me" played. Again, I was comforted.

Are you feeling alone or helpless, or are you mourning the loss of someone special in your life? Take a moment to know that our God is a God of comfort! Let Him wrap His arms of love and support around you. It doesn't take the trial away, but it makes it more bearable and gives you the strength to get through the day. Our world has a lot of pain and loss, but the day is coming very soon when that will all be gone forever. In the meantime, while we wait, remember: "The Lord has appeared of old to me, saying: 'Yes, I have loved you with an everlasting love; therefore with lovingkindness I have drawn you' " (Jeremiah 31:3, NKJV).

Mona Fellers

To Be the Chosen Mother

Gabriel greeted her:
Good morning!
You're beautiful with God's beauty,
Beautiful inside and out!
God be with you.
—Luke 1:28, *The Message*

Mary was a young woman when the angel came to tell her she would be the favored one to birth the Messiah; the One women had hoped to birth for many years. Shaking, Mary wondered how this could happen because she had never been with a man. Sure, she was engaged to Joseph, but they weren't married yet. How could she have a baby without a husband?

Mary accepted the responsibility in faith, trusting her Lord and the angel's explanation. I'm sure her parents were disappointed when they were told she was pregnant. It reflected badly on them too. But Mary didn't let the shame, embarrassment, and rejection that would come her way during her pregnancy keep her from being faithful to her Lord. Understandably, it was a struggle for Joseph to accept her being pregnant when he knew it wasn't his doing! Talk about confusing! His faithfulness shows in his accepting what the angel told him and immediately acting on the angel's directions. God knew this couple would be the best parents to raise His Son. I'm sure they prayed daily for God's guidance to prepare them for such a responsibility. As Mary taught Jesus each day, the angel's words were at the back of her mind, causing her to feel the importance of "getting it right." I know as a young mother, I would worry about making the wrong decision with my boys, but praise the Lord, He promises to always be our Helper, giving us the wisdom and discernment needed to make wise choices.

Mary's love for Jesus grew stronger each year, so when He was mocked, rejected, and finally killed, her pain and loss were deep. She, too, felt His pain. She tried to understand the deep love that made Him willing to give up His young life. She stood at the foot of the cross, faithful in her love and commitment. Despite His incredible pain, Jesus honors His mother and makes provision for her continued care. God does the same today, loving, guiding, and honoring moms as they faithfully serve Him.

Louise Driver

May 8

The Widow of Nain

Jesus said unto her, I am the resurrection, and the life: he that believeth in me, though he were dead, yet shall he live.
—John 11:25, KJV

The Jewish widow of Nain (Luke 7:11–15) is in deep mourning; her only son is dead. Lying with him on the bier are her hopes, dreams, and means of earthly support. Soon the last trace of his lifeless body will rest in its burial place, and she will be left alone in her sorrow. As she mechanically places one foot in front of the other, she realizes that there will be no son to love, touch, or converse with. Her heart is frozen; she is shattered by grief.

Although friends sympathize and encourage, their words do not console the emptiness, loneliness, and brokenness of her heart. And then she hears the compassionate words of Jesus, "Weep not." Through her blinding tears, she looks into the eyes of Him who truly feels her pain, whose words evoke hope, faith, and courage within her. Her weeping turns into laughter and praise; her despondent heart leaps with unbounded joy and then overflows with gratitude and thanksgiving when Jesus touches the bier and bids her dead son, "Arise." Life flows into him; he speaks and then is delivered to her. He is whole again, and it is a miracle.

Mothers, you may have a child that is spiritually dead in trespasses and sin, but don't give up hope; do not despair. As Jesus met the funeral procession at the gate of the city of Nain, He can meet you at the gate of the mercy seat where you weep and mourn for your child to live again in truth and righteousness. His touch can rejuvenate the callous heart and make it glow with love for his Maker again. If you are an abandoned mother, without any interaction with your child, remember the words of Jesus, "Weep not." You may be a mother of a runaway, impudent, or unthankful child, but remember that at the touch of Jesus and the voice of His command, life can be restored: your child can have life and be delivered unto you again. Latch on to the promises of faith, hope, and courage, for all is not lost. Do not despair or become discouraged, for Jesus can restore relationships. He can save lives. "The thief cometh not, but for to steal, and to kill, and to destroy: I am come that they might have life, and that they might have it more abundantly" (John 10:10, KJV). Be consoled; the compassionate Jesus still works miracles.

Maureen Thomas

A Mother's Prayer

"What ails you Hagar? Fear not, for God has heard the voice of the lad. . . . I will make him a great nation."
—Genesis 21:17, 18, NKJV

In Hagar's darkest moments, just when she thought all hope was gone, she remembered the God of Abraham and Sarah and the lessons of faith she learned from them. She lifted her voice to God and wept, expecting her only child, Ishmael, to die from thirst in the wilderness. God responded immediately, opening her eyes and showing her a water well. God not only provided water to quench their thirst but also, through His angel, assured Hagar that her son would be the father of a great nation.

Bible students are familiar with the story, but let me remind my readers. When Abraham and Sarah fled Egypt, Sarah took her servant, Hagar, with her. Sarah became impatient with God in fulfilling His promise to give Abraham and her a son who would be Abraham's heir. However, when Sarah conceived and had her own child, Isaac, she felt that there would now be competing interests in the family between the brothers. (Definitely a self-fulfilling prophecy!) Sarah devised another plan to help God out. But as my mother would say, "Only God could be God!"

When Abraham and Sarah banished Hagar and her child to what appeared to be certain death in the wilderness of Beersheba, they could not have imagined the plans God had in store for mother and child. As of 2019, Ishmael's descendants, the world's Arab population, stood at approximately 428 million. God truly is faithful in keeping His promises—on that we can depend! We know of God's promise to bless Isaac, the promised child, but there is no evidence that God cannot and will not pour out His blessings on all His children. He did it for the unloved and unwanted child Ishmael. Are you feeling unloved and unwanted? Do not despair. God has a plan for your life. If you are blessed with a praying mother, the fulfillment of God's promised blessings is assured. To all the mothers out there, I encourage you never to grow weary of praying for your children. Their circumstances might seem impossible at this moment, but remember that God knows the beginning and He sees the end. He is truly omnipotent. God hears the cries and prayers of mothers everywhere, even in the midst of the wilderness of life!

Avis Mae Rodney

May 10

A Mother's Gift

Train up a child in the way he should go,
And when he is old he will not depart from it.
—Proverbs 22:6, NKJV

One of the greatest gifts in this universe is the gift of a godly mother. I was blessed to have such a mother. Mrs. Leila HoShing was always a full-time mom. She mothered ten biological children and still found time to mother many others who needed a mother's help. Mama, as we affectionately called her, was always at home attending to the domestic needs of her large family. She always hummed or sang a hymn as she worked.

As a young child, I wondered if Mama could ever get tired because it appeared that she was always so very busy. Mama seldom got sick—strength and excellent health were among her blessings; it is no wonder that she lived ninety-three years! Mama was very God-fearing. Her private devotional life has left the most indelible images on my mind. I can still see her in my mind's eye diligently reading her Bible very early each morning. Her favorite Bible passage was Psalm 27. She memorized it and allowed its message to order her life. I still remember her carefully chosen quiet place, where she took delight in meeting with God day after day. As a young child, I lovingly observed and admired her devotional life—and oh, how I longed to be like her! I think this was her greatest impact on my life.

Mama was devoted to whatever she was engaged in. Humanly speaking, I think my mother had reason to be unhappy because having more than ten children and being a full-time mother must have been challenging, yet Mama had a cheerful spirit. She was industrious, generous, thoughtful, kind, and always singing about Jesus' love!

I am a grandmother now, and I find that even in my senior years, I still practice nearly everything my mother modeled to me as a child. Children indeed live what they learn. My mother passed this earthly life and now awaits the second coming of Jesus. I eagerly look forward to meeting with Mama again when we will never ever part.

"Her children rise up and call her blessed. . . . But a woman who fears the Lord, she shall be praised. . . . And let her own works praise her in the gates" (Proverbs 31:28–31, NKJV).

Jacqueline Hope HoShing-Clarke

Thriving on God's Meal Plan

And God said, "See, I have given you every herb that yields seed which is on the face of all the earth, and every tree whose fruit yields seed; to you it shall be for food."
—Genesis 1:29, NKJV

I was blessed to have a mother who loved God and was faithful to Him even in the most unfavorable circumstances. She, like Daniel in the Bible, took God at His word. At seventeen, she was captured by the Nazis, along with thousands of other Ukrainian young people, to work in German work camps. Unlike Daniel's being placed in a royal court, though, my mother was consigned to a labor camp. Like Daniel, she made a commitment to God that she would obey all His commandments. Therefore, she kept Sabbath holy by not working on that day. The commanding officers determined to ship her to a concentration camp as punishment. However, God intervened, and Mother was sent to work for a nearby farmer's family.

Mother had been nearly starving at the labor camp because she wouldn't eat the biblically unclean meats that were provided, such as horsemeat. She hoped she would have food to eat at the farm. However, she soon learned the farmer's family ate mostly pork, so she went hungry there too. She was assigned to care for the cattle. However, the farmer's wife made it very clear Mother was not to drink any of the milk. Mother was aware of the woman often spying on her though Mother had resolved not to dishonor God by stealing even a few drops of milk.

Among her other taxing responsibilities, Mother had to chop fodder for the cattle to eat: kohlrabi, turnips, rutabagas, beets. Wait—no one had ordered her *not* to eat what the cows ate! So, like Daniel and his God-honoring friends (Daniel 1:8–16), Mother began eating raw vegetables. Summer came. One day in the pasture cutting hay, she discovered rose hips and began to eat them by the handful. Earlier, before being taken captive by the Nazis, Mother had been having some health issues even at her young age. But her diet of water, raw vegetables, and rose hips helped her body become strong and healthy again. Mother lived to be ninety-four!

God will also bless our faithfulness and obedience—in all circumstances—when we choose to abide by His health laws. And His reward for our doing so will last into eternity.

Galina Gritsuk

May 12

Just in Time

Be careful for nothing; but in everything by prayer and supplication with thanksgiving let your requests be made known unto God.
—Philippians 4:6, KJV

We have three children: Alyssa is ten, Natalia is eight, and Eric is fourteen months old. Natalia loves grapes and apples. When she was a baby, she couldn't wait long enough for me to cut the grapes for her, so she popped them into her mouth whole and swallowed them. Then, she passed them in her poop whole, which we thought was quite impressive. All our children love fruit.

Yesterday Natalia asked for an apple, so I cut it up for her. As she was eating it, Eric decided he wanted some too. So she gave him one wedge of her apple. Eric has two teeth in the front bottom row of his mouth and two teeth on the top beside the middle teeth that are just starting to burst through his gums. I kept an eye on him as he ate the apple to make sure he was eating it with no problems. He ate three-fourths of the apple wedge and then was full because he had already eaten.

Today I gave Natalia most of an apple cut into wedges and gave Eric one wedge. He was biting and chewing the apple with no problems. He coughed a few times but settled OK. My husband, Alan, was getting ready to leave for work. I went to tell him goodbye and had started back to the kitchen when I heard Eric choking while gasping for breath. He was sitting on the floor, so I quickly pushed him forward and patted his back to dislodge the apple with no success.

I quickly picked him up and put him across my arm and the arm of the couch with his head down and then gave him five back thrusts to dislodge the apple that was still stuck in his throat as I prayed for the Lord to help me dislodge the apple piece quickly. He made a heave and then gasped for breath, leaving the piece of apple on the couch. It was such a frightening experience. I breathed a "Thank You, Lord" when he finally got a full breath in again. Nothing ever sounded so sweet, I tell you!

I took him to Alan and told him what had happened, and he said he was glad I was at home and able to act quickly. Thank You, Lord, for answered prayers.

Noella (Jumpp) Baird

My Mother's Flowers Still Bloom

Honour thy father and thy mother: that thy days may be long upon the land which the Lord *thy God giveth thee.*
—Exodus 20:12, KJV

Many years ago, my mother was in the hospital 250 miles away from where I lived. When I visited her, I noticed a container with daffodils on the nightstand beside her bed. However, the blooms were dead and the stems brown.

Mom said, "Now, Vonda, you take these daffodils home and plant the bulbs. They will come back up next spring."

Mom certainly knows about flowers, I thought. *I will do as she asks, and then I will see what pops up from the soil next spring.*

I followed through on my mom's instructions to the best of my ability. I even put the leftover planting soil from the daffodil container into the ground at home when I planted the bulbs. All winter long, the bulbs "slept" in the soil. Then spring arrived.

What a blessing I was in for! The flowers that pushed through the soil that year were delicate, tiny, beautiful "baby" daffodils. Oh, how I loved those daffodils, and what a delight when I looked at them and thought of my dear, sweet mom—of her life and giving!

As the years went by, the daffodil bulbs doubled and doubled again. I dug them and spread them on the edge of my flower garden. They continued to multiply, allowing me to share them with family and friends many times.

Through the years, my mom would often say to me, "Vonda, go out there and dig some of those lilies" (or any other perennial she might have growing). She even had me dig a bit of the old rosebush that grandpa had and said to take care of it as it was very old.

Today, when I stepped outside and saw my mother's flowers blooming, I realized that all my mother had to give me years ago was her flowers. But she gave gifts that still give hope and glory in the many years since her passing. My mom knew life was in those dead-looking flowers, just as there will be life anew in us when Jesus comes to redeem His flock.

How I look forward to seeing Mom again and planting flowers with her and discovering all the things that God will have for us to do in His kingdom.

Avonda White-Krause

May 14

A Degree for Mothers

"And these words which I command you today shall be in your heart. You shall teach them diligently to your children, and shall talk of them when you sit in your house, when you walk by the way, when you lie down, and when you rise up. You shall bind them as a sign on your hand, and they shall be as frontlets between your eyes. You shall write them on the doorposts of your house and on your gates."
—Deuteronomy 6:6–9, NKJV

In 2010, I received an interesting call from my son. He had just completed his MBA and was excited. However, what he said next was what grabbed my attention.

"Mom," he said, "you are the only one now without three letters behind your name."

"You are right," I quickly responded. "I don't have three; in fact, I have six letters: M-O-T-H-E-R. And I got that title before you were born because your older sister qualified me."

I can still remember his chuckle as he admitted I had outwitted him with my response. Over the years since then, I have reflected on this statement and encouraged many mothers who think they have not accomplished much because they are "just moms" and never earned a degree. Acquiring a degree is commendable, but mothering is one of the greatest responsibilities given to feeble humans. It is a lifetime work for which God guides you through the endless internship. You remain in training as long as you live.

In one of the most profound statements on motherhood, Ellen White says, "Next to God, the mother's power for good is the strongest known on earth."* Only the One whose power exceeds yours can help you make a success of the motherhood experience. When God gives you the mother degree, He stays with you long after the degree is conferred.

God is good and kind. He knows your mother degree does not make you ever know it all. You need to keep your certification current by renewing your connection with Him daily. Claim the many promises in His Word. I encourage you to search and find many more to keep your mother degree current and relevant!

Claudette Garbutt-Harding

* Ellen G. White, *The Adventist Home* (Hagerstown, MD: Review and Herald®, 1980), 240.

When God Answers No

"For as the heavens are higher than the earth,
so are My ways higher than your ways,
And My thoughts than your thoughts."
—Isaiah 55:9, NKJV

What do you do when God answers no?

Working on my master's program was the hardest twenty-four months of study in my life! I can't remember how many times I wept with frustration because I didn't understand the assessments. I experienced overwhelming stress and felt I couldn't see how I was ever going to keep ahead of the course content. I remember the highs when I received better marks than I expected. Throughout the roller-coaster ride, I continued to picture myself in a cap and gown while attending the graduation ceremony with my parents.

I completed my degree and was looking forward to celebrating my achievements. Then came the most devastating news—my graduation ceremony was going to be held on Sabbath. I asked my prayer warrior friends to intercede on my behalf that God could provide a way for me to attend on another day. As days came and went and the ceremony was fast approaching, I received another email asking me to confirm my attendance, but the date had not changed. With a heavy heart, I decided not to attend. I confess that I cried several times because of the disappointment that I felt. I remember telling my mum that I had sent in my RSVP, declining my attendance. Mum hugged me and said, "I'm sure you sent it in with a heavy heart. In this life, we will always have moments of disappointment, but imagine if you missed out on entering heaven. Wouldn't that be a greater disappointment?"

As I write this, my graduation ceremony would have been two days ago. After that chat with Mum, I changed the way I prayed. I asked God to take away the hurt and disappointment because I just couldn't deal with it anymore. I also acknowledged that despite this answer of no to my first prayer, I would continue to praise Him because He is in control of my life. Although I may never discover the reason this side of heaven, I have the reassurance that God wants only what is best for me. Sometimes we need to stop banging on closed doors and turn our focus to trusting our heavenly Father. He wants to give us only the best, and that should be our aim too.

Jenny Rivera

May 16

Her Crown and Glory

Blessed is the one who perseveres under trial because, having stood the test, that person will receive the crown of life that the Lord has promised to those who love him.
—James 1:12, NIV

Beauty is said to be in the eye of the beholder. But in many societies, a woman's beauty is often associated with long hair. In these cultures where much emphasis is placed on long hair, the pressure often results in women going to many extremes to meet this demand. In my teen years, I was told that a woman's hair was her "crown and her glory"—likely a spinoff from a Scripture passage (see 1 Corinthians 11:15). While the intended meaning of this passage is widely debated, that is not my focus today. Instead, I want to look at what happens when a woman begins to lose her "crown and glory."

The consequences of sin batter us both spiritually and physically. Many women lose their hair because of aging, cancer, lupus, or even stress. The trauma associated with seeing one's hair fall to the ground, collect in clumps in one's hand or brush, or clog the bathroom drains can be terrifying. But thankfully, there are options available to remedy such a situation. Many women across the world cut their hair and donate it to organizations that make beautiful wigs for those in need. This and other options help ladies who struggle with hair loss.

While losing one's hair is a major matter, there is a greater "crown and glory" that we could lose. Christ gave His life on Calvary to save us from our sins and offers us a crown of eternal life. The choices we make each day will help determine whether we will inherit that crown. So while we can try to find ways of coping with losing our earthly "crowns" (our hair), there is a greater crown that we must not lose—the crown of eternal life.

Let us dedicate ourselves to spending time each day with Jesus so that He can transform our characters in preparation for His heavenly crown, which we can lay at His feet when we meet Him in glory. Pledge to recommit your life to Jesus today and be saved in His kingdom.

Taniesha K. Robertson-Brown

War-Time Love Letters

For we wrestle not against flesh and blood, but against principalities, against powers, against the rulers of the darkness of this world, against spiritual wickedness in high places.
—Ephesians 6:12, KJV

From 1939 to 1945, more than 100 million personnel from more than thirty countries were involved in World War II (WWII). Many wondered whether this global combat would ever end.

My father, Harry, was a part of this conflict. He enlisted in the United States Army and served overseas at a small island in the South Pacific called New Caledonia. He had met my mother, Rose, on a blind date before his deployment, and they were apart for thirty months. For almost three years, they wrote letters to each other every day. Mail took one to four weeks to cross the ocean. The dedication in these daily letters kept them connected and began forming a bond of love that would forever link their hearts. My father returned to the United States when the war ended in December 1945 and was married to my mother for sixty-two years.

As I was journaling prayers to my heavenly Father (which I have done now for more than fifteen years), it struck me how much my daily letters to Him were like my parents' letters during the war. Just as my father was enlisted to fight in WWII, as a believer in Christ, I am enlisted in Christ's army. For over six thousand years, this planet has been in a war with evil forces. These spiritual conflicts with evil continue to rage about us though many are oblivious to them. But we know from prophecy that this war will end, and Satan and sin will be destroyed forever. And just as my father came back from war and married my mother, Jesus will come to marry His bride (the church) and take her home to heaven with Him.

The preface to a book by a favorite writer of mine states, "Prayer is the channel of communication between our souls and God. . . . We cannot weary or burden Him by our frequent heart-to-heart communications."* Let us commit to developing that love relationship with our Lord so that when He comes, we will be ready for that marriage with Him, which will last forever.

Karen M. Phillips

* Board of Trustees of the Ellen G. White Estate, "Preface," in Ellen G. White, *Prayer* (Nampa, ID: Pacific Press®, 2002), 3.

May 18

Love Story

A man's heart deviseth his way:
But the L*ORD* *directeth his steps.*
—Proverbs 16:9, KJV

I searched genealogy sites for several years, looking for my father's military service record. Recently, I was delighted to discover his honorable discharge document on a genealogy site I don't usually frequent. The document bore truth to the story of how my parents met. Mama had told us that her older brother, Uncle Jimmie, met our father while in training. Uncle Jimmie told our future father that he had a sister he might be interested in, and the rest is history. Mama and Daddy communicated via letters throughout the war and finally met when Daddy was discharged. Soon after, they were married.

The document revealed that Uncle Jimmie and Daddy trained together for about seven months. While Daddy was deployed overseas to Africa and Europe, Uncle Jimmie received an honorable discharge and went home. What was interesting to me was the time frame when my uncle and father met. If not for their meeting, who knows whether my parents would have ever met. They lived about ninety minutes from each other. Neither had strayed too far from home.

My father had given his heart to the Lord as a young boy soon after his father had passed away, leaving his mother a young widow with seven children to raise alone. Daddy dropped out of school and helped on their farm. My mother was raised on a farm by God-fearing parents along with eight siblings and led a pretty sheltered life.

Being a Christian, I'm sure my father had mixed feelings about serving in the army during the war. However, God worked everything out for his good. He got to travel the world, was awarded medals, came home uninjured, and finally met and married the love of his life. They were married for nineteen years and had five children, four of whom survived to adulthood. Daddy died at the young age of forty-five, and Mama never remarried. Theirs was a marriage of love and respect. They taught their children about God and lived their lives to His standard.

As He orchestrated the beginning of this world, He orchestrates the beginning of our lives. How we choose to live is up to us. If we trust in Him, He will order our footsteps all our days so that we can safely navigate our life's journey into His kingdom. We serve an awesome God!

Barbara Burris Neequaye

Bearing Patiently

My brethren, count it all joy when ye fall into divers temptations; knowing this, that the trying of your faith worketh patience. But let patience have her perfect work, that ye may be perfect and entire, wanting nothing.
—James 1:2–4, KJV

The road of troubles and difficulties comes in many forms and has numerous twists and turns. We sometimes do not identify with and see our circumstances as troubles and difficulties, and at other times, we cannot focus on or deal with them how we ought to. We often go through trials feeling alone, without the physical help and emotional support we need and crave. It does not matter the circumstances that affect us; it is how we deal with those circumstances and relate to others while going through them that will help us overcome victoriously.

It is also encouraging and comforting to have the support of family, friends, and church brethren during and after difficult times so that we can grow above the circumstances that prevail against us. The Word of God admonishes us to bear patiently, live in hope, and wait for our deliverance and blessings (see Ephesians 4:2, James 5:8, Philippians 4:6, and Romans 12:12). If, over time, we overcome by God's will, we will be able to tell our story to strengthen others and go on living more fulfilled and happier lives in Jesus.

Sisters in Christ, Jesus is our only hope in times of difficulty. Let us remain focused and bear patiently because He who promised will surely come and save us. The Word of God always prevails no matter how long it takes, and we overcome through Jesus Christ. Our personality and character will make each of us shine like one who is molded by God's hands, and others will come to know Jesus Christ as their personal Savior because of His beauty shining in and through us. So let us be patient in tribulation each day and allow the Lord to lead the way; we may be surprised by the outcome.

I pray that our heavenly Father will help us trust Him in trying circumstances as we grow from day to day, allowing the Lord to work out His purpose in our lives.

Elizabeth Ida Cain

May 20

Be More Than Patient

I charge you, O ye daughters of Jerusalem,
by the roes, and by the hinds of the field,
that ye stir not up, nor awake my love,
till he please.
—Song of Solomon 3:5, KJV

There are times in a woman's life that I look forward to: a time to be married, a time to have babies. I thought I would be married before I turned thirty and have three kids. However, I have none of that. God knows me, and if it's not the time, He knows the reason. Thus, I have learned how to wait with no limits.

I found hope and, therefore, don't despair. I asked God for what I wanted. I know that I will regret it if I run ahead of God's timing. So I prefer to wait and respect God's will and timing. He sees what I don't see.

Patience is a seed of the Holy Spirit that will help me be victorious in my "inner fight." Sometimes, I will be content to wait; other times, I may suffer and cry. Indeed, being patient is being in training with the Holy Spirit as a coach. God's patience has no limit. Thus, He will help me wait, putting no demands on Him, though sometimes that is hard to do.

During the wait, I think of the reasons I would like to marry, have children, and move elsewhere. In the past, I wanted these things to satisfy myself without asking whether these were God's plans for me. I have studied my motives and goals. I now see that marriage should lead me to a mission at my husband's side, like Adam and Eve in the Garden of Eden. Marriage should not be only about relieving my loneliness. I also accept that I'm not yet ready. "Patient" is also the word for a person waiting to see a doctor to obtain a cure for illness or wound, and that takes time. So while waiting for my prayers to be answered, I am also waiting for God to heal and prepare me for a fulfilling marriage relationship. He will tell me when I am ready.

Do not be discouraged in your wait on God. Ask for patience to wait for the blessings God has for you. Respect the divine process of heart preparation and the steps you may need to take (even if difficult) to be ready—in God's timing. Don't give up. Show faith and wait in confidence, as if your dreams have already been fulfilled. Then smile on your life.

Lynn Mazarin

My Song in the Night

"But as for you, be strong and do not give up, for your work will be rewarded."
—2 Chronicles 15:7, NIV

It was the first time. A time I will long remember. There I stood, singing and strumming a guitar for a small choir. I was the lead singer directing a small group who responded with the fullness of a large choir. This moment produced such a fine blend of voices that it appeared other instruments accompanied us, and those few seconds were so ecstatic as we sang the plain, simple, short song together about the heavenly gates.

Then I awoke. The dream ended as the morning light filtered through the windows into my room. Now, I am a person who dreams every night. Seldom do I recall much of anything . . . unless it is relevant. On this morning, I did not want to stir; I just wanted to mince through my thoughts until I could recollect every part of this dream! I didn't want to forget it! It had been only as long as the song but sufficient to convey the spiritual message I would draw from it.

My special song occurred several years ago. The details of the unfamiliar faces, the place where we rehearsed, and the accuracy of the melody have since grown dim to my memory. But the song's words were so permanently etched in my mind that even after many days, I could recall and write the words down.

In Revelation 21:12, 21, 25 (NKJV), I get a much clearer picture of those gates I only sang about in my dream. John describes the twelve gates surrounding the Holy City, and each one is made from a single enormous pearl. He tells us that the Holy City, with its great high wall and twelve gates, has twelve angels guarding the gates. And on the gates are written the names of the twelve tribes of Israel. "Lord," I pray, "that I might so live that I will be numbered with that number that no man can number!" (See Revelation 7:9.)

As life on this planet has become increasingly challenging, uninviting, and complex, hope must prevail. Christ's return is imminent! We must daily claim His promises to carry us through . . . until then, I'm forever grateful that He gave me my song in the night.

Jayne Byrd-Moody

God Will Fight for You

"The Lord will fight for you; you need only to be still."
—Exodus 14:14, NIV

In 2015, I was in my second year studying theology at Peruvian Adventist University. I was the only woman student in the classroom. Most of my friends were sure that God had called them to be pastors. I was also very sure that God had called me to do a work for Him, but I could not imagine the way that God was preparing for me.

At the time, I attended a Faith and Science Conference in Peru. The speaker was Dr. Ben Clausen, who works at the Geoscience Research Institute at Loma Linda University, California, United States of America. I felt very impressed about the relationship between science and the Bible. I asked God, "If You have a plan for me in this area, please help me learn more about that."

One year later, I emailed Dr. Clausen. I shared with him my story and my interest in faith and science. He told me, "I know God has a plan for your life." In 2018, I graduated from theology and started applying for a master's degree in geology at Loma Linda University.

As an international student, I had to take different exams. When I failed my English exam, I was so disappointed with myself. I prayed and told God that I did my best on the exam. I asked Him, "If You want me to stay in Peru, please help me find a job, but if You want to take me to Loma Linda University, open the doors because I cannot do any more."

Everything happened after that prayer; it was a miracle from God. In 2019, Loma Linda University accepted me as a graduate student. Now Dr. Clausen is my advisor and is a friendly and passionate scientist. He teaches me to love igneous rocks and minerals!

Sometimes we do our best; we work hard to achieve our professional and family dreams, but we do not have many results. However, I encourage you to wait on God if you have done your best because He wants to fight for you as He fought for the Israelite people.

Dear friend, nothing is impossible for God! The Lord will fight for you. Search for God with all your heart!

Raquel Bendita Larico

Share Your Bread

Is it not to deal thy bread to the hungry, and that thou bring the poor that are cast out to thy house? When thou seest the naked, that thou cover him; and that thou hide not thyself from thine own flesh?
—Isaiah 58:7, KJV

I arrived at church for a class of teachers one morning and found a young woman sitting on a bench crying. I approached and asked how I could help her, and she told me her story. She was a single mother with a daughter who was studying at the local Adventist school. Due to financial difficulties, she would be forced to put her daughter in a public school. Her young daughter could not accept the decision and just kept crying. Without having a way to solve the problem herself, she went to the church hoping to find help.

At the time, I was married and had no children, so I offered to help her by paying the school tuition so that her daughter could continue studying at the Adventist school. The tears turned to joy, and she was grateful.

Five years after being married, I had a daughter, and fifteen years later I had twin sons.

When my twins were three years old, my husband passed away, leaving me in a difficult financial situation. When they were ten years old, I had to put them in a bigger, more expensive school. In the middle of the school year, I saw that I would not be able to afford the tuition and would need to move them to a public school. This situation made me very sad because the quality of teaching would be much lower than they had in their school.

I didn't tell anyone about the situation, but at night I cried out to God in prayer.

After a tearful night of prayer, my nephew (whom I had raised) called and said that he had received a promotion at work and wanted to begin paying the school tuition for my children beginning that month.

I remembered God's promise in Isaiah 58:9, "Then shalt thou call, and the LORD shall answer; thou shalt cry, and he shall say, Here I am" (KJV).

God's promises are fulfilled without advance or delay and at the exact time we need it most.

God is always faithful.

Isabel Cristina de Almeida

May 24

My Sister

Dear friends, since God so loved us, we also ought to love one another.
—1 John 4:11, NIV

"You and your sister are closer than most twins," my father-in-law observed. Even with our three-year age difference, we joke that somehow God made us twins! We know what the other is getting ready to say before she says it. We talk on the phone daily, and when we hug each other, it is a warm, powerful, healing hug. For the question "What amuses baby?" in my baby book, my mother wrote, "Tibby. She adores Tibby."

To say my sister and I are close is an understatement.

Everyone loves my sister. She is many people's "best" friend. She has been my best friend throughout my life, too, helping me through difficult times and sharing in the best of times. She has the greatest sense of humor, like our father had. She makes me laugh so hard that I can't catch my breath! No one does it like she can.

Tibby truly reflects the golden rule, "Do to others as you would have them do to you" (Luke 6:31, NIV). She spends time with friends, family, and perfect strangers, meeting them where they are. If someone is going through a difficult time, she will spend hours with them and has helped so many, including me. She celebrates with me through my joys and helps me through difficult times—always with a waiting hug.

Wouldn't it be wonderful if more people were like my sister? There is pain in many families where people haven't reflected love, so I know how truly blessed I am to be from a family where love prevailed. My sister truly reflects God's love.

Tibby has faced difficult times in her own life and recently had a scare with a lump in her breast. Thankfully, she did not have cancer. She felt it was one of the best experiences in her life because she knew she was totally in God's hands, and she was grateful to meet wonderful ladies through this experience. What a great outlook and faith!

Ladies, if you don't have a best friend or sister, know that all the ladies who write for this devotional are your sisters in Christ. Please know that Jesus is your Best Friend. You can always count on Him. He is always with you. Every day, I thank God that He gave me a sister who reflects His love to me and so many others.

Jean Dozier Davey

The Perfect Gear for the Perfect Storm

Therefore put on the full armor of God, so that when the day of evil comes, you may be able to stand your ground, and after you have done everything, to stand.
—Ephesians 6:13, NIV

The *Andrea Gail*, a successful commercial swordfishing boat, left port from Massachusetts looking for a good catch. The vessel sank after being caught in the perfect storm, killing its crew of six. This northeaster in 1991 caused damage along the North American coastline from Nova Scotia to Puerto Rico.

Following Jesus doesn't mean we will not face any storms. The disciples ran directly into a storm while obeying Jesus. Yet God has provided us with the perfect gear to withstand the storm.

The first gear needed to withstand a storm is a jacket that keeps you warm. In our spiritual gear, this is like the shield of faith, which is needed to daily endure Satan's ungodly attacks on us.

When headed out to sea, we also need a raincoat with a hood to cover our heads and faces from the rain. This is like the helmet of salvation, which protects us from thinking bad things, listening to bad things, saying bad things, and watching bad things.

A personal flotation device is crucial to stay afloat. The breastplate of righteousness enables us to stay afloat and live a Christlike life through storms, knowing God overcame this world for you and me and covers us with His righteousness.

Water shoes prevent us from slipping off the boat and protect our feet in waters filled with rocks and coral. When our feet are covered with the gospel of peace, we are ready to share the gospel with anyone. Jesus told His disciples to preach the good news to everyone, making disciples of all nations.

A harness tied around the waist that latches on to the boat prevents people from falling out of the boat. The belt of truth will keep us connected to God as we follow Jesus' example of prayer and studying the Bible, preventing us from falling out of connection with God.

Finally, a knife is needed to defend those at sea against deadly creatures swimming in ocean waters, ready to attack. The sword of the Spirit is the Word of God in our hearts and minds, preparing us to defend ourselves against Satan's lies while facing temptations.

Suhana Chikatla

May 26

Lord, Save Me!—Part 1

You have put away my acquaintances far from me;
I am shut up, and I cannot get out.
You have made me an abomination to them.
—Psalm 88:8, NKJV

I got my mask on and opened the door to my brother's knock. When I opened, he was at a distance, all decked out in goggles, mask, and gloves. We called out a greeting from behind our masks and laughed a little, but it didn't last. We stood there looking at each other, and then my brother shouted, "This is not right!"

In March 2020, the Canadian government mandated social distancing and strict quarantine measures because of the COVID-19 pandemic. My brother called to inform me that he was on his way to visit. I am not sure that *visit* is the correct word because the meaning had changed due to COVID-19. Family, neighbors, friends, and coworkers were to stay at least two meters (about six and a half feet) apart. This affected some frontline workers who shared the same space with family members whom they were protecting.

I agreed, it wasn't. As a family, we are very cuddly. We are accustomed to warm, passionate hugs, kisses, laughter, and smiles when we visit. We are so close we can see the twinkle in each other's eyes, and we benefit from the radiance of the joy that emanates from each face.

My brother took the package I offered with a quick grasp and pulled back; he was ensuring my safety. Before he left, he prayed a heartfelt prayer for the family and a world in crisis.

Sadly, it was not meant to be like this. In the Garden of Eden, God said, "It is not good that man should be alone" (Genesis 2:18, NKJV). The news is replete with the emotional and psychological effects of this social isolation on parents, grandparents, children, and friends. Lord, please save us from sin's isolation; we long to be with You!

A few days later, my friends who are also my neighbors saw me coming. They withdrew from me and quickly closed their door. As they retreated, we laughed and shared greetings from behind closed doors. Then, when I entered my apartment, they exited theirs. On all my errands, people avoided me, and I avoided them. We were protecting each other from one of the deadly effects of sin, COVID-19.

Sonia Kennedy-Brown

Lord, Save Me!—Part 2

"And the LORD, He is the One who goes before you. He will be with you, He will not leave you nor forsake you; do not fear nor be dismayed."
—Deuteronomy 31:8, NKJV

It was 2:59 A.M., the first day of May 2020. According to the clock, I had only a very short nap. I had been turning and twisting for several hours. I needed answers for a few church-related issues. As the lead elder, I was expected to have a broad back and stiff upper lip, but I felt helpless. To compound the situation, my COVID-19 stress level was increasing. Just that afternoon, I had learned that a few positive cases were in my condominium building. Who were they, and what level were they on? Were they close to my apartment? Had I met and spoken to them recently? I felt threatened and unsafe. I recited a litany of Bible promises and hymns to settle my mind, but I felt no peace.

I was aware of several distant family members and friends affected by the virus; some were recovering, and others had succumbed. I have a compromised immune system, so I was very concerned about exposure. Of course, I followed all the necessary guidelines for my protection, but I needed spiritual strength.

I got out of bed and went to my prayer corner, where I talked to God. With tears, I laid my cares and concerns before Him. At last, I began to feel His peace in my heart as I placed my COVID-19 fears, my tears, and my church concerns before Him. He spoke to me with several promises, including today's text, "And the LORD, He is the One who goes before you. [Sonia,] He will be with you, He will not leave you nor forsake you; do not fear nor be dismayed" (Deuteronomy 31:8, NKJV). This was the promise Moses gave to Joshua when he handed over the leadership mantle to guide Israel into the Promised Land. A promise that no matter what we face, God is with us, and we do not need to be afraid.

Gradually, God's peace filled my heart, and I was reassured that all would be well with Him as my leader. My fear and concerns were gone. I returned to bed, and after a few moments, I slept soundly for the remaining two hours of the night.

Again, I prayed, "Lord, please save us from the greater pandemic of sin and its consequences. Please safely guide us to Your heavenly home. Amen!"

Sonia Kennedy-Brown

May 28

A Voice Behind Me

Whether you turn to the right or to the left, your ears will hear a voice behind you, saying, "This is the way; walk in it."
—Isaiah 30:21, NIV

Have you ever heard someone give a testimony and say, "God spoke to me and said . . ."? If you are a Christian or have been around Christians long enough, you may have heard this statement at least once. I used to wonder why when I prayed or asked God for signs, I never heard His voice. Ever. I began to chalk it up to others having a better relationship with God than I did—before something quite curious happened.

A year ago, I was about to make a really bad decision. In what can only be described as presumption, I declined to pray about it because I already knew I was in the wrong. That night, I had one of the most vivid dreams of my life. In the dream, I saw the direct consequence of the action I was about to take. I even heard a voice saying to me, "Don't do it!" I woke up in cold sweat. Could that be the voice of God? As a self-proclaimed "modern woman" not given to the traditional Caribbean emphasis on the significance of dreams, I shrugged it off as being just the result of an overactive conscience. Ignoring the warning I had been given yielded the exact results I saw in the dream. I realized then that God had spoken to me, but in not recognizing His voice, I chose to ignore it.

Since then, I've come to realize that God speaks to each of us in different ways, and every time since then, I've perceived God speaking to me through that "gut feeling"—my conscience. The Bible says in John 10:27, "My sheep hear my voice, and I know them, and they follow me" (KJV). As Christians, as followers of Christ, we must be able to not only recognize God's voice speaking but also heed His wisdom when He gives it to us. As the ever-loving Father, He only desires our good and wants to give us direction. While we may never be able to say that we have heard an audible voice telling us which path to take, through dreams, a word from a friend, a Bible passage, and yes, through our very consciences, we can still hear God's voice behind us, saying, "This is the way, walk in it" (Isaiah 30:21, KJV).

Olivia D. Valentine

The Things We Don't Do

If anyone, then, knows the good they ought to do and doesn't do it, it is sin for them.
—James 4:17, NIV

The fire trucks sat in our driveway for five hours while a fire raged in the hills behind our home. They were prepared to protect our home along with a dozen others on this side of the hill should the fire move our direction. For most of those five hours, I felt impressed to share some Christian literature I had with the men. But I didn't do it. Even though the impression was very strong, I didn't act on it. And then the fire was out, and they were gone. That was several years ago, and the fact that I refused to act on that impression still haunts me. It's not that I have never acted on an impression that I believe God sent me. It's just that for some reason, I didn't do it that day. We are all very much aware of the sins of commission—the things we do that we ought not to. But have we thought about the sins of omission? The things that we don't do but should?

There have been other times when I felt impressed to do or say something, and I didn't. There have also been times when I felt strongly impressed to do something and followed through. Or I would find myself saying or doing something that I know God impressed me to say or do. Why the difference? Why are there times when it is so easy to follow through and other times when it is so very difficult? I have determined that for me, the problem is one of focus. When I focus on myself, when I let insecurity, doubt, or fear of failure or ridicule dominate my thoughts, the result is obvious. But when I forget about myself and focus on the other person or on the thing God impresses me to do, then it's a different story.

Obviously, Satan wants us to keep our focus on ourselves, our feelings, our fears, our hesitations. When we do that, we are doomed, and he knows it. Since the day of the fire, I have had a lot of time to think about my response to God's impressions. I wish I could say that I am 100 percent better about following His lead. Unfortunately, I can't say that. But what I have learned from that experience—and what I hope and pray I never forget—is that it isn't about me. It's about God. And with His help, I really can be His hands and feet and reach out so that I am not guilty of sins of omission.

Sharon Clark

May 30

Taking Orders From Jesus

Verily, verily, I say unto you, He that believeth on me, the works that I do shall he do also; and greater works than these shall he do; because I go unto the Father.
—John 14:12, ASV

Taking orders from someone is something I prefer *not* to do. I am not sure about you. Human nature equals wanting to be in control of my life, my day, and my profession. Some people prefer controlling others and telling them what they think they should do and how to live life—specifically religiously speaking.

I am reminded of a song sung by Frank Sinatra, "I Did It My Way." The words to that song reflect our thinking when we were born into this world. I believe this song was played at Senator John McCain's memorial service as people exited the solemn service. McCain was a respected American politician, statesman, and United States Navy officer who served as a United States Senator for Arizona and was known for doing things his way. While Sinatra sings about doing it his way, "Me do it!" and "I do it!" are words I heard our children say when they began to talk.

As I began my quiet time with my *God Moments* prayer journal today, I read October 17. The opening sentence in the powerful devotional book *My Utmost for His Highest*, by Oswald Chambers, reads, "Prayer does not equip us for greater works—prayer is the greater work. . . . Prayer is *the* battle, and it makes no difference where you are."* Prayer takes away the control battle. It places the control in the hands and will of my Father and Lord.

From whom do you take orders? As I studied and listened to God today, He assured me that His way is "He has my back." When I give Him permission, He takes my will and allows His express will to be lived out in my life. I choose to give Him my day, my desires, my passions, my thoughts, just because I want Him to control me, "simply because [I've] been in the habit of taking [my] orders from Jesus Christ."† I choose each day, each hour, and each moment to take orders from my awesome Creator, beloved Redeemer, Lord, and Lover of my heart and soul. From whom do you take orders?

Mary H. Maxson

---

* Oswald Chambers, "The Key of the Greater Work," *My Utmost for His Highest*, October 17, https://utmost.org/the-key-of-the-greater-work/.

† Chambers, October 17.

Gifts for the Class of 2020

Let your light so shine before men, that they may see your good works, and glorify your Father which is in heaven.
—Matthew 5:16, KJV

When COVID-19 began and then escalated, I knew I wanted to make a difference. I longed to show my small community, my neighbors, and my friends who God is. I wanted them to know that they do not need to fear or panic but that they can trust God, even in a pandemic.

I started thinking, *What can I do?*

Suddenly a brilliant idea came to me. Why not present the students in the neighborhood with a graduation card and a small gift?

Each evening as I walked through my neighborhood, I saw "Class of 2020" signs in yards celebrating a graduating senior. I immediately went out and bought a few cards. Two days later, as I took my walk, I decided that this would be the evening to present a card to one of the graduates as I passed his house.

I walked bravely into the driveway and asked for the student. His mom was a bit hesitant, but when I explained that I was a neighbor and a former teacher, she happily went and got him. I gave him the card. He was very happy and grateful—especially when he saw the gift inside the card. His mom took a picture of us together.

I plan to return as soon as the COVID-19 precautionary measures are lifted and invite them to church. I am almost positive that mom and the children will come. Showing kindness to our neighbors is one way of leading them to Christ. The Lord requires us to love Him with all our hearts and our neighbor as ourselves. My prayer is that God would use us to shine for Him in this dark world.

Patricia Hines

Graduation Ceremony

"For I know the thoughts that I think toward you, says the LORD, thoughts of peace and not of evil, to give you a future and a hope."
—Jeremiah 29:11, NKJV

Have you ever had a dream that you desperately wanted to be fulfilled? Or asked God for something, but the answer was no? After completing the graduate certificate of stomal therapy nursing, I started thinking of studying again. I prayed as I applied for this course. I was accepted into the Master of Clinical Leadership program and began studying with gusto. I regularly spoke to God and told Him that my aim was to achieve a grade point average (GPA) of six (seven being the highest) and that I was looking forward to traveling down to New South Wales to attend my graduation ceremony with my parents.

As I completed all subjects and came to the end of the master's program, I did achieve a GPA of six (thank God!) but was disappointed when I received notification of the graduation ceremony—it fell on a Saturday. I started praying that God would change the date. My close friends joined me in prayer for this change because I didn't want to dishonor God by attending my graduation ceremony on the Sabbath. Sadly, the day did not change. You can imagine how disappointed I was because God chose not to intervene in this situation, even though He can do the impossible.

As an associate lecturer for the faculty of medicine at one of the leading universities in Brisbane in 2020, I was invited by this university to be part of the graduation procession for the 2021 medical student graduation ceremony. As I drove to the university on that graduation day, got ready in my cap and gown, and joined the academic process, I was still shocked by the turn of events. The procession got a standing ovation round of applause, and while I reveled in the pomp and ceremony, I felt out of place. I mean, it is rare for a registered nurse to be part of a ceremony for the school of medicine, let alone teach medical students, but there I was—a place I never expected to be—but where God had graciously placed me. I burst into tears on my way home and thanked God for allowing me this opportunity—so totally humbled by the whole experience. God answered my prayer in His time, and it exceeded even my expectations. When we are faithful to God, He is faithful to us and will give us blessings that overflow.

Jenny Rivera

Hope

O Lord, you alone are my hope.
I've trusted you, O Lord, from childhood.
—Psalm 71:5, NLT

There is no disputing that 2020 was a difficult year. A pandemic caused restrictions on our lives. Businesses closed. Children attended classes virtually. Parents struggled to juggle jobs and help their children with schoolwork. Churches closed their doors and moved services online. Relatives and friends passed away. And yet, we pressed on.

How? Trusting that God is our hope no matter what the world looks like.

We can have hope as we trust Him. Hope for a brighter future. Hope to look forward to the future. Hope to know that no matter how bad things seem, things will get better. Hope that with every passing day and every leaf that falls in the autumn months, a new one will grow and take its place come spring.

We must and should look forward with expectation. With hard work, yes. Hard work enables us to reach our goals. We are not to sit idle; these are busy days. We can work together with God, trusting Him to bless our work and give us the courage and hope each day.

I was thinking of a rose and how strong its roots must be to sustain it and how its thorns protect it. The strong roots and thorny protection enable it to go on to produce a beautiful, sweet-smelling flower. We need to stay strong and be protected to live a life that produces a sweet-smelling aroma that reveals Christ to others. As the thorns protect the rose, we also have protection in the armor of God, which enables us to "stand firm against all strategies of the devil" (Ephesians 6:11, NLT).

Paul encourages us, "Therefore, put on every piece of God's armor so you will be able to resist the enemy in the time of evil" (verse 13). So, stay rooted, my friend. Be strong in Jesus with the armor of God: the helmet of salvation, the breastplate of righteousness, the belt of truth, the sandals of peace, the shield of faith, and the sword of the Spirit.

"I pray that God, the source of hope, will fill you with joy and peace because you trust in him. Then you will overflow with confident hope through the power of the Holy Spirit" (Romans 15:13, NLT).

Laura A. Canning

June 3

Moving-Day Miracle

"Before they call I will answer;
while they are still speaking I will hear."
—Isaiah 65:24, NIV

It was moving day, and I (Edith) had been helping my son's family pack and get ready to move. I love to pack because packing always reminds me of new beginnings. My task had been to pack the kitchen, bathrooms, and children's room. On the morning of the moving day, I awoke energized for the move, stripped my bed, and completed packing the guest room. We were expecting the movers at any moment. I remember reflecting that things were going smoothly for this move. Just then, my daughter-in-law came downstairs, looking anxious and concerned.

I (Alta) woke up exhausted because the baby was up all night and worried because there was so much to do. I began to pack. After feeding my son, Sebastian, I checked on my husband, who was breaking down the baby's bed. When I saw him on the phone, I knew immediately something was wrong. "The movers just called to say they couldn't come today because of a staffing shortage. They will try the next day," he said with a forlorn expression.

Since he was so upset, I said, "Don't worry; we are going to fix it." I suggested we get a moving truck, move whatever we could, and put out an SOS to our friends. He did. Then, I went downstairs and told my mother-in-law.

What my daughter-in-law shared was shocking! I thought of all the work we had done and realized we had to move that day. I agreed with her suggestion for a self-move; it was the best alternative.

I said, "Let's pray." We begin to pray audibly. My son rushed downstairs; he had been able to secure a truck and was going to pick it up. I kept praying, asking God to intervene. Then, I remembered something my niece had shared about hiring movers when you rent a U-Haul truck. I shared this information with my son. He was able to hire two young men to help us move. Within three hours, we were at the new location. The miracle continued. When I (Alta) asked for the cost of their services, I was shocked. These young men who worked diligently charged us only one-third of the cost of the previous movers. We received three hours of moving for the price of one hour! What seemed to be a disaster, God turned into a blessing.

Edith C. Fraser with Alta Ventura Fraser

Miracles Still Happen—Part 1

I waited patiently for the Lord*. . . .*
He lifted me out of the slimy pit . . .
and gave me a firm place to stand.
—Psalm 40:1, 2, NIV

My husband, Adjei, makes it his duty to help me carry stuff upstairs from my car every day when I get home from work. Because of that, I call him every time before I start the journey home. But when I called this Friday, he answered softly, "I am sick, so I won't come down." Sick? He was well when I left in the morning, although he had been complaining of backaches for some time. His doctor sent him for an MRI, and we waited for the results. That was it. Adjei was crippled from that day, and our daughter, Abby, had to arrange for her sister-in-law, Bibi, to bring us a wheelchair.

The MRI showed a tumor in his lower spine, and the doctor referred him to an orthopedic surgeon. The first surgeon checked the images and referred him to a spine specialist. With hope, we informed the church and the pastor, and they started to pray for him. My brother-in-law, Lewis, a pastor in England, also started to pray with his church over this very sudden development.

We met the spine surgeon, who explained that the situation was so serious we needed a neurosurgeon. It took a struggle and a long wait amid COVID-19 restrictions and protocols to meet this neurosurgeon. This surgeon was very nice and reassuring. He told us that he and his team would take up the case and go ahead with emergency surgery to remove the tumor.

I know that our God is able. By faith, we trusted and waited on Him. We were afraid for Adjei to go through the surgery because he was over seventy. But we were encouraged by this neurosurgeon. He explained that my husband might not be able to walk without the surgery to remove the tumor, and the pain might only get worse. No medication helped. He could not stand, and even sitting down for a while was an ordeal. God is great. He never fails. He has the answer to every situation. Our faith was strengthened by the fact that people like Abraham and Hannah and the woman with the issue of blood believed, and it worked for them.

Mabel Kwei

June 5

Miracles Still Happen—Part 2

I will exalt you, my God the King. . . .
Great is the LORD.
—Psalm 145:1–3, NIV

The prayers of friends, family, and church members never stopped as we waited for the Lord's will to be done. By His grace, after several tests, imaging, and trials, a date was set for Adjei to get into the hospital for a pre-surgery procedure. As we prepared for the admission, we received a call to the effect that Adjei's insurance would not cover him under that particular neurosurgeon's treatment because he is not in Adjei's insurance network.

Discouraged? Yes! But we prayed, believing that somehow it would be all right. Suddenly, a call came again from the doctor's nurse that my husband was to report to the emergency department and a nurse would take care of him. No one is denied care in the emergency department—network or not. In that way, the surgeon would be able to do the surgery as planned.

Because of COVID-19 restrictions, when I took my husband to the hospital, only he was allowed to enter. I was sent home in tears. I called the nurse, and she assured me that the doctor would call me after the surgery, two days later. After I had waited alone for three days in agony, the phone rang, and the neurosurgeon was on the line. "Good news. Your husband's surgery went well, and after seven hours, we did it. Oh, he is moving his legs."

"Amen. Glory to God." This was great news. He was moving his legs, and the tumor had been removed. That gave me hope that my husband would surely walk again. I am very grateful to God and this neurosurgeon and his team. After a week of pain and suffering, my husband was transferred to a rehab facility, and even though I was still not allowed to visit him, we communicated by phone. Prayers continued unabated, and by God's grace, after six weeks, everybody, including the doctor, was surprised that my husband stood up and walked without a walker or cane, never to go back.

Yes! Just like that. And if this is not a miracle, what do you think it is? For me, my church, my coworkers, my friends, the neurosurgeon, and my family, it is the greatest miracle in our lives. So, I ask, are miracles still happening in this sinful world? Yes, they are. Only believe!

Mabel Kwei

God Paid for My Bus Pass

But my God shall supply all your need according to his riches in glory by Christ Jesus.
—Philippians 4:19, KJV

It was the last day of the month, and I only had money left for my monthly bus pass, which cost about US$148.

I had about $60–$70 in the bank and about $70–$80 in cash. I made my way to the local 7-Eleven store to make my purchase. You know you're broke when you pay for something half in cash and half on a debit card!

I walked up to the cashier to make my purchase. "How would you like to pay?" he asked.

"I'll pay half in cash and the rest with debit," I replied.

The cashier took my cash and then punched in the key for the debit machine. I inserted my card and waited to input my pin. I noticed that the number on the debit machine did not move or allow me to put in my pin. Then suddenly, the machine beeped, and a receipt came out.

"Do you want a receipt?" the cashier asked chirpily as he ripped the receipt from the machine.

"But I didn't punch in my pin," I said to him, astonished and not sure what happened. It seemed like no money had been removed from my account.

"Well, it looks like it went through to me," he replied as he handed me the receipt.

I was still in shock, so I went straight to the bank to see if the money was taken out of my account. Sure enough, the money I had left in my account for the remainder of my bus pass was still there.

Whenever I think about that experience, I wonder if it was a glitch in the system or an issue with the debit machine that day. Regardless, I know that there was divine intervention in the mix. God in His wisdom covered the cost of my bus pass, which allowed me to have money left over to purchase groceries and have food until my next paycheck.

Some people may question how God would have possibly paid for my pass through the debit machine, but for me, anything is possible when my heavenly Father owns the whole world and everything in it. The God I experienced that day knew what I needed before I even asked!

Jonsaba C. Jabbi

June 7

Unspoken Prayer Answered

And it shall come to pass, that before they call,
I will answer; and while they are yet speaking, I will hear.
—Isaiah 65:24, KJV

After the recent death of my stepfather, there were just no ifs or buts about it: the most logical thing to do was to have my mom live with me. This meant that her house had to be sold, her furniture had to be gotten rid of, and the whole house cleared out.

My mom could not assist in all this activity because she is ninety-five years old and has dementia. There just was not anyone to help. Well, at least that was what I thought. God, on the other hand, had other plans in mind for me. Day after day, I could see Him working in so many ways that it was just a bit overwhelming at times. However, there was one unasked prayer that He answered for me.

A dear friend who was visiting in another part of Florida offered me help the day before he flew back home. While planning for his stay, I thought it would be nice if I could get some green bananas to complement the ackee and saltfish that I planned to cook for our breakfast. The problem was that I did not have anyone to stay with my mom while I went to the store, and I certainly did not want to leave her alone while I went to get it.

The following morning, while I was still trying to figure out how to get the bananas, my telephone rang. I answered it, and a friend who usually gets up quite late in the day was on the line. I inquired why she was up so early, and then she asked, "Would you be interested in some green bananas?" I could not believe my ears! Did the Lord just answer my unspoken prayer before I even got a chance to voice it? I gladly accepted her offer and shouted for joy!

What a God we serve! He has promised that He will take care of us, no matter what. As the text says, He also has promised that He will answer before we call and hear even while we are yet speaking. Friends, trust Him where you cannot trace Him. He is there, waiting to help us even if we have not asked.

Maureen H. Moncrieffe

Wrong Car Was an Answer to Prayer

"Before they call, I will answer;
And while they are still speaking, I will hear."
—Isaiah 65:24, NKJV

My husband had a trip overseas for his meetings. I had taken him to the nearest airport before, but this time he was flying out of Reagan National Airport (DCA), which was new to me. For this reason, I asked him to call a taxi. The driver was delayed, and my husband was getting anxious—fearing he would miss his flight. So he asked me to drive him. I was not happy because I had never been to this airport before. However, I had no choice but to take him. We prayed and left for the airport.

I could not use the GPS on my phone because the battery was running low, and I was saving it for emergencies. While at the airport, I asked a man how to get to Route 395. I knew my way home from that spot. The man figured out I was not grasping the directions and politely told me to just follow him. We started off, and I watched his car faithfully until, at one point, another car cut in between us. It was a strenuous drive trying to keep up with the driver because there were many similar cars. I tried everything possible to get behind my guide, and eventually, I did. After a few minutes, the car took an exit, and I followed, only to realize that it was going to a hotel. When the driver stepped out of the car, he was not the person I had spoken to earlier, and he was with his family. I went back into my car as if I had forgotten something. I whispered a prayer to God for direction.

I then decided to go into the hotel, although I was afraid the driver might be thinking I was following him. I went to the front desk and explained my predicament, and the lady was so understanding. I gave her my home address, and she printed a MapQuest for me. I studied it carefully and then started home to get ready for work.

God knew how hard it would be to follow behind a car in that busy street. So He directed me to a wrong driver who ended up at a hotel just for me to get printed directions. I was a little late for work but safe and less stressed out.

Gertrude Mfune

God Can Still Be Trusted

And it shall come to pass, that before they call,
I will answer; and while they are yet speaking, I will hear.
—Isaiah 65:24, KJV

I am convinced that God can be trusted, and I will continue trusting in Him until I die.

We are all aware of the type of year 2020 was. Difficult. Lots of changes, adjustments, and the like. But through it all, our God has been good.

On Tuesday, May 26, 2020, I used the last egg from the box and said (more or less to myself), "Lord, this is the last egg, and You will have to help me find money to buy more."

Less than half an hour after making that statement, I looked through the window and saw a car parked in front of my house. I did not hear a horn or hear when the car pulled up. I told my son, "Go and see if that person is here for us."

In a few minutes, he returned with a smile and a box with a dozen eggs in his hand, saying, "The neighbor brought this and said, 'they are on the house.' "

I shouted, "Thank You, Lord!"

My son did not understand why I thanked God for the eggs, so I explained to him how I had used the last egg and told God He would need to provide more.

Afterward, I prayed, "God, You said my bread and water is sure, and now you have sent eggs also; thank You for looking out for me."

God continues to provide the eggs. As of writing this (in February 2021), the eggs are still coming and are always "on the house." They have become a regular reminder of a God who cares, who hears, and who provides.

Immediately, today's text came to mind, and I was reassured that the eggs were on the way before I called. God had already known my need and provided before I had even asked.

I want to reassure you today that God loves you and desires your good. If that was not so, why did He take time to number the hairs on our heads? Let us trust Him even though we don't understand all that is happening around us. Call on Him today, and trust Him to take care of your situation. No matter how big or small your need, God cares.

Brenda Browne-Ashe

God's Timing

Humble yourselves, therefore, under God's mighty hand, that he may lift you up in due time. Cast all your anxiety on him because he cares for you.
—1 Peter 5:6, 7, NIV

Thunk! Hurrying from the kitchen, thinking one of the dogs had knocked something over, I looked to see what had fallen in the dining room. I was startled to see my husband flat on his back on the hardwood floor. Lying there, dazed, he stared at the ceiling. After a few moments, he stood up. He appeared to be fine, but as I turned toward the kitchen, he collapsed again.

"I'm taking you to the hospital." I reached for my car keys, unsure how I would get him to the car.

"No. Call an ambulance. You can't lift me."

Fumbling for my phone, I dialed 911.

As he lay there, I corralled the dogs and gathered our four-year-old daughter. I told Rebecca that her daddy was going to the hospital and that she was going to Grandma's house.

The paramedics arrived very quickly, loaded him up, and sped to the hospital.

Buckling our daughter into her car seat, she settled in with her "Grandma blanket" (a baby blanket Grandma had crocheted) and her favorite stuffed animal. Trying not to exceed the speed limit, I drove to my in-laws' home. My mother-in-law took Rebecca, and my father-in-law accompanied me to the hospital. We settled into the waiting-room seats.

Finally, the doctor appeared with a report. "Your husband had a stroke. Since he arrived here so quickly, we administered TPA [tissue plasminogen activator]. I believe he has an excellent chance of recovery."

I sat back down in gratitude and amazement. Earlier that day, I had returned from my exercise class and intended to leave shortly thereafter for a MOPS (Mothers of Preschoolers) event. My husband collapsed during the hour and a half that I was home. How differently his outcome could have been if I had been away. Ten years have now passed; he is strong and healthy, with no side effects from the stroke.

God lifted him in due time. God cared for us during those anxious times, and He still cares for us today.

Sandy Kolb

June 11

No Signal

For God has not given us a spirit of fear,
but of power and of love and of a sound mind.
—2 Timothy 1:7, NKJV

Our daughter, her husband, and their son had just that day moved to another state. Two other daughters, a son-in-law, and two great-grandchildren were on vacation in another state. My husband's brother was in hospice care and not expected to live many more days, and our niece was also in hospice. We did not have a landline for our phone anymore, just our cell phones. Then that dreadful evening came. My husband was going to make a call when he got the message that there was no signal. I quickly looked at my phone and was able to send a text, but when I tried again to send another text, the message popped up that the text could not be sent, and I also was told there was no power.

My husband and I went into the office and rebooted everything. We looked at our router, and there was a very weak signal for the Wi-Fi, and we realized that our router would probably need to be replaced, but it was nine-thirty at night, and the stores were all closed, so we would have to wait until morning.

I was so concerned. I worried that one of our daughters might need to call about something and would be worried that she could not get through to us, but there was nothing I could do. I felt helpless as I realized I had no power over the situation.

I remembered that God has told us not to fear and that the spirit of fear had not come from Him. Instead, He gives us a spirit of power, of love, and of a sound mind. I prayed He would give me the peace I needed to leave my family concerns in His hands and that our signal would be working in the morning or that He would help me find a simple solution. He sent me His power to fall peacefully asleep.

The next morning, when I woke up, I looked over at my phone, and there was just what I needed to see—my phone had a strong signal once again. I called my husband in the next room, and we thanked God that when we seem to have no power, God is still watching over us. His power is ours when we feel we cannot carry on. Let us never forget: we can trust in Him always.

Anna May Radke Waters

Slow Down

But those who wait on the L*ORD*
Shall renew their strength;
They shall mount up with wings like eagles,
They shall run and not be weary,
They shall walk and not faint.
—Isaiah 40:31, NKJV

Many will describe the pace of their lives today as "warp speed" or "out of control." Cellular phones, voicemail, email messages, a demanding job, twelve to fourteen hours of work a day—the list goes on. All contribute to this life in the fast lane.

People seem to be always rushing. In the hospital where I worked, doctors walked in the hallways with their cup of coffee or soda cans in their hands; they had no time to sit and enjoy the drink before they went from one patient to another. One early winter morning, I saw a nurse drop off her sleeping baby in the arms of the babysitter who was waiting in the parking lot. Some women apply makeup in the car while waiting for the light to turn green. I once saw a driver brushing her teeth during the morning traffic. "Crazy!" we may say.

Some of us feel like we are "running to and fro," having way too many things to do and feverishly attempting to accomplish them before the day is over. Students have the stress of finishing a term paper due the next day or anxiety before a final exam. Others have the never-ending chores at home. Families with school-age children endure the everyday cycle of dropping off the kids at school in the morning and picking them up in the afternoon and then ball practice, music lessons, or other extracurricular activities at the school.

Before our kids could drive, Henry and I spent weekends attending football or basketball tournaments in academies as far as three hours' drive away. We cherish the memories of these weekends and were glad to be part of the children's growing years.

To those caught in this mad rush who often feel the need for more hours in a day, slow down!

Are you are burdened by a busy schedule today? Slow down! Let the Lord take control. "Cast all your anxiety on him because he cares for you" (1 Peter 5:7, NIV).

Evelyn Porteza Tabingo

June 13

That Unneeded Tool in the Toolbox

Be diligent to present yourself approved to God, a worker who does not need to be ashamed, rightly dividing the word of truth.
—2 Timothy 2:15, NKJV

My husband is a master carpenter. He has many, many tools that he uses for various jobs. Of course, not every tool is needed for every job. He knows which tools are needed at each job and takes those along with a few extra things just in case he might need them after all.

He has added to his tool collection over the years. Some tools in his toolbox he needed frequently once upon a time. Then there came a time that he didn't need them as much, and those tools found their way to the bottom of the toolbox. He knows they have served him well and knows he will someday need them again, so he holds on to them.

I've been feeling a bit like those unneeded tools lately. My son has moved out, and my daughter has one foot out the door. I know this is the natural progression of life, and it's good to watch your children spread their wings and fly. But I've been a stay-at-home mom for the past twenty-one years, and to be perfectly honest, I don't know how to be anything else.

They needed so much from me while growing up: meals, snacks, dressing, bathing, emotional support, advice, as well as help with friendship strife and broken hearts. Now they are grown and don't need these things from mom.

It feels bittersweet. I am grateful they are equipped to move into the next phase of life, yet I'm not quite ready to let go. As they tote their new toolboxes with their own set of tools, I remain at the bottom. Underneath the shiny new tools sits the old trusty but rusty tool. But you know what brings me a little comfort? I'm still in the toolbox.

My husband may not need his old tools on every job, but he keeps them in the toolbox in case he needs them. And when he does, he is always grateful that he kept that old trusty tool in the toolbox.

I want to be used by God in whatever capacity He has in mind. I'll just be here in the Master Carpenter's toolbox if anyone needs me.

Cyndi Woods

To God Be the Glory

I shall not die, but live,
And declare the works of the Lord.
—Psalm 118:17, KJV

In my despair, it seemed as if the Lord was nowhere to be found. I was overwhelmed with grief. Clouds of disappointment and discouragement enveloped me. To accuse God of abandonment was not an option, for He had delivered me numerous times from what appeared to be the impossible.

Abraham and Sarah frequently come to mind. They prayed in desperation for a child, and God promised to bless them with a child. He kept His promise, but while they were waiting, their faith wavered. They felt the wait was too long, ran ahead of God, and attempted to fix it themselves. This caused mass confusion. When we run ahead of God, we always find ourselves in trouble.

Are you waiting for an answer to a situation that you've been praying over for what seems like forever? Does it seem as if God has reneged on His word? He promised never to leave us. He also said, "Before they call, I will answer; and while they are yet speaking, I will hear" (Isaiah 65:24, KJV). Does it seem as if He has turned a deaf ear? Have you fasted as well as prayed, and you're still waiting for the yoke to be broken?

Don't run ahead of God. Utilize your faith and put your trust in God. He says He knows the thoughts He has toward us, "thoughts of peace and not of evil," to give us "an expected end" (Jeremiah 29:11, KJV).

Satan is doing everything he can to get us to turn our backs on God. But God does things in His own time, and His time frame is not the same as ours. We must have the mindset of Shadrach, Meshach, and Abednego (Daniel 3:17, 18). I am claiming 2 Corinthians 6:2, "For He saith, I have heard thee in a time accepted, and in the day of salvation have I succoured thee: behold, now is the acceptable time; behold, now is the day of salvation" (KJV).

Regardless of how much time He takes or what decision He makes, I know He has my best interest at heart, and I am going to praise Him anyway!

Claim His promises and praise Him anyway.

Cora A. Walker

June 15

The Missing Passport

"Do not let your hearts be troubled.
You believe in God; believe also in me."
—John 14:1, NIV

My husband and I went on a ten-day Taste of Europe tour with two of my girlfriends. There was a lot of fun and laughter as we breezed through six countries. Highlights of the tour included a visit to Stonehenge and Bath City in England, the Atomium in Brussels, Belgium, a Rhine River cruise and the walled city of Rothenberg in Germany, the famous balcony of Juliet in Verona and a gondola ride in Venezia, Italy, the scenic view of the Alps in Austria and the fascinating city of Innsbruck, the boat ride around beautiful Lake Luzerne, and a cable car ride to the top of Mount Stanserhorn where we could see Lake Luzerne, the Swiss Alps, and the surrounding communities nestled on the mountain slopes of Switzerland.

The tour ended in Paris, France, where the bustle of city life was a far cry from the serenity of the countryside. We visited the Cathedral of Notre Dame, Eiffel Tower, Versailles Palace, and the Louvre, among other places. We walked along the city streets of Paris, sightseeing and searching for souvenirs to take back home.

We parted ways at the Charles De Gaulle airport in Paris when it was time to return to the USA: one friend was flying to Florida while two of us flew to Maryland. As I was wandering near the gate waiting for our flight, I reached into my bag and realized that my passport and ticket were missing. I knew that I had them when I went through security. I wasn't sure whether they fell out or someone took them. I breathed a prayer heavenward and looked for an airport security officer to report the loss. I didn't want to miss my flight home, and I prayed that God would help me find the missing documents. The security officer told me to go back to the person in charge of the aisle where I went through. Praise the Lord! They had found my passport and ticket in one of the bins! I must have neglected to pick it up in my haste to get out of the security area.

We are going on another journey someday. Our heavenly Father is preparing a beautiful mansion for us, grander than any earthly palace we may have seen. My prayer is that we will be ready when He comes to take us home. We do not need passports or tickets. The only thing we can bring is our character made clean by the blood of the Lamb poured out on Calvary's cross!

Rhona Grace Magpayo

Are You My Father?

He is a father to the fatherless.
—Psalm 68:5, *The Clear Word**

My parents divorced when I was four. My mother, sister, and I lived with my grandparents. I have no childhood memory of my father. When I was seventeen, I convinced my grandparents to take me to find my father. Grandpa drove to my paternal grandmother's home in Flint, Michigan, USA—and she still lived there!

As I stepped onto the porch and the light shone on me, my grandmother announced, "She's the spitting image of Jimmy!"

She immediately called her oldest son—my father, James Milton Hook—and he and his wife, Grace, came over to join us. Though he was sitting next to me, the conversation was mostly between my three grandparents and my father. I just sat there, numbed by the realization that I had finally met my father, who was a stranger to me.

On the way home, Grandma chastised me for not hugging and kissing my father. I told her it would have been like walking down the street in the city where we lived and just asking the first man I saw if he was my father.

I saw my father three times that year. I never saw him again until I was forty. I called him and set up a time to visit. I looked at photos of my cousins, aunts, and uncles that I had never met. His wife gave me my birth certificate.

When he turned seventy-five, I convinced my father to come visit me in Cincinnati, Ohio, USA, for the weekend. At the end of his trip, I was totally exhausted. That is when I knew I was my father's daughter. I talk as much as he does. I am *exactly* like him.

I saw my father as often as I could, especially the last year of his life. When he was moved to hospice, I told him I wanted to introduce my earthly father to my heavenly Father. I told him about God and how He loved us and encouraged my father with the hope of heaven. When he died, I did the eulogy for his funeral.

I can only imagine how wonderful it will be when I do see my heavenly Father face-to-face, and I do so long to be just like Him!

Patricia Hook Rhyndress Bodi

* Jack Blanco, *The Clear Word* (Hagerstown, MD: Review and Herald®, 2003), 625.

June 17

Children of the Same Father

"Look at the birds of the air; they do not sow or reap or store away in barns, and yet your heavenly Father feeds them. Are you not much more valuable than they?"
—Matthew 6:26, NIV

I met him on the beach. He was slim and smiling and at that age where he could easily be twenty-one or thirty-one. He was walking with his landlord, who, in an attempt to poach me from my own landlord, invited us to dinner at their place. They were complete strangers to me, but my housemate knew them, so I went. They served us chicken biryani, and though I am vegetarian, I ate it because I can never seem to resist South Asian food. Then he shared his story.

He was from Pakistan and on his way to Canada. He had been on a layover on the island for three and a half years. He was a refugee, evacuated from his country due to a threat of death. Why? Because he is a Christian and because he worked for an organization that often succeeded in converting Muslims to Christianity.

He looked like a kid. And yet here he was, about to start life in a new country while desperately missing his old one. He showed me pictures of his home in Pakistan. It is nicer than my home in Canada. He showed me pictures of his mom and sister, both young and beautiful. He showed me pictures of himself—his old self. The self that he used to be, flashy clothes, nice car, expensive haircut. I looked at the person he was now. The resemblance was faint.

But I did see the resemblance between us. Like him, I had come to this island for what should have been one month but had turned into three and counting. There was similarity in our uncertainties. However, he was doing much better with his unknowns than I was with mine. While he was keeping a positive attitude and not complaining, I was silently shaking my fist at God. I despise uncertainty. I much prefer knowing what is coming, even if it is unpleasant. With knowledge, I can prepare myself for whatever I have to deal with. But not knowing means all I can do is surrender myself to the hand of God, believing that He will take care of it. Take care of me. This is where I see again similarity between me and my new friend; even though we have no certainty about our immediate future, we do have a certainty that our common Father will take care of us both, no matter where we find ourselves. And though I may not always like it, really, that is the only certainty that matters.

R. Bowen

Daddy's Home

Fathers, do not exasperate your children; instead, bring them up in the training and instruction of the Lord.
—Ephesians 6:4, NIV

When my siblings and I were very young, our daddy would kiss us goodbye when he left home for evening church meetings. As we grew into adolescence, Daddy became stern. We were living in the Jim Crow era. It must have been challenging to raise children to be God-fearing and at the same time stand up for themselves in a sometimes racially hostile environment.

In my early teens, I sometimes dreaded when Daddy came home from work. We had to be careful what we said and couldn't always speak freely lest he perceived it the wrong way. He didn't tolerate what he considered sass. It wasn't so much sass as it was the growing curiosity about the world around us. My older brother and Daddy would butt heads over simple things.

Daddy must have realized that he didn't want his children to dread his coming home. So, each Wednesday, he began bringing a treat home (such as a half-gallon of ice cream). I noticed Daddy began changing as we matured and listened to what we had to say. He evolved from being gentle to our younger selves to being strict with curious adolescents to listening to his emerging young adults. He was still very gentle and lenient with my younger sisters. He passed away before reaching fifty and left my mother a relatively young widow.

I think our relationship with our heavenly Father also changes as we mature in our relationship with Him. When I was younger and began reading the Bible, I viewed God as somewhat harsh in His dealings with humankind. But as I have grown in my spiritual relationship with Him, I have come to realize that His discipline is steeped in mercy and unconditional love. He desires us to live a life that will fit us for His kingdom.

Sometimes parents must be strict or stern with their children to keep them from harmful situations. My earthly father, in his own way, taught his children to respect and obey God. When our heavenly Father seems strict with His ten rules, it's really to protect us and to give us guidelines for navigating life in this world. He desires that we obey Him until His Son comes to take us home to be with Him forever.

Barbara Burris Neequaye

June 19

Five-Dollar Blessing

"Truly I tell you, whatever you did for one of the least of these brothers and sisters of mine, you did for me."
—Matthew 25:40, NIV

I was standing in line at the bakery to buy eight burger-sized loaves, not realizing that this transaction would end in a totally different way than it did every other week. The customer ahead of me, an older gentleman, was placing his order for "fungi," a Caribbean delicacy of boiled cornmeal and okras. He took his time selecting something to eat with the starchy dish. He finally decided on stewed chicken with lots of gravy. Then he asked for a little more gravy. The pleasant clerk happily complied. The price? Five dollars.

The customer checked his cargo pants, but the search turned up nothing. So he went outside to his vehicle, I supposed. He returned with a puzzled look on his face. I have had this expression before on my own face before—credit card left at home, cash in my other bag.

"I don't know what happened," he stuttered to the clerk, still checking his pockets in disbelief.

"I will pay for his meal," I heard myself saying. I had at least an extra five dollars, I knew. I had not planned this. It was truly a random act of kindness. The customer looked at me, beyond puzzled. "Yes," I said, putting the Styrofoam container into his hands, and paying the attendant five dollars.

"I will pay you back." I can imagine his conversation at home that night. Maybe he shared his fungi and chicken with someone at home, telling them about the lady who paid for his meal. A lady he had never seen, who materialized out of nowhere it seemed. I can imagine him still with the puzzled look on his face. I hope that as he reflected, he realized that his forgotten five dollars had resulted in an unexpected blessing from God.

But the blessing was two-part—not just for the receiver but also to the giver. "Inasmuch as ye have done it unto one of the least of these my brethren, ye have done it unto me" (Matthew 25:40, KJV), said the Master. If I had not "done it," what a blessing I would have lost!

Annette Walwyn Michael

Budget Buddies

"For every beast of the forest is Mine,
And the cattle upon a thousand hills."
—Psalm 50:10, NKJV

"I am the LORD, that is My name;
And My glory I will not give to another,
Nor My praise to carved images."
—Isaiah 42:8, NKJV

I can't give all that to one person; certainly, You know that there is someone else I need to help. God, You can't be serious. Why should I add more to the amount?" In response to my question, God asked me a question: "Will you do as I say?"

Still a little confused yet resting in the fact that God has always been faithful, I proceeded to give as God had instructed. Sometime later at a prayer-and-fasting session, the person I had gifted shared a wonderful testimony of God's faithfulness. She shared that she was in need of funds to pay an outstanding debt, and God had sent her the exact amount—not only to pay her debt but to faithfully return her tithe and offering!

Tears came to my eyes. Who but God? It was one of those "stand still and see" moments. At that moment, I immediately realized that the "extra" was so she could faithfully return to God what He commanded. She was blessed, but I was immensely blessed by this experience! What if I had not listened to Him? Sure enough, God owns the cattle on a thousand hills and would have provided for His child, but I would not have been gifted such an invaluable lesson in giving, obedience, and trust. Sometimes God may ask us to do things that seem irrational, unreasonable, or even sometimes downright impossible, but He owns and knows it all. He will work it out to bring glory and honor to His name.

Will you listen to Him and follow His leading? Choose today to make God your financial planner; after all, He is the best budget buddy anyone could ever have!

Simone E. Johnson

June 21

Sixty Fives

Delight thyself also in the Lord*:*
and he shall give thee the desires of thine heart.
—Psalm 37:4, KJV

It was a cool fall morning. I was preparing myself for a great day with God at church. I got up, finished my morning routine, and prepared breakfast for my husband and me. It was almost time to go, so I began gathering my things together. Then I realized I needed my tithe envelope.

I got my envelope out and started counting the money. *Wait a minute, I'm US$5.00 short*, I thought. How could that be? I put my tithe aside last week. I recounted my tithe, thinking I had miscounted. No, still short. I thought, *Well, it is just five dollars; God won't hold that against me.* You see, I only had $12.00 in my wallet. If I took the $5.00 from that, I wouldn't have much left. What if I wanted to go somewhere? My mom always told me never to go out with empty pockets in case of an emergency.

Suddenly Malachi 3:10 came to my mind, "Bring ye all the tithes into the storehouse, that there may be meat in mine house, and prove me now herewith, saith the Lord of hosts, if I will not open you the windows of heaven, and pour you out a blessing, that there shall not be room enough to receive it" (KJV). Convicted, I quickly added the $5.00 and trusted God to bless.

At church, I greeted my brothers and sisters in Christ. I enjoyed the service and gratefully placed my tithe envelope in the offering plate. At home that afternoon, I listened to another sermon via the internet, and can you guess what the sermon was about? Yes, tithing!

Later that evening, I went to the mailbox. In it was a letter from my sister. The letter was unusual because she had written my first name in large letters. Very few people know my first name. I always use my middle name.

When I opened the letter, I found a check for US$300.00! Three hundred dollars! I couldn't believe it!

I think God smiled down on me and said "What did I tell you? Trust Me."

I gave God one five-dollar bill, and now I have sixty five-dollar bills. God truly opened the windows of heaven and poured out a blessing bigger than I ever imagined.

Elaine J. Johnson

Called and Chosen

Before I formed thee in the belly I knew thee; and before thou camest forth out of the womb I sanctified thee, and I ordained thee a prophet unto the nations.
—Jeremiah 1:5, KJV

Did you ever feel that you're not good enough? Have you failed to measure up to the worldly standards to fit into a world laced with pitfalls? Is the pressure too great to bear? Sadly, some of us feel that way. But God cares. He molded you into His image. He knows you. God sculpted you to reflect Him. He chose you and loves you. He calls you into His righteousness, His truth, and His light to partake in His promises. Imagine having a Creator and Father who knows you and called and selected you before you were even a thought. A God whose love is boundless and unreserved. He calls us "a chosen generation, a royal priesthood, an holy nation, a peculiar people" (1 Peter 2:9, KJV). You are royalty and an heir.

The devil, our enemy, tells us a different story. He constantly reminds us of the mistakes we've made. He will make you feel despicable and deserted by God because that's what the devil whispers. The agonizing thoughts cripple us. The voices start to shout, "You're unworthy and unforgiven!" Thoughts of unhappiness and gloom envelop our hearts, leaving us numb, dumb, and forsaken.

But Jesus, our Savior, wants us to know that even our vilest sin, whatever it is, He will forgive. There's no sin in this world too great or small for Him to forgive. There's no heart that is riddled with hate that He cannot supplant with love. He is the Potter, and you're the clay. When clay is dry, it cracks. Once it's entrenched with love, water, and care, it lives again. It experiences invigoration and is ready to fulfill its tasks. This can happen only when the clay master ministers to its needs. He will put his being into restoring its image, and he knows how to mold it into its new state, just like our heavenly Father. He can fix any cracks, broken spirits, and dreams. When your heart needs repaired, just call upon the One and only Source who will reinstate you into His image. The One who covers your sin. The One who calls you heir. Your sins are justified by having faith in Jesus Christ. Therefore, permit the Holy Spirit to purge anything that is in your path of reclaiming your rights as an heir to God's throne. Remember, He called you first. He chose you first. So go to Him in His secret tabernacle. He's waiting.

Corletta Aretha Barbar

June 23

Forever in My Heart

The Lord *hath appeared of old unto me, saying, Yea, I have loved thee with an everlasting love: therefore with lovingkindness have I drawn thee.*
—Jeremiah 31:3, KJV

My church will soon be having a seminar on depression," said my doctor one day during my visit. "It might be helpful for you to attend. Here's a phone number if you'd like to register." Sure, I could use a depression seminar, but at a church? What did I know about church? Well, I knew some Christmas carols, though they didn't hold much meaning for me. What did I care about a baby born in a manger? Yet I *did* need help with depression, so I registered.

The night of the first meeting, I drove by the church three times before going in. The friendliness of the people, including the pastor, surprised me. Over time, the pastor began to chat with me, and one particular woman sat by me, showing interest in me. I began to think, *Maybe I should be a part of this church.* Before long, I purchased a Bible from a local bookstore. At home, I just sat and looked at it. *Now what?* But God was leading. I told the pastor and my doctor, an elder in the church, that I was interested in joining their fellowship. The woman sitting by me (my doctor's wife, I learned) invited me to a women's Bible study. At the end of the seminar, I was asked, "Will we see you at church Saturday?"

Saturday? Don't people go to church on Sundays? Oh, well. I'd go at least once. Though nervous upon arrival, I soon relaxed. The friendly people greeted me so warmly, saying, "Happy Sabbath!"

OK, what is Sabbath? I wondered.

I soon learned why these people attended church on Saturday—and what *Sabbath* means. At my second prophecy seminar, I looked at the baptismal invitation card. A conviction arose within: *Yes, I want to give my heart to Jesus, my Savior.* In mid-June, my beautiful, sun-filled baptismal Sabbath arrived. That day, our church was worshiping with another congregation on Mackinac Island. I would be baptized in one of Michigan's great lakes.

The pastor, my doctor, and I waded into the waters of Lake Huron. After a few words, the pastor baptized me. I heard no angels singing, but my heart was—for Jesus was there! As for the baby in the manger, I now know who He is: my very own personal Savior, forever in my heart.

Gail Dotski

The Obituary Notice

But the fruit which the Holy Spirit produces is totally different: love, joy, peace, patience, kindness, generosity, faithfulness, humility, and self-control. There is no law against such things.
—Galatians 5:22, 23, *The Clear Word**

I was living in South Korea when I received an obituary notice in the mail from my brother—about himself. It had his date of birth and the date of his death—which happened to be the same except for the year. My first thought was Herman must be losing it. However, as I spoke to him about it, I learned he actually died on the date he had in his obituary because he had a massive stroke that day and was never the same again.

While he was in an unconscious state during recovery, he had a dream that he was living on borrowed time and God was giving him extra time to get his life together—and that he did. You see, before his stroke, he lived only for work and pleasing his family; therefore, he had no time for spiritual matters. But now, after his ordeal bringing him so close to death and then his dream, he was a new person, living to gain all the knowledge he could about our Savior.

Jesus is returning to this earth someday very soon for a church whose character is similar to His. Therefore, we should be growing daily like Him.

God gave my brother nine additional years after surviving that massive stroke in 2004 on his birthday. He was never the same again, and in reality, he died that day to be raised a new creature, learning, living, loving, and growing in our Father which art in heaven. Those around him saw the change. Isn't this the way our lives should be? Shouldn't others see a change in us that will draw them to the person we are modeling?

Let us be like Naaman, who came up out of the Jordan River completely and obviously changed. *Lord, please help us live the fruit of Your Spirit so that it will be evidence of You living in us. Let our lives become contagious and draw all men unto You. Come quickly, Lord Jesus, and help us to be ready!*

Bessie Russell Haynes

* Jack Blanco, *The Clear Word* (Hagerstown, MD: Review and Herald®, 1980), 1210.

June 25

Where Do You Stand?

And he died for all, that those who live should no longer live for themselves but for him who died for them and was raised again.
—2 Corinthians 5:15, NIV

I love fresh fruit—especially for breakfast. I like to slice and dice apples, melons, strawberries, kiwi, and bananas on a plate, then add blueberries, cherries, raisins, nuts, and a sprinkle of coconut. For variety, I'll vary the melons, adjusting to my taste for the day: honeydew, cantaloupe, or watermelon. As appetizing as this all may sound, there are occasions when I reach for the container of strawberries and upon close examination discover that one has started to rot. Disappointed, I discard that one strawberry and begin to select others. But then my heart sinks realizing that those strawberries closest to the rotten one have softened, and they, too, are no good. On mornings like this, if I can savage three to five of this tasty, eye-pleasing fruit, I count myself blessed.

It took only one strawberry to destroy much of the batch. Just one strawberry to spread its bacteria to all the others, causing them to lose their firmness, their beauty, and their taste. I can't help but view this occurrence in a different way—wondering whether God is trying to show me something. It took only one negative person in heaven, Lucifer, to cause one-third of the heavenly host to lose out on a closeness with the Father. Too often, I have seen the negative effect of just one person's action or attitude on a meeting, a group project, a committee, or even a congregation to cause rot to occur.

A while back, I was sitting in a meeting observing the discussion of a serious matter. The matter would ultimately determine the direction this committee would take in recommending funding for a much-needed program. As the discussion proceeded and a positive consensus was about to be reached, one person interjected a negative comment that challenged and ultimately killed the proposal. Enough people chose to believe misstated assumptions rather than clearly articulated facts.

Father, make us aware of the impact of the things we say and the actions we take. While we may not see ourselves as leaders of the masses, someone is likely listening and observing us. May our behavior model You so that no one is led astray.

Yvonne Curry Smallwood

June 26

Stop Hiding Behind the Baggage!

The eyes of the LORD are in every place,
keeping watch on the evil and the good.
—Proverbs 15:3, ESV

Saul, from the tribe of Benjamin, was the first king of Israel. When Samuel told him he had been chosen to be king, he responded, "Am I not a Benjamite, of the smallest of the tribes of Israel, and my family the least of all the families of the tribe of Benjamin? Why then do you speak like this to me?" (1 Samuel 9:21, NKJV).

On the day of his coronation, Saul was nowhere to be found. This was an amazing accomplishment because the Bible tells us that he stood head and shoulders above the people (verse 2). How could such a tall man remain hidden in a crowd?

First Samuel 10:22 gives us the answer: "He is hiding among the baggage" (NLT). Bible commentators theorize that Saul had hidden among the baggage because he didn't feel worthy. He had been chosen to be king by God, but he still didn't feel qualified to do the work he had been called to do.

You and I also hide behind the baggage of our lives. We hide behind a perfectly presented image because we're afraid that if people see the mess we are behind closed doors, they won't want anything to do with us.

We hide behind our social media presence, thinking if we only had enough likes or followers, we'd be good enough. We hide behind so many pieces of baggage, we forget that God always sees us exactly as we are.

My friend, what are you hiding behind? Come out from behind the stuff and trust that God will be with you every step of the way.

Lord, I've been faced with my unworthiness and know that I can't do this task on my own. Remind me that I don't have to because You will never leave me nor forsake me. Hide me under the shadow of Your wings and give me the courage to face the challenges ahead. In Your name, I pray. Amen.

Aminata Coote

June 27

God Is My Helper—Part 1

God is in the midst of her . . . ;
God shall help her, just at the break of dawn.
—Psalm 46:5, NKJV

In preparation for special music for our church service, I prayed, "Lord, help me find just the right music to sing." As I searched through my music, I was impressed with one piece, "Follow Me" by Ira Stanphill, written in 1953. The song talks about our traveling a hard road and complaining to Jesus or thinking we've done so much in order to follow Christ; the refrain is Christ's response—His understanding of the hard road because He, too, walked a hard road to the cross and invites us to take up our cross and follow Him.

I sat down at the piano and played and sang through the music, but the words didn't fit my experience. I asked God, "Help me make the words my own!" I took out a piece of paper and began writing. It only took a few minutes. I sat down at the piano with the "new" song. It felt right for me. While I tweaked the first two verses slightly from the original and kept the refrain the same, I wrote a new verse three that is my heart's prayer:

Lord Jesus, help us day by day
To follow Your commands
To serve You with a joyful heart
And be your feet and hands.
Guide each step along the way, and
Show us what to say.
Let's listen to His Words
And bow the knee.

I praise the Lord for His help! This song has become my testimony song, and I share it whenever I get the opportunity.

Sharon Follett

God Is My Helper—Part 2

Blessed be the Lord,
For He has shown me His marvelous kindness!
—Psalm 31:21, NKJV

The Sabbath came that I was to sing. I looked forward to sharing my testimony song, "Follow Me"!

A storm was brewing as the service began. Soon we could see lightning flash and hear loud claps of thunder. I began praying that this storm would not be happening when I was singing and drown out the words!

As I walked up to the pulpit, there was one more loud clap of thunder! The introduction was played, and I began to sing my special song. I was blessed to be able to share it with my church family.

Following the service, I was talking with a friend, Scott Clarke, who was taking care of the sound system as I was singing. He asked me if I realized that the pulpit microphone was not working during the service. I told him I was oblivious. Then, I recalled being handed a handheld microphone to sing with and that those on the platform were also using handheld microphones because the pulpit microphone was not working.

Then Scott shared the rest of the story, "All during the service, I couldn't get the pulpit microphone to work. So I made sure that two handheld mics were working. When you stepped up to the pulpit, there was a loud clap of thunder—then you began to sing, and the microphone began working!"

Wow! What a miracle for God to do! I was blessed because there was no confusion up front and no distraction for the congregation.

Praise the Lord for His loving-kindness!

Sharon Follett

Bringing Hope to Strangers

But since we belong to the day, let us be sober, putting on faith and love as a breastplate, and the hope of salvation as a helmet.
—1 Thessalonians 5:8, NIV

I used to work on the eighth floor of a building full of medical and dental offices in Belo Horizonte, Brazil. After finishing my shift one day, I waited for an elevator. Coincidentally, two opened their doors at exactly the same time.

Quickly glancing at both of them, I saw a family crying in one and nobody in the other. My first natural impulse was to go to the empty one. But in a fraction of second, I felt impressed to get in the elevator with the family.

Even though they were standing in the back of the elevator and I was facing the door, I could hear them crying all the way to the lobby. My heart ached because they had certainly just received a devastating diagnosis.

When the elevator stopped, I held the door and waited for them to leave. At this moment I heard a voice telling me to give them *The Great Controversy* CD that I had in my purse. Everything happened so quickly that they left the building without the CD. Their car was right in front of the building, but I was not brave enough to stop them.

While crossing the street to go to the bus stop, the voice insisted. So I turned back. I glanced at the car, and the driver's window was closed. Getting closer, I noticed that the passenger window was open. I stretched out my arm and offered the CD to the wife, telling her that God had asked me to give it to them.

On its cover, she read, "A biblical study series that will bring hope to you and your family." She told me that for sure God had used me because I had no idea how much their family needed hope. I smiled, and we followed our different paths. I never met them again.

Many are suffering and searching for hope. I invite you to never leave your home without a book or a CD in your purse. God will place somebody in your path who needs these words of hope. Just be willing to stretch out your arm and be a blessing. One day in heaven, we will learn how God used us to give courage and hope to others—just as I will know about that family.

Ana Maria de Souza Gonçalves

Hold My Hand

He doth execute the judgment of the fatherless and widow, and loveth the stranger, giving him food and raiment.
—Deuteronomy 10:18, KJV

Today, I found a sunny little part of the day and mulched my favorite rosebush. It has given me two dozen roses every year since my husband, John, planted it for me on a long-ago Mother's Day. We both tenderly cared for it, enjoying sharing bouquets of its fragrant pink blossoms each season. Oh, what memories!

Twenty years later, I'm still facing life without John. We had thirty-six wonderful years of marriage; but what a struggle without him. Our families have dealt with the grief in their own way. Such feelings of hopelessness, especially when our three-year-old grandson kept watching for his grandpa to come home. "Is he just playing hide-and-seek, Nana?" he asked every day for the longest time, refusing to be comforted by mere mortals. "Is he gonna come down the driveway today?"

I'm thankful the Lord of comfort and hope has been a faithful friend to His sorrowing children, "to comfort all who mourn" as promised in Isaiah 61:2 (NKJV). Our family tombstone, with far too many names listed, reminds us of "that blessed hope, and the glorious appearing of the great God and our Saviour, Jesus Christ" (Titus 2:13, KJV).

As I have walked into the unseen days, Jesus, my forever Friend, has been with me and continues to remind me that He is and always will be present. From Him come promises of deliverance, "for the Lord [has] sustained me" (Psalm 3:5, KJV).

Despite my great loss, or maybe because of it, I have been able to minister to other widows—my neighbor most recently. I handed her a vase of pink roses from John's rosebush with a note, "These bloomed just for you!" Listening to her, crying with her, taking her tasty dishes, sometimes just holding her hand, have all helped her heal, and I am grateful I could be a part of that.

Ladies, my heart breaks for you if you have had to experience the loss of a husband, but I am a firm believer in Jesus as the Great Healer of sorrows. I desire to help Him defend the cause of the defenseless, (grand) fatherless, and widows.

Jane Wiggins Moore

Compassionate Call Center

Are they not all ministering spirits sent forth
to minister for those who will inherit salvation?
—Hebrews 1:14, NKJV

When traveling home for permanent return from mission service in Africa, my nine-year-old son, Kent, and I flew into Charles de Gaulle Airport in Paris—but somehow, our luggage was shipped to Orly Airport on the other side of that vast city. My husband, who spoke fluent French, had come to Paris a week earlier for a choral conducting workshop. Our plan was for the three of us to rendezvous at a downtown hotel for two days and then continue home to the United States of America.

One two-hour bus ride later, we reunited with our luggage at Orly. The luggage attendant gave us free train passes to the downtown station nearest our hotel. As we pulled away from the airport, a dour conductor passed through the crowded coach checking tickets and train passes.

"These are *yesterday's* passes!" he snapped at me. "What are you trying to do here—get a free ride? Free passes are just for those who have flown in on that day!" He ignored my weak "But we just did!" in French and moved on with his work, shouting an "I'll be back!" at us.

O God, I silently prayed, *what do we do now?* Suddenly, I remembered our airline ticket stubs with today's arrival date. The returning conductor snatched them from my hand, took one look, and threw them back into my lap. *Thank you, God!* I sighed. At the station, we dragged our heavy luggage onto the sunbaked platform. *God, we're hungry and thirsty and lost. Now what?*

"Say, that train conductor back there was pretty rough on you two," said a kind voice in perfect English just behind us. I turned to see two clean-cut young men smiling at us. "We saw the whole thing. If you need a taxi, it's a one-block walk. Since your hands are pretty full, may we carry those two biggest suitcases for you?" Thirty hours without sleep, Kent and I tightly held hands and wordlessly trudged behind them. "There you go." The men set down our bags before hailing a cab for us. And that is the last memory I have of seeing them. Within minutes, a jovial cabbie had driven Kent and me to our hotel, where we reunited with my very relieved husband.

I've always wondered whether those young men were compassionate *angels* sent to a weary, overwhelmed missionary mom by a compassionate God who hears and answers prayer.

Are you feeling weary today? Overwhelmed? All of heaven is just *waiting* to receive your call!

Carolyn Rathbun Sutton

Commit Your Way to the Lord

Delight thyself also in the Lord:
and he shall give thee the desires of thine heart.
Commit thy way unto the Lord; trust also in him;
and he shall bring it to pass.
—Psalm 37:4, 5, KJV

As Christians, we frequently forget that God honors the desires of our hearts and, according to His will, makes them come to fruition. A few years ago, I wanted to go on a mission trip and invited my daughter to go with me. She agreed but had two obstacles: her job and the necessary funds. She was living in another state, but her training as a nurse would benefit the team greatly. However, her place of employment didn't approve leaves for more than fifteen days at one time, and she needed three weeks. Nevertheless, she submitted her request and waited for a response.

For her to make the trip, two things needed to happen: (1) raise the money for the trip and (2) have her request approved despite the length of time. God took care of both. She didn't like the idea of soliciting funds, so we prayed about it. With the help of friends and my husband, I raised my funds, but for my daughter, it was a different story. She filed her income tax return papers, and the unbelievable occurred. Her return was double more than what she needed to cover the trip. Her request to be away from her employment was approved without question. God removed the obstacles and cleared the way for her to go.

Then something unexpected happened: the director of nursing (DON) asked her when she would return from her trip, and she told her the date. Surprisingly the DON said, "But, this is three weeks of absence from work; it's not possible." My daughter replied that she had signed the request and proceeded to show her the signature. The DON responded, "This is my signature, but I would not have approved that. I don't know how it happened." Well, we know what happened. The angel of the Lord held the DON's fingers and made her sign the request without questioning the length of the trip. God is so awesome! He can perform amazing things beyond our comprehension if we come to Him and ask, even the desires of our hearts. He has an ultimate plan for our lives, and He delights in making us happy. Indeed, we serve an awesome God!

Flore Aubry-Hamilton

July 3

Trusting in God

Trust in the Lord *with all your heart;*
do not depend on your own understanding.
—Proverbs 3:5, NLT

Do you believe God answers prayers? I always thought so, but recently I had doubts. What I believed God was going to bless me with didn't happen.

I had some issues that caused me to possibly lose my ability to have children. I was peaceful in the knowledge God would allow me to accept that. I almost did lose that ability, but the doctors were able to save it. I thought God would allow me to have children.

Not too long after this, I had a vision of God telling me to keep trusting in Him. I thought that meant in time, I would be given my dream and desire to have a child of my own. After many tests and procedures, things didn't progress as I had hoped.

I got to the point where there was no chance to have a child even through in vitro fertilization. I was told that the next time I was in a hospital, I would lose my uterus. Even a miracle child wouldn't be able to come after that. Over the next little while, there was always that little bit of hope in my heart.

Finally, the time came. I needed to have a hysterectomy; there was no other way. I was in pain almost daily. I was trying to be positive, but part of me kept going back to the vision God had given me. He didn't say He would give me what I wanted; regardless, I had to keep trusting in Him.

I have a hereditary condition that causes muscle weakness and other issues. I noticed there were things I could no longer do. Things that would need to be done if I had a child. I did want a child, but God knew I would not be able to take care of one. Trusting was hard when I so badly wanted a child.

So God does answer prayers, just not in the way we think. I had people praying for my desire for a child. I think my heart's desire is to live a life that gives glory to God in all things, though, as you all know, that is not always easy. We can't know God's decisions because He alone knows all. He knows what is best for us. We can't comprehend how many things we ask for may not be good for us. But God does know what is best and loves to give His children the best gifts.

Melanie Carter Winkler

My Baptism

I have been crucified with Christ; it is no longer I who live,
but Christ lives in me; and the life which I now live in the flesh
I live by faith in the Son of God, who loved me and gave Himself for me.
—Galatians 2:20, NKJV

I grew up in Kilimanjaro, Tanzania, where my parents and their parents were Lutheran. I loved being a Lutheran. My mother sang in a choir. My dad was an elder in the church. We went to church every Sunday.

After moving to the United States in the late 1990s, I met and married my husband, John. He was an Adventist, but I kept going to the Lutheran church. We agreed that when we had children, we would raise them as Adventists. After our first child was born, I was committed to attending church every Sabbath. But nothing changed in my spiritual life. Our pastor at the time tried to talk to me about the importance of following Jesus' example and being baptized, but I brushed him off, telling myself that I was already baptized when I was a baby, so that was enough. However, the thought never left me. It kept bothering me, but I did nothing.

As my boys grew, I found myself getting frustrated and angry most of the time. I continued to search for answers to my parenting issues and started praying with other mothers. The devotions we read each morning were very helpful to me. I learned a lot, but the question of baptism began to bother me again. I wanted my children to obey and follow Jesus, but was I? I considered baptism when my youngest son and his friends were baptized but again put it off.

When you know the right thing to do but don't do it—that's disobedience. I realized that the best thing I could do for my children was give my whole heart to Jesus. So I gathered my courage and emailed our pastor, telling him that I wanted to be baptized. On January 15, 2021, I was baptized. I didn't think people would be able to attend because of the pandemic, but I received so much support! My mother-in-law watched from Kenya with my sister-in-law and her children. My brothers-in-law tuned in. My mom, sisters, and brother also tuned in to watch. Women from my prayer group drove from so far to come witness. It was a blessed day! My sister's children watched with a lot of curiosity. I pray that I will get to tell them one day why I was baptized the way I was so that they, too, can learn about the true baptism.

Judith Mmari

July 5

The Handpicked Ones

"Before I formed you in the womb I knew you,
before you were born I set you apart."
—Jeremiah 1:5, NIV

My parents had a two-year-old boy and a nine-month-old baby girl when they found themselves unexpectedly pregnant with me. My mom had quit her job to take care of my siblings, so the budget was really tight.

Today, as an adult paying my own bills, I understand their feelings. But growing up hearing the story that I was not planned made me feel loved but not desired. Please, don't misunderstand me. My parents have always been loving, and I would not choose another family even if I could.

One Saturday when I was already an adult, we were in church, and the sermon was about cases like mine. The preacher said that everyone is very special to God, but the ones whose births were not planned by their parents have a higher purpose in this world because God Himself planned their existence. Wow! This thought had a huge impact on my life. I felt specially chosen by God.

I dedicated my life to following God's plans, spending more time with Him, and asking what and where He wants me. It has been an adventure since then. I have put aside my plans to live His. I can tell you that it is not easy not being the one who plans your own life—what you will study, where you are going to live, where you will work, whom you are going to marry, or even smaller things—but I can guarantee it is wonderful because God never makes a mistake. He knows everything and everyone better.

Many things have happened since then—some of them I never would choose, and others I would make them happen sooner—but I am learning day by day to live God's way in His timing.

This is my story. I don't know yours, but I am sure God has a higher purpose for your life. Wonderful things or even hard tasks that you never would dream or plan. Let Him show you. Your part is to obey, wait when necessary, and trust Him. Search for Him with all your heart, and He will make your paths straight and guide you in the middle of the storms and the bright sunshine. Always keep in mind that His plans are far better than yours.

Kênia Kopita

Be Careful What You Wish For

"The very hairs of your head are all numbered."
—Luke 12:7, NKJV

For a long time, I had been wishing for a hairstyle that was in tune with the times—one that would be easier to care for and take less of my time and attention. How little I knew that my desire was about to be realized in an unexpected way!

One day while vacuuming, I tripped over the cord, and down I went. I moved tentatively, fearful of broken bones. What a relief when everything worked! However, I felt blood on the right side of my face. I phoned my younger daughter, a surgical technician, hoping she could stop the bleeding and apply appropriate dressings. She alerted my son who lives nearby, and he came right away.

Though the bleeding continued, I resisted anyone calling 911 until after I had passed out. Then, I had no choice. So just two weeks shy of my ninety-fourth birthday, I was headed to the emergency room for the first time in my life! It turned out an artery in my scalp had been cut and had to be sutured. During this procedure, the right side of my head was shaved, and the left side was cut extremely short. Because of blood loss, I was kept overnight at the hospital. The next day, I was released only because my older daughter, a nurse, put her life on hold to care for me for the next several days. She was relieved by my sister for almost another week.

So, you see, I now have a hairdo that fulfills all my wishes: I no longer have a dated hairstyle, it takes a minimum of care, and I have no idea when it will be otherwise because my hair does not grow fast!

Lessons learned: (1) independence (or stubbornness) can sometimes cause inconvenience and even hardship in one's life and the lives of others; and (2) if I watch where I walk and step high enough, tripping will not be a problem.

I have facetiously wondered whether it might be harder for God to number the hairs of my head now that my hair is like stubble. However, we know that nothing is too hard for the Lord. It seems to me that a Father who loves us to that extent is more than worthy of our loyalty, praise, and thanksgiving. Incidentally, whatever hair the redeemed have or don't have really won't matter, for we all will be content.

Lila Farrell Morgan

July 7

In the Firewood Bush

The LORD *is nigh unto them that are of a broken heart;*
and saveth such as be of a contrite spirit.
—Psalm 34:18, KJV

When we were growing up, my parents often told us that the three best gifts they owe us are speech (language), knowledge of God (the Bible), and education (cultural or other). Early in life, I learned the value of educating girls. My father was raised in a traditional religion in a polygamous home where it was not acceptable to send daughters to school. Therefore, his sisters never saw the four walls of a classroom. Nevertheless, they received a culturally rounded education, considered good grooming for a girl's future home—marriage being the goal. My parents felt education was a gift, so my siblings and I were able to attend school.

Fresh out of a devastating civil war, my father uprooted his entire family, and we traveled to the western part of Nigeria, where he wanted to pursue a degree in theological studies. While there, Papa and Mama struggled to put food on the table. The good thing was that fertile soil was abundant, so my industrious mom worked extremely hard! We farmed, collected firewood for cooking, cut bushes, and harvested and sold big bunches of green, luscious vegetables. The bad thing was that we were unable to attend school. We missed our friends and our previous lifestyle.

One morning, while collecting firewood, I was emotionally exhausted as I reminisced about school back home. My mind rebelled as I imagined the classes I was missing. Following an explosive sigh, I dramatically exclaimed, "Where is Ekele Ukegbu?" Frustratingly but laughingly, I answered my question, "In the firewood bush." Everyone laughed! The burden I carried in my heart regarding my halted education was exposed. Little did I know that Mama heard me. She was saddened and grieved, but she painfully kept it in her heart.

Although my comments became a big joke in the family, my revealed brokenness was taken very seriously and became the beginning of another episode in my life. My parents sacrificed their plans and transported us back to our beloved school. I was happy to return to complete my education.

Dear reader, are you carrying a heavy burden on your heart? Tell Jesus. He knows how to work out all things for your good.

Ekele P. Ukegbu-Nwankwo

Nature's Plastic Surgery

And I say unto you, Ask, and it shall be given you; seek, and ye shall find; knock, and it shall be opened unto you.
—Luke 11:9, KJV

Have you ever been dissatisfied with your physical appearance? I was OK with mine except for one thing. It seemed that I was forever having to push my glasses up, for they kept sliding down to within an inch of the tip of my nose!

"Oh, for a more prominent nose," I sighed. I didn't want a beak—just enough bridge that my glasses would stay in place!

Since I knew of so many people who needed help with problems or disabilities far more serious than mine, I never once thought of mentioning it to God in prayer. I didn't want to seem vain. So I didn't ask God to reconfigure my nose.

One day, my godchild, Kai, and I were outside painting. When we reached the kerosene tank, we did the top and sides first. Then I stepped under the tank to show Kai how to paint the bottom with a roller. The wooden rack that held the tank had crosspieces that stabilized it. They were about level with my knees. I forgot about them when I went to step back out. My knees hit the braces, and I overbalanced, falling straight forward and hitting the ground hard! My glasses were pushed into my face! Amazingly enough, the lenses stayed intact, and the strong titanium frames were fine once I bent them back into shape.

Kai helped me into the house and gave me first aid. Every part of me that slammed into the ground was bruised and painful except for my face. Looking into a mirror, I saw that my face was unhurt except for an indented line across the top of my nose between my eyes. It wasn't very noticeable when I wore my glasses. But I wondered whether I'd have that sunken look forever!

My fall had been the result of my carelessness. And I hope I never have another such accident. I believe that my guardian angel kept me from suffering a broken neck.

As time passed, extra cartilage or bone grew enough that my glasses stayed put. Nature's plastic surgery at work!

Only God can take something bad and bring something good out of it, granting my wish in such a unique way! Now I talk to Him about everything!

Bonnie Moyers

July 9

Quilts and Christians

And over all these virtues put on love, which binds them all together in perfect unity.
—Colossians 3:14, NIV

Tea parties were fun when I was a child, even if I could only have water for pretend tea. So I was surprised when our women's ministry team decided to have a real tea party at the church's fellowship hall.

After a great deal of planning, everything was ready when the day arrived. All the tables were adorned with various kinds of teapots and beautiful table decorations. Refreshments were typical of old-fashioned tea parties: petit fours and other little sweets, dainty sandwiches, various finger foods, and of course, a variety of herb teas.

The guests were told that, except for the back, which had been made ahead of time, they would make a quilt from start to finish during the meeting.

Everyone decorated a precut quilt block with fabric pens. There was no theme. As each person finished her design, it was taken to two ladies with sewing machines, who would then stitch the squares together right there.

One square of fabric won't make a quilt. If you're cleaning house, you can use it as a dust cloth. If you are eating and get food on your chin, you can use it as a napkin. If you sneeze, you can use it as a handkerchief. But you cannot use it as a quilt.

Quilts are made up of many pieces, all different sizes, colors, and shapes. Laid side by side, each piece supports the ones around it. Each contribution adds interest and beauty to the rest. No one piece is more important than the others. All are needed, and all add something special and unique. When stitched together, it becomes a beautiful quilt.

A quilt and a church family have some of the same qualities. You have a group of Christians of different sizes, shapes, and colors. They support those around them. Every member is important and contributes something special and unique. Bonded together with Christian love, they bring others the warmth of friendship, comfort in trials, and the love of Jesus.

It's surprising what you can learn about Christian living from a simple quilt.

Marcia Mollenkopf

Lady, Your Angel Was With You

For he shall give his angels charge over thee,
to keep thee in all thy ways.
They shall bear thee up in their hands,
lest thou dash thy foot against a stone.
—Psalm 91:11, 12, KJV

I had just come off the Interstate-95 highway ten minutes earlier and was overjoyed that I had done so safely. After all, it was my first time driving on the busy roadway during my first year in the United States. I was less than five minutes from home when I heard a deafening explosive sound! My small Toyota Corolla was out of control and heading for the median. There was nothing I could do to change its course.

"Jesus, help me!" I cried as the car headed over the median for the second time. Suddenly an Unseen Driver was at the control, and the car stopped in the turning lane, just where I needed to make the last right turn toward home.

I grabbed my handbag and jumped out, fearing a fiery explosion was imminent. It had barely come to a complete stop. A bright pink fuel was flowing from under the front part of the car. My right front tire had blown out. Thank God it happened on the quieter Miramar Parkway and not the busy I-95!

The first to arrive on the scene was a kind cop. "Lady, your angel was with you!" he exclaimed. "I saw the whole ordeal," he continued. "I have never seen the parkway clear in both directions at this time of the day."

"God cleared the east- and westbound traffic," I assured him.

The kind cop called my husband, who was at church only fifteen minutes away. He soon arrived with the mechanic. He had our other car—a rental we had picked up at the Miami International Airport.

God's promise of protection had been proven true again. He had given His angels charge over me, and they had kept my feet from dashing against the stone! You can claim that promise as you drive or go out today. His angels have your feet and back! Praise God!! He will protect you over and over again! Trust me; He will!

Claudette Garbutt-Harding

July 11

Miracle Bed

And it shall come to pass, that before they call,
I will answer; and while they are yet speaking, I will hear.
—Isaiah 65:24, KJV

I never thought I would be a caregiver but found myself taking care of my brother-in-law, who suffered a devastating stroke in 2015. He was bedridden and partially paralyzed on the left side. He also had to be fed through a tube. In our home, my husband and I took care of all his needs with assistance from family and friends.

Being caregivers consumed a lot of our time, but I was OK with doing the daily tasks of bathing and feeding him. He was content but not happy because he desired to live with his daughter and grandchildren in his birth country. Being there would be psychologically better for him, as would the year-round warmer environment, so his daughter had a room added to her house for him. We just needed to transport him by plane to get there. The problem was that because he was bedridden, we had to ship an adjustable hospital bed to his daughter, and we couldn't use the one he was currently lying on. We had already exhausted a lot of money for the trip and other needs, and hospital beds in his home country were expensive. Therefore, we decided to find one here in the United States and ship it to her.

I prayed about it and solicited prayers from others. The time frame also was limited. We needed to ship the bed a month before we traveled. That same week at church, I was eating lunch when our first elder came and told me a lady at the next table was asking if anyone needed a hospital bed. I couldn't believe it! I jumped up and was quickly introduced to her. This wonderful woman had been taking care of her sister, who had died earlier that year. She was moving to Florida and wanted to donate the bed to someone.

We arranged to pick up the bed and shipped it to my brother-in-law's daughter. I was so overjoyed at how God took care of this situation. I was deeply moved by how He provided for such a specific need as an adjustable hospital bed. God knows our desires and will supply all our needs according to His will. We just need to have faith and trust Him. Why don't you ask Him for your specific need today?

Raquel Gosling-George

Promises!

[Cast] all your care upon him; for he careth for you.
—1 Peter 5:7, KJV

My husband had lost his long battle with cancer, and his memorial service had just ended. My children, grandchildren, and I were greeting those who had come to honor him. One kind gentleman from the church, in a rash moment of generosity, assured me that the deacons would keep my lawn mowed in the summer.

However, promises made in January can be forgotten when spring and summer make the grass grow! Fortunately, I have never remembered who made that grand but unrealistic gesture, and I'm glad I don't, for he meant well.

Warm weather came, the grass grew on my large lawn, but no deacon appeared with a lawnmower. Two of my kind neighbors noticed my predicament, and each took a turn or two with their riding mowers.

Finally, remembering the promise that the deacons would help, I picked up the phone to call the head deacon to ask for help. Then I put the phone down. Picked it up again and put it down and cried. I did this several times before actually making the call. The head deacon and his wife were some of our close friends, but he came himself and did the job rather than enlisting someone else.

Realizing that the promise was made in a moment of unrealistic sympathy, I knew it was up to me to find someone I could pay to do the mowing. First, a young man in my church mowed the grass, and when it was no longer convenient for him, he passed it on to another church member, who years later is still faithfully doing it every summer—and being paid for his work!

Even though the deacons didn't take turns mowing my yard, there was a day when men and women from the church devoted a whole Sunday morning to do a general cleanup of the premises, trimming trees and shrubbery, cleaning gutters, weeding, hauling in mulch to go around trees—and mowing!

Years ago, my husband and I started memorizing promises from the Bible. After his death, I continued working on them and occasionally added others that spoke to my heart. I see God fulfilling these memorized promises. He truly cares and takes care of our needs.

Mary Jane Graves

July 13

Where the Lord Wants Me

Then I said, "Here am I! Send me."
—Isaiah 6:8, NKJV

I grew up listening to summertime evangelists under insufferably hot tents. I was fascinated by the pictures of children sitting on Jesus' lap, the glory of His second coming, Adam and Eve in an un-sinful garden, and of course, the serpent in the tree tempting Eve.

But the pictures that intrigued me the most were of Jesus and His disciples and the bright, brilliant pictures of His return! It may have been because the elders of my church seemed much like disciples and were held in high esteem. They seemed more relatable to my juvenile mind.

For many years, my father was a deacon. He often turned down eldership. I couldn't understand in my seven-year-old mind why he made this choice. I was a little girl who often saw my peers with more than I had—they seemed to have prettier dresses and new patent leather shoes—and I felt that if my daddy became an elder, that would give me a step up and more prestige. But Daddy would always say, "I'm where the Lord wants me." I was in college before he accepted the position of elder. He became one of the church's most noted elders, serving until his death at eighty-two.

Fast-forward to my adulthood. Marriage. Three beautiful children. Great professional accomplishments. Financial rewards. Restlessness. Backsliding. Forgetting those summer crusades. Losing faith. So many valleys of doubt and hills of renewed faith are a part of my journey. Now, it is so beautifully clear to me what Daddy meant and what he was experiencing.

Becoming an elder was not something I sought after either. There was so much opposition, mostly by women, for all kinds of reasons. The scrutinization and demeaning statements drove me as far away from this position as I could get. God was still grooming me, and I wasn't ready. I still cared about what people said. My faith and trust in Him grew. I learned to answer His call, His will, and His way.

I've been an elder for more than four years now. I am so blessed, and it's such a joy to be doing God's will, no matter the title it's given.

Edna Thomas Taylor

What's in Your Head?

"Blessed is the one whom God corrects;
so do not despise the discipline of the Almighty."
—Job 5:17, NIV

I was feeling great that day. I had just had an invigorating workout at the gym, and I was waiting to cross the street. While standing there, I was bopping my head to the music in my headphones. The walk signal appeared, and I entered the intersection.

As I was happily crossing the street, a man in a big white truck came speeding into the crosswalk to turn the corner. I looked at him in disbelief because it was obvious that I had the right of way. I was so upset that he almost intentionally killed me that I turned around and gave him a very un-Christlike gesture. I expected him to just keep on driving, realizing that he was in the wrong. But no, he slowed his vehicle down to yell obscenities at me, which I readily yelled back at him. I was furious! I couldn't believe it!

I immediately called one of my girlfriends on my cell phone to tell her what had just happened and get things off my chest. I walked home, kind of in a fog. I felt scared and ashamed all at the same time. What would Jesus have done? He certainly would not have done what I had. Was the irate man in the truck in the wrong? Yes. Did he deserve to be treated the way I treated him? By the world's standards, yes. By God's standards, definitely not.

What made me lash out at him like that? I didn't feel like myself when I was yelling at him. Then it hit me. It was the music in my head! I had been listening to hip-hop when it all happened. I had tried to rationalize that it was OK for me to listen to this genre of music. I would tell myself, "It's OK for me to listen to this because I am an adult. I am no longer impressionable like those young teens. I have my morals already in place. It's just good workout music." Boy, was I wrong.

That night, I prayed for forgiveness for my sins and for the man in the truck. I prayed that whatever he was going through that made him so angry would lead him to the feet of Jesus. I now praise God that I gave up hip-hop, and I enjoy singing hymns!

Mary C. D. Johnson

July 15

Trust the Process

"Behold, God is my salvation;
I will trust, and will not be afraid;
for the LORD GOD is my strength and my song,
and he has become my salvation."
—Isaiah 12:2, ESV

On January 23, 2020, I had a total hip replacement surgery as a result of injuries from a car accident. After surgery, I had to learn to transition from a walker to a cane to no assistance, plus dress myself, drive, and do my everyday activities.

My orthopedic surgeon cleared me to go back to work on April 13, 2020. Unfortunately, that very day, my company decided to furlough approximately 85 percent of the employees, which included me. This occurred during the COVID-19 pandemic. I was one of approximately twenty-three million Americans who were collecting unemployment. It took six weeks for me to receive any unemployment benefits. During this time, I had zero income. I live on the south shore of Long Island, and my budget is tight. It was a very difficult time, but God took care of all my needs.

I was blessed to be able to go back to work full-time with my company in July. Unfortunately, not all my coworkers came back.

One challenge was my commute, especially during COVID-19. I take the train to work and was very concerned. I contemplated asking my boss if I could work remotely. God clearly told me, "Do *not* contact anyone. I will tell them what to tell you! You still don't trust Me after your major surgery, recovery, furlough, and getting your job back?"

My mouth was wide open, and I humbly said, "I trust You, Lord!"

I'm not sure how I missed the email from my boss stating, "Until further notice, I would like you to work from home." Our God is amazing!

Sometimes life may seem like things are overwhelming and you are in a whirlwind. I'm here to tell you no matter what's going on, God promises to take care of you! He taught me to trust His process—to stay still, listen, and obey. Our timing is not God's timing. Let's continue to keep each other in prayer during this journey called life!

Andrea D. Hicks

Only Trust Him

Trust in the L*ORD with all thine heart;*
and lean not unto thine own understanding.
In all thy ways acknowledge him,
and he shall direct thy paths.
—Proverbs 3:5, 6, KJV

There are Sabbath days when I need to decompress: no people, no smiling, just quiet. The only sound I want to hear is gospel music and a sermon—while I'm still in my pajamas. On those days, I like to "visit" Oakwood University Church and listen to their online sermon. One such occasion caused me to reminisce.

I was a single mother and wary about relationships after the failure of my first marriage. I wasn't looking for any new relationship, and my burgeoning feelings for my eventual second husband scared me. I felt that this time should be devoted to my young daughter, to my relationship with God, and to developing a healthy love for myself once more, which had suffered tremendous blows and was only just recovering. One morning, I poured this out to God, begging Him, "Please remove this man from in front of me and set my gaze on You alone!" I told Him that whatever He wanted me to do was what I would do. As I completed my prayer and got off my knees, my cell phone rang. It was Arnold. He had called for us to pray together.

The timing was an indication that God had heard me and was reminding me that He was in control. The more time I spent with Arnold, the more I recognized God's leading. He constantly sought to develop a spiritual relationship with me and showed respect and regard for my daughter and other family members. Fast-forward fourteen years, and I recognize that God was answering a prayer I had been praying when I first got married "for a man who loves You more than he loves me." I figured if he had that kind of relationship with God, I would be in a loving relationship. The memory that morning reminded me that when God is first in every decision, goodness and mercy follow. He never steers us wrong. Since then, there have been times when I forgot that lesson, but God never leaves me to my own devices for long. When I compare those occasions with trusting God to guide, I can attest that His way has always been the better—no, the best—way!

Greta Michelle Joachim-Fox-Dyett

July 17

Watch and Pray

"Watch and pray that you may not enter into temptation. The spirit indeed is willing, but the flesh is weak."
—Matthew 26:41, ESV

From my "God Moments" Prayer Journal:

> 2-20-18–Paradise, CA—37 degrees this morning:
>
> My beloved Father, I have been reading through the last chapters in Matthew. Upon reading Matthew 26:36–46, verse 41 hit me over the head like a thunderbolt [see text above]. Father, how many times have You said to watch and pray, and I've entered into temptation by following my plan and my direction? That phrase "that you may not enter into temptation" means to me that I must be alert to You each moment of every day or I will be following my way, not Yours. This scripture is for me today—I lay before You my day—my plans must be pushed aside so that if today were my last day, I would be watching and praying so that the Holy Spirit's conviction would be my guiding path.
>
> As You pursue me each day, dearly beloved Lord, I surrender what I think are today's duties as I watch with You and pray that I will be about what Your will is for me instead of my plan. Jesus came to the disciples three times, asking them to pray for Him, yet they went to sleep. Their weariness was greater than their prayerfulness for their Friend—Jesus.
>
> Oh, dear Lord, how often do I follow this same pattern of lifestyle? You pursue me to spend time with You—oh, this precious time with You—and yet my plans for the day are more important to carry out (what I think I need to do) instead of watching and praying, allowing the Holy Spirit to shower upon me what I so desperately need.
>
> In verse 46, Jesus said, "Rise, let us be going; see, my betrayer is at hand." If I do not choose the Holy Spirit as I choose to "watch and pray" during the God moments in my day, the devil (my betrayer) will take advantage of that time. He will snuff out my day with his plans which I choose . . . *if* I do not watch and pray.

My dear sister in Christ, as you enter the day's activities that God has orchestrated, may you choose to watch and pray with Him as the Spirit guides you throughout this day. In Jesus' name. Amen. Blessed be the name of the Lord.

Mary H. Maxson

Free of Fear

I sought the L*ORD*, *and he answered me*
and delivered me from all my fears.
—Psalm 34:4, ESV

We always think that we have a plan and that when things get crazy or situations become stressful, we will do OK and get through them. We got this! I got this! This is what I thought until the COVID-19 pandemic started sweeping the world. All it took to prove that I didn't have this was, of all things, toilet paper.

I know you are thinking, *Is she crazy? What does toilet paper have to do with anything? How could that be scary?* That's what I thought until the morning I was picking up some prescriptions and noticed that the drugstore was out of toilet paper. Now, I had heard that people were running out in places in the country as fear of the virus spread, but I didn't think it would happen in the middle of Nebraska where I live. My husband had no luck finding any at our local Walmart either. I figured surely the grocery store would have it. I walked quickly to that aisle only to see a wall of empty shelves where it should be. I then started to panic. *What would happen next? What else wouldn't I be able to purchase? How much worse would it get? How will I make it through the end times?* A panicked phone call to my husband calmed me down some. A few minutes later, he called me back to say he found some.

I realized that I need to remember who is ultimately in control of things. We need not be afraid if we put our trust and faith in Him. He has promised to take care of us and take away our fears. On my drive home, I started thinking about how He cares for us. Staying connected to Him will get us through anything. I need to keep myself in His Word daily to strengthen my faith and relationship with Him. These are the keys that will help get us through the difficult days, the trials, and yes, even times of no toilet paper! God doesn't want us to be fearful. In fact, the phrase *fear not* is in the Bible 365 times—one for every day of the year. God knew we would be afraid and provided a "fear not" for each day. That's pretty amazing and comforting to me.

No matter what we are facing, God will carry us through the difficulties and fears we face. We only need to hold on to Him, and He will deliver us out of them all.

Debra Snyder

Come, Lord Jesus—Today!

He who testifies to these things says, "Surely I am coming quickly." Amen. Even so, come, Lord Jesus!
—Revelation 22:20, NKJV

I sat on the bank of the lake where I had just completed a summer working as a ski instructor and camp counselor. I talked to God for about thirty minutes before I needed to pack for the drive back to college in the morning to finish my final year.

The sun was sinking toward the horizon, and I sat in nature's silence watching in wonder! I watched the beautiful artistry of God's creation with its changing colors. I listened to the twittering birds settling down to sleep. Feeling a deep need for Jesus right then, I whispered, "Please, Jesus, come right now!"

The feeling was so intense that tears washed down my face. And then I felt Jesus sitting beside me. "Not yet," He whispered back. "You have a life ahead. You will serve me, raise a family, travel to many places, and witness in My name to many people. I have an amazing plan for your life. I will walk with you as you move toward the time of My second coming."

Now, as I work for God in Nepal, where there is a great need for people to know Jesus, I remember that special moment at the lake talking to Him. Every day, I still want Jesus to come, right now! But here in Nepal, I have the opportunity to shine for Him, fulfilling the plan for my life just as He explained to me long ago. God has been with me for forty years since that day beside the lake, and He still has not come back—but I believe He will. Jesus will come again!

So each day, when the sun comes up, I sit and talk to my God. A song I often sing during my devotional time is "I'll Walk with God." I pray every day that I will serve Him faithfully wherever I go.

Dear Jesus, please come soon. Help me share Your love with those who desperately need to know You. May we all be waiting for Your soon return to take us to live with You in heaven. Come, Lord Jesus—today! Amen.

Susen Mattison Molé

Miracle Wife

For He shall give His angels charge over you,
To keep you in all your ways.
—Psalm 91:11, NKJV

My pastor husband, Abel, and I had talked excitedly for months about our plans to attend a large ministerial convention in Austin, Texas, United States of America, and afterward drive to San Antonio, Texas, to attend our denominational church's sixtieth General Conference session, which is held every five years. We count it a great blessing to belong to our worldwide church family, and it is always a pleasure to see many acquaintances during the week of meetings. A special joy came from the gracious invitation of friends to stay with them at their spacious San Antonio home.

The night we arrived, I took note, even pointing out to Abel, that the guest bathroom was close to the stairs. That knowledge should have guided my feet to the bathroom during the night, but it didn't. I took a misstep and tumbled down the entire flight of fourteen steps, landing in a heap at the bottom.

Abel heard the terrifying noise and rushed down the stairs to find me lying awkwardly in a pool of blood. His first impression was that I was dead, and he was now a widower. Even when it was determined I was, in fact, alive, everyone in the house anticipated the accident would have caused broken ribs, a hip, an arm, a leg, or all of them. After an ambulance rushed me to the hospital, the doctor determined that I had broken only my left wrist and ring finger. He put my wrist in a cast and stapled the lacerations on my head.

I was kept at the hospital for a couple of days for observation. When the staff technician tested my cognitive skills the next day, he was happy to congratulate me for passing the thirty-minute interrogation. Nothing was wrong with my brain, although I did need some therapy later to regain wrist and finger mobility.

When tragedy strikes, many people question God. They wonder whether God truly cares about them. Even I have questioned God, and I'm a follower of God—a pastor's wife! However, the fall down the stairs during which my life was spared reminds me to thank God, daily and profusely, for showing me that He truly loves me and protects me. That is why Abel calls me his wife with a new life, his miracle wife.

Ofelia A. Pangan

July 21

The Journey

"For I know the plans I have for you," declares the L*ORD*,
"plans to prosper you and not to harm you, plans to give you hope and a future."
—Jeremiah 29:11, NIV

The idea of traveling from one place to another can be interesting, exciting, or heartbreaking. Taking a long trip long usually calls for patience, endurance, and discipline. In life's journey, all can choose to serve God and journey with Him. Whether you are a widow, wife, single mother, motivator, encourager, or counselor, embrace the gift of life on the journey.

On this journey with God, we're promised, "If we confess our sins, he is faithful and just and will forgive us our sins and purify us from all unrighteousness" (1 John 1:9, NIV). Once God's cleansing is asked for and received, the journey will continue with His support.

The journey to heaven is vivid; nonetheless, some encounters along the way will be marked as troubles and trials. However, understand that once God has allowed them, He will mend them. The journey is not an easy road, but nothing is too hard for God to conquer. The Word says, "Consider it pure joy, my brothers and sisters, whenever you face trials of many kinds, because you know that the testing of your faith produces perseverance. Let perseverance finish its work so that you may be mature and complete, not lacking anything" (James 1:2–4, NIV). As you walk along the life's journey, know that God is beside you.

Like James, have a positive attitude toward trials. Do not complain. Instead, take the opportunity to welcome the many trials along the way and look beyond the present experiences of discomfort. By faith, you will see the blessings as they blaze the hallelujah horizon of praise and thanksgiving. Rest assured, "blessed is the one who perseveres under trial because, having stood the test, that person will receive the crown of life that the Lord has promised to those who love him" (James 1:12, NIV).

Believers, love the journey! God offers recurring strength during the journey, so become strong long-distance journey-walkers. You will make it to the very end—"For he will command his angels concerning you to guard you in all your ways" (Psalm 91:11, NIV).

The journey leads to heaven. Stay the course!

Juliet L. Lucas Languedoc

Be Still, My Soul

Be still before the Lord
and wait patiently for him.
—Psalm 37:7, NIV

The pedestrian traffic lights in Berlin, Germany, depict a man with a hat quickly moving with big steps in green or a man with a hat standing with outstretched arms in red. These were the pedestrian symbols of East Germany, and now most of the traffic lights in united Berlin use them. People just love them because they show so much energy. The man has a paunch and a snub nose, making him somehow sympathetic, something we can identify with. They are also safer because the shining surface is larger.

I use pictures of these figures on my Facebook page for my profile photo. I usually post the little busy green man when I am away from home for a while, and when I return, the red one takes over again.

I had returned from a holiday, but I forgot to change my profile picture from green to red due to a busy schedule. Our granddaughter saw the green figure on my Facebook page and wondered, "Where are they now?"

I just happened to change my profile picture on a Friday evening. Soon a friend posted a comment on my stout red man who almost looks like a cross, "Aha, Sabbath."

I hadn't thought of that, but the idea was great! Stop and wait for God's blessings. Stop rushing about with hurried steps and enjoy the Sabbath. I normally hate to wait. But Sabbath is different. Even though I am often involved in church services, the Sabbath is a day of rest. Facilitating praise through music soothes the hassle of my "green" days and directs my attention to the red figure with outstretched arms, filling my heart with gratitude for Jesus' sacrifice on the cross.

Why is being still often so difficult? Letting go? Waiting? The Lord is on our side. We can let God provide because He is our best heavenly Friend who loves us and wants to soothe our sorrows and fears.

I need to learn to wait patiently for the Lord, commit my ways unto Him, and trust Him. I am sure that is something we all need to do.

Hannele Ottschofski

July 23

The Millionaire

Trust in the Lord *with all your heart,*
And lean not on your own understanding;
In all your ways acknowledge Him,
And He shall direct your paths.
—Proverbs 3:5, 6, NKJV

Who Wants to Be a Millionaire is an American game show that gives away not less than a thousand dollars. The games consist of about ten questions with three lifelines. The person who can answer all the questions correctly wins one million dollars. The contestants come from all walks of life.

I have not watched this show for several years, but one morning in 2021, I got out of bed early and decided to turn on the television before starting my chores and morning worship. Usually, I have my morning worship first in the morning, but this particular day I was intrigued and tempted to turn on the television. The show was on with a contestant who was a returnee, which means that he was playing for the second day. He had thirty thousand dollars and still had his three lifelines.

He had difficulty answering his next question. It was obvious that he didn't know the answer. I was surprised and astonished when he refused to use his lifelines to help him answer the question. He had three choices: the audience, fifty-fifty, and an individual help. He guessed the answer to the question, and his answer was wrong. If his answer had been right, he would have gone up to fifty thousand dollars, but he chose not to ask for help.

I was amazed and shocked that he didn't use his lifeline. And yet, many times, I find myself refusing to seek help when I am not sure what to do. Sometimes we think we don't need help—that we can do it on our own, especially when things are going well. But often, we find ourselves failing or missing out on peace, joy, and blessings.

Lord, help us to come to You for help and answers. Forgive us for trying to do it on our own and forgetting that You are there. Thank You for promising that whatever we ask the Father in Your name, He will give it to us. We want to be Yours!

Patricia Hines

Apples of Gold

A word fitly spoken is like apples of gold
In settings of silver.
—Proverbs 25:11, NKJV

In personal relationships, the way we communicate is paramount. On many occasions, misunderstandings are generated that can ruin relationships or, in the best of cases, create conflict between people.

Psychologists and communication professionals give guidelines and even courses for conflict resolution and ways to restore relationships.

Conflicts often begin with the way we talk to each other or with words that we speak without thinking. These can be the first steps to hurting the other person and thus begin to generate a conflict even with someone we appreciate or whom we want in our lives.

How do we usually express ourselves—with aggressive, derogatory, ironic words, or attitudes of superiority?

It is very important to think about how we are going to say things, especially when we are angry, because once the words are out your mouth, you can no longer retract them or go back. They can damage the feelings of the people they are addressed to.

I do not remember who told me the story of the wrinkled paper, but the story says that when you wrinkle a paper very hard with both hands, even if you try to stretch it out again later, it is no longer the same. There are both big and small wrinkles throughout the paper, depending on how many times and how hard you squeezed it. There will come a time when the wrinkles deteriorate the paper, almost unrecognizably, from its initial form. The paper is a metaphor for a relationship; the harsh words, the wrinkling.

Let's meditate on Proverbs 25:11 and think about how we speak to others—and improve our general way of communicating before it is too late because the relationships of our friends and family are already too "wrinkled."

Maite Lavado

July 25

Table Talk

The Lord is nigh unto all them that call on him,
to all that call upon him in truth.
—Psalm 145:18, KJV

Our makeshift congregation—scattered across three states—met on a conference call each Sabbath morning during 2020 to study the Bible. To me, our weekly quest for fellowship and straight truth was like the groups that Martin Luther, the Protestant Reformer, called together in the 1500s in his book *Table Talk*. Though not seated at a table, we felt the Lord was nigh as we shared research and insights by phone for three hours or more.

Luther's five-hundred-year-old book vividly presented the historical perspectives of the Protestant Reformation. Luther's notes about his Spirit-filled sessions referred to events and personalities and the stuff of life—common peoples' lives. Luther valued the priesthood of believers—salvation seekers not just being ministered to but sharing in the delivery of the gospel.

When I happened upon Psalm 145, I found that David reveals a passion like Luther for talking with believers. Envision with me how David, consummate worship leader that he was, orchestrates conversations with an impromptu choir, each contributing insights about praise (verses 1–3). He urges a mature person to share with a younger one about God's acts and to utter personal memories about God's goodness (verses 4, 7). Men speak about a terrifying time when they witnessed God's intercession, and they commemorate it with a tune about His righteousness (verses 6, 7). Someone snapshots God's future kingdom in all its glory and majesty (verses 11–13).

Some tender and inclusive soul then reminds fellow believers that the Lord is good to *all*, that *all* depend on Him, and that God upholds *all* who fall and raises *all* those who are bowed down (verses 9, 10, 14, 15). A concerned God interacts with His human creatures, fulfilling their desires, hearing their cry, and preserving them that love Him back (verses 19, 20). Sadly (or is it justly?) the wicked will He destroy (verse 20). David concludes that he is inviting all flesh to make their calling and election sure to meet in heaven where the saved will bless God's name forever (verse 21).

To God be the glory. No one can steal the joy of our salvation if we pledge "every day" (verse 2) to "make known . . . [God's] mighty acts and the glorious majesty of his kingdom" (verse 12, KJV).

Elinor Harvin Burks

Before You Call

"It shall come to pass
That before they call, I will answer;
And while they are still speaking, I will hear."
—Isaiah 65:24, NKJV

Since several of my friends had fallen and broken bones recently, I tried to be very careful, especially when I was caring for my elderly husband. I knew that if I broke any bones, there would be no one to care for him. Later, when I was living with my youngest daughter and her husband, I didn't want to cause them any problems either. And then it happened. Early one morning when I got up to use the bathroom, I fell. When the pain eased enough for me to try to move, I was thankful that I could get to my feet, because that meant I hadn't broken any bones. But I did have a black eye on the left side and a painful bruise on my right arm.

When my doctor daughter heard that I had fallen, she insisted that I go to the emergency department at the local hospital and get checked out. Because of my advanced age, they were happy to do that. After hours of x-rays and other tests, they decided to admit me for further examinations. Because of the pandemic, my daughter was unable to see me once I was admitted, so I almost felt like a prisoner. Although they treated me very well, I had different tests every few hours during the night. They assured me that I could go home the next day, but as the hours passed, no doctor came to give the orders for dismissal. By then, I was very anxious to get out of the hospital bed and go home.

Meanwhile, my daughter had been told that I couldn't go home until I had an appointment with my primary care doctor to see me within a week. But my doctor was three thousand miles away! Because of the pandemic, doctors weren't taking new patients. While my daughter was at home stressing about what to do, her friend, Dorothy, stopped by. When my daughter shared the problem with Dorothy, she quickly responded, "My husband isn't taking any new patients either, but I'm sure he would see your mother." And that's how the Lord provided my new primary care doctor, a kindly, caring man, and soon I was able to leave the hospital and be home again.

Thank You, Lord, for answering my prayer before I even knew what to pray for!

Betty J. Adams

July 27

Watching and Waiting

"Therefore keep watch, because you do not know on what day your Lord will come."
—Matthew 24:42, NIV

As I listened to our pastor's closing story in his sermon one Sabbath morning about anxiously watching and waiting for his parents to come home from a day of shopping, I was reminded of something similar from my childhood.

My favorite cousin lived in another state, but quite often she came to visit. We loved to spend time together at our grandparents' house. Our grandfather was still working, and he rode the city bus back and forth to work. Every afternoon, when we knew it was almost time for him to arrive home on the bus, we would station ourselves on the front sidewalk to watch for him. The bus stop was about a block and a half away, but we could look down the sidewalk and see the bus pass by. Sometimes it was right on time; sometimes it was late, and we would have to amuse ourselves in some way. But we always kept a watchful eye for the bus.

Finally, it would come, and our grandfather would get off and start walking home. As soon as my cousin and I saw him, we would run as fast as we could down the sidewalk to meet him. What a happy time we had walking back home with Grandpa!

As I listened to our pastor's story and thought about this from my childhood, I wondered whether I was really waiting that anxiously for Jesus to come. I have believed in the second coming of Jesus all my life. I have never for one minute doubted that it will happen someday. I remember sitting in an adult Bible study class many years ago, and the teacher asked the question, "How do we know Jesus will come back?"

A simple question, but everyone sat there quietly and said nothing. Finally, my husband answered, "He will come back because He promised He would." Of course! Jesus tells us, "I will come back and take you to be with me that you also may be where I am" (John 14:3, NIV).

As I write this, it has been an unusual year. We have experienced a worldwide pandemic. The news has told us about unprecedented fires, hurricanes, civil unrest, and other disasters. I hope and pray that as I watch these events unfold, I will be reminded anew to watch and wait for Jesus as anxiously as I did for my grandfather years ago.

Sharon Oster

July 28

Examine Me, O Lord

Examine me, O Lord, and prove me.
—Psalm 26:2, NKJV

I mostly hated tests in school. I especially loathed multiple-choice tests where there are three answers to choose from followed by two more choices of "A and B" or "A and C." It immediately put me into a panic trying to figure out whether it was a trick question. Have you ever felt that way about spiritual things? Like God is giving you an exam, and you better come up with the right answer or you fail?

God likes trick questions. No, I am serious, He does. If you read the Gospels, Jesus constantly challenged the Pharisees with questions that stumped them because their brains were so stubborn and saw through the glass narrowly. Christ gave them trick questions because they were tricky spiritual leaders leading people astray.

I don't know about you, but I *do* want to get the answer right! So am I left with a God who dangles the right answer in front of me like a pendulum, always a little elusive, and anxiety ensues? I say a resounding *no*! "For God is not the author of confusion but of peace" (1 Corinthians 14:33, NKJV). Exams produce peace only if you are fully prepared to take them and have confidence in your knowledge of the material.

Here is the good news! We can have confidence in the material. The material is Jesus Christ. My confidence is not in *my* ability to pass the test, but my confidence is in the One who has already passed the test and knows all the right answers. So when the devil tries to confuse you, just call on Christ, your Test Taker! That was the issue with the Pharisees—they did not trust in the Test Taker; they trusted in themselves.

God wants us to understand His loving-kindness as we walk in the truth of Jesus. As we set our mind and heart on Him, He will lead us to truth and obedience. We will know the truth, and the truth will set us free. Free from condemnation, free from the chains of sin, free from doubt and worry, we will walk in integrity and not slip.

Lee Lee Dart

July 29

The Sin Virus

Finally, be strong in the Lord and in his mighty power. Put on the full armor of God, so that you can take your stand against the devil's schemes.
—Ephesians 6:10, 11, NIV

When Australia first went into lockdown in response to the COVID-19 pandemic in March 2020, it was a bewildering and anxious time. I was particularly concerned to avoid infection, not just for myself but for the sake of my ninety-three-year-old mother, who lived with me. I carefully followed the advice of health experts and government leaders regarding social distancing, mask use, and so on, but this was an invisible foe. How would I know, on any given day, whether I had managed to avoid contamination or had inadvertently come into contact with the unseen organisms? I soon concluded that, no matter how hard I tried, I could never be sure of success—I needed to turn over the problem to God.

Some reassurance came via a devotional presented by a local church leader. He shared the story of King Ahaz, who was fearfully facing human enemies. Ahaz knew that he and his people were no match for these foes. God promised that the threatened invasion would not happen and sent King Ahaz this message through the prophet Isaiah, "Be careful, keep calm and don't be afraid. Do not lose heart" (Isaiah 7:4, NIV). What this story said to me was, yes, it was important to follow sensible advice, but my main role was to rest in God and trust Him to win the battle.

It struck me just how much the pandemic situation is like the problem of sin. The devil is an unseen enemy, and the insidious contamination of sin is everywhere. No matter how faithfully I try to follow the rules or how hard I try to be free of sin, I can never succeed by my own efforts—I must turn the problem over to God. Scripture contains advice for everyday living and "personal protective equipment"—the "armor of God" (Ephesians 6:11)—but my main role is to accept Jesus' cleansing blood, shed on my behalf. I must rest on His promise of salvation and trust Him to win the battle. Like His people of old, I take comfort in the promise, "Do not be afraid or discouraged. . . . For the battle is not yours, but God's" (2 Chronicles 20:15, NIV).

Jennifer M. Baldwin

Sins Be Gone

If we confess our sins, he is faithful and just to forgive us our sins, and to cleanse us from all unrighteousness.
—1 John 1:9, KJV

Recently, my husband and I retired and relocated to sunny Florida. Having eagerly looked forward to this chapter of our lives, we bought a house soon after arriving in the state and embarked on our "new" life together. A new home is always a major project, and ours was no exception. While we waited for our furniture to arrive, we did what little we could with the inside, and I began work on the outside. Unfortunately, my new garden was filled with weeds, and I hate them with a passion! There were so many different kinds. While some with shallow roots were easily plucked out, others had deep roots and required a lot of effort to remove them completely. Some were so stubborn that the stem and leaves broke off, but the roots were still in the ground. The stubbornness and persistence of these weeds and their resistance to being pulled out reminded me of how dogged sin is and how difficult it can be to uproot it from our lives.

Like weeds, sin comes in all shapes and sizes and can sometimes be deceiving and difficult to spot. Left unchecked, sin takes root in our hearts and eventually affects our behavior. Some sins are so deeply rooted that they can become quite difficult to eradicate, especially through our own strength. Some sins appear to be easily overcome and eliminated completely, and other sneaky sins can *seem* to go away with some amount of effort, but the roots of those sins are still there, ready to spring to life again. The truth is that in either case, we cannot get rid of sin on our own; we need our Father's help.

God is our strength, Deliverer, and Forgiver. There is nothing too hard for Him to do for us. All we need to do is confess our sins, and He will cleanse us completely and make us pure. Let us stop pulling the weeds of sin with our own strength and, rather, rely on our heavenly Father to remove sin from our lives.

Maureen H. Moncrieffe

July 31

Wildfire

Be ready in season and out of season.
—2 Timothy 4:2, NKJV

As I write this, a large wildfire is burning in Klamath County, Oregon, United States of America, where I live. So far it has destroyed over four hundred thousand acres—an area half the size of the state of Rhode Island. People who lived near the fire were told to be prepared to leave if it became necessary. When the order came to evacuate, the people had two choices: obey evacuation orders or stay without emergency assistance.

Most people heeded the warnings and left the area. Some, because the fire had burned the area around them without destroying their property, thought they would be safe if they stayed. That was true. But they soon ran low on food and water for themselves and their animals. No one was allowed into the area to help them. They were stuck.

All through history, God has given warnings to help people avoid disasters. God told Adam and Eve, the first people He created, not to eat fruit from the tree of the knowledge of good and evil. We know all too well the sadness of death caused by their disobedience.

Noah tried for 120 years to warn people of the destruction that was coming on the earth. When the Lord told him to build an ark, he started building. The people laughed. After all, they reasoned, there was no water, and the boat was way too big to float. They missed the big picture—and they missed the boat.

After the Hebrew people had been slaves in Egypt for more than four hundred years, God told Moses to command Pharaoh to let the people go. Pharaoh refused. God gave him ten opportunities to change his mind or reap the consequences. Not until it was too late did he obey. Losing the firstborn in every family, including his own, was an awful price to pay for his stubbornness.

This planet is becoming a dangerous place, but it is not our real home—heaven is. If that's our destination, we need to start preparing for it now. God is giving us signs to show that this world is not going to last much longer. May we all be ready for His coming is my prayer.

Marcia Mollenkopf

Male and Female He Created Them

So God created man in his own image, in the image of God created he him; male and female created he them.
—Genesis 1:27, KJV

The Bible tells us that God created mankind in His likeness, and mankind included males and females. I read this verse to mean that both males and females can reveal aspects of God's character. If this is so, it's reasonable to believe that human relationships that embrace, accept, and employ both masculine and feminine traits will be the most successful.

In my field of research, composition studies, different forms of writing have, at times, been gendered either "male" or "female." In the eighties, for instance, personal writing styles—sometimes gendered "female" writing styles—suffered attacks of being anti-intellectual and antagonistic to academic writing. Since then, however, both male *and* female scholars have defended personal writing, arguing that it is the logical counterpart to more traditional, more "male" forms of writing. Scholars of rhetoric and composition have also suggested that *listening* to opponents (and finding areas of agreement) is just as important as constructing an argument. In short, my profession has recognized that a blended style of communication—a "masculine" *and* "feminine" style, you might say—brings the best results.

I can't tell you how often I've applied these concepts to my marriage. My hubby is a "typical male" in that he is logical, facts-driven, and blunt—whereas I might be called a "typical female" based on my big emotions and frequent need to express them. So we have been working hard to accept and embrace one another's communication styles. While *I* am trying to respect his need for clear, "bullet-point" communication, *he* is trying to appreciate that sometimes I simply need to express without being "fixed." Indeed, I have observed that when we embrace and employ both male *and* female styles in our communication, we both win.

If your communication skills could use a tune-up, I encourage you to pay attention to your words—as well as your silences. Do you communicate your needs clearly, and do you also *really* listen to the needs of others? If you take a balanced approach, prioritizing both listening *and* speaking, both expressing your emotions *and* arguing your points clearly, you will be on the path to successful communication—because balanced communication is godly.

Lindsey Gendke

August 2

Primary Colors

I am the way, the truth, and the life.
—John 14:6, KJV

My daughter-in-law likes to give me activities to do with my granddaughter, who is three at this writing. On my last visit, she brought out a tie-dyeing kit for me to use with my granddaughter. How could I get out of it? Tie-dyeing was not really my thing. Is it even age-appropriate for a three-year-old? I set it on the table for a couple of days, then picked it up and read the directions. *Oh my, I may as well get started with this!* I thought.

After getting all the materials we needed, my granddaughter and I headed to the patio. Surprisingly, she was adept at wrapping the rubber bands around the material. Although the gloves were too big for her little hands, she was really into this! She didn't waver one second. Plus, I was starting to enjoy it.

I realized this could be a teachable moment about primary and secondary colors. Starting with yellow and blue, I explained that those two colors make green. The color came through beautifully. Red and blue make purple. *Huh, that's an unusual purple color.* We continued. Red and yellow make orange. *Oh, no!* We looked at each other. *That's not orange. What happened?* By now, her mom had come outside. She picked up the bottle of dye and said, "It's not red; it's pink." And, as we all know, pink is not a primary color. So, the desired colors we expected could not come through.

How many times have we been disappointed when things didn't come through as we hoped? Were they planned with faith or with presumption—which is a close look-alike? So why were we disappointed? Number 1, as immature Christians, we may not have been spiritually attuned to seeking God's way for our lives. Number 2, we may have thought we were strong spiritually but wanted so much to carry out our way we were unwilling to just wait on Him.

Father, please increase our faith in You, the Source of all knowledge, and Your Word so that we not only look to You for guidance but can be enabled to wait on You for all that we desire to do. Keep us from the alluring appeal of presumption.

Sharon M. Thomas

The Game Called Life

But the LORD has become my fortress,
and my God the rock in whom I take refuge.
—Psalm 94:22, NIV

My husband and I enjoy playing Qwirkle, a game that uses colors and shapes. Points are earned based on how many cubes of the proper color and shape are in an acceptable configuration.

It is challenging and fun. Sometimes one person will earn the most points at the beginning of the game but not necessarily end up the winner. Various players may take the lead throughout the game, or one may dominate the whole game. Sometimes we play Qwirkle quite often, and at other times, we may go months without playing.

We are all engaged in a game—the game of life. It is not a game of choice. To be alive is to be in the game. It is played every hour of every day. The choices we make determine, in large part, how well the game goes. Even when we make choices, sometimes there are adverse effects. We live in a sinful world. Our adversary, the devil, delights in bringing misery, temptations, and discouraging events into our lives to keep us from being winners.

Unlike the game of Qwirkle, the good news is everyone can win in the game of life. Like any game, there are principles that, if followed, lead to a fulfilling conclusion. To top it off, we don't have to play this game without guidance. No matter how poorly we play the game at the beginning, we can turn our lives over to God, and He will guide, encourage, and strengthen us. He has promised to be with us in every play that we make. He delights in making us winners and assures us in Isaiah 41:10 that we don't need to be afraid or discouraged because He is our God and will strengthen and help us each step of the way.

These promises don't give assurance that every day will go exactly as we plan or hope, filled with sweetness and smooth sailing. However, they tell us that we aren't going it alone. The Creator of the universe knows and loves each of us so much that He chooses to be there for us every moment of every day. He intends to make each one of us a winner. It is up to us to use His strength to give us victory in this game called life.

Marian Hart-Gay

August 4

GPS

The heart of man plans his way,
but the Lord *establishes his steps.*
—Proverbs 16:9, ESV

When the movers arrived, they loaded the truck up lickety-split.* The only problem was that they left for our apartment before we did! By the time we headed out, the movers were at least ten minutes ahead of us. We worried they would arrive first and end up standing around, waiting on us. The first half of our route is interstate; nothing exciting there, all very normal. The second half consists of regular roads. The previous Sunday, we had driven over to pick up the keys to our new place and check it out. All went smoothly as planned. On moving day, however, the GPS told us to use exit 136. *Didn't it tell me on Sunday to get off at exit 159?* I wondered. Within a few minutes, we both knew, beyond a shadow of a doubt, that this was a very different way. The GPS turned us down a dirt road in the middle of farm country! Already running late, we decided to follow wherever the GPS led us.

We bumped along, blazing down at least two different dirt roads before popping out onto paved but unfamiliar territory. After making a wrong turn and needing to try again, we finally made it back to a recognizable street. "That GPS is crazy!" my husband said. While talking smack about the GPS, we arrived at our apartment. I then noticed the estimated arrival time on the GPS had changed from what it initially said at the beginning of our trip. The farm road detour shaved ten minutes off our time. Astonished and bewildered, we were happy to find the movers were still in transit. We parked, opened the door, and walked back out just in time to see them pull up.

Later that week, we drove back to give our house a final cleaning before the Friday closing. On Friday, we wondered which way the GPS would take us to our apartment this time, and it used the Sunday route—no dirt roads in sight. We thank God for how He orchestrated our timely arrival on moving day. God helps us with big and little problems and guides us the whole way. Why would we ever doubt Him and His plan when it is so much better than ours!

Deidre A. Jones

* This devotional was previously published on the Highland Seventh-day Adventist Church's blog. "GPS," *Highland Seventh-day Adventist Church: Sabbath Thoughts* (blog), June 6, 2020, http://highlandcounty22.adventistchurchconnect.org/sabbath-thoughts-blog/gps.

A Big Jolt

For thou hast been a strength to the poor . . . a refuge from the storm.
—Isaiah 25:4, KJV

It was a typical summer afternoon in August 2018, with temperatures in the high eighties and lower nineties. For the past month, the weather had been giving us a reprieve from the heat with brief rain showers. One afternoon, I was in the kitchen preparing dinner. My husband, who is legally blind, enjoys listening to the local and national news. It was raining lightly outside, nothing serious. I told him his news was coming on. Just as he turned on the television and sat back down, a large bolt of lightning flashed through our window. Even as my husband called for me, I was already there. I had heard and seen it from the kitchen. It shut down my television, telephone, cable box, and Christian satellite box. Yet we were extremely blessed. Our house could have caught on fire, or my husband could have been struck by lightning.

That was not the first time that lightning struck our home. We live on a hill, surrounded by a lot of trees. The tornadoes and storms have blown down about five of them. I know God has His angels surrounding our home. We had no telephone or television service for five days. We had to purchase a new TV set, cable box, satellite box, and telephone.

We called an electrician, wanting to make sure our home was grounded since it seems as though our property is prone to incur damage during severe storms. The electrician walked all around, checking inside and outside. "You are definitely grounded," he assured us.

In God's Word, we read about Christ's disciples in a boat during a storm. Jesus was asleep in the boat. Out of fear, the terrified disciples awakened Him. Jesus arose and rebuked the storm. Mark tells us that "the wind ceased, and there was a great calm" (Mark 4:39, KJV).

Jesus can also calm our storms—not just the driving rain, howling wind, and lightning bolts but the fierce storms of life. Those times when we're struggling to pay our bills. Those times when our car breaks down and we have no transportation. Those times when we get laid off from a job or our marriage fails. Yes, we all have storms in life, but the good news is that we may experience another type of lightning jolt—from the Holy Spirit. It wakes us up and reminds us that we're not alone. We have a Father in heaven who loves us and strengthens us. He neither sleeps nor slumbers. He is standing at the door, waiting for us to invite Him in.

Elaine J. Johnson

August 6

A Raging Storm

Then He arose and rebuked the wind, and said, to the sea, "Peace, be still!"
—Mark 4:39, NKJV

On January 13, 2020, I had a heart attack! It hit me across the chest like a ton of bricks, which sent shock waves through my body. Thank goodness, God saved my life! While reflecting on my life-altering experience, I thought, *What if I had died? Was my soul right with God? Had I repented of known and unknown sins, and God had forgiven me?* That was a stormy year of physical, emotional, and spiritual turmoil. I prayed and asked the Lord to show me His way.

Although some struggles may seem insurmountable, God promises us "that if we ask anything according to His will, He hears us" (1 John 5:14, NKJV). God revealed to me my need to completely surrender all my burdens and rest in Him (Matthew 11:28–30).

As the COVID-19 pandemic was raging around the world, I began listening to sermons in various ways—YouTube, Zoom, telephone—and participated in online Bible studies, praying and meditating on His Word. Later, I believe, God opened the way for me to receive counseling by telephone on coping with stress and anxiety. God gave me physical healing and peace to my troubled mind and heart. He is our guiding light to move forward in life! I am reminded of a story of hope from the Bible.

In Mark 4:35–40, Jesus and His disciples were in a boat, crossing over to the other side of the sea. Jesus was asleep on a pillow, and a great windstorm arose. The disciples were doing the best they could to keep the boat upright. They remembered that Jesus was asleep in the boat and called to Him. He awoke and "rebuked" the wind. Jesus said, "Peace, be still!" (verse 39, NKJV). Amid their fear, He was there for them. Jesus asked them, "Why are you so afraid? Do you still have no faith?" (verse 40, NIV). God will calm the seas of suffering and show us the way. We can trust in Jesus and feel peaceful and protected in His arms (Psalm 91; 46:1, 2). Day by day, we must surrender to Him and walk in His ways through His Spirit.

Each day, I am "confident of this very thing, that He who has begun a good work in [us] will complete it until the day of Jesus Christ" (Philippians 1:6, NKJV).

Carolyn Venice Marcus

Seven

Thus the heavens and the earth, and all the host of them, were finished. And on the seventh day God ended His work which He had done, and He rested on the seventh day.
—Genesis 2:1, 2, NKJV

I had knee replacement number 7 in June 2021. I pray this ends my knee journey. I decided this time not to focus on asking God when the surgeries will end but rather to research the significance of the number seven in God's Word.

The number seven signifies completion and perfection. God completed His work of creation in six days and rested on the seventh day (Genesis 1; 2:1, 2). This is our example from God about how we should balance our lives. Six days for us, one day to give God all our time and worship.

The number seven is also part of Christ's death on the cross. Seven times Jesus spoke from the cross, showing completion of His work of salvation. "Father, forgive them, for they do not know what they are doing" (Luke 23:34, NIV). "Truly I tell you, today you will be with me in paradise" (verse 43, NIV). To His mother, He said, "Woman, here is your son," then He said to the disciple, "Here is your mother" (John 19:26, 27, NIV). "My God, my God, why have you forsaken me?" (Matthew 27:46, NIV). "I am thirsty" (John 19:28, NIV). "It is finished" (verse 30, NIV). "Father, into your hands I commit my spirit" (Luke 23:46, NIV).

The number seven denotes promises. God's promise not to destroy the earth again (Genesis 9:8–15) is visible in the seven colors of the rainbow. (Did you include indigo?) My favorite number seven is seen when God instructs Joshua to march around the walls of Jericho once a day for six days and then seven times on the seventh day—and the walls of Jericho fell (Joshua 6:1–20).

These and many more examples in the Bible give meaning to the number seven. I do not know what it means for my knee journey, but I thank God for using this number to point me to His perfection and completion and fulfillment of His promises.

Heather-Dawn Small

August 8

From Struggle to Ease

Then spake Jesus again unto them, saying, I am the light of the world: he that followeth me shall not walk in darkness, but shall have the light of life.
—John 8:12, KJV

Growing up in the Caribbean meant that I had experienced many nights without electricity. We were accustomed to that, so we never skipped a beat when those times occurred. We carried on with our regular duties and activities with the help of kerosene lamps or candles.

Coming to live in America brought a new normal. Not having electricity was unusual. Those times were clustered around severe storms and high-velocity winds, which came infrequently. We humans tend to adapt to new circumstances quite easily. We adjust our expectations as our new life unfolds. I am no different.

While on a mission trip with my daughter, I was jolted out of my complacency of taking for granted that the light I need will always be there. In spite of our heavy schedule, I had vowed to keep my personal devotions time and format the same as when at home. To do that, I had to awaken slightly earlier than usual. The lighting in the home where we stayed was poor, and I struggled to see the words on the pages of my Bible. Even though I was using the same reading materials during my devotional time there as at home, I strained to see clearly to read.

When I mentioned my challenge, my daughter offered me one of her photography lights. It was a small light, perhaps about two inches by three inches, but it made a significant difference in my vision, thus increasing my comfort level and ease of study. Though small, what a difference a bright light made!

That experience caused me to reflect on the importance of having sufficient light. All human-made lights need a source. In the same way, Christians need a source and they get their light from the Son. Jesus told us He is the Master Light, and we are little lights reflecting His light. Therefore, He commissions us to shine and dispel the darkness of this sinful world.

In the same way that little light illuminated my books and changed the nature of my study from agitation to ease, we can share Jesus with others to change their lives of struggle to lives of triumph over sin.

Florence E. Callender

For the First-Time Callers

For he saith, I have heard thee in a time accepted, and in the day of salvation have I succoured thee: behold, now is the accepted time; behold, now is the day of salvation.
—2 Corinthians 6:2, KJV

I've been driving myself to and from work for the past three years. The journey takes more than an hour from the Borough of Point Fortin to the City of San Fernando and vice versa. This means that for almost three years, I've listened to the afternoon gospel radio programming of 107.1 FM "The Word."

I played this gospel station to keep me company on the journey. On a Wednesday afternoon, Jamie Thomas (a.k.a. JT) conducted a call-in segment for first-time callers. He would say in Trini dialect, "Alyuh know what time it is! This time is for YOU, the first-time callers!" Then came his standard line, "Yuh nehvah [never] call before . . . You're not the call-in type . . . Yuh call and yuh nehvah get through before? This is your opportunity!"

I would have a good laugh when people would call and say, "This is my second time." I shook my head as he politely told these callers repeatedly that this was not their segment.

There would be times when I got a strong urge to call, but I would jokingly tell myself, *This is not my time to lose my first-time-caller status.* Sometimes there would be pauses, and in my mind, I knew that I would get through if I called. It was as if he was speaking to me and waiting for me to call. I can't believe how many times I silenced the urge.

When it was reported on the news that JT had suddenly died of a heart attack, I thought, *I will never get the opportunity to be a first-time caller on his radio program ever again.* A lost opportunity.

It is the same way when we hear the voice of God pleading with us and don't respond. We listen to His call to overcome our sins and turn over our lives to Jesus. We can even repeat God's verses, but we don't budge, often for no plausible reason. We make no attempt to heed His call, even laughing along the way at others who heed the call repeatedly. May I urge us to act now? God has cleared the airways for you! It is the right time to heed His appeal. We know not the unexpected day when our opportunity will be lost forever.

Delina Ashley Roberts-James

August 10

A Vivid Dream

How shall we escape if we neglect so great a salvation.
—Hebrews 2:3, NKJV

In June 2020, I woke up feeling amazed from a vivid dream reassuring me of my salvation. I found myself in a dark jungle and an impossible situation—bound on an altar for something serious I had done. Menacing figures chanted in victory at a distance. I desperately prayed for God's deliverance as Satan was about to light the fire. Escape was impossible. I felt so hopeless. Suddenly, I felt the ropes that held me fall away. I lay motionless, fearing I would be seen and caught again.

From the shadows, Jesus whispered to me, "Don't be afraid, just come down onto this side of the altar." After carefully climbing down, He gave me a Bible, saying, "This will be a light to your path so you can see where to go in the darkness and escape to safety." Then He quickly put Himself on the altar in my place, the crowds not noticing I had escaped.

As I started walking along in the dark, I was given a pair of special glasses and instructed, "You must use these. They are the Holy Spirit and will make the Bible instructions clear and unfuzzy." As I followed the path with the Bible lighting my way, I came to a fork in the road. A sign pointed to the left, but the Bible instructed me to go right. When I did, the path lit up.

As I went along, I could see that the left path led people closer to a cliff edge, where people fell into the lake of eternal destruction. People who chose that way came to several more forks in the road with opportunities to turn right, but many ignored the Bible instructions and fell to their destruction. Others tried following their Bible instructions but didn't use their special glasses and, after more wrong turns, also fell over the cliff.

As I kept going with my Bible and special glasses, dark shadowy figures kept menacing me on the sides of the path, making me feel afraid and stressed. At times, I doubted I would ever get out of that dark place, but I was reminded of the song "I Just Keep Trusting My Lord," which calmed me. At that point, I woke up feeling relieved and reassured of my salvation!

I pray you, dear reader, choose today to accept Jesus' great salvation, and remember that His Word is a light to your path (Psalm 119:105).

Merian Richardson

Faith and Fortitude

I keep my eyes always on the Lord.
With him at my right hand, I will not be shaken.
—Psalm 16:8, NIV

As I reread Psalm 16:8 recently, the verse suddenly came alive to me in a new way. "I keep my eyes always on the Lord" (NIV). Another version says, "I have set the Lord always before me" (ESV). It's very difficult to focus on something that is beside you or behind you. Focusing requires that we face it. Focusing on Jesus means we keep Him "before us." Doing so helps me view the world and everything happening in my life through the lens of my relationship with Christ.

"With him at my right hand." I was reading about this idea of someone being at our right hand. This position represents someone you can trust, someone dependable. Christ is definitely trustworthy. I have found Him faithful for many decades. When people ask me about being alone when traveling, I remind them that I haven't been alone since I accepted Christ when I was thirteen. He promised never to leave us or forsake us. Jesus is always at my side. I can't think of anyone I would rather have as my traveling companion through life.

"I will not be shaken." A lot is going on in this world that could "shake" us. Not just physically but socially, financially, mentally, even spiritually. Knowing that Christ is in front of me and beside me gives me the fortitude I need to keep moving forward. Author Ellen White writes, "We have nothing to fear for the future, except as we shall forget the way the Lord has led us, and His teaching in our past history."*

Too often, as human beings, we make the same mistake the Israelites did in the wilderness. They forgot. They forgot the miracles that got them out of Egypt. They forgot the miracle that brought them across the Red Sea on dry land. They forgot to focus on the Lord and focused on the problem instead. Big mistake.

Today I read (again) how Christ was treated at His trial. There's no way in His humanity He could have withstood that horrible treatment if He hadn't kept His focus on His Father. We need to follow His example and keep our focus on Him. Fortitude will follow.

Sharon Clark

* Ellen G. White, *Life Sketches of Ellen G. White* (Mountain View, CA: Pacific Press®, 1943), 196.

August 12

Letting God Lead

Trust in the L*ORD* *with all your heart*
and lean not on your own understanding;
in all your ways submit to him,
and he will make your paths straight.
—Proverbs 3:5, 6, NIV

Coming from a family that feels the need to control everything, I have never been the best at putting my trust in God. Anytime I had the opportunity to trust in God and give it to Him, I went the opposite direction and did my own thing. I was given the opportunity to transfer to a boarding school in Colorado during my junior year of high school. My parents said I needed to go, and I was not happy about it. Instead of embracing an exciting, new opportunity, I tried to hate everything about the school. Because of my stubbornness and inability to let go, I had a miserable year. My parents listened to me constantly complain about how much I wanted to leave. After much consideration, they decided to give me the option of going to a different school back home for my senior year.

Although I was happy and ready to be back home, something was still off. I had dreams consistently about returning to the school I hated so much.

As the dreams continued, I felt God was pulling me back there. I had never been so uneasy before, but God was making it clear that it was the place I needed to be to learn to trust Him. Finally, after a summer of dreams and mixed feelings, I decided to return to Colorado. Just two weeks before the start of school, I asked my parents if we could even afford for me to go back. A few days later, we found out that the school would help pay exactly what we needed to enable me to go. Even though I wanted to be in control over this decision in my life, I knew I needed to let God take over and trust He knew what was best for me.

Looking back at my experience, I can see that was the best place for me to be. I went in struggling spiritually and mentally and came out closer to God and stronger in every aspect. During times in my life when I want to be in control, I look back on my experience and know to trust in God. Although it may not be easy, I know God will continue to pull me out of the darkness and into Him.

Haley Enochs

Count It All Joy

And she was in bitterness of soul, and prayed to the LORD and wept in anguish. Then she made a vow and said, "O LORD of hosts, if You will indeed look on the affliction of your maidservant and remember me, and not forget Your maidservant, but will give Your maidservant a male child, then I will give him to the LORD all the days of his life, and no razor shall come upon his head."
—1 Samuel 1:10, 11, NKJV

As a young girl, I held the conviction that it was not right to bring children into the world when there are so many kids who need a loving home. So it was no surprise when I got married that it took some years before I began to feel the maternal bug. When I finally realized that there would never be another human being from my family line to love and to share our family's history, there was an immediate shift.

Having a child of my own became crucial to me. So I prayed as Hannah prayed, "Lord Almighty, if You will only look on Your servant's misery and remember me." Praise God! We became pregnant with our daughter, Alyssa. It was such an exciting time. I was so excited about the arrival of a new baby, and I couldn't wait to hold my little one in my arms. Things were going very well until one Sabbath, after a very long day at church, we went home, and there was a problem—spotting! I was rushed to the hospital, and the unthinkable happened—we lost our precious Alyssa. We were devastated. All my hopes and dreams were shattered and replaced by hurt, guilt, disappointment—but the most impacting was depression. I could not see myself living in this world without my precious Alyssa. Life held no meaning for me.

Eventually, I sought help in dealing with my loss. And with the help of our very supportive family and friends who prayed for us and encouraged us, we began the healing process. When the mourning of loss is matched by our faith in our Lord Jesus Christ, new mercies come with each dawn. Although I will always ache at the thought of my beloved daughter, it gets easier with time. I have learned to give God thanks in all situations.

Little did I know that five years later, after a long drive on a beautiful sunny day, two beautiful identical twin baby boys would be placed in my loving arms. Oh, what joy! What incredible tiny hands and feet! I was in love. The Lord had answered my prayer.

Anysia Alexander-Archibald

August 14

The Wait

"For I am the Lord, I do not change."
—Malachi 3:6, AMP

What do you do when darkness is the only thing to greet you during the "wait"? When nothing happens after you've read scripture after scripture about God rewarding patience and being faithful to those who wait? You're still waiting, still in the "darkest hour before the light." Platitudes aren't believable. Friends don't understand. Promises seem unfulfilled. Questions remain unanswered. You've tied the knot at the end of the rope, hung on with cramping fingertips, barely avoided plummeting into the yawning abyss below, but you are still . . . waiting. What do you do? The only thing left to do. Know in your head, even if you cannot feel it in your heart, that God is unchanging.

After receiving visions that he interpreted to show his destiny, Joseph was thrust into a waiting season, not once, not twice, but multiple times. During his waiting, he endured the pit, the long month's trek, the slave auction block, the false accusation, the jail sentence, and the cupbearer's broken promise. But just when it seemed that disappointment and injustice would prevail, the wait finally ended. And he was able to say, "You meant evil against me; but God meant it for good" (Genesis 50:20, NKJV).

I am still in a waiting season and feel like I am free falling. Perhaps this continuing rejection and the overwhelming sense of loss is preparing me to participate in God's ultimate plan. Sitting here watching yet a different judge, clothed in black, glasses perched on the end of his nose, I feel helpless and hopeless. So many courtrooms. Did I qualify for protection from an abusive spouse? Yes. More waiting. Will my husband plead guilty to his crimes? Yes. And still more waiting, yet again, I don't know what the next verdict will be.

But still, in some corner of my mind, I remember that the God who was with Joseph in the pit is the same God who spoke the world into existence. The same God who promises that He will walk through the valley with me is still here with me. That God strengthens me.

So what do you do as you find yourself waiting and waiting? Keep praying, keep expectantly hoping. Even though another round of waiting may be just beyond the bend, remember, God is unchanging.

Charmaine Houston

Do You See Right?

Yet the Lord *hath not given you an heart to perceive, and eyes to see, and ears to hear, unto this day.*
—Deuteronomy 29:4, KJV

I was focused on my problems. Many things were not the way I wanted. The gap between my wish and reality was big. I finished projects. They looked perfect but weren't and turned into a nightmare. However, the Lord never gave up on me, and I learned a new lesson.

How do you see right when you are struggling? God invites us to ask and promises we will receive. I pray to have new eyes, more spiritual. I ask the Lord to see things as He sees them—through Heaven's eyes.

My human eyes have two problems. They are limited to appearances, desires, or problems. I always "fall in love" with things that alter my judgment. My eyes are never satisfied; I always want more. "Hell and destruction are never full; so the eyes of man are never satisfied" (Proverbs 27:20, KJV). Thus, I must keep working on my character.

I pray to have temperance, godliness, patience, love; if not, I will stay blind. "But he that lacketh these things is blind, and cannot see afar off, and hath forgotten that he was purged from his old sins" (2 Peter 1:9, KJV). The reality can be disappointing sometimes, especially when you have a dream. It is time to keep believing that what you want is coming. Have hope.

However, to see right, I also need to listen to God's voice to synchronize my will to His will. That's why my favorite part in my daily prayer time is when I let God talk to me. I ask Him for a message for the day, and I open my Bible. I receive strength and direction step-by-step. I just need to listen to His voice by opening His Word.

Let me share with you my little prayer. *God, give me Your eyes to see as You are seeing people or my situation. I'm tired of being sad, angry, and in despair. Come, help me; I need a real change. Show me the way out. Amen.*

It is constant work to see right because the enemy wants us to be blind. Always repeat to yourself, "Victory belongs to Jesus; the enemy already failed." Then always stay closer to Him.

Lynn Mazarin

August 16

With All Your Might

Whatever your hand finds to do, do it with all your might.
—Ecclesiastes 9:10, NIV

It was a special program for residents at the retirement center. Several individuals had been invited to participate. One young woman brought her violin. Melissa had decided to play Pinto's "Run, Run!" on the piano. "It's a happy song, and they will like it," she explained.

The program went very well. At the conclusion, Melissa and the violinist walked around, greeting each guest. Approaching a distinguished-looking lady in a wheelchair, Melissa held out her right hand for a friendly handshake. The woman stretched out her left hand and took Melissa's. Looking at the violinist, the woman said, "I used to play first chair in the symphony. Unfortunately, a stroke damaged my right hand. I miss the violin and loved hearing yours. Sometimes I still play in my imagination."

"Once a violinist, always a violinist," said the young woman. "Let's play something."

"I don't have my right hand," the woman replied, softly.

Standing behind the wheelchair, the violinist placed her violin in the woman's left hand. Holding the bow in her own right hand, the violinist said, "OK, what do you want to play?"

Startled, the woman named a familiar violin solo. Melissa watched, fascinated. The young woman bowed; the older woman fingered the strings. It was hauntingly beautiful. The other residents stopped in their tracks as they listened intently. One violin. Two musicians. One using her right hand; the other, her left. A collaboration. A duet. Playing in harmony. Connecting with the music—and with each other.

When the last notes of the song floated away, the woman's face was wet with tears. "The best gift," she whispered, handing back the violin.

"How did you think to do that?" Melissa asked as they left. "It was simply wonderful!"

"I read about a man who did that for his father," replied the violinist. "I am always looking for ways to help people. Happy it worked so well today."

Everyone has a talent. You do, too. Are you using yours to bless others? Yielding your hand to God's *whatever* is truly the "best gift." Especially when you do it with "*all* your might."

Arlene R. Taylor

Not on My Watch

The angel of the Lord *encamps all*
around those who fear Him,
And delivers them.
—Psalm 34:7, NKJV

As my husband and I surveyed the damage done to our vehicles parked in front of our home, we had to praise God. We knew it was the angel of God who intervened in this mayhem.

A woman had driven her truck into my husband's new car, which hit the electric pole; his car hit my van, and then my van hit the neighbor's car. It was a domino effect.

This all happened at four o'clock in the morning when we were all sleeping, including my neighbors. God be praised that no one was hurt. Unbelievable! As the woman walked toward me, I asked her if she was OK. I tried to reassure her and told her that it was going to be OK. I told her to be thankful—a car we could always replace, but a life we could never replace, so let us thank God for His grace.

Another amazing thing about this occurrence is that the police had to call the electric company out to replace the pole because my husband's car was lodged in the pole. It took two attempts to release the car. The worker also showed my husband a faulty connector on our house that would have eventually caught fire and burned the house. If this accident hadn't happened, we never would have known about the fire hazard, and the pole could have fallen on our house. The enemy would have tried to take our lives, but the angel of God standing by us said, "Not on my watch."

God never promised us that we wouldn't have troubles in this world, but He does promise us that He will be with us during our times of trouble. We might not always understand or know the reason things happen, but we are given the reassurance that all things work together for good to those that love the Lord. God is always turning it around and working it for our good. God is always worthy of praise and honor.

Avis Floyd Jackson

August 18

The Stuck Window

Ask, and it shall be given you; seek, and ye shall find;
knock, and it shall be opened unto you.
—Matthew 7:7, KJV

One day my husband discovered that the window on the driver's side of our car would not go up. He gave it a quick knock, and surprisingly, it went up. Three weeks went by, and it was working like a charm—until the day it was not. After a long, hot summer day of running errands, we got into the hot car and put down the windows. A cool breeze flowed through the car. When we got home, we put up the windows. The driver's side window did not budge. My husband and I took turns trying to push and pull the window button. Nothing happened. My husband gave it a little nudge as he did before, but nothing happened. The window was stuck.

For the next few days, the car's window was down. We could not afford to get the car fixed, so what were we going to do? Afraid that the interior of the car would get wet, we decided to invent our own window. We covered the window with plastic. After a while, the plastic could not protect the inside of the car from the elements. I had faith that God was going to take care of our window.

My husband was worried about the safety of our car. When he went to work, he needed to park the car in an open parking lot. He could not have the window like this. Having faith, he went out once more to the garage to see what he could do to the car. I later met him in the garage and suggested that before he did anything, we should pray. At first, it seemed a bit comical, both of us standing and praying over the window. Nevertheless, after we prayed, an idea popped into my husband's mind. He pulled the window's buttons apart and fiddled with the wires. To our surprise, the window came back up as if nothing had been wrong. My husband and I turned to each other with big grins on our faces, admiring God's power.

There is nothing impossible for God to handle. Here we were trying to fix the window on our own; we should have called on our heavenly Father to begin with. Nothing is too hard for God. He sees and knows all. He wants us to call on Him. He wants us to seek Him. Today's verse reminds us that we are not alone; we should ask, seek, and knock because our heavenly Father will answer.

Dianatha Hall-Smith

One Room Left and Two Hours Late

Before they call, I will answer. While they are still speaking, I will respond.
—Isaiah 65:24, *The Clear Word**

Vacationing in Europe, I found myself in Rudesheim on Friday, June 16, 1995, for my last weekend in Germany. That morning, I read the devotional entitled "Take Time" in the women's devotional *A Gift of Love*. Turning to the biographical section, I learned that the author, Sylvia Renz, lived in Darmstadt and had a connection with Adventist World Radio (AWR). I had to go to Darmstadt!

The hotel clerk called information for me. There were fifteen people with the last name Renz, so I couldn't call Sylvia. I went on the Rhine cruise as I had planned. Later, I retrieved my suitcases, walked to the station, boarded a train for Wiesbaden, and transferred to Darmstadt.

I wrote in my journal, "I'm going on faith, Lord. Can I find the Adventists in Darmstadt and lodging for tonight? I'm testing You. Let me know I am Your child, please. Amen."

My "angel" was a clerk at the bookstore at the Bonhof in Darmstadt. I'd attempted to call AWR, but the coin-operated phone booth was out of order, and I didn't have a telephone card. I explained this to the clerk. He just grabbed his business phone, called AWR, and handed the phone to me. The English-speaking secretary, Yvonne, told me to take a taxi to Marienhohe, the Adventist seminary, and said she would see me at church tomorrow.

The next morning, I attended church, and afterward, I met and thanked Yvonne for her help. I even met Sylvia Renz, who was only at this particular church because of graduation!

The next morning, transportation to the Frankfurt airport was a challenge. I had to be at the airport three hours early for my flight. My new friends at AWR made the arrangements for me. I did not get to the airport until 10:40 for my 11:10 flight—but my flight was delayed two hours! God enabled me to arrive on time, even though I was two hours late!

God saved a room for me and held the flight to enable me to get on board. What a loving God who cares about every detail of our lives.

Patricia Hook Rhyndress Bodi

* Jack Blanco, *The Clear Word* (Hagerstown, MD: Review and Herald®, 2003), 760.

Getting Ready

Therefore be ye also ready: for in such an hour as ye think not the Son of man cometh.
—Matthew 24:44, KJV

Christians talk about the last days and the end time and how God's children should be ready for Jesus to come. It seemed as though we weren't ready, the way people were stockpiling store items like toilet tissue, paper towels, food, and hand sanitizer during the COVID-19 pandemic.

Jesus said we should remember the birds of the air and the lilies of the field (Matthew 6:28, 30). We forget that God is our Provider who takes care of us each day and has promised to supply all our needs. Remember, He made us a little lower than the angels.

Have we as God's children lost our faith in His promises? It really amazed me how neighborhoods turned into ghost towns during the height of the pandemic. Churches, businesses, and schools were closed, and we were mandated to stay home unless we were essential workers, needed treatment or medicine, or had some other necessary business. Instead of focusing on God as our Creator, using this quality time with God and each other, we kept busy complaining about trivial things. Some church members complained because the church doors were closed (many had services online), which they felt was wrong. They failed to realize that the church is just a building, and we the people are the church. Attendance greatly increased by having services online.

During the pandemic, a lot of our minds were focused on the news and negative things going on in the world, allowing Satan to draw our attention away from God and the Second Coming. We acted like Satan wanted us to act—being defiant, refusing to wear a mask, not social distancing, and being violent. God's children really lost their faith in His promises. His Word has more than three thousand promises. When the real time of trouble comes and the last days are upon us, it will be too late to turn to Him when Jesus is seen coming through those clouds.

He wants us to spend eternity with Him. If this were not true, He wouldn't have continued this world after the first Adam failed. He had the second Adam, His Son, ready to die for all humanity to give us eternal life. God's plan is to give life and save us because of His love for us.

Camilla E. Cassell

Heart Blessings

Bless the L*ORD, O my soul:*
And all that is within me, bless his holy name.
—Psalm 103:1, KJV

My son grew up on the west coast of the United States of America (USA). While in college, he took a year off to serve as a task force worker with young people in northern Georgia, USA. When he'd come home for vacation, he'd say, "I love the South! But I haven't figured out some of their expressions." Years later, I met, fell in love with, and married a Tennesseean. Eventually, we moved to the South to be closer to his birth family. During a family reunion, my son and I sat amid dozens of in-laws and listened to happy people recalling—in beautiful southern drawl—the good ol' days. After a while, I quietly asked my son, "Have you noticed the frequent use of the expression, 'Bless your heart'?"

"Yes," he answered. "I think I'm noticing its use right before someone is about to say something, uh, less than charitable about someone else. On the other hand, after I told someone about my jetlag, she said, 'Bless your heart!' and I felt like I'd just been hugged."

Since that family reunion, I've learned some of the nuances of "bless your heart." This expression was directed at me most frequently the summer I fell down a flight of stairs. Puffy black and blue bruises from neck to hairline made me look like a raccoon—one that had been hit by a truck. Every time someone looked at me with horror and exclaimed, "Bless your heart!" I sensed they were expressing heartfelt empathy. One Southern writer pointed out that *bless your heart* can be an expression of cattiness but, perhaps more important, is said "as an expression of genuine sympathy, murmured with hugs and casseroles in funeral parlors."* I like that.

Did you know that God also wants to be included in this bless-your-heart dialogue? Psalm 103:1 tells us to "bless the LORD" with all that is within us. The word can mean to "bestow good of any kind upon . . . extol . . . glorify."† Not only can we bring God joy when we pray, "Father God, bless Your heart of love," but we can also bring comfort to one another when our heart blessings—however we word them—are spoken as spiritual hugs of encouragement.

Carolyn Rathbun Sutton

* Candice Dyer, "Your Southern Decoder," *Atlanta*, November 1, 2012, https://www.atlantamagazine.com/southern/southern-decoder/.

† Dictionary.com, s.v. "bless,"accessed February 22, 2022, https://www.Dictionary.com/browse/bless.

August 22

Apricots

Taste and see that the Lord *is good.*
Oh, the joys of those who take refuge in him!
—Psalm 34:8, NLT

When I was in college, someone told me apricots were "sooooo good." Having only eaten the canned version served in the dining hall, I thought they were OK, but nothing great.

While home on break once, I saw some at the grocery store. I can still see them in one of the square displays that were like islands in the produce department. I bought some because they were supposed to be "sooooo good." They weren't garbage, but I couldn't imagine why my friend thought they were "sooooo good."

Years later, I now live where apricots grow, and they are soooooooooooo good—like eating candy! We eat lots and lots of them when they are fresh and freeze them for smoothies later.

The ones I bought at the store that day had been grown in another part of the country and shipped to the store for sale. The farmer, the shipper, and the grocer had all been involved in getting those apricots to my hand. The ones I eat now come from a tree in our garden. My husband usually brings them to the kitchen counter, and then they go from my hand to my mouth. When discussing why the store-bought apricots weren't all that great, he said ours almost get bruised just coming from the garden to the kitchen, they are so perfectly ripe. They come directly to me—though I can pick them off the tree myself if I just walk out to the garden.

God said, "Taste and see." If what I am tasting of God's goodness is coming to me through a pastor, a devotional book, or a women's ministry leader, or even if I got it a long time ago from my Primary teacher, then it is like that apricot I bought at the store. It just isn't fresh and delightful to my taste buds. Maybe the only message you're getting from God has been processed a bit and is as good as the canned apricots, but it's not soooooooooooo good. The third-party sources can be very helpful at pointing the way to the garden, but go there yourself and pick the fruit; go directly to the Source. Read the Word, talk to God, and see if He doesn't give you something that is better and sweeter than you ever knew existed.

Summer Stahl

Rotten Potatoes

For the Son of man is come to seek
and to save that which was lost.
—Luke 19:10, KJV

I love potatoes. Anyone who really knows me knows that I can never seem to get enough of them. The one thing that you can always find in my kitchen? Potatoes. Potato salad, potato pie, creamy-style potatoes, red-skinned potatoes, herbed potatoes, mashed potatoes, grilled potatoes, or just plain old fries—I love them all.

However, as much as I love potatoes, there is one kind of potato I can do without, and that is a rotten potato. You may be thinking, that's not strange; no one likes a rotten potato. Indeed, that is true; however, in my case, it can seem somewhat extreme. Even if it is just a small section of the potato, instead of cutting it off and throwing that part out, I am always ready to throw the entire potato out.

When I am peeling a potato, my husband knows very well that if he hears his name being called with urgency and desperation, it usually means there is a rotten potato or a rotten spot, and I am calling him to deal with it. After he handles the problem, I go back to being happy again while continuing to prepare my potato dish.

One day as I was cooking, I thought about myself as a potato with not just one but many rotten spots of sin. The difference is that God is the cook in the kitchen preparing me for the banquet table in heaven. But instead of throwing me out, which He has every right to do, He cuts away the sin because He sees the good in me. It's a painful process, but God knows that once He cuts out the sin, I am as good as new. And with the right ingredients, I can be presented at the banquet table. I am so thankful that God sees the good in us, sinful though we may be, and He is willing and able to make us good as new and worthy to be used for His service.

So the next time you are preparing a meal and you happen upon a rotten spot on your favorite fruit or vegetable, just cut it out and remember that God sent His Son to cut out the sin in your life and to save the lost (rotten potatoes) of this world.

Candy Monique Springer-Blackman

Hosting the King

" 'For I was hungry and you gave me something to eat, I was thirsty and you gave me something to drink, I was a stranger and you invited me in, I needed clothes and you clothed me, I was sick and you looked after me, I was in prison and you came to visit me.'

"Then the righteous will answer him, 'Lord, when did we see you hungry and feed you, or thirsty and give you something to drink? When did we see you a stranger and invite you in, or needing clothes and clothe you? When did we see you sick or in prison and go to visit you?'

"The King will reply, 'Truly I tell you, whatever you did for one of the least of these brothers and sisters of mine, you did for me.' "
—Matthew 25:35–40, NIV

One Saturday when I was the youth director of the Seventh-day Adventist Santa Efigênia Church in Belo Horizonte, Brazil, our youth group visited the Cancer Hospital for Children in Baleia, Belo Horizonte. We prayed with the kids and their parents. In an isolated room inside the nursery was a young mother with her six-month-old baby girl. They were a very humble family from another city. I learned that the baby had a serious sickness called visceral leishmaniasis. I prayed with them and offered my phone number in case they needed help with anything.

After a week, my phone rang. A social assistant told me that the baby's situation had worsened. They needed to transfer her to another hospital where the mother did not have a place to stay. They also called the father since the baby had little chance of surviving.

At the hospital, the doctor called me aside. The baby had blood in her diapers and was bleeding through her mouth and ears. My heart ached for them! I had two little girls and could not imagine how much these parents were suffering. I brought the mother, and later the father, to my home to stay. They attended church with my family, where everyone prayed for this precious baby and her family.

The baby's health improved little by little. Finally, they could bring her home, and we dedicated her to God in our church. They were ready to go back to their city and promised to follow Jesus. I am sure they never forgot the miracle we all witnessed. I certainly won't.

Ana Maria de Souza Gonçalves

To the Hills

I will lift up my eyes to the hills—
From whence comes my help?
My help comes from the Lord*,*
Who made heaven and earth.
—Psalm 121:1, 2, NKJV

When my husband was a teenager, his parents exchanged their home in a college town for a 160-acre ranch in the foothills. This was a good place for him because he got a job at a sawmill and later drove a lumber truck when he finished high school. After serving several years in the air force, he returned to the ranch and started working as a self-employed logger. After we were married, we bought 120 acres of the ranch and found it to be a good place to raise our family.

For a few years, we worked in logging during the summer and fall, but when the rainy season came, we looked for dryer weather. For several years, we went to different places in Mexico, and then we heard of a new school starting in the mountains of southern Mexico. There, we found a place we could volunteer. My husband helped by cutting down trees for the sawmill and bringing supplies for the school from the city. Later, when our children were in school, I helped by teaching English as a foreign language. Our three children finished grade school and academy there and headed to college.

With three children in college, we needed to spend more time working, so we spent more time in and around our foothill ranch. That's where we were living when I received the message, "Don't come into town. You're too old. And you're taking care of someone who is too old." Yes, the years had passed, and my husband no longer felt safe driving at ninety-nine. I would go into town once a week to help at our church and take care of errands. But my husband always worried until I got home. While the restrictions of COVID-19 stressed many other people, we were already in a safe place. We were together, and I kept busy cooking, cleaning, and caring for my husband. For three months, I didn't go into town. It was a happy time for us, and once again, we were thankful for our home in the hills. We didn't realize what a blessing it would be to our family many years ago, but the Lord provided.

Betty J. Adams

August 26

Birds in Flight

The heavens declare the glory of God;
the skies proclaim the work of his hands.
—Psalm 19:1, NIV

I am lucky enough to have a multipurpose path right in front of my house. It is one of the amenities the state built as consolation for putting a six-lane toll highway in the middle of our neighborhood. The neighborhood is now joined by a conciliatory bridge.

Along the path, about three-quarters of a mile from my front door, is a stormwater management pond. In a rainy year, the pond is always full of water—and with Canada geese and ducks. Some days, more than a hundred geese are on the pond, plus a few mallard ducks and the occasional great blue heron.

I like to look at the water-loving birds on the pond. As a person fascinated by aviation and flight in general, I am particularly taken by the geese as they leave the water or return. The geese honk constantly. I imagine they are planning their next foray.

As I watch, the geese start paddling their feet, and in a second or two, their feet are out of the water. Their necks crane upward, and then they are heading for the sky, quickly getting into the well-known V-formation. As geese return to the pond, they land toward the back of their feet and skid on the water until their necks and the rest of their bodies come down to a level position and they are floating on the water.

The first time I observed this, I realized that the birds take off like an airplane, and when they land, they look like the retired Concorde aircraft or the space shuttle. It occurs to me that the people who invented and developed aircraft must have studied birds, including geese, to perfect this method of transportation that we all take for granted today. Humans did not invent flight; God did. He made the whole world. And God laid out a plan and gave humans the insight and wisdom to adapt it for our use.

Just a bit of observation opens our eyes to the intricacies of nature. Nature provides us with answers to many problems—from flight to medicines and everything in between. Nature demonstrates that it was all created by someone who loves us—God. How can we not recognize the love of an all-powerful God?

Jean Arthur

Angels' Food

Can God furnish a table in the wilderness?
—Psalm 78:19, KJV

During the COVID-19 pandemic, I enjoyed trying new recipes. My husband and I enjoyed gleaning instructions to new taste sensations we never knew existed. Webpages exposed us to *maqluba*, an upside-down lentil and eggplant casserole. We transformed cauliflower into pizza crusts and ground cauliflower and walnuts into burgers. We snacked on black-bean brownies, rice paper "pigskins," Asian steamed coconut bread, turnip "potato" salad, and Spanish mango salsa. I not only investigated edible recipes but learned to formulate medicinal salves from manuka honey and fresh comfrey leaves. We reduced our blood sugar by ingesting mulberries and sweet potatoes.

I compared our experiments to Israel's introduction to manna. Manna took some getting used to. Many despised that white, coriander-seed-like, honey-flavored stuff (Exodus 16:31), calling it "worthless" (Numbers 21:5, ESV). It could be milled in the "food processor" of Moses' day, the mortar and pestle. It was versatile enough to be baked or boiled (Exodus 16:23). Manna had the property of melting when the sun grew hot, but a Friday batch could last through the Sabbath (Exodus 16:21–25). It was included as a souvenir in the ark, the box containing the Ten Commandments (verses 33, 34; Hebrews 9:4). Asaph described the mystery food as "angels' food" (Psalm 78:25, KJV).

I admire George Washington Carver, the scientist who called God Mr. Creator. God showed Dr. Carver that peanuts, soybeans, and the sweet potato held the nitrogen cure for the American South's deteriorating infrastructure, the land itself. He could make milk from a bean and plastic, soap, and diesel from plant parts. There were members of the House of Representatives in 1921 who mocked Carver as he spoke. But wise listeners among them sought to implement his suggestions to heal the land and the former cotton-based economy.

This COVID-19 interlude reminded me of several things. The Lord made fruits, vegetables, nuts, and grains. Each is unique. All are useful. He has given us minds to discover new ways foods can be enjoyed. How can anybody hate vegetables? Learn new ways to eat. God made this stuff. And appreciate Jesus, the real Bread sent from heaven (John 6:35).

Elinor Harvin Burks

August 28

The Hezekiah Effect

Hezekiah received the letter from the messengers and read it. Then he went up to the temple of the LORD and spread it out before the LORD. And Hezekiah prayed to the LORD: "LORD, the God of Israel, enthroned between the cherubim, you alone are God over all the kingdoms of the earth. You have made heaven and earth."
—2 Kings 19:14, 15, NIV

The story of Hezekiah is written twice, in 2 Kings 19 and in Isaiah 37. When Hezekiah received a threating letter from Sennacherib, king of Assyria, he took the letter to the temple, spread it out before the Lord, and prayed. God answered Hezekiah's prayer in an amazing way. God sent an angel to solve the problem. The angel killed 185,000 men in the Assyrian camp. When Sennacherib returned to Nineveh, his sons killed him.

I decided to take Hezekiah's method to solve my problem. I wrote the problem on a sheet of paper, spread it out on the table before the Lord, and prayed. Then I waited on the Lord for His answer. God blessed me abundantly. Thus my Hezekiah effect prayer ministry was born. I shared this ministry at church, women's retreats, and with many who came to me for prayer.

When my friend Charlotte and her husband, Doug, had a housing problem, they could not find a home at a specific reasonable price. I had them write their problem on a sheet of paper. I placed the sheet on the floor. Then I had each of us put a foot on the paper and hold hands, and we prayed. God solved the problem.

What problems are you facing that you cannot solve? What debts are you in that you cannot pay? What situation are you facing that you have no idea what to do or where to turn?

Please do not try to solve it yourself. Give your problem to Jesus. Write it on a piece of paper, spread it out before the Lord, and pray. No matter what you are called on to face in this life, learn to turn to God first for the help you need. Even though God doesn't always answer yes, we must trust Him when He answers wait or no.

Remember, prayer, trust, faith, and obedience to God are the solutions to all our problems. Try the Hezekiah effect today. Write down your problems and requests on a piece of paper, lay it before the Lord, and pray. God will amaze you with what He can do with your situation.

Ruth Cantrell

Who Touched My Clothes?

And Jesus, immediately knowing in himself that virtue had gone out of him, turned him about in the press, and said, Who touched my clothes?
—Mark 5:30, KJV

It was the teacher's birthday! She was all smiles as she arrived at school. Dressed in her brand-new turquoise dress with matching shoes, she strolled toward her third-grade classroom. The students, seeing her approaching, rushed toward her like the waves of the sea. Some held her hands, others tugged on her new dress, and one boy threw his arms around her neck. When she was finally able to free herself, she looked down at her clothes, and there was a huge brown stain on the front of her skirt.

Hysterically, she shouted at the band of cheerleaders, "Who touched my dress? You've ruined my birthday dress!" In shock and amazement, the children scurried away. They couldn't figure out who messed up the teacher's dress. They regretted that their well-meaning gesture caused her so much discomfort.

The question the teacher asked reminds me of a similar one asked by Jesus. One day, a large crowd thronged Him. Suddenly Jesus stopped, looked around, and said, "Who touched my clothes?"

This question astounded the disciples and left the crowd dumbfounded. The disciples responded, "Thou seest the multitude thronging thee, and sayest thou, Who touched me?" (Mark 5:31, KJV).

The disciples did not realize that Jesus recognized an extraordinary touch. The multitude brushed against Jesus, but someone deliberately touched Him in faith. In response to His question, a woman came trembling before Him and told Him all that she had been experiencing over the years and the healing miracle that had taken place in her body because she came into direct contact with Him. Jesus affirmed the woman's faith and confirmed her healing.

The woman's response to Jesus expressed her faith in Him and her acceptance of His pardoning grace. We can rejoice that we have the opportunity of coming close to Jesus through prayer and study of the Scriptures. May we experience God's transforming grace as by faith we reach out and touch Him today.

Gerene I. Joseph

August 30

The Red Stain

"Come now, and let us reason together,"
Says the L*ORD,*
"Though your sins are like scarlet,
They shall be as white as snow;
Though they are red like crimson,
They shall be as wool."
—Isaiah 1:18, NKJV

Years ago, I taught a Vacation Bible School kindergarten class at our church. We made crafts, played games, sang songs, and enjoyed stories. We also enjoyed a refreshment break. Everyone was pleased with the juice and chocolate chip cookies. All went well until five-year-old Debbie reached for her Hawaiian punch. The cup tipped over and splashed her juice onto the table, the carpet, and my slacks.

Debbie's brown eyes filled with tears. "Oh, Mrs. Moyers," she wept, "I didn't mean to ruin your pants! I'm so sorry!"

As I wiped myself off, her classmates cleaned the table and the floor with wet paper towels. Debbie kept sobbing. Patting her shoulder, I said, "It's OK. It was an accident. Look! My pants are the same color as your juice. Nobody will notice the stain once it dries. I'll wash them when I get home. They'll be just fine!"

"Really?"

"Yes!"

What happened made me think of God's promises, such as, "For all have sinned, and come short of the glory of God" (Romans 3:23, KJV). Whether on purpose or unknowingly, we have all done wrong. And as a result, our lives and characters are stained. That's when we need to read today's text from Isaiah 1:18. We can start with a clean slate.

God says, "And I will give them one heart, and I will put a new spirit within you; and I will take the stony heart out of their flesh, and will give them an heart of flesh: that they may walk in my statutes, and keep mine ordinances, and do them: and they shall be my people, and I will be their God" (Ezekiel 11:19, 20, KJV). I want that spiritual heart transplant, don't you?

Bonnie Moyers

A Provider for Complainers

"Consider the ravens: they neither sow nor reap, they have neither storehouse nor barn, and yet God feeds them. Of how much more value are you than the birds!"
—Luke 12:24, ESV

There I went, complaining again. I know that God never becomes impatient with us, but as the complaint escaped my lips, I suddenly felt conscious of the fact that as I vented about the things that had gone awry, I had neglected to remember the many times that God had provided for me just when I needed it.

One such incident happened a few months earlier while battling a financial issue at my school. To compound the issue, I added to my list of gripes the need for money to get through the coming week. I prayed—rather, I complained and argued with God for the entire week, even becoming upset about the cashless predicament that has become quite characteristic of my academic life. In almost comedic timing, I then received a call from a family member of a fellow national at my school who needed me to do a favor for them. "Sure, no problem," I said. "That's what compatriots are for!"

The person replied, "A part of the money is yours—sorry it wasn't more." Sorry it wasn't more? It was more than enough for my personal needs! At that moment, I thanked God with enthusiasm that was nonexistent just two seconds before. I think I got the divine eyeroll just then. And if I did, I deserved it.

How easily we forget the many times that God has provided for us, rescued us from impossible situations, and showed up for us when it seemed that there was no way out! We praise Him for the victory won—whether small or great, and then just a few minutes go by before we forget the miracles He wrought, and we begin to mount our list of complaints again. Life is riddled with its challenges, and we will never live a life of complete ease until Jesus comes again to take us home. But we can be assured that the God who feeds the birds, sends rain for the plants, and continues to give us new opportunities with each new dawn will continue to provide for us when we most need it. The next time we think about complaining, let us thank God for what He did for us in the past and pray in faith, knowing that He will provide for us, His children, once more.

Olivia D. Valentine

September 1

Observation From Estes Park

And the Lord has laid on Him the iniquity of us all.
—Isaiah 53:6, NKJV

When our son and his family came to visit us in Colorado, they wanted to spend some time in Estes Park, a mountain resort town. After a picnic lunch there, we started walking along the river. Unable to keep up with everyone, I decided to sit on a bench by the river and "people watch"—a very interesting activity in Estes Park. Earlier, from a distance, I had noticed a family with four children—two grade-school-age children and toddler twins in a double stroller. As I was sitting there, the family walked by, and I could see them better. The twins were no longer in the stroller. The little boy was walking with the dad. I could now read the little boy's shirt: "My first name is trouble; my last name is trouble."

I had to laugh and was still smiling when his mom and twin sister walked past. I said, "I saw your little boy's shirt and thought it was funny."

"Yes," she responded, "funny, but so true! That shirt is perfect for him." We both laughed, and she walked on.

Well, I thought, *I'm glad I don't wear a shirt advertising my negative character traits!*

The Bible, however, does put on display the negative character traits of many people. Abraham, a friend of God, lied about his relationship with his wife, Sarah. Jacob lied and deceived his father to obtain the birthright blessing. Peter, after spending three years with Jesus, denied he even knew Him. Saul (later Paul) persecuted Christians. David, a man after God's own heart, committed adultery and murder. But when confronted by the prophet Nathan, David readily admitted he had sinned. Without hesitation, Nathan said, "The Lord has taken away your sin" (2 Samuel 12:13, NIV). Instant forgiveness—just like that!

Perhaps if we Christians wore a shirt like the little boy in Estes Park, it would say, "My first name is sinner; my last name is forgiven." Author Ellen White wrote, "[Christ] has borne the burden of our guilt. He will take the load from our weary shoulders. He will give us rest."* Jesus even says that, someday, He will give us a new name (Isaiah 62:2). How special that will be!

Sharon Oster

---

* Ellen G. White, *The Ministry of Healing* (Mountain View, CA: Pacific Press®, 1942), 71.

Loop Trails and New Trails

I will be glad and rejoice in Your mercy . . . ;
You have set my feet in a wide place.
—Psalm 31:7, 8, NKJV

Walking a loop trail is a beautiful thing. One can enjoy the convenience of "walking a circle." Taking such a trail regularly, one gets to know every obstacle along the path and learns how to deal with them. Everything becomes familiar.

Unfortunately, not every loop trail in life is wholesome. I realized an area in my life where I was running an inner loop trail, trapped in compulsive circular thinking. A painful experience forced me to take a closer look at that old pattern of "thinking."

Preceded by many prayers for healing and growth, I started to experience my situation differently. It felt like a breakthrough into something new. My prayers are being answered.

When I was hurting, I would go on about my pain in endless circles, condemning the perpetrator. Now, I let my friends help me find a different line of thought. We briefly talk about the pain and the person who caused it before steering the conversation in an empathetic and inspiring direction. The process challenges me to take new steps, and my friends reassure me that I can do it. I don't want to think and walk along the same paths anymore. A new resolve is growing inside of me.

Being nurtured in such a patient and loving way helps me realize how paralyzing a negative life pattern is. Together, we identify further steps that correspond to my conviction deep down inside. Staying true to my feelings, I see how liberating this is. In my heart, I contemplate how to express this best.

Hikes in nature help me bring everything before God in few words. Thoughts swarming in my mind are reduced to what is important, offering a refreshing sense of clarity.

I rejoice that God has seen my affliction and the anguish of my soul (Psalm 31:7). He has not given me into the hands of the enemy. He makes growth possible. He sets me in a spacious place (verse 8). Bits and pieces of what I had previously perceived are now falling in place. A process of healing and liberation is given room. I am ready to embark on new roads to wide places.

Sigrid Hruby

September 3

Order My Steps

And thine ears shall hear a word behind thee, saying, This is the way, walk ye in it, when ye turn to the right hand, and when ye turn to the left.
—Isaiah 30:21, KJV

We got the news that my brother-in-law, Trevor, had died in Jamaica after a battle with cancer. The funeral was scheduled for October 10, 2019. I decided to attend and pay my last respects. Later, it dawned on me that my brother, Wesley, would turn sixty on October 14. I weighed my options and decided to go to Jamaica on October 6, then to Montreal, Quebec, Canada, after the funeral for the birthday celebration on October 12. Since I live in western Canada, this plan made sense because I was already connecting in Toronto, Ontario, Canada.

Three days before my departure, my right leg began giving me pain. By Friday, I could hardly walk! I messaged the travel agent and requested wheelchair assistance at the airport. By the next Sabbath, I was using a cane to help me walk. Because of the intense pain, I went to see a doctor immediately after church. The doctor looked at my swollen knee and said, "You have a lot of inflammation in your knee. I'll prescribe an anti-inflammatory for you." When I told him I was planning to fly out that night to our family funeral, he asked, "May I give you a letter to get your money back in case you can't travel tonight because of your medical issue?"

The thought of not being able to make the trip weighed heavily on me. The truth was that I was in a lot of pain and could not bend my knee nor lift my leg. I took the medication, rubbed and iced my knee, and kept watching the clock. I prayed, *God, please order my steps. I really want to go on this trip*. Since I was flying out ahead of my husband, my family was concerned because I would be traveling alone. I left the situation in God's capable hands, and my husband drove me to the airport. I was put in an area to wait for assistance before being escorted through security. Safely at the gate, I boarded the flight ahead of the other passengers and was delighted that no one was seated beside me. It was a red-eye flight, so I made myself comfortable and went to sleep. By the time I arrived in Toronto, the swelling in my knee had gone down. I could even bend my leg a bit. Hallelujah!

The rest of the trip was pain-free. God knows everything we are going through, and He will make a way where there seems to be no way. What a mighty God we serve!

Sharon Long

Waiting on the Lord

Wait for the Lord;
be strong and take heart
and wait for the Lord.
—Psalm 27:14, NIV

Several years ago, I participated in a devotional program at church. The program consisted of forty days of prayer and reading the Bible very early in the morning. At the time, I was studying chemical engineering in Peru. My goal was to work as an engineer and have my own business; however, reading the Bible and learning more about Jesus changed everything. My heart was very impressed. I told God, "I want to serve You."

I decided to ask for God's direction, so I prayed for two years. One day, I cried out to God in prayer, "What is Your plan for my life?"

Sometimes we look for many answers in our life, but if we wait on the Lord, He will lead us and provide for our needs in His time. He will show us a way when sometimes we do not see anything. I can tell you how wonderful our God is!

At the time, I was doing missionary work. During my devotional, I found an answer in the Bible. I read the story in Luke 5:1–10 about when Jesus called His disciples. I felt that this is my opportunity to follow Jesus with all my life. I decided to study theology and serve God as a missionary.

After four years, I graduated as a chemical engineer. I studied theology from 2014 to 2018 at the Peruvian Adventist University. Now I am studying for a master's degree in geology because I want to do geochemistry research. At the same time, I want to preach about the message of God's creation and spread the three angels' messages (Revelation 14:6–12).

Dear friend, I am sure God has a special plan for you! He will reveal it to you as you pray, study the Bible, and ask Him for direction.

"Many, Lord my God, are the wonders you have done" (Psalm 40:5, NIV).

Depend on God with all your heart!

Raquel Bendita Laric

September 5

Always Enough

There was always enough flour and olive oil left in the containers, just as the Lord *had promised through Elijah.*
—1 Kings 17:16, NLT

Zarephath means "smelting furnace," and surely the widow of Zarephath feels the heat of the drought is sweltering, smelting hot. Even the severe testing of her situation may seem like her own burning, fiery furnace. Perhaps she is expected to offer her only son as a sacrifice to Baal to survive the famine. Possibly she sees the futility of worshiping Baal, the harvest/storm god who doesn't provide a harvest and doesn't send a storm. Maybe she is secretly praying, "If there is a true God who can hear my cries, please work a miracle here."

Elijah arrives near the gate and asks for a cup of water. A traveler can expect that much, but then he asks for more. Does Elijah feel he is entitled to a meal? Is he selfish to demand all she has? No, the widow needs a miracle, and he knows that God is ready for action.

Elijah foreshadows Jesus. This is Elijah's divine appointment with a woman at the well. Traveling from Judaea, he arrives in a foreign country to answer her cry for the Bread of Life to satisfy her hunger. She has no husband, but God wants to husband her.

When Elijah asks for bread, the widow must respond. She cannot take time to ponder her decision. She must choose instantly between self-preservation and self-denial. She is at the end of her resources, and she has no way to replenish them. Is it foolish to meet the needs of this stranger while depriving her only son of his last supper?

Perhaps one meager flatbread will not make a difference in the starvation schedule, but being asked to make the last loaf for Elijah is the greatest test of her lifetime.

The woman chooses to act in self-denial and with compassion and generosity. Ironically, her choice against self-preservation allows God to preserve her and her entire household and to act toward her with compassion and generosity far beyond her comprehension.

Trusting in the promise that her jar will never run dry and her bin will be replenished makes the difference between serving her life's last meal and her meal lasting a lifetime.

When we give our all to Jesus, we allow Him to give His all to us throughout eternity. The miracle is how far beyond comprehension His compassion, generosity, and riches extend.

Rebecca Turner

September 6

Talents

Then Peter said, "Silver or gold I do not have, but what I do have I give you. In the name of Jesus Christ of Nazareth, walk."
—Acts 3:6, NIV

Sometimes in life, we have low self-esteem. We believe that we are insignificant and have no value, that we have nothing to offer. But let's look at Peter's example.

Peter was a simple man, a fisherman, but in the company of Jesus, he became a man full of talents given to him by the Holy Spirit.

Like Peter, we can each have all the talents and gifts that God can give us through His Spirit. We should not feel inferior even if we have less money or less education or less success than other people. The Lord expects us to be brave and use those gifts to help others. That, in turn, will fill us with joy, and we will develop more talents.

Talents are given by God according to His will. We all have at least one, so we shouldn't feel inferior to others because, like Peter, we can be humble but be filled with the Holy Spirit and do great things.

"And [Christ] Himself gave some to be apostles, some prophets, some evangelists, and some pastors and teachers, for the equipping of the saints for the work of ministry, for the edifying of the body of Christ, till we all come to the unity of the faith and of the knowledge of the Son of God" (Ephesians 4:11–13, NKJV).

Spend time with God, and He will fill you with His Holy Spirit.

Maite Lavado

September 7

The Sabbath Test

Commit thy way unto the LORD; trust also in him; and he shall bring it to pass.
—Psalm 37:5, KJV

When I was a teenager, God became a friend to me who would never betray or deceive, unlike earthly friends. I saw God's hand in my life when I had to choose between my future education and faith. In eleventh grade, I needed to take exams to get a certificate. I prayed throughout the year that the exams would not be set on Saturday. However, I learned that all exams would be on Saturday. I was very upset but decided to trust God. I tried to study well so that the teachers would allow me to take the exam on another day.

Once in a geometry lesson, a teacher called me to the blackboard and asked me to do a sum. After I had done the sum, she told me, "You have done everything right, and I'll give you the best mark. But you must understand that you are ruining your future. You won't be able to find a job where you won't have to work on Saturdays. You will not be able to study at the university; you will simply fail all the exams." Everyone around me thought that I was going to make the wrong choice.

Sometimes I thought, *What if my teachers and classmates are right? What if I don't achieve anything in life?* All my relatives are believers, but even they told me that there would be nothing wrong if I took the exam on Saturday. I prayed a lot and decided that I would be faithful to God to the end and trust Him to take care of me and my future.

On the Saturday of the exam, I went to church and tried to focus on the service. After worship, the headmistress of our school called my father. After a short conversation, my father said, "Masha, you can pass the exams on other days. They will try to make sure that the authorities of our city won't know about this." Hearing this, I almost burst into tears of joy. God heard my prayers! I was able to pass all the exams and received a certificate.

I am grateful to God for all those difficulties because I learned to trust Him. I was also able to testify to the whole school and teachers about God. It may be easier to live in the world, where you do not need to defend your principles, but in fact, God wants us to be salt and light, even if other people do not understand you and see no point in your commitments.

Khametova Mariia Sergeevna

The Best Day

Let us rejoice and be glad
and give him glory!
For the wedding of the Lamb has come,
and his bride has made herself ready.
—Revelation 19:7, NIV

Teachers never experience a dull moment in the classroom. When I was a first-grade teacher, one of my adorable students declared, "Today is the best day of my life!"

She proclaimed this because she was allowed to eat lunch with her classmates in my classroom. To her, this simple treat was something she'd remember for the rest of her life. One of my colleagues was helping me facilitate this lunch in the classroom. Later, we spoke about my student.

I told my colleague that my student doesn't know it yet, but she's going to say that again with even more meaning as she grows up and experiences life events that will feel like "the best day," such as when she falls in love with a wonderful man, he proposes, and her wedding day arrives!

As this sweet memory returned to my mind years later, God inspired me with a spiritual lesson: the best day for humankind is the day when Jesus will return to earth to take His faithful followers home to heaven. The Bible describes this grand event as a bridegroom coming to meet his bride (Matthew 25:6).

For me, this will truly be *the* best day of *my* life! Our trials on earth will be over, and we will enjoy being forever in the presence of God! We will continue growing into all God intended us to be. Never will we suffer or sorrow again.

Satan doesn't want us to focus on heaven and all that awaits those who faithfully follow Jesus Christ. He works hard to persuade us to build our dreams here on earth. He wants us to be so focused on working hard to make our earthly dreams come true that we forget about the bigger picture.

That bigger picture is that God has prepared a place for us and He's coming back to take us home! Let us look forward to that "best day" and live for it!

Alexis A. Goring

September 9

Whose Hand Are You Holding?

I have set the L*ORD* *continually before me;*
Because He is at my right hand, I will not be shaken.
—Psalm 16:8, NASB

Not long after falling asleep, I awoke with a start from a dream. In my dream, I saw two hands: my husband's and mine, but in between, there appeared another hand. It was then that I woke up abruptly. Whose hand was that? Did this dream have any significance? I don't know. It kept me awake for a while, and then I went back to sleep.

The Bible uses the word *hand* fifty-six times. The hand often represents power, authority, and self-confidence, particularly the right hand. In one place, the right hand is spoken of as being used to restore life. Among many other things, it speaks of the hand giving support, the laying on of hands for healing and blessing, hands smitten together in extreme anger, and hands raised in thanksgiving. Jesus often put His hands on the sick when He healed them. The Lord's right hand is said to be exalted, full of righteousness, majestic in power, and valiant.

One of my favorite verses in the Bible is, "See, I have inscribed you on the palms of My hands" (Isaiah 49:16, NKJV). That means Jesus knows each one of our names—yours and mine—and loves us so much He has engraved our names as a permanent record where He can see them any time He chooses.

Hands are such a vital part of much that we do. If we were to lose one of our limbs, it seems to me that the hand, particularly the dominant one, would be the hardest to do without. Think of no longer being able to do the many things we do with our hands that are necessary, such as eating, dressing, grooming, cleaning, and many other things, not to mention the things we do for pleasure: playing games, cuddling a baby, or touching a loved one.

Jesus invites us to put our hand in His and do what He would have us do to bring joy to our lives. We are told we will be recompensed for the work of our hands.

Whose hand are you holding? Are you holding the hand of Jesus so He can lead you and recompense you with a home in His company throughout eternity?

Marian Hart-Gay

Reverberating or Wiggling?

And a little child shall lead them.
—Isaiah 11:6, KJV

Grandparents' Day in the United States is celebrated annually in September, and I looked forward to celebrating with my four-year-old granddaughter's preschool class.

As my granddaughter and I enjoyed the festivities of her class, set against a backdrop of sparkles, bows, and tulle fabric, we laughed, talked, took photographs, and met her teachers and friends. The grandparents sat at the breakfast tables decorated with their individual grandchild's photograph. The preschoolers danced and pranced, climbed on their grandparents' laps, and had snotty noses, and their faces were filled with a conglomeration of food that had to be cleaned by the gentle, loving hands of the grandparents. In an extraordinary manner, the grandparents were entertained with an exhilarating grandparent-grandchild dance and a show-and-tell session.

It was now time for grandma to leave her granddaughter. I told her I was leaving. "I can go home," she replied. So I inquired of her teachers. They stated it was fine to take my grandchild after following the school's sign-out protocol. I checked with my daughter, who also stated it was fine to take her to their home.

The journey in my car to her home was quite hilarious. My 2004 car was having trouble maintaining a smooth ride. Several days before, I made numerous telephone calls to my service advisor, informing him that my car was vibrating, oscillating, reverberating, palpitating, dancing, and acting up. He gave me a date in October 2019 to bring in the car for its diagnosis. During our ride, my granddaughter asked, "Grandma, why is your car wiggling?"

I tried to give her an explanation. Immediately, I called back the service advisor for my car. I relayed the conversation between my four-year-old Kelcee and me about the troubled car. He repeated, "Wiggle! Wiggle! Bring in the car right away."

Are we like little children: true, honest, matter-of-fact? Can we become childlike believers in our everyday ride with Christ? Do we listen to our Savior and practice to have an attitude of forgiveness and humility to others and ourselves? Let us be once more like little children, where love is boundless and where our Omnipotent Father can lead us.

Pauline A. Dwyer-Kerr

September 11

My Very Present Help

God is our refuge and strength,
a very present help in trouble.
Therefore will not we fear, though the earth be removed,
and though the mountains be carried into the midst of the sea.
—Psalm 46:1, 2, KJV

I was returning to New York from Florida in the United States, where I had gone to visit my sister. My itinerary included a layover at Hartfield-Jackson Airport in Atlanta, Georgia. There, I boarded a much smaller plane for the next part of my journey. Although I have always been fascinated with aerodynamics, flying has always been challenging for me.

Approximately halfway through the Atlanta to New York flight, the captain turned on the seat belt sign and announced that the weather had changed. He told us that we would encounter some degree of turbulence. My alarm bells started to ring!

My eyes were glued to the window where the entire view had changed to thick white clouds with zero visibility. It felt as if the plane was at a standstill!

The captain then announced that a storm had developed in and around the New York area, resulting in unfavorable weather conditions. Our scheduled landing at John F. Kennedy Airport, New York, had to be diverted to Newark Airport, New Jersey. By this time, we were in a holding pattern. I knew that we were in trouble. My alarm bells pealed loudly!

The captain tried unsuccessfully to land. Nevertheless, he calmly reassured us that as soon as we were cleared to land again, we would do so. My fear of flying loomed largely before me. I had two choices—panic or pray. I chose to pray. The silence throughout the cabin was palpable. Some people were praying. Others looked worried. I begged God for mercy.

After further failed attempts at landing, we finally broke through those thick, dense clouds and, shortly thereafter, touched down on solid ground! Words cannot adequately explain the euphoria I felt when I heard the sound of wheels connecting with ground! God heard my plea and extended mercy! I am alive to tell the tale and glorify our mighty God!

Whenever we are faced with a crisis and fear grips us, we must remember that God is our refuge and strength. He is, most assuredly, our very present help in trouble.

Winsome Joy Grant

The Filing Cabinet

And we know that all things work together for good to them that love God, to them who are the called according to his purpose.
—Romans 8:28, KJV

In 2020, the entire world was plagued with the COVID-19 virus, which caused many deaths and loss of jobs. As a result of this situation, my position was terminated, and I had the option to retire. I was very glad to retire, and I knew it was God's leading.

No longer heading to work each day, I wanted to set up my home office and have everything organized, especially my files. One day, I was shopping online to find a steel two-drawer filing cabinet with wheels and was glad to find one on sale. I immediately placed the order. I was glad to receive a prompt email confirmation from the company, indicating that the filing cabinet would be shipped in three days.

After three days, I received another email from the company stating that the shipment would be delayed another two days. I waited patiently, and after ten days, I tried to call customer service to find out what was causing the delay. To my frustration, I was not able to speak to anyone by phone or get a response by email. Each time I wrote an email, I got a standard response saying they would get back to me in three business days; yet no one ever responded. I finally lost my patience and wrote a serious email, asking them to cancel the order and refund my money. Only after that did I receive a response from someone, who did refund my money. I was relieved and thanked God for helping me get my refund.

While still hoping to get a filing cabinet, I went down to my basement one day, and I suddenly noticed a steel cabinet with wheels in the corner of the room, which I had not noticed for years. When I pulled it out, it was the perfect filing cabinet for my need! I was thrilled and thanked God for delaying the shipment, grateful that I did not have to spend money unnecessarily.

This experience encouraged my faith and reminded me that no matter what happens in our lives, God always works it out for our good. Always put your trust in our loving God, for He loves you and will take care of all your needs.

Stella Thomas

September 13

Free From Entanglements

"So if the Son sets you free, you will be free indeed."
—John 8:36, ESV

I was walking in the park one morning when I noticed a stag with its antlers tangled in a branch. I watched from a safe distance to see whether it would untangle itself. Sure enough, the deer untangled itself, but seconds later, it went back to the same position—tangled up in the branch. There it was, butting its head around, trying to free itself. It freed itself again but went back to do the same thing.

I stood shaking my head. Why is this deer not realizing when it's free? I approached another walker nearby and pointed out the situation. He advised that we leave the deer alone because visitors are not allowed to go near them; the stag would eventually figure out what to do. I kept watching for a few minutes, encouraging the stag, "Go, go, you're free." After what looked like several painful entanglements, the stag finally walked away free. "Yeah!" I cheered, so happy that it was free to wander the rest of the park.

This is how God looks at us, pleading for us to walk free in the path that He has made plain for us. God hurts when He sees us making the same mistakes again and again. He patiently waits for us, ready to intervene and cheering us on when we do the right thing.

Entanglement became a meme word of 2020 when a famous actor's wife used this word to describe her extramarital affair. Many laughed at her choice of words, including me, but when I reflect, I realize I have some entanglements of my own. There are some things that I need to walk away from, and even when I do, I sometimes find myself in the same situation again. Other times, we may not even realize that we are entangled, and even worse, we may not see the way out.

Let's pray that the Holy Spirit enlightens us to see our condition, and if we are entangled, pray for the courage and strength to walk away from entanglements that are not good for us. God promises us that we can find freedom through Jesus Christ. When we are free, we can walk in that freedom, truly accepting and believing it is ours. I remember a song about being wrapped up and tangled up with Jesus—that's the only entanglement I want.

Kimasha P. Williams

In Hot Water

You prepare a table before me in the presence of my enemies;
You anoint my head with oil;
My cup runs over.
—Psalm 23:5, NKJV

I had been planning a restful overnight away with my husband. Instead, several unplanned appointments drained me dangerously close to empty. He, too, showed signs of running his energy down to a vapor.

I woke, prayed about the conflict in the coming workweek, and hoped we could glean a few restorative hours in the day. After steaming a bit of frustration, I berated myself over such a stupid prayer. How could one day possibly undo the entire week and the stress of the previous hours? It was too much to ask of God and certainly too trivial.

An exhaustive internet search rendered a couple of romantic and appealing plans that quickly evaporated as I discovered each one was already full. Maybe we should just stay home after all and clean the house? No, we had not had a day together since he returned from school.

We packed our things into the car and began driving, based on a hunch that there surely must be a hot spring in the mountains somewhere. The first discovery was a lukewarm pool. My husband suggested we settle for what was before us since any place worth having would probably be taken before the end of the day. Something didn't feel right, though, and I insisted we keep looking. We hiked along the river, seeking a warmer hot spring.

We found one that looked promising and submerged ourselves as another couple arrived close on our heels. I silently boiled like a kettle ready to whistle when they joined us, mourning the alone time that had been my last hope of sorting out the questions bubbling inside.

From the first moments of testing the conversational waters till we surfaced over three hours later, the words of life from our companions bubbled into springs of hope, purpose, and inspiration that poured over my heart. The realization of this divine appointment enveloped us in depths of grace. Fear drained away.

Praise God for failed plans, emptiness, the shadowlands. He is the Water of Life that restores the soul. He will surely cause your cup to overflow in the presence of all.

Wendy Williams

September 15

Deal Gently

He can deal gently with the ignorant and wayward,
since he himself is beset with weakness.
—Hebrews 5:2, RSV

What would cause a teen who was only nineteen years old to grab a knife, present himself to his mother, and say, "Kill me!"

What caused that same young man to turn to drugs and alcohol? Broken home, jobless market, lack of ambitious friends—all contributed to pulling him into a deep, dark chasm. He was a leader in his school—but now? Why?

He had been involved in church and youth activities but, alas, had fallen by the way!

"Many, many have fainted and become discouraged in the great struggle of life, when one word of kindly cheer would have strengthened them to overcome."*

"I am inviting you to church this Sabbath," I said to this young man.

"I am not the kind who goes every week, but I go the Sabbath of my birthday to give thanks, and my birthday is next week," he replied.

"OK, next week then!" I responded.

True to his word, he was in church that week, sitting beside his mother in the congregation.

I watched the circle that surrounded him after church—old, young, and middle-aged—all were clamoring for his attention to let this young man know that they missed him and were glad to see him back. I also welcomed him and encouraged him to keep on attending. "Attending church will give you courage for all you face each day," I shared.

"The angels of heaven look upon the distress of God's family upon the earth, and they are prepared to co-operate with men in relieving oppression and suffering."†

Let us heed the exhortation found in Hebrews 5:2 and "deal gently with the ignorant and wayward, since [we ourselves are] beset with weakness."

Hyacinth V. Caleb

* Ellen G. White, *The Desire of Ages* (Nampa, ID: Pacific Press®, 2005), 504.
† White, 500.

A Flexible Christian

My son, give me your heart,
And let your eyes observe my ways.
—Proverbs 23:26, NKJV

I have discovered four different exercise routines online: stretching, weight exercises for the arms, a dance-cardio workout, and a happy walk. Doing all of these routines takes close to an hour to complete. I do not like some of the yoga and arm exercises, but I do them anyway because my body needs those muscles to stay strong. One example is push-ups. They are hard, and I break into a sweat every time I do them, but I can do fifteen regular push-ups then drop to my knees to do another fifteen. My body does not want to do these, but as I push through, they become easier.

I'm thankful that at the age of sixty-one, I can move easily and can do the same things I did when I was half this age. At an American Indian reservation, it was explained that the boys learn the Hoop Dance. The reason is they will be happier people if they are flexible. Flexible—can that be related spiritually? Can we be happier Christians by being flexible?

I envision a flexible Christian as loving, smiling, and thoughtful of others. A flexible Christian thinks positively and upholds God's Word. In the Bible, Jesus met a lot of inflexible people—people who had hard hearts and wouldn't give up their ideas to learn what true worship is. The Bible says God wants to give us a heart of flesh—a heart that can be molded and shaped (flexible).

Maybe physically, we want to say no to certain exercises or just skip them altogether because they are not easy or convenient, but over time, the result will be less flexibility. Likewise, spiritually, if we say no to God's Holy Spirit by neglecting to read the Bible, pray, or follow His commandments, our souls will become hard and rigid.

In the exercise videos, the instructors say things to encourage their viewers: "Great job, everyone," "You can do it," "Stay accountable," and "Fifteen minutes is all it takes." God also encourages us by promising us eternal life in heaven, where we will run like a deer.

My prayer is that we each catch this vision so that God can really live inside our yielded hearts. Let's stay flexible for Him!

Rosemarie Clardy

Get Ready, Get Set, Go

"So you also must be ready, because the Son of Man will come at an hour when you do not expect him."
—Matthew 24:44, NIV

I am going through each room of the house and grabbing items we might need and setting them at the entrance to that room. Then if we go to the next level (Get Set), we will put those items in the truck. And if we get to the last level (Go), we are ready to leave," my husband Ron said to me on the phone. I was at my mom's house, asking her to pack some items in case she also needed to leave.

It seemed surreal to me. *Is this really happening?* I thought. It was September, and a few days earlier, some fires had started miles from our house. We could see the ominous tall plumes of smoke. A few days later, smoke totally engulfed us and turned the air an eerie, ominous yellow that was hazardous to health. Meanwhile, the fire spread and destroyed towns and vegetation as it moved closer and closer to us. At work, I found a room away from the smoke and stepped inside to inhale deep breaths of normal, clear air for a while before going back to my office with the smoky air that had seeped in the windows. Never do I want to take fresh air for granted again. The destroyed cities close to us barely had any time between the levels: Get Ready, Get Set, Go. The fire came too quickly, and they were suddenly in the Go level and had to leave without possessions. Many lost homes. We never moved from the Get Ready level to the next level. But we were ready.

This situation was a great example of how I should likewise be in ready mode for Jesus' coming. He, too, is coming unexpectedly. Jesus said, "The Son of Man will come at an hour when you do not expect him" (Matthew 24:44, NIV). Jesus spoke those words to His disciples rather like a personal warning—be set for immediate evacuation. John 14:1–3 counsels us not to be troubled because Jesus will return for us. Thankfully, I won't have to have bags packed from our various rooms. Jesus already has what I will need. Let's be in ready mode for when we hear similar words from Jesus: "Let's go!"

"But our citizenship is in heaven. And we eagerly await a Savior from there, the Lord Jesus Christ" (Philippians 3:20, NIV).

Diane Pestes

Whoa!

Trust in the L*ORD* *with all thine heart;*
and lean not unto thine own understanding.
In all thy ways acknowledge him,
and he shall direct thy paths.
—Proverbs 3:5, 6, KJV

I hadn't been horseback riding in a long time, but my employer recognized how challenging teaching had been during the pandemic and sent my colleagues and me away to camp for rest and rejuvenation and to enjoy the great outdoors! After watching the instructional video, we paired up with our horses, and off we went. My horse's name was Mr. Dusty, and within a few minutes, he began giving me hints that my ride would not be easygoing. He repeatedly veered off the trail, stopped, and refused to move with the group, and a couple of times, he suddenly decided to make a U-turn and face the stables.

I quickly realized that horses, like my students, have personalities. Some are very calm and obedient; they follow directions very well. Others need constant redirection, correction, and gentle guidance, just as I had to constantly pull Mr. Dusty's reins to guide him back onto the trail. At times, I wondered why my daughter and most riders in our group had no problems whatsoever. As a matter of fact, at the end of the ride, my daughter didn't even remember her horse's name because she didn't have to keep calling it!

At one point, Mr. Dusty reared up suddenly, and I thought I was going to fall off for sure. The wrangler commended me for holding on and handling him. I was fully aware that he was a tall, robust, majestic animal who could easily throw me off his back with minimal effort. The wrangler explained that Mr. Dusty had some "challenges" and apologized for the antics. I assured her that I was OK with Mr. Dusty. I told her I had handled children with "challenges" throughout my career. In addition to that, I had a child with special needs.

I am convinced that as we lined up in the stable before the ride, the wranglers sized us up and decided which horse best suited each of us. God knows what's best too. Yes, some children present extra unexpected challenges, but we must remember that He knows what's best for us and what we need.

Michelle Vanessa O'Reilly

September 19

Is Anything Too Small for God?

Hear my prayer, O LORD,
And let my cry come to You.
Do not hide Your face from me in the day of my trouble;
Incline Your ear to me;
In the day that I call, answer me speedily.
—Psalm 102:1, 2, NKJV

It had been a busy week with the regular things I do. But this week, I needed to change the program and classroom for the children's class I teach at church. With the coming of fall, I began redecorating the room. I put a beautiful fall tree in the front of the room along with a small hay bale, a stump with an owl on it, squirrels in the trees and on the ground, pumpkins in the field, and apples on a tree and in a basket.

As I looked over the songs, I realized I needed the little tractors that would be "gathering" the hay! I looked and found the baskets I had used before but did not find the tractors. I prayed and asked God to help me locate them. Again, I went to the closet in the classroom and noticed a container filled with empty plastic bags. I was impressed to look for them there. When I put my hand down to the bottom of the container, there were the tractors!

On my own, I would not have thought they would be under a stash of plastic bags, but God knew! He blessed me by helping me find them. Then He blessed the children in my class as they used them. I am blessed when I share about the miracle God did for us!

Isn't this so like God? He is so kind and helpful to His children! It excites me to realize how a request for something so small and insignificant to God still pleased Him, resulting in an answer to my cry for help! "God sees the little sparrow fall; it meets His tender view. If God so loved the little birds, I know He loves me too."*

Really, there isn't anything too small for God to care about! He is interested in our lives and willing to help us in the little things! This gives me courage as I walk through life day by day, knowing He will take care of the big things in my life, too, as I take them to Him in prayer!

Sharon Follett

* Maria Straub, "God Sees the Little Sparrow Fall," public domain.

A Wise Decision

I will praise thee; for I am fearfully and wonderfully made.
—Psalm 139:14, KJV

A short time ago, I watched a documentary on Thalidomide, a drug used to cure morning sickness in the early 1960s. The results of that drug have been disastrous for the babies of mothers who used it. These children were born with malfunctioning or missing arms or legs. The courage with which they face each day is amazing. What troubles me most is that the drug is still produced and used in many third-world countries. Thalidomide babies are still being born.

I shudder every time I hear the word. I could have been one of those mothers. In 1961, I was desperately sick every day, not just in the morning but all day, every day.

My doctor assured me that it was a good drug and safe to use. He had been sold a bill of goods by the manufacturer. I prayed about the whole thing for several days. Then I decided that I would suffer through the next few months. I remember carrying a small pail everywhere I went. It was a good thing that I carried it.

When I had free time, I began to read my Bible. Through the stories of Eve, Hannah, Ruth, Miriam, and others, I learned to love and trust God's Word. Every time I was ready to give up, there was another Bible woman whose struggles made mine seem easier.

What mother could happily see the body of a son murdered by his brother as Eve did? What mother could easily give up her child to the care of a faithless priest as Hannah did? What young woman could happily give up her homeland to travel to the unknown as Ruth did when she went home to Naomi's world in Bethlehem? What big sister would hide in the bulrushes to guard a baby brother as Miriam did? And then be brave enough to show herself to the princess and offer a nurse to care for baby Moses? Their stories gave me the courage to persevere.

In May 1962, I held my sweet little Patti in my arms. As I checked her tiny fingers and toes, I praised God for the perfection that she was. God promises in Scripture that He knew everything about us before we were even born. That is a promise that I remember every time I look at her dear face and remember God's protection.

Patricia Cove

September 21

Everything Beautiful

He has made everything beautiful in its time.
—Ecclesiastes 3:11, NIV

Botanists know that shortening daylight time and falling night-time temperatures trigger biochemical reactions in deciduous trees and shrubs, including the shutting down of photosynthesis and reduction in the green pigment called chlorophyll. This allows other compounds, such as yellow flavanols, orange carotenoids, and red to purple anthocyanins, to become more prominent. Does all this sound a bit too complicated? You don't have to be a botanist, or a scientist at all, to appreciate the glorious autumn colors that these processes produce and to wonder at our amazing Creator God, who not only conceived this complex biochemistry but also made it beautiful!

People interested in botany also know that the principal purpose of flowers is reproduction—their colors and shapes facilitate pollination, seed growth, and seed dispersal. Their bright hues and sweet fragrances attract pollinators, such as certain insects and birds. But again, it is awe-inspiring that our Creator has not only made such intricate living organisms and the biological processes that sustain them but also made them beautiful. Flowers are a delight to our senses in all their incredible variety. And that's not all. Flowers speak to our emotions as well. Flowers often form an important element of special occasions, whether joyful celebrations or times of mourning, and serve as expressions of love and affection. Fittingly, they may also be used to enhance our worship experience.

The beauties of creation are indeed wonderful, but the true wonder is how much God cares for each one of us. Jesus used flowers to illustrate God's sustaining love. He gently chided His listeners, "If your heavenly Father takes the trouble to make even the common and short-lived wildflowers beautiful, how much more attention will He give to the needs of His children?" (see Matthew 6:28–31).

Despite this old world being marred by sin, there is still so much beauty to enjoy that I can't wait to see what God has in store for us when we reach our heavenly home, where His creativity will be perfectly displayed. I'm especially keen to see His marvelous tree—the tree of life—with its healing leaves. "Amen. Come, Lord Jesus" (Revelation 22:20, NIV).

Jennifer M. Baldwin

Sound an Alarm With the Trumpet

"Blow the trumpets in times of gladness, too, sounding them at your annual festivals and at the beginning of each month. And blow the trumpets over your burnt offerings and peace offerings. The trumpets will remind your God of his covenant with you. I am the LORD your God."
—Numbers 10:10, NLT

I was standing in a line at the hospital where I work, waiting to get my booster shot for the COVID-19 vaccine. I could hear all the chatter from other staff members who were waiting. Some were apprehensive about the side effects; others felt it would be no problem. So many different opinions as to what would happen to us. This was the first week the second round of vaccines was being given, so as you could imagine, many were afraid or anxious.

As I stood there, I prayed for peace and protection because I was apprehensive about getting this dose. Staff members were told to take our second dose on our day off in case we experienced any side effects. I have several allergies, which was an added stressor for me. I decided to take out my phone and read a Scripture promise to calm my thoughts. I tapped on a Bible devotional app and started reading. The thought for the day was on Numbers 10:10. After reading the passage, I heard God's assurance that He is near when we hear a trumpet.

Soon after my reading, the chaplain from my unit passed by and said, "I got my second vaccine yesterday, and all I have is a sore arm, so don't worry, you all will be fine." Little did he know, his words were "the trumpet sound of the Lord" that encouraged me. Immediately, all my fears were gone. I felt at peace as I boldly approached the nurse to get my injection. It was an assurance of the Lord answering my prayer that all would be well.

Remember that God is near, and we can use our voices as trumpets when we pray to call on Him. "His ears are open to their prayers" (1 Peter 3:12, NLT).

Judie Lewis

September 23

Don't Ignore the Signs

"So you also, when you see all these things, know that it is near—at the doors!"
—Matthew 24:33, NKJV

On a recent trip from Tennessee to our home in New Hampshire, USA, I abandoned my post as my husband's navigator to take a short nap. During this time, my husband thought he saw a sign indicating a delay up ahead, but he wasn't sure. When he noticed a lot of traffic on an overpass, he assumed that the delay was for that road instead of the interstate that we were on. However, about a mile later, we came to a grinding halt and were stuck for five hours because of a tractor-trailer accident. We realized too late that the sign was meant for us.

That immediately brought to my mind another time that I missed some signs. I was at home working on some notes for my next lecture when the birthing center at my local hospital called, saying that a woman in labor needed a doula.

I immediately left for the hospital, which is just twelve minutes away. When I arrived, the circumstances had changed dramatically, and my services were needed for only about fifteen minutes. I was back home within forty-five minutes. As I drove up my driveway, I noticed a vehicle parked on the side of the road, which I found unusual, but no red flags were raised.

Upon entering my garage, I noticed the lights were on. *Hmm, that's odd.* I thought I had turned those off. I climbed the stairs from my basement into the house and resumed work on my lecture notes again. But my laptop was lying on the floor—*I didn't put that there. Hmm. Oh well, I must have.* I then remembered that I had a load of laundry in the dryer that needed to be folded. As I walked to the laundry room, I noticed that my back door was unlocked. *Hmm. Did I forget to lock that when I waved goodbye to my husband that morning? That's not like me.*

I had gathered my laundry and was heading upstairs to fold it when my husband called. We were chatting as I entered my bedroom and screamed! My whole bedroom was torn apart. We had been burglarized!

How many signs had I ignored or rationalized away? Am I guilty of that in my spiritual walk as well? *Lord, You have given us so many signs of Your soon return. Help us to pay attention, not to rationalize away or ignore signs. Help us to be watchful as we wait.*

Diane McLean Gaspard

Noah's and Ours

"Just as it was in the days of Noah, so too it will be in the days of the Son of Man. They were eating and drinking, and marrying and being given in marriage, until the day Noah entered the ark, and the flood came and destroyed all of them."
—Luke 17:26, 27, NRSV

Our world today is truly in trouble, just as it was in the time of Noah, a time when people were grossly intemperate in nutrition and deportment. It was a time when the marriage institution was highly desecrated; it was a time of great pomp and pride as people showed ingratitude to God, their Creator and Sustainer, and many others engaged in human-debasing attitudes. Above all, it was a time when creatures bestowed with gifts and talents abused such privileges and man trampled upon the character and standard of God's judgment.

Ellen White elaborates and clarifies the current state of our world through this statement:

> That which is lawful in itself is carried to excess. Appetite is indulged without restraint. . . . Multitudes feel under no moral obligation to curb their sensual desires, and they become the slaves of lust. Men are living for the pleasures of sense; for this world and this life alone. . . . The picture which Inspiration has given of the antediluvian world represents too truly the condition to which modern society is fast hastening. . . .
>
> As the time of their probation was closing, the antediluvians gave themselves up to exciting amusements and festivities. Those who possessed influence and power were bent on keeping the minds of the people engrossed with mirth and pleasure, lest any should be impressed by the last solemn warning.*

As Christ's coming draws nearer and while the time of probation lasts, God charges us to warn the world that the people might be led to repentance, prepare for that great event, and thus escape the threatened destruction.

I have always prayed and longed for my family to always live in harmony with God's precepts. God is willing to redeem and restore families as they hearken to this call of repentance from their sins. All who will put away their sins by repentance toward God and faith in Christ are offered pardon.

Dear merciful God, help us live for you and in harmony with your divine precepts.

Joy Bakaba Igwe

* Ellen G. White, *Patriarchs and Prophets* (Nampa, ID: Pacific Press®, 2005), 101–103.

September 25

Living in Babylon With God

Be strong and of a good courage, fear not, nor be afraid of them: for the Lord *thy God, he it is that doth go with thee; he will not fail thee, nor forsake thee.*
—Deuteronomy 31:6, KJV

We are living amid dangerous, climactic changes. Turbulence threatens livelihoods. Health and homes are in jeopardy. Pink slips come in the mail. Tensions multiply, and people are scattered for fear. Poverty, disease, famine, and drought exist in many places. Nothing is the same anymore. We look for a secure haven but cannot find it. There's no refuge. *Is this it, Lord? How am I going to cope amid all these trials?* Then "Why me?" comes to mind. *I've been serving You all my life, faithfully, and now I am being robbed of everything. How am I to live and take care of my family? Where are You, my God?*

But God is right there, going through the pain and sorrow with me. When I permit my situations to dictate my responses, I fail to remember that when all else perishes, I still have my God. His words are life. David said, "If I make my bed in hell, behold, thou art there" (Psalm 139:8, KJV). In the midst of trial, David could still praise God. So did Job, despite his losses. And Esther, despite her danger. Joseph eventually saw God turn his disappointments into blessings. Daniel praised God. Even though Daniel was living in Babylon, God was with him. Daniel could praise God in the lions' den. God was with His Son, Jesus, when He went through His storms on this earth, and Jesus always gave glory to the Father. Since God is also with us, we can praise Him too. When we're in doubt, Jesus says, "Cast all your cares on Me" (see 1 Peter 5:7). When your faith is shaky, He says, "Trust Me; lean on Me" (see Proverbs 3:5, 6). When you feel that you cannot go on, He says, "My grace is sufficient for you" (see 2 Corinthians 12:9).

Know this, my sister: you may experience unfathomable losses in life, but you can still praise God in "Babylon." It may not be easy, but you're not alone. Jesus is with you.

I do not know your pain, but I am here to encourage you that Jesus will see you through your storms. Jesus said, "My Father, which gave them me, is greater than all; and no man is able to pluck them out of my Father's hand" (John 10:29, KJV). How powerful is that scripture! If you always abide in Christ, nothing can shake you. Someday soon, the storms of this life will end, but until then, you can live in Babylon—with God.

Corletta Aretha Barbar

God Is in His Silence

Now Jesus loved Martha, and her sister, and Lazarus.
—John 11:5, KJV

As believers, we've all been there—finding ourselves in a crisis, praying about it, and expecting God to come through, but nothing happens. We have quoted every promise we know about the situation, and in return, we sense God's silence. I know. I have been there too many times to count, and the silence can be difficult, frustrating even. But here's what I always learn through the silence: God is not obligated to answer all my prayers. He doesn't have to inform me or let me know anything. Why? Because He is God! He understands what I am going through and speaks louder in His silence. Too often, we are so focused on the crisis at hand that we forget to listen to what God is saying in and through what appears to be His silence.

My sisters, I want to encourage you to stop and listen to what God is saying. Recognize that His silence can be intimate. The Gospel of John tells a story about Jesus' friends Lazarus, Mary, and Martha. When Jesus found out that Lazarus was ill, rather than rush to Lazarus' house to heal him, He stayed where He was for two more days (John 11:6). And before Jesus arrived in Bethany, Lazarus died. To Lazarus's sisters, Mary and Martha, Jesus' silence could have been interpreted as neglect—that Jesus did not care about or want to help them. This mirrors many of the emotions we feel when God does not immediately answer our cries for help. But in Jesus' silence, we, along with Mary and Martha, are drawn into a new closeness to God and understanding of His power.

Although God may seem silent regarding a specific request or petition, remember that He is constantly communicating with us. In fact, it is possible that you already have an answer from God. The Bible is full of specific answers about what is right and wrong as well as information about God's character and His intentions for us as His children and His followers. So don't forget to dig into God's Word—His written communication to us—to find out what He has to say about the problems you are facing or the questions you are asking. As you read the Bible, ask God to speak to you through the Holy Spirit, who lives inside of you. Just because God seems silent doesn't mean you should doubt Him or stop praying. His silence may be a call for deeper intimacy. Trust that God is in control, and look for what He is doing behind the scenes.

Beverley Martin

September 27

Without Understanding

My son, do not forget my law,
But let your heart keep my commands.
—Proverbs 3:1, NKJV

I had just completed vacuuming the house when my grandson, Doug, came inside to use the bathroom. When he decided to take the shortcut back to the sandbox by way of the dining room, I told him he could not use the dining room door because the carpet had just been vacuumed and I didn't want sand brought in. He would have to use the back door.

He looked up at me with his beautiful dark eyes and began to inform me with great respect and seriousness that he could not use that door. I replied that I was very sorry, but he must use the back door. Doug then put his hands on his tiny waist, and shaking his head back and forth, he repeated, "You don't understand, Grandma Dottie, I have to go out that door."

Again, I said, "Doug, I'm sorry, but you cannot use the dining room door to walk to and from the sandbox."

Doug climbed onto the kitchen stool, holding up four little fingers and speaking in his most convincing yet patronizing voice, he said, "I am four years old, and you are an old woman, almost a hundred! You just don't understand. I *need* to go out that door!" as he pointed toward the dining room.

Again, I repeated, "I'm sorry, Doug, you must use the back door." Without further comment, Doug shrugged his shoulders and jumped off the stool. His tiny feet raced to make up for lost time, so I thought, as he headed out the back door to the sandbox. I remember standing there in my kitchen wondering what that was all about. Years later, I learned that Doug was a little boy who had a need to be safe from the wasps flying around the back door.

Throughout God's Word, He repeats, emphasizes, and frequently asks us to remember. When we see this repetition and emphasis in the Bible, we need to pay close attention, for He is telling us something of great importance. Although He understands our reasons for not wanting to really listen or obey Him, God cannot change those requirements "written in stone," for they speak of His character and exist for the good of everyone, both now and throughout eternity.

Dottie Barnett

Gone but Not Forgotten

"Never will I leave you;
never will I forsake you."
—Hebrews 13:5, NIV

When I was a nurse in the United States Air Force, I had to go to another base for training. This training required me to be away from my family for one month. One weekend, when I came home to visit, my husband and my two sons decided to accompany me on my return so we could all spend the night together. We decided to drive two cars. My husband would have the older son in the car with him, and I would have the younger one, Michael.

For some unknown reason, we had forgotten to leave extra food and water for our dog before loading up in the car. Knowing this, Michael got out of my vehicle and proceeded toward the backyard to complete those chores. In the meantime, I saw my husband drive off.

Hmm, Michael must have gotten in my husband's car, I thought. I drove off behind my husband, not realizing that Michael was still in our backyard at home.

Twenty minutes down the freeway, I saw my husband's car. However, there was only one other person's head in his car—not two! At that instant, I realized that I had left my son at home!

Michael was only ten years old. I could barely even breathe when I envisioned him being home all alone. Quickly, I turned my vehicle around and sped toward home. My husband followed. I think I reached our house in ten minutes, much less time than it should have taken me to return.

Michael was sitting on the front porch crying. "Momma" he sobbed, "I was running behind the car, and you did not stop. I did not think you were coming back." I embraced him, trying to comfort my hurting child.

You know there is an enemy among us named Satan, and he wants us to believe that the heavenly Father has left us on this earth alone, never to return. That is not the truth. So today, I encourage you to believe that God loves us! His promise to us is, "I go to prepare a place for you, [and] I will come back" (John 14:3, NIV).

All heaven is waiting and preparing for the Son, Jesus Christ, to bring His children home!

Ann Hickman Smith

September 29

Lost and Found

"What do you think? If a man has a hundred sheep, and one of them goes astray, does he not leave the ninety-nine and go to the mountains to seek the one that is straying?"
—Matthew 18:12, NKJV

After my mother died, my father gave most of her things away to the college where he worked in Virginia. One day, I asked my father what happened to my mom's cedar chest. He replied that he gave it away to a college student. It had never occurred to him that his own family may have wanted it. Our niece wanted the cedar chest to remember her grandmother. But it was too late.

Many years later, I visited a friend in another city about one hour away and went to her church. After the service, she invited a young couple to join us for lunch. As we were talking, I realized she knew my parents from attending the college where my parents worked. As I continued to visit with her, I realized that my dad had given her the cedar chest. Later, her grandmother gave her a cedar chest. This young woman offered to give my mother's chest back to me. The cedar chest traveled all the way to Illinois from Virginia and back up to Michigan, where my niece lived. As you can imagine, I was thrilled to have found this treasure!

I like to think that God was smiling down on me when I found this chest. He loves us in a unique and special way. He cares about us in a very personalized fashion. He has given us our own personal guardian angel (see Psalm 91:11). Our angel guards and protects us every step of the way from unknown danger. God knows our wants and needs. He will give us whatever we need but not necessarily what we want because He knows what's best for us in our Christian growth. In Matthew 7:11, Jesus says, "If you then, being evil, know how to give good gifts to your children, how much more will your Father who is in heaven give good things to those who ask Him!" (NKJV).

God surprised me many years later after I had pretty much forgotten about my conversation with my dad regarding my mom's cedar chest. What have you lost? A prized possession, a job, a pet, a relationship, or a spouse? In 1 Peter 5:7, Jesus says to cast "all [our] care upon Him, for He cares for [us]" (NKJV). Jesus loves to surprise you with good gifts! Why not see what He has in store for you today?

Gyl Moon Bateman

September 30

Be Ready

Therefore thus says the Lord GOD:
"Behold, I lay in Zion a stone for a foundation,
A tried stone, a precious cornerstone, a sure foundation;
Whoever believes will not act hastily."
—Isaiah 28:16, NKJV

Some years ago, my close friend Shirley lived in a building where there was an apartment above her. When a new neighbor moved in overhead, renovation began in that upper-floor unit. One day, Shirley was walking toward her kitchen. Suddenly, she was amazed to see a concrete stone drop from the ceiling of her kitchen—just over by the windows. Fortunately, she was alone at home and not under the large stone when it fell through her ceiling.

This astounding event started her wondering, *How can a concrete stone just drop through a kitchen ceiling?* As she visualized the astounding scene she had witnessed, she was reminded about the second coming of Jesus Christ. Daniel saw "a stone" in a vision that he referred to as Christ's kingdom, and it was "cut out without hands" (Daniel 2:34, NKJV). The stone in the prophet's vision came in the context of worldly kingdoms (represented by various metals in a great image) that would rise and fall until Christ's kingdom was forever established. The stone represents Christ, the Son of man, coming "in His glory, and all the holy angels with Him. . . . He will sit on the throne of His glory" (Matthew 25:31, NKJV).

Shirley's experience led her to maintain a daily relationship with Christ, making things right with Him, abiding in Him (John 15:5), and accepting Him as her personal Savior, Redeemer, Intercessor, Advocate, and High Priest. She resolved to live a godly life within a saving relationship with Him, by God's grace, mercy, and compassionate love.

No matter what happens, my friend now knows Christ will surely come again (Revelation 22:20). More important, she knows she must be ready for Him every day—as must we.

Yan Siew Ghiang

October 1

A Laugh a Day

A merry heart doeth good like a medicine:
but a broken spirit drieth the bones.
—Proverbs 17:22, KJV

I love to laugh, and I smile widely when I think about meeting a baby for the first time and how everyone reacts when the baby smiles or laughs. Laughter is our most basic emotional response, but we aren't taught to laugh or even to smile; they're as natural to us as breathing.

What happens when we laugh? Laughter releases endorphins, neurotransmitters that have effects similar to those of such drugs as morphine, which are responsible for feelings of euphoria.

Laughter is more than just a sound—it's a whole-body experience. Within our immune system, laughter increases the amount of T cells, which are the body's natural defense against viruses, cancer cells, and other disease-causing cells. Laughter boosts the immune system, so it would be safe to assume that laughter makes us healthier.

Some researchers suggest that laughing one hundred times gives you the same workout as fifteen minutes on an exercise bike. Laughing works the cardiovascular system and lowers blood pressure, so it's like a cardio workout. It also increases memory and cognitive functioning.

Laughter is clinically proven to make you look younger. As many as fifteen facial muscles work together to help you smile and laugh. This increases the blood flow around the face, bringing the circulation into even the smallest of capillaries which, in turn, helps to make you look younger and healthier.

Be contagious. Laughing lifts not only our spirits but also the spirits of those around us. Happy people lift the spirit of those around them. Remember, a smile or laugh shared is a smile or laugh doubled.

What a difference we could make if we would share a laugh a day or give someone a reason to laugh. "Freely [we] have received, freely give" (Matthew 10:8, KJV). A laugh a day just might help keep the doctor away.

Sylvia A. Franklin

It Started With a Song

But I will sing of your strength,
in the morning I will sing of your love;
for you are my fortress,
my refuge in times of trouble.
—Psalm 59:16, NIV

It was Communion Sabbath, and I was feeling emotional. For many months, my husband had been having ill-health, and we were at a loss of what to do. The special music began, and while I was listening, the most amazing thing happened to me. The song faded, and I felt God reminding me of all the times Jesus was with my husband and how He carried him through so many health crises. Then I saw what I felt was the future and also a time in my past when I was in trouble and Jesus was with me and got me through it. Then I could hear the song again. It was truly a remarkable experience. I started crying, feeling the assurance of how God is with us no matter what problems we face.

Five nights later, I dreamed that my husband had gotten up from bed and fallen. In my dream, he said he forgot he didn't have a foot! The next morning when I awoke, my husband had a high fever, and his foot did not look well. After a visit to the emergency room, he was admitted to a major hospital. Four days later, he had surgery for a below-the-knee amputation on his right leg. The surgeon found a bone infection that was traveling up his leg. Within two days of the amputation and prescribed antibiotics, my husband looked like a new man! He had color to his cheeks, was smiling, and was out of pain. We praised God that he was getting well after so many months of being so sick.

We know God was preparing me for what was to come so that I could be my best for the man I love. God carried us through this experience that also included setbacks. Eight months after the amputation, my husband was able to walk again with the help of a prosthetic leg. The support and prayers we received during this time were such a source of strength and encouragement for both of us.

God's promises are real. I am so thankful for a loving God who not only prepares us for the hard things we face but also walks with us every moment of every day.

Jean Dozier Davey

October 3

Harvesting

Then saith he unto his disciples, The harvest truly is plenteous, but the labourers are few; pray ye therefore the Lord of the harvest, that he will send forth labourers into his harvest.
—Matthew 9:37, 38, KJV

Daily I traverse the highway from Saint Catherine to Kingston, Jamaica, and back for work. The vast fields of sugarcane stand regimentally as vehicles speed along the highway. It is refreshing to watch the harvesting process as the seasons pass from spring to summer, to autumn, and to winter, with the effects of the seasons generally the same except for when the rains come. There is great patience as we watch the tropical sunshine ripen the fruit, enhancing the texture to be savored by taste buds when the crystal grains reach supermarket shelves and, ultimately, kitchen tables.

The tractors clean and ready the fields, and soon, new suckers are planted. Daily sprays of water are seen wetting the fields—soon, streams flow into the surrounding river. The huge watering machinery will be taken away, and as the weeks pass, the plants mature, and extensive watering is no longer necessary. The fields become covered in a sea of dense green sugarcane plants, swaying in the wind, heavy, ripe, and ready for harvest. The morning dew is still fresh on the ground in the cool air as the day awaits the rising sun, when the harvesters converge on the fields, their frames small and insignificant among huge sugarcane plants. They are few, and the fields are plenty. When will their task be o'er?

The disciples had just completed a tour of duty and were no doubt tired, tested, and tried. Jesus called the Twelve and gave them power and authority over devils and to cure diseases; then, He sent them to preach the kingdom of God and to heal the sick (Luke 9:1–6). The work was great, so after these things, the Lord appointed another seventy-two and sent them also, two by two, into every city and place where He would come (Luke 10:1). The work of the harvest continues with us today. As with the sugarcane, hardly anyone remembers the process of planting and growing or the labor of the reapers as we enjoy the sweet crystals at our table in their various forms. Still, there is victory in spirit when the harvest is reaped, lives are changed, and others come to know Jesus Christ as their personal Savior. May we continue to give glory and honor to God through harvesting!

Elizabeth Ida Cain

More Than Wonderful!

And the peace of God, which passeth all understanding, shall keep your hearts and minds through Christ Jesus.
—Philippians 4:7, KJV

It was Friday afternoon, and I was running a few errands before the coming sunset. I was at my next-to-last stop—gassing up the car. The autumn air was somewhat brisk, and the sunshine delightful. With the tank full and the transaction complete, I started the car to make my final stop and head home. Surprisingly, the start of the car produced sounds totally unfamiliar to me: fluttering and misfiring never heard before. What should I do? I pulled out of the station, stopped in a nearby spot, and began to pray. It was reassuring to ask Christ to lead me through this predicament.

My next concern involved getting to church the next morning. I was scheduled to play the piano and needed to be at the church before class began. After thanking God for a forthcoming answer, I made calls seeking a ride. Some dear friends offered to pick me up and invited me to their home for a meal after church and a delightful Bible study group after our lunch fellowship. The day was lovely!

The following Monday morning, I took my car to a repair shop. A friend took me back home while the work was being done. Soon the shop receptionist called, saying they were finished. All they could do was change one spark plug. They advised me to go to the dealership for specialized attention. I followed through and prayed that God would let the cost be financially friendly. An appointment was scheduled for the next day.

Upon arrival at the dealership, I briefly described what had happened and told the serviceman the notices that had been flashing on the dashboard. It displayed at least three prominent repair codes. Settling into a comfortable waiting-room seat, I prayed and then started some paperwork I brought with me. Within fifteen minutes, the serviceman came and said the car was ready. He said none of the repair indicators could be found. He didn't know what had happened. Tears welled up inside as I realized what God had done for me.

I'm trying to live knowing that Christ is always with me and He's always ready to hear and answer humble petitions. Hopefully, we will expand our prayers with thanksgiving and our trust in the One who is more than wonderful!

Cherryl A. Galley

October 5

Beauty Restored

And we know that all things work together for good to them that love God, to them who are the called according to his purpose.
—Romans 8:28, KJV

As you know, 2020 was an unprecedented year for all the wrong reasons. COVID-19 changed nearly every aspect of our lives.

By fall, many of us had become somewhat used to the "new normal," but as if to add insult to injury, the Oklahoma City area of the United States of America experienced a catastrophic ice storm in late October.

The trees still had most of their leaves, which were soon covered with a thick layer of ice. The combined weight of the leaves and ice was too much for many of them. For days, we could hear limbs breaking and falling day and night.

I stood in my backyard and watched a huge tree fall on the back of my neighbor's house. Praise the Lord, it caused only minor damage, and nobody was injured, but it certainly frightened the family!

After the storm, the devastation looked like the aftermath of a tornado. Many people were also without electricity for days or weeks.

Down the road from my house stands a very large tree, tall and majestic, with beautiful leaves in the summer that become even more colorful in the fall. After the storm, that tree was a sad sight indeed. Its branches drooped almost to the ground under the weight of the ice, and one huge section of the tree had fallen into that neighbor's yard. I mourned the damage.

As the sun came out and the ice began to melt, I was amazed to see the tree's branches springing back up, many of them with the yellow leaves still intact. It did not look exactly as it had before the storm, but it was still beautiful.

All winter, people cleaned up the fallen limbs. Many yards looked rather forlorn for several months, but with the coming of spring and the sprouting of leaves, the neighborhood began to look much as it had before the storm.

As I looked at the transformation, I thought about how our awesome God takes our mistakes and the ugliness of our lives and cleans them up, often creating something even more beautiful than before from the devastation we go through. What a wonderful God we serve!

Robin Widmayer Sagel

When the Devil Comes to Church

Don't sin by letting anger control you.
Think about it overnight and remain silent.
—Psalm 4:4, NLT

Did you know that the devil comes to church?

I really didn't consider the idea until one Sabbath when church felt like anything but a blessing to me. I was doing my best to pay attention to our lesson study but kept hearing two older women talking rather loudly in the back of the church. Then someone criticized the lesson. To make matters worse, when I spoke up to make a point, another church member said something hurtful to me. I had enough sense and respect for the church and the other members not to say anything back or make a scene; however, my mood and attitude were about as far from wanting to worship and be in church at all as they could get. I left as soon as the service was done, not staying to talk with anyone afterward.

Later, I confided in one of my dear friends what had happened in my heart and how upset I had been at church that day. When I learned she had a similar experience, I suggested, "Maybe we need a sermon, 'When Satan Comes to Church.' " I was not being totally serious, but the thought stuck in my mind. I had no doubt that Satan had been present in the complaining of members, the comments carelessly stated, and most definitely in the way that I chose to let my anger and irritation over what happened affect the remainder of my day. I let it grow and fester and turn into something that wasn't productive or in the spirit of God. Yes, the devil had certainly been in church that day, and he sat right next to me, feeding me with his spirit of discontent.

How about you, friends? Have you ever let the devil come to church with you—or to the grocery store or a restaurant? There is hope. When we realize we are listening to the devil, we need to turn to Christ and pray for His strength to help us. He promises He will. Christ is stronger than the devil. Let's stop bringing the devil to church or anywhere with us. Life is so much better when we unfriend him and his bad company.

Lord, help us stop bringing the devil with us throughout our day; fill the spot we are happy to have him vacate. Amen.

Debra Snyder

October 7

The Intruder

Good Sense will scout ahead for danger,
Insight will keep an eye out for you.
—Proverbs 2:11, *The Message*

In 1987, I managed a group home where ten adults with developmental disabilities reside. Another staff member and I were on duty one night when I heard a thumping on the wall of the western side of the ranch-style building around three o'clock in the morning. I looked through the glass sliding door and saw a man sitting on the pavement with his back against the wall, banging both arms simultaneously on the wall.

I shouted to my coworker to call 911. She shouted back for the man's description, but he was gone. Relieved, I told her, "It's OK; never mind, he's gone." Suddenly, a loud crash and shattering glass from the back of the house startled us. We ran to the front office and listened for the next sound. Nothing. Holding hands, we cautiously walked toward the back.

As we entered the passageway, a man staggered toward us, holding a sharp, bloody piece of glass. We retreated to the front office and called 911 again only to discover that the operator was still holding and that the intruder was on the same line telling her that people were trying to kill him. As we talked over each other, trying to tell her that he had broken into the group home, the operator seemed confused. I knew then that I had to find another way to get help.

I told my coworker to stay on the line. *Oh God, we need Your help*, I thought, tiptoeing stealthily out the door. "Pull the fire alarm," my mind told me. The fire alarm was two steps away, and I remembered that it was linked to a nearby fire station. I pulled the fire alarm. In thirty seconds, the sirens approached. Two fire trucks and a police car arrived within a minute. Drops of blood trailed from the back bedroom to the kitchen, and a bloody knife was on the kitchen floor. The police apprehended the intruder as he scaled the fence.

The ten residents slept through the ordeal. No one in the house was harmed. Thank God for giving me the good sense to pull the fire alarm.

Maureen Nembhard

October 8

The Dreaded Phone Call

For the eyes of the Lord are on the righteous,
And His ears are open to their prayers.
—1 Peter 3:12, NKJV

The phone rang that night around eleven o'clock. "Ms. Phillips, your daughter has taken almost an entire bottle of pills." The voice on the line was the dean of women at her school. "We are transporting her by ambulance to the nearest hospital. We hope to get her to the hospital in time." In time? What did that mean? I was in shock. I'd heard about suicide but never dreamed someone in my family would attempt it. I began throwing things into a suitcase as the gravity of the situation sank in. My sixteen-year-old daughter was three hours away from me. *Will I be able to get to her in time? Will she be OK? How many pills had she taken?* I thought as I called my family and friends, asking them to pray.

As I backed out of the driveway, tears began to flow. "Dear Lord, take care of my baby. Please don't let her die!" I prayed. The roads were clear, but I would have never known it through my tears and tissues. I arrived at the hospital and raced through the emergency entrance. I soon learned emergency room personnel had pumped my daughter's stomach of the eighty-plus Tylenol and Midol tablets. They were stabilizing her condition as her blood levels were elevated four hundred times above the normal numbers. God had spared her life. But was there any organ damage?

She was placed on the psychiatric floor on suicide watch. The nurses watched for her reaction to me as I entered the room. I didn't know what to expect as I looked into her eyes. I mouthed the words, "I love you," as she rolled over to sleep. Later, a doctor arrived to share she had not suffered any kidney or liver damage. Her life was something she needed to value.

The next few days were a strange mixture of assuring my daughter that I loved her and wondering why she would do such a thing. I found myself becoming increasingly angry. What loss we would have had to endure if she had succeeded in taking her life! I asked God to help me forgive her and get her the help she needed.

God's hand of mercy brought us through that night of uncertainty. Will there be more uncertain times? Yes, there will be. But that night, I learned to lean on the One who hears my prayers and can answer in miraculous ways.

Karen M. Phillips

October 9

God Is My Strength

My health may fail, and my spirit may grow weak,
but God remains the strength of my heart;
he is mine forever.
—Psalm 73:26, NLT

I was walking two or more hours a day, eating a vegetarian diet, and drinking nothing but water. Praise God, I felt wonderful! Then I awoke one morning with a bad stomachache, nausea, and vomiting. I couldn't eat or drink. *OK, maybe it's just some stomach bug, and it will go away very soon.* I prayed and asked God to help me. My doctor gave me some medicine to try, but it didn't help. He had to hospitalize me for dehydration.

Two months later, my miserable symptoms were still with me: more dehydration—and hospitalizations. After performing a test on my gall bladder, my doctor scheduled me for surgery. "Oh, please God, help me," I prayed over and over regarding the surgery. A few days after surgery, my earlier symptoms worsened, and I could not eat or drink. Medical personnel inserted a feeding tube into my body. For four long years now, I have lived with the tube, all my previous symptoms, and infections too numerous to count. I've lost count of my many doctors, tests, procedures, and hospital days. Each time I am wheeled in for another test or procedure, I ask God, "Hold my hand, and don't let me go."

I have often asked God, "Why?" I have also asked for strength to push on. And He answers that prayer, helping me out each day. Even on the many days I no longer feel like pressing on, He is there with me. Whether I read His Word or listen to an uplifting song, I know He is helping me through all my pain, fatigue, and nausea. He loves me too much to let me walk this painful path alone. My body has not responded well to the tube feeding with the many formulas doctors have tried. I still have chronic pain and such fatigue that I can scarcely pull myself out of bed. Yet the strength I do have, God gives me, and I make it through each day.

Yes, I am scared about tomorrow as doctors continue to run tests, try new meds, and formulate new plans. But I am not going through this alone. Many people are praying for me. God will answer those prayers and heal me in His time—though that may not be before Jesus returns to take me home to a life free of fear, pain, tears, and feeding tubes. But for today, He is the strength of my heart and the love of my life. If you ask Him, He will be your strength too.

Gail Dotski

God Still Speaks to His People

"Therefore keep watch, because you do not know on what day your Lord will come."
—Matthew 24:42, NIV

About eighteen months ago, I started having dreams that speak of unpreparedness. I've forgotten the content of most. The first one, however, etched itself firmly in my mind. It was terrifying. In it, I received an urgent phone call telling me that the president of the United States would be coming to dinner and was on his way. I started panicking. I had absolutely nothing prepared. Frantically, I started calling folks trying to get food, help, anything, but to no avail. No one offered any kind of assistance.

The president arrived, and all that was on the long table, which was covered with a white tablecloth, was one dinner plate and a fork. I can tell you that the president was not happy.

Ashamed, I did not go out to meet or greet him. I hid in the kitchen. He sat at the table alone and made no effort to speak with me. I awoke from the dream perplexed. What did it mean?

For many months, the dreams about unpreparedness kept coming. I kept asking myself, *Why am I having these troubling dreams?*

As we read through the Scriptures, we see that dreams are one way God communicated with His people. I will cite just two such people. God began to prepare Joseph for a leadership role when he was still a child. Through two dreams, God showed Joseph that he would rise to a position of power and that his family would bow to him (Genesis 37:5–10). In the New Testament, God used dreams to inform Joseph (Mary's husband) of his upcoming responsibility to care for and raise the Christ child. I believe God still uses dreams to speak to His people.

I have contemplated whether God is using the dreams to warn me that I am not ready for the coming of the Lord. But looking at patterns in the Scriptures, I feel that I need to share the urgency of these dreams. The signs of the times—wars, rumors of wars, huge out-of-control fires, floods, earthquakes, crimes—all point to Christ's warning in Matthew 24. I've decided that I've got to love others as I love myself. That means I've got to encourage anyone who will listen to prepare *now* for the soon-coming Lord and Savior Jesus Christ.

Jasmine E. Grant

Jesus, My Strength and Stay

Thou wilt keep him in perfect peace,
whose mind is stayed on thee: because he trusteth in thee.
—Isaiah 26:3, KJV

October 22, 1844, was the Great Disappointment to the Millerites, but for Jason Nebres, my husband, and me, August 12, 2021, is our great disappointment. Not having gone home for two years, we excitedly headed to Suvarnabhumi airport. It takes about two hours to travel to Bangkok from Asia-Pacific International University (AIU) in Saraburi, Thailand, so we left earlier to have plenty of time to check in and do all the paperwork that needed to be done.

While approaching the check-in counter, a guy met us and said that we could not fly to Cebu via Hong Kong because the Philippine government had banned ten countries, including Thailand. We knew about this travel ban, but with the assurance of our travel agent that there was no problem with our flight, we thought everything would be all right. We tried to convince the gentleman that Cebu knew we were coming and showed him the QR code to prove we had registered for quarantine. He was willing to accommodate us if someone in authority could assure him that we could go home without any problem. With the help of our son, Jojie, we received a copy of the travel advisory, which states that citizens are allowed entry provided they haven't been to any of the ten countries within the last fourteen days.

We felt like the full-blown balloon pricked by a needle. High hopes of going home vanished. What do we do now? We called the AIU human resources director to tell her of our predicament. She called our travel agent, who assured us that she would rebook our tickets. Our children Jun and Kaye invited us to stay with them in Bangkok but warned that we would stay in the room all day because Bangkok was locked down. We hired a taxi to take us back to AIU. Fortunately, we could still go back to our empty apartment. Praise the Lord for a place to stay and for friends who eased our disappointment by providing for our needs—pots, pans, bedding, towels, curtains, and food!

This hard experience could have easily driven me to depression. But I cling to God's promise for peace to the one whose mind is stayed on Him and who trusts in Him. With Jesus as my strength and stay, I have decided to live one day at a time and let Him lead.

Forsythia Catane Galgao

Faith Must Have an Object

And it is impossible to please God without faith.
—Hebrews 11:6, NLT

I have been discouraged several times. But by faith, I become a conqueror. The Bible tells us of a woman who was also discouraged. For twelve years, she had been hemorrhaging blood. My sisters! You can imagine how it feels. Though she had gone to doctors, it was in vain. She must have been weak to the extent that even leaving her house was hard. In addition to her discouragement, she had no money, having spent everything she had trying to regain her health. Her condition rendered her ceremonially unclean. No one wanted to be around her, for whoever touched her would also be unclean (Leviticus 15:25–27). She had no hope of getting well nor of being accepted as a normal woman. Horrible!

Many times, we find ourselves in different crises. What is the object of our faith?

One day, Jesus visited the area surrounding the Sea of Galilee to minister to God's people, to teach, and to heal. In the process, He delivered a man from unclean spirits, and the news spread. People were excited. They all wanted to see the One who had performed miracles.

As the crowd gathered on the seashore, the woman slipped in unnoticed. Because people were excited, no one saw her resolutely inch her way toward Jesus. "If I can just touch his robe, I will be healed," she said to herself (Mark 5:28, NLT). She believed that Jesus had the answer to her problem. A slight opening in the crowd gave her a glimpse of Jesus. When she touched the hem of His garment, she knew instantly that she had been healed. What faith! Strength flowed into her.

Jesus immediately turned and asked, "Who touched Me?" The woman, fearful and trembling, came and fell before Him and told her story.

"Lord, it was me. I knew if I could just touch the hem of Your garment, I would be healed," she answered, head bowed, and waited. What would He do?

Jesus said, "Daughter, your faith has made you well. Go in peace. Your suffering is over" (verse 34, NLT).

The woman reached to Jesus in faith, and this impressed Jesus. May God help me impress Him in my dealings and actions as I reach out to Him in faith.

Pauline Gesare Okemwa

October 13

The Tiniest Details Are Not Too Small for So Great a Love

And may you have the power to understand, as all God's people should, how wide, how long, how high, and how deep his love is.
—Ephesians 3:18, NLT

Our neighbor, Richard, has been renovating a home in our neighborhood ever since purchasing it and recently invited my husband, Carl, and me to stop by to see his progress.

We stepped into a lovely house—large, spacious, and elegant with fascinating custom details, unique fixtures, elegant trimmings, and exotic touches. The kitchen was a chef's dream; the bathroom floors were heated; the bedroom was outfitted with gorgeous French doors that framed a perfect lake view. The house was a work of art. However, the reason claimed my attention: the house was a labor of love—Richard's best effort to create a dream home for his wife of forty years. For the past eighteen months, his singular agenda has been to fulfill to the smallest detail whatever it was that his wife preferred or specified, no matter how minute or time-consuming. He had stripped and stained the wooden floor in one hallway three times before getting the shade just right. Why? "Because I wanted it to be exactly what she wanted." His face reflected not the slightest trace of resentment or impatience, only love and joy.

That's when my mind turned to the sanctuary. Though I have studied it many times throughout my life, I was once again reading the many minute instructions found in Exodus, Leviticus, and Numbers. If I were honest, in the past, it has always seemed to me that God was being incredibly picky and rule-oriented and that no detail was too small for Him not to legislate. However, it had begun to occur to me that maybe the sanctuary provides a tiny glimpse into a mind so great, so omniscient and omnipresent, that there isn't even the slightest detail of a microbe that can escape His thoughts, attention, and planning.

After visiting Richard's house, though, I realized something more than God's infinite mind at work. Not unlike Richard's attention to every detail in the house because he loves and wants to please his wife and give her the very best, the detailed nature of the sanctuary is an outgrowth of God planning every facet of how to redeem us because of His eternal love for us. The many minute instructions related to the sanctuary provide just a tiny window for us to understand "how wide, how long, how high, and how deep His love is"! (Ephesians 3:18, NLT).

Rachel Williams-Smith

Called—Part 1

Beloved of God, called to be saints: Grace to you and peace from God our Father, and the Lord Jesus Christ.
—Romans 1:7, KJV

Do you feel called? Sure, there are certain things we enjoy doing, but that doesn't mean any of those things are necessarily our "calling." After all, some things we enjoy may not be good for us. These thoughts whirled in my mind one evening as I left Unit 28, the women's prison. I'd just had to tell a young mother her ten-year-old daughter was in the hospital dying of cancer and, according to the doctors, would be gone within a week. This inmate was almost done serving her sentence and had hoped to be home in five weeks—now, too late to see her daughter again. What heartache and anguish! What need of the comfort only a loving God can provide!

My husband and I volunteer at a medium/maximum prison in Tennessee, where he started giving Bible studies twenty years ago. I first went along as a support for him, though doing so wasn't very comfortable for me. We didn't see much growth in our Bible study group for the first few years. We'd been told not to teach anything that might be potentially controversial or cause the inmates to be uncomfortable. Around 2012, the elderly, longtime volunteers' leader retired and asked my husband and me to lead out. After much prayer, we accepted but also decided to teach what we believed the Bible taught regardless of who might be offended. Things began happening. Bible study group attendees became more interested in the studies and invited fellow inmates to join our group, which began to swell. Exciting? Yes! But I still didn't feel as though I quite fit in. I still didn't know if prison ministry was, indeed, my "calling." So I kept praying about it and searching the Scriptures even as I continued to volunteer. Around 2013 an expansion project swelled the prison population from eight hundred to three thousand inmates. A new unit was added for women prisoners. A new chaplain came aboard . . . but was *I* in the right place?

During those years, I learned that the best ways to discern God's calling for your life include (1) keeping your complexities before the Lord in prayer; (2) seeking His will and guidance through daily time in His Word; and (3) being ever watchful for His opening and closing doors of opportunity as daily life unfolds around you. Sooner or later, "thine ears shall hear a word behind thee, saying, This is the way, walk ye in it" (Isaiah 30:21, KJV).

Diana Halverson

Called—Part 2

"Yet who knows whether you have come to the kingdom for such a time as this?"
—Esther 4:14, NKJV

Five years ago, the new prison chaplain phoned me. "Do you know anything about computers?" he asked. "My predecessor used only paper files and had just a few volunteers helping him. Now I arrive, and the inmate population has swelled to three thousand! I am overwhelmed and need to get all these statistics and this information in a database. My present workload is impossible! Would you be able to help me with the database?" Was this God's answer to me?

"Yes, of course! I'd love to help you!" Though I am not a computer expert, I sensed God's opening a door of service for me. Besides, I'd been praying and knew God would help me learn. As I assisted in the chaplain's office, I became convicted this was my *calling*—and I loved it! One day the chaplain said, "I need help in the women's unit, where we now have three hundred inmates." I encouraged some of our ministry team to start Bible studies there. A retired pastoral couple had been volunteering every Monday night since 2013. With their help, these once-weekly group studies increased to five Bible-study groups, spread out over the entire weekend. These studies were in addition to ministering to the inmates in protective custody and solitary confinement. God just threw all the doors wide open! Literally!

Today, the most exciting part of my calling is ministry at the women's site. I work with the chaplain office's team planning Christmas programs and services and have the thrill of assisting at all baptisms. Yet I treasure most my one-on-one Jesus-sharing times. The day I had to tell that young mother that her ten-year-old daughter was about to die of cancer, we held hands and begged God for her to be released in time to see her child before it was too late. My husband and I shared this prayer need at the men's services, and they prayed as well. Then the little girl, surprisingly, got somewhat better and went home. The young mother *was* able to finish serving her sentence in time to be reunited with her daughter before the little one passed away.

I now know God has called me to be where I am. Not just for the ladies in Unit 28 but also for me. As a family member challenged me years ago, I challenge you today: "If you have any question about God's calling on your life, get on your knees. Ask Him to use you." He *will*!

Diana Halverson

Jesus' Touch—Part 1

Then Jesus, moved with compassion, stretched out His hand and touched him, and said to him, "I am willing; be cleansed." As soon as He had spoken, immediately the leprosy left him, and he was cleansed.
—Mark 1:41, 42, NKJV

Of all our senses, touch may be the one we think about the least. We know the importance of sight, hearing, taste, and smell, yet COVID-19 has made it evident that touch and the ability to feel someone else are important. We hear heartbreaking stories of the elderly suffering and dying in isolation while their loved ones long to be there to touch and hold them but are not able to do so. We hear of wonderful, compassionate caregivers who try to bridge the gap by providing some human touch during this difficult time. All of us suffer from not being able to hug and be hugged, to shake hands, or to receive a gentle touch of affirmation.

Our loving Lord Jesus knows the importance of touch for His created beings. His touch accompanied so many instances of His healing miracles during His time on earth. The touch of His hands also healed emotional wounds and spiritual scars.

When a leper came to Jesus begging to be healed, Jesus touched the man first. That poor man probably had not received human touch for years. Even if anyone had touched him, he probably couldn't feel it with his damaged nerves. How much it must have meant to him when Jesus touched him—and then for that touch to also heal and cleanse him!

The woman with the issue of blood expects only to touch the hem of His garment. Jesus stops immediately when He feels the power go out from Him. Right there, Jesus acknowledges the woman's emotional need, calling her "daughter," and recognizes her spiritual need, publicly declaring her healed—meaning she is cleansed and able to touch others and be touched (Matthew 9:20–22). Jesus continues to the home of Jairus (who asks Jesus to simply touch his daughter) and takes the hand of the little girl, bringing her back to life (verse 25).

Matthew 14:36 tells us that all who reached out to touch Him were healed. Jesus is as ready today as He was then to meet us at our point of greatest need when we reach out to Him and request His touch upon us. He is as willing to touch us as He was the leper. He will heal us. He will restore life itself.

Myrna Hanna

October 17

Jesus' Touch—Part 2

But Jesus answered, "No more of this!" And he touched the man's ear and healed him.
—Luke 22:51, NIV

Many verses in the Gospels reveal that Jesus showed compassion and healed the sick. Often, the stories describe Jesus' healing people by touching them. Jesus touches Peter's mother-in-law's hand, and her fever leaves her (Matthew 8:15). He touches the coffin of the widow of Nain's son, and the young man comes to life (Luke 7:14, 15). To heal the deaf man who did not speak clearly, He touches his ears and tongue (Mark 7:33, 34). He restores sight to the blind—He touches the eyes of the man born blind (John 9:6); He touches the eyes of two blind men (Matthew 9:29); He touches the eyes of two more blind men on His last journey to Jerusalem (Matthew 20:34).

At other times, His touch gives more than physical healing. He takes children in His arms and puts His hands on them to give them a blessing (Matthew 19:15; Mark 10:16). At the time of Jesus' transfiguration, the disciples fall to the ground in terror at the cloud and the voice from heaven, but Jesus comes to them and touches them, telling them not to be afraid (Matthew 17:7). Jesus reaches out His hand and catches Peter to prevent his drowning (Matthew 14:31).

Then, imagine this, as Jesus is being arrested in Gethsemane, He touches the high priest's servant's ear and restores it (Luke 22:51) after Peter cuts it off (John 18:10). Here He is, hours before His death, still reaching out, touching, and healing—even His enemies. What a compassionate, loving Savior!

I love to think of these stories of Jesus' touch because He still wants to touch our lives. When we are afraid, terrified, or bewildered, He is ready to touch us with His peace, His calm, His presence. He knows our needs, our desires, and what is best for us. Hebrews 4:14–16 tells us, "Seeing then that we have a great High Priest who has passed through the heavens, Jesus the Son of God, let us hold fast our confession. For we do not have a High Priest who cannot sympathize with our weaknesses, but was in all points tempted as we are, yet without sin. Let us therefore come boldly to the throne of grace, that we may obtain mercy and find grace to help in time of need" (NKJV).

May His touch of love, strength, and courage touch your life and change your destiny.

Myrna Hanna

The Mailbox

"A new commandment I give to you, that you love one another: just as I have loved you, you also are to love one another. By this all people will know that you are my disciples, if you have love for one another."
—John 13:34, 35, ESV

As I drove up into the parking lot at the post office, I noticed there were many cars, and many people were coming and going from their vehicles. I parked, closed my windows, and went into the building. As I collected my mail and exited the building, I heard a voice calling, "Ma'am, Ma'am, can you give me twenty cents?"

I was surprised. I kept thinking, *Why would someone ask for just twenty cents? What can twenty cents buy these days?*

I turned around and saw a young man coming toward me. I told him I had to retrieve the money from my car, so he walked to the car with me. When we got to the car, I gave him a dollar instead of twenty cents. He was extremely happy and thankful and left the parking lot immediately.

As I drove off, I pondered and asked myself, *What did that young man see in me that he bypassed everyone else and chose me to ask for twenty cents? Many people were going in and out of the post office. Was he embarrassed to ask the others, or was there something different about me that he chose me to ask for help?*

When I work in schools, I always pray that the students will see something different in me. I pray that the beauty of Jesus will be seen in me. I really want people to see the presence of Jesus through me—in my actions, walk, and especially the way I dress. If we say we are a child of God, there should be something different in every one of us. My prayer is that we allow God to work in our lives so that the world may see Jesus in our day-to-day living.

Patricia Hines

October 19

What Did I Forget Now?

For He shall give His angels charge over you,
To keep you in all your ways.
—Psalm 91:11, NKJV

A friend and I were traveling to a women's retreat, but I needed to stop for an appointment. As I waited for my friend to pick me up afterward, I realized I had left my water bottle inside, so I went and retrieved it. We stopped about an hour later to eat—that's when I realized I had forgotten my purse at my appointment . . . sigh.

I shared my story at the retreat, and someone asked, "Can't someone bring it up with them?" Yes! A friend hadn't left yet and was able to stop and pick it up on her way.

At the end of the weekend, I had my hands full carrying a bag and my suitcase to my car when I met a friend. While we chatted, I set down my bag next to my suitcase. As we said goodbye, I grabbed my suitcase and headed home. On the drive home, I needed something from my bag and realized I had left it behind. Sigh . . . I called the director of the retreat, who had found the bag and sent it home with a friend.

We had stopped at Costco to shop, so while there, I texted my friend to see if she was home so I could swing by and get my bag. She texted back that she was at Costco! We looked around, and there she was, just a few cars away. Wow! Thank You, Jesus!

As we were leaving, my youngest daughter asked if she could borrow my Costco card, and you guessed it . . . I couldn't find it. We went back in the store, didn't see it, and no one had turned it in. I whispered to the Lord, "What are You going to do with me?" Before I could pray to find the card, my daughter found it on the pavement by the driver's door of my car. "Jesus, I have no words! You are so, so good to me!"

I have a history of forgetting things. It's so frustrating, but I usually don't put the Lord through so much work like I did that weekend. But maybe I do. I just don't realize how much He does as He watches over me. Everyone I know has forgotten, misplaced, or lost something. Someday soon, won't it be fun to talk with our angels and laugh at our forgetfulness?

Jesus, please, continue to keep watch over us. We need You desperately. Thank You!

Mona Fellers

Saving the Baby

Fear not, for I am with you.
—Isaiah 41:10, TLB

My two sons are "miracle" babies. I was pregnant with our first one when an examining doctor unexpectedly asked my husband this disturbing question: "Are you sure you want to abort the baby?"

"No, I want to save the baby!" replied my shocked husband.

"Oh, everything is fine then," she said with a broad smile. "I am happy to tell you that your wife is healthy, and the growing baby is fine." The doctor returned to the examination room, where I was still waiting for her. "You can get ready to go home now. Everything is fine." In the waiting room, I found my husband with a very pale face. He told me about the doctor's question. We were in Brazil, visiting my husband's brother and family. Since I wasn't feeling too well, I had asked if I could see a doctor to check on my unborn baby's health. My brother-in-law (who practices spiritualism) recommended a woman doctor. We learned he had asked her to abort the fetus without consulting us. Had she not queried my husband, we could have lost our first child without knowing why. My husband immediately found a hotel where we could stay, leaving his brother's house to avoid confrontation.

Some years later, when I wasn't feeling well, I tried to make an appointment with my doctor—only to learn he was on holiday. The consulting doctor sent me for one barium meal and seven full-body x-rays. They revealed nothing. Then I was able to see my own doctor when she was back at work. She simply pressed my tummy and declared, "You're pregnant." I froze. She continued, "It's too late in your life now to have a normal delivery. You could easily give birth to a defective child. You should probably have the baby aborted. In fact, you could probably easily sue the medical staff who misdiagnosed and treated you before I could see you." Again, I decided to refuse an abortion. I simply submitted my future child to our Creator God.

"You should listen to the doctor," someone reprimanded me. "I know somebody in your situation who had a blind baby."

My husband alone prayerfully supported my decision to do the right thing by honoring human life. And today, our two sons are miracles of God's grace.

Monique Lombart De Oliveira

Work Is a Blessing!

Whatever your hand finds to do, do it with your might.
—Ecclesiastes 9:10, NKJV

When I was growing up, my mom owned an adult foster home that had eleven residents. This enabled my mother to always be at home when my sister and I returned from school. We helped mom get the meals on the table, wash dishes, help the residents get in bed, wash laundry, and do other chores. I enjoyed the work and told my mom that I would take over the business after finishing my education.

We had a female resident named Florence who enjoyed helping my mom. She knew who wanted coffee and who wanted tea. She would set the table. Occasionally she would wear her white nurse's uniform with matching white shoes and order my mother around, thinking she was Florence Nightingale. This made my mother smile and my sister and me giggle.

In the Garden of Eden, even before sin, God's plan was that Adam and Eve were to tend the garden (Genesis 2:15). Before sin existed, this was not considered hard work but part of the fun of doing things together. I imagine that God came and walked with them, enjoying what they were learning each day. Imagine Adam and Eve showing God all they had done that day—sharing what they learned as they cared for the garden and the animals. I think God may have smiled to Himself as He saw the joy they experienced in their work.

God has given us work to do too. In Acts 18:1–4, Paul worked with Aquila and Priscilla as a tentmaker. Jesus worked as a carpenter before He started His ministry (Mark 6:3). God desires us to work and enjoy what He's created us to do and to find satisfaction in our labor, learning and growing as we serve Him, no matter what our job. But some of us take work to excess. Our society tends to encourage working to the point of burnout, which affects our health and our relationships—sometimes crowding out time to walk and talk with God. Because of this, we may miss out on the blessings that God has in store for us. God gives us work so that we can provide for our families, learn, grow, and be a witness for the people we meet as we share Him and reflect His love and character. Imagine walking with God at the end of each day, talking to Him about your day and job, and seeing Him smile as He hears the stories of all you have learned and how you've enjoyed serving Him.

Gyl Moon Bateman

Pressing On to the Prize

But as the days of Noe were, so shall also the coming of the Son of man be. For as in the days that were before the flood they were eating and drinking, marrying and giving in marriage, until the day that Noe entered into the ark, and knew not until the flood came, and took them all away; so shall also the coming of the Son of man be.
—Matthew 24:37–39, KJV

As I reflect on our world today, I am reminded of Matthew 24. Many today are living for themselves. There is no respect for persons, especially the elderly, nor is there appreciation, gratitude, thankfulness, or reverence for God. As of this writing, there is a pandemic upon the land with no immediate cure. Schools are going virtual, creating anxiety issues for parents choosing between staying home with their children to help support their virtual learning or leaving them home alone so that the household remains intact financially. Churches are closed and going virtual, allowing us to worship from our living rooms. But online church does not compare with face-to-face contact, visiting the sick and shut-ins, Communion, or the other programs that we usually experience in worship. Some say this is the "new normal."

In the midst of all this, we are to seek and serve. We are to pray and make our requests known to God. Second Chronicles 7:14 tells us that if we pray and turn from our wicked ways, God will hear and heal our land.

God promises that nothing can separate us from His love no matter what is happening in our world. "Nay, in all these things we are more than conquerors through him that loved us. For I am persuaded, that neither death, nor life, nor angels, nor principalities, nor powers, nor things present, nor things to come, nor height, nor depth, nor any other creature, shall be able to separate us from the love of God, which is in Christ Jesus our Lord" (Romans 8:37–39, KJV).

It takes the unity of like-minded Christians to seek the Lord in prayer for the healing of the land. It takes the unity of like-minded Christians to fall humbly before the throne of grace to seek the Lord with reverence and holiness so that He will hear and forgive, trusting His love and pressing on to the prize before us.

Sylvia Giles Bennett

October 23

Forbidden

You know every bad thing we have done; even what we have done secretly.
—Psalm 90:8, *The Clear Word**

My husband, Harold, had a wonderful childhood growing up in a quiet, rural community called Pleasant Hill. He enjoyed exploring with friends and an assortment of wild critters. Around the age of ten, Harold welcomed a friend into his life. Ringer, a large raccoon, became his constant companion. His pet coon learned to drink soda pop by holding a bottle with his front paws. He became a regular passenger on Harold's bike by gripping the crossbar with his hind feet and the handlebars with his front feet. Ringer loved to sneak through an open window in the dark of night and play a game of hockey with a bar of soap in the bathtub.

A major restriction was placed upon Ringer by Harold's parents, who owned and operated a country store in Pleasant Hill. Ringer was forbidden to be in the store at any time! Harold complied by supplying his pet regularly with snacks outside on the porch. One day, his parents announced that they had sold the store. The new owners were scheduled to take ownership the following day. Harold was reminded again to keep Ringer outside while the transfer took place. However, curiosity prevailed! Thinking his parents were too busy to notice, he slipped inside with Ringer on a leash. All went well for a few moments. Suddenly, chaos broke loose! However, Walt Disney could not have planned a more dramatic escape! Ringer scampered up and along food-laden shelves with his owner in hot pursuit! Boxes, jars, and cans of food tumbled to the floor below. After the chase ended and Ringer was captured, one small boy began cleaning up one big mess.

How often do we, as adults, reason as a ten-year-old, "God is too busy with the affairs of the universe to notice? It won't hurt this one time!" Such deceptive reasoning gives license to just about anything without regard for the well-being of others. The mess resulting from these indiscretions, moral or legal, many times cannot be cleaned up within a lifetime. Psalm 90:8 reminds us, "You know every bad thing we have done; even what we have done secretly."†

Dottie Barnett

* Jack Blanco, *The Clear Word* (Hagerstown, MD: Review and Herald®, 2003), 638.
† Blanco, 638.

Rising Tides Lift All Boats

Whatever you do, work at it with all your heart, as working for the Lord, not for human masters, since you know that you will receive an inheritance from the Lord as a reward. It is the Lord Christ you are serving.
—Colossians 3:23, 24, NIV

I have the privilege of being surrounded by some amazing women.

I am in awe as I watch what God is doing in my friends' lives. I am a relatively new entrepreneur. When I felt called on this journey, I knew that there were women I could call on who had gone ahead of me. I'm not one who believes I need to do it on my own—I believe I can borrow someone's template and tweak it and make it my own.

As I reached out to each of these amazing women and listened to their stories, I was in awe as I heard how God had moved for them.

One friend's story struck a chord. She had had some experiences that would be considered cringe-worthy. They had made her angry at the things that she had to do on her own. She'd had to go some places that she couldn't even fathom, but as part of her duty, she had to go.

As I listened to her recount the story three years later, it was evident God had not wasted any of her experiences. As I listened to her, my mind quickly put two and two together and saw how as she went through those cringe-worthy experiences, God was setting her up for her current role. Because of the grueling schedule she had been put through, she had mastered the art of being both creative and detailed, a necessary trait in her profession.

As I sat with her recently and listened to her success, I beamed with joy for her. Why? Simply because if God can do it for her, He can do it for me too.

When my friends do well and are accomplishing their dreams, I am cheering on the front lines. I might even be one of the loudest cheerleaders because I know what it takes to realize the dream. And I also continue to be reminded, if God can do it for her, He can surely do it for me too. It keeps me both encouraged and joyful when my friends are in a season of abundance.

Dear heavenly Father, thank You for the examples before us, even as we navigate uncharted territory. Please continue to prepare us in all the areas necessary so that when we get there, we will know what to do.

Kaysian C. Gordon

October 25

Delivered From Dangerous Dogs

The angel of the Lord *encampeth round about them that fear him, and delivereth them.*
—Psalm 34:7, KJV

Not long after we had moved into our new home in Montego Bay, Jamaica, I warned my four- and six-year-old children to always play inside our well-fenced yard. I stood by the stone wall and showed them two stray dogs walking by.

My daughter's six-year-old mind did not remember that advice for long. Her curiosity won, and one morning she sneaked out of the gate and crossed the road. In a matter of seconds, she was surrounded by the neighbor's dogs plus a few strays—a combined total of seven dogs.

She dashed across the road at the speed of lightning and flew up the side attempting to get over the wall before the dogs got her. Her getting up and over the wall was nothing short of a miracle.

As she shared the story during the recent Christmas holidays, she is still convinced her guardian angels took her over the wall. There was no way her six-year-old feet could get her over.

Two decades later, my daughter was returning home from her regular evening walk. Suddenly, growls caught her attention. This time it was two unfriendly stray dogs she had never seen before. Barking and snarling, they blocked her path. There was no way to go.

Just when it seemed there was no way out, a car stopped beside her. The driver rolled down her window and asked, "Do you need help?"

"Yes," she responded, more frightened than polite. My daughter opened the door and hopped in before the woman could finish inviting her to get into the car.

"Where do you live?" the lady asked.

My daughter was happy to let her know she was only a minute drive from home.

My daughter thanked her over and over again. She never saw that lady in the neighborhood again. God had sent His angel to deliver her again! She was reminded that God had kept His promise in Psalm 34:7. Two decades later, her guardian angel had done it again. This time, she met her!

Claudette Garbutt-Harding

Lavender Epsom Salt

Purge me with hyssop, and I shall be clean;
Wash me, and I shall be whiter than snow.
—Psalm 51:7, NKJV

I'm lowered—I use a wheelchair—into warm, soapy water to soak my tired limbs and scrub them clean. When I learned that Jim, the resident bird artist, was using Epsom salts to moisturize his skin that had become dry and scaly, I was intrigued, especially when told it also came in lavender. Even though I knew it would be more costly, I begged my sister-in-law to send me some. When she did, I splashed it into the water. Calming lavender fragrance filled the air. Changing three of the words I had seen on the tub wall, I wrote a metaphor of my own. "Lavender is to the body what fragrance is to the soul." That became my life mandate.

Almost immediately, my mind traveled to a moment that occurred some two thousand years ago just before Jesus' crucifixion. This incident was so important that all four Gospels record it. Jesus was at the recently-cured-from-leprosy Simon's house. But He was not guest of honor, though He, as the Healer, should have been. Nobody washed His feet, though somebody should have because the roads were dusty. The very grateful, very tearful Mary Magdalene filled the gap. While everyone else was otherwise occupied, she anointed His feet with a very costly flask of alabaster oil. Tearfully, she washed His feet with the oil and her long hair.

Reading from the pen of inspiration, we understand a critical point in the story. "She had sought to avoid observation, and her movements might have passed unnoticed, but the ointment filled the room with its fragrance, and published her act to all present."* She had wanted a private moment with her Lord, but the aroma had a totally different effect. It attracted the attention of everyone in the space.

I want to be the fragrance that delights the souls of those around me; the element that inspires the joy in our hearts. Joy effuses the perfume of our souls and diffuses it on those around us. No wonder Mary Magdalene's story will be remembered wherever that gospel narrative is shared. I can't wait to meet her.

Glenda-mae Greene

* Ellen G. White, *The Desire of Ages* (Nampa, ID: Pacific Press®, 2005), 559.

October 27

Ruth's Encounter in the Church

The angel of the L*ORD* *encamps around those who fear him,*
and he delivers them.
—Psalm 34:7, NIV

It was a beautiful Sunday morning when Ruth Bixby volunteered to clean her little church in southern Maryland. She was cleaning the church by herself that day. When she entered the church, everything looked so peaceful and calm that she felt impressed to meditate and read God's Word before starting her cleaning. So she went outside to her car to get her reading glasses and then came back inside the church and sat in the last pew to read the Bible. She read for some time and then started to pray. Just then, she heard a floor creaking sound. She stopped praying and listened, thinking that maybe someone was coming inside, but no one came. Yet the creaking sound continued.

For some reason, she was not afraid and felt that it was an evil spirit. Fearlessly she commanded in a loud voice, "Leave God's house. You have no right to be here. Do not disturb me. Get out of God's house immediately." She repeated this several times, and finally, the noise stopped, and everything was silent.

After that, she quickly went around to check that everything was locked and make sure nobody was around. Then she began cleaning the church by herself without any fear. She felt God's presence was with her, and she knew that His angels were watching over her.

God gave her the strength and courage to get the church cleaned that day. She went home rejoicing, knowing that God's presence and help were with her that morning.

Although this experience shook her up, she knew that God was real and that He was watching over her. She felt the assurance that God was taking care of her in every way. This experience has greatly strengthened her faith and trust in God.

We also can have the same assurance, under any circumstances, when we commit our faith and trust in our God!

Stella Thomas

Everything Was in Its Place

God is my strength and power:
and he maketh my way perfect.
—2 Samuel 22:33, KJV

My husband has always been a very energetic man. For years, he was a building contractor and never seemed to be tired. He could go for hours and was strong. Even in old age, he could outdo anyone, it seemed. So while visiting our local primary-care doctor, we were shocked to learn that he had a bad leakage in his heart and needed to see a cardiologist as soon as possible.

He was set up for an echocardiogram. Then he had a catheterization of his heart and was told he would need a new valve. Before that surgery, he was to have a stent placed in one of the arteries in his heart. All went well with these procedures. A trip to Spokane, Washington, United States of America, was arranged to do five more tests to see when the valve would be replaced.

At the time of the catheterization, the physician, who was in the hospital in Walla Walla, Washington, only for two weeks out of each month, happened to be there at that very time. He wanted to place the stent in my husband's heart as soon as possible and was able to do so the very next day. He also checked to see whether any other arteries needed stents, which they did not.

We had no idea that we would need anyone special to do that procedure; we just thought it could be any cardiologist, but God knew just who needed to do that procedure and made sure that just the right person was there at just the right time. The stent was placed in his heart in time so everything could proceed in a timely manner for replacing the heart valve.

As I write this, my husband is in Spokane, having five pre-op exams before he will know just when the valve can be replaced. How we thank the Lord that His timing was perfect and the right person was in the right place to take care of his needs.

God is *so* good!

Anna May Radke Waters

October 29

I Spy With My Little Eye . . .

Be careful what you think,
because your thoughts run your life.
—Proverbs 4:23, NCV

The sound of a big sigh floated in from the family room. Looking up from making hummus, I saw Melissa slumped in her favorite bean-bag chair, a tear rolling slowly down one freckled cheek. She was busily typing on her iPad and slowly repeating: "I don't want to fail!"

"What's all this about?" I asked, surprised.

"You know. Geography class," she sniffed. "I don't want to fail, but it doesn't look good, even with all the homework I've done." More tears rolled over freckles. Both cheeks now.

"Melissa, Melissa," I said kindly, "you are caught in the white bear phenomenon."

"Have you told me about the white bear phenomenon?" she asked, sitting up, alert.

"It is research by Dr. Daniel M. Wegner," I explained. "When you say, 'Don't think about the white bear,' a mental representation of a white bear goes into working memory and that's all your brain wants to think about. In effect, you think about the white bear even more."

"So when I say, 'I don't want to fail,' a mental representation of failing goes into my brain's working memory?" asked Melissa.

"What do you see in your mind's eye?" I asked, nodding.

"A big red F on my test paper," Melissa said. "What could I tell myself instead?"

"What mental picture would represent what you want to have happen?" I asked.

Melissa brushed tears from her cheeks and, chin in hand, looked off into space. "I spy with my little eye a big A+ on my test!" she said. (Melissa and I had often played this game.)

"There you go," I said. "Depending on how much you've studied, an A+ may not materialize immediately, but you'll get further when you aim higher."

As we went about our day, I periodically heard Melissa quietly repeating to herself, "I spy with my little eye a big A+ on my test. I spy with my little eye a big A+ on my test."

Are you failing to achieve your goals? You may have missed a key admonition from the Scriptures. Stop thinking about what you do not want to happen. Instead, picture in your mind's eye what you *do* want to happen. You are what you think.

Arlene R. Taylor

October 30

Someone Needs What You Have

I have been crucified with Christ and I no longer live,
but Christ lives in me. The life I now live in the body, I live by
faith in the Son of God, who loved me and gave himself for me.
—Galatians 2:20, NIV

It seems as though this story would have had a much different ending from how it started. Jesus came to the well to meet a woman who He knew had been living in sin. When she saw Him, she didn't realize she would become an evangelist.

As the conversation carried on, Jesus let her know that He knew all about her. Her husbands. The man she was now living with, who was not her husband. He knew all about her and still accepted her and invited her to a life-changing relationship with God.

This conversation and His acceptance changed her life. He didn't even need to tell her what to do next. When He set her free from sin, shame, and guilt, she became the head of His sales department. The woman began telling everyone her story, inviting them to come and see this man who had changed her heart and offered her acceptance and forgiveness and hope.

People needed to hear her story. They could relate to her story. Soon, the entire town was joining her to listen to Jesus.

Being the head of sales for Jesus was a great job. The woman would never get another offer as great as this one. She could never be fired. The woman just needed to tell her story. The benefits lasted long after she died—they will last through eternity. We know she started her job right then as she ran back to her village and shouted to everyone, "Let me tell you about a man," but I'm sure the woman continued to tell her story—and that people heard about her and came to hear it in her own words.

Sister, someone needs to hear about how you became who you are and how you got here. They need to know what God did in your life, how Jesus spoke to you, and what He offered you. Whatever your job, business, or life may be, it's only a vehicle to tell them who your boss is. Jesus invites you to be His head of sales.

D. Renee' Mobley-Neal

October 31

Never Fail You

"Never will I leave you;
never will I forsake you."
—Hebrews 13:5, NIV

This morning I was led to Hebrews 13:5, where the writer counsels us to be content because God has said He will never leave or forsake us. That has always been such a reassuring promise to me, and I love to remember it! My Bible cross-references this back to Deuteronomy 31:6. There, Moses is encouraging the children of Israel as they face the future in the Promised Land, even as he is also telling them goodbye because he won't be going with them. That verse in the New International Version (NIV) is the same as it is in Hebrews. It says that God will never leave us. But the really neat thing I found this morning is that in the King James Version (KJV), this text is rendered in these words: "He will not fail thee, nor forsake thee." Interesting, because the KJV rendering in Hebrews also says "leave" and not "fail." I find both words meaningful. I love knowing that God won't leave me and that I am never alone. God is with me! I also love the thought that He won't fail me. God won't let me down! He will always come through for me!

Since our God will never leave us or fail us, we can confidently ("boldly," KJV) say, "The Lord is my helper; I will not be afraid. What can mere mortals do to me?" (Hebrews 13:6, NIV).

This verse refers to Psalm 118:6, 7. In reading that text both in the NIV and the KJV, I found another very special message. The KJV says, "The Lord is on my side" (verse 6), and He "taketh my part with them that help me" (verse 7). Both of those phrases give such a rich and expanded meaning to the thought of God being my Helper. Just think! The Creator and Sustainer of the universe—my Savior and Redeemer—is on my side. He takes my part. He stands up for me! With a God like that, we don't need to be afraid, discouraged, or dismayed. The devil wants us to forget the kind of God we serve and whose child we are. He wants us to try to take care of everything on our own. The good news is, we don't have to go it alone!

May you be richly blessed today and celebrate the fact that your God is with you. He won't leave, fail, or forsake you because of His surpassing love. God is your Helper, always on your side, taking your part. You are not alone to face any challenge you may encounter today!

Myrna Hanna

Tears and More Tears

"And God will wipe away every tear from their eyes; there shall be no more death, nor sorrow, nor crying. There shall be no more pain, for the former things have passed away."
—Revelation 21:4, NKJV

It was the middle of the afternoon, and I had agreed to talk to a friend. After a question was asked, I could see where the conversation was headed. In minutes, I was on the verge of tears. At first, my eyes watered. It was all I could do to continue the conversation. When it ended, I cried. I cried for what I had lost, facing the truth once again and understanding that the friend cared and wanted what was best for me.

At the time, I thought that I had done enough crying. But that evening I cried some more. You know how it is. Every time you think of the incident or person, you cry more. You cry so much that you wonder, *Why am I still crying?*

By night, my eyes hurt from all the crying. I would like to say that was the end of my tears, but it was not. I cried often for the next several days. Then Friday night, I felt a peace that I knew could only come from God. For the first time in three days, I slept through the night and had a peaceful rest.

I would like to tell you that tears are not necessary, but they are. Tears are a clear liquid secreted by the tear gland found in the eyes of all land mammals except for goats and rabbits. Their functions include lubricating the eyes (basal tears), removing irritants (reflex tears), and aiding the immune system. Tears also occur as a part of the body's natural pain response. Humans are the only mammals known to produce tears as part of an emotional response, such as joy or grief. Tears have symbolic significance among humans. Emotional secretion of tears may serve a biological function by excreting stress-inducing hormones built up through times of emotional distress.

We need to cry. Our reasons may be varied, but we need to shed tears. It seems we cry more out of pain and sorrow than happiness. There will come a day when God will wipe away our tears. Oh, I cannot wait for that day! My eyes will not hurt anymore! God will give eternal rest! Hold on, my sister!

Dana M. Bean

November 2

The Soccer Coach

You will increase my greatness,
and You will encircle and comfort me.
—Psalm 71:21, MEV

He stood on the sideline of the playing field, adjusting his shin guards and tugging at his jersey. Clearly, my seven-year-old grandson was nervous.

This was the first soccer game of the season. On top of that, it was his first soccer game ever, and because of a holiday and a problem with communication, the team members had never practiced together.

Suddenly a coach walked over. She squatted by him so they'd be eye to eye. "Derion, you're playing soccer this year! That's really great!" He nodded solemnly, his eyes still worried. "Let me give you a few pointers," volunteered the coach, putting her arm around him. He stood a little taller, looked at her seriously, and listened to her instructions.

"Now," she said, "go join your teammates!" They exchanged a high five, and he ran down the field, his orange jersey blazing in the summer sunlight.

The coach smiled, turned, and called, "My team—the blue team—come on over! Let's talk!"

She wasn't Derion's coach! She was a coach for the other team, yet she had taken the time to build the confidence of a small boy facing a big moment.

I'm a long-distance grandmother, so I couldn't watch many of the games that summer, but when I arrived at my grandson's house in December, he greeted me with an excited grin. "Do you want to see my soccer medal?"

"Of course! How did your team do?" I queried.

"We didn't win one game—not even one!"

"Are you going to play soccer next year?"

He laughed and answered, "Of course I am!"

From his response, it was clear that members of the team had experienced plenty of fun. They built their skills, learned teamwork, and grew in confidence. They may not have won any games, but the coaches made sure that they experienced a multitude of victories.

Denise Dick Herr

When Things Don't Work Out

I know the plans I have in mind for you, declares the Lord.
—Jeremiah 29:11, CEB

Have you ever tried to do something and been met with 101 distractions that seem to limit you to making any progress at all and wondered why?

That sometimes happens to me. Then there are times when everything goes well and things just click perfectly into place, and you make so much more headway that it's phenomenal.

As I started to write this, I sat at my desk pondering. I looked outside. It was raining. I reminded myself that the rain would stop eventually, the sun would come out, and I would be able to do the things I needed to outside. Realizing that the weather and my thoughts were distracting me from writing, I looked back to my paper and the words I wanted to write.

The distractions didn't stop. My cat pushed the pen out of my hand and nuzzled me for attention and then wanted to sit on the piece of paper I was writing on. I gave him some of the attention he demanded before moving him off the paper so I could go back to writing.

There are distractions that interrupt what we are trying to accomplish, but there are also times when everything knits together perfectly, when nothing can prevent us from achieving what we are attempting to accomplish. I waited for that time.

Soon the words began to come. First a trickle, then they gained momentum and began to flow like a faster running stream. I knew exactly what to write. It became so easy.

As I read over what I had written, I wondered whether it was like this when the Bible writers wrote down the Scriptures. Did they face distractions and moments the words wouldn't come? Or did everything flow with a real sense of peace? I am sure the words came easily because God ordained it to be so.

It is reassuring to know that we can leave it all for God to work out, in His time, in His way. God's Word reminds us, "Unless the Lord builds the house, the builders labor in vain" (Psalm 127:1, NIV).

So let's wait on God's time and blessing in all we do and not be frustrated when things don't seem to be working out the way we want and distractions and interruptions delay us. We can trust that things will and do come according to His time and purpose.

Laura A. Canning

November 4

Give Thanks

Rejoice always, pray continually, give thanks in all circumstances;
for this is God's will for you in Christ Jesus.
—1 Thessalonians 5:16–18, NIV

The Bible records the story of Hannah in 1 Samuel 1:2–2:21. Hannah was depressed and bitter. Not only was she barren, but also her husband, Elkanah, had married a second wife who had children for him. Peninnah, the other wife, and her children mocked Hannah. When her heart couldn't take the pain any longer and her humiliation reached its peak, she went to the place where she felt closest to God, and the priest thought she was drunk. She had innocently gone to the temple to plead with God over her barrenness when the priest saw her muttering something and misread her actions.

At first glance at the story, I recognized a possible cause for her utter distress and shame. The Lord had uttered a blessing on the womb of His people. Yet, though a godly woman, she was barren. Her womb had not received the blessing that God promised. What had she done or not done to deserve this curse?

A second look revealed another side of the story—a woman loved by an attentive husband. He gave her a double portion of the meat for the sacrifice. He playfully assured her that he was worth much more than ten sons. He did not condemn her but loved her and was willing to invest more in the sacrifices if that would help her feel better. Hannah, however, was blinded to the many blessings because she was so focused on what she did not have.

In our most distressing moments, we often focus only on the immediate problem but forget to count our blessings. We forget to refocus and see the number of good and wonderful things in our lives. Pause right this minute and begin to count or acknowledge them. I imagine a smile curling on your lips as your shoulders relax and you are relieved of tension. I hear you saying, "Indeed, I have so much for which to thank God."

Godly woman, there is nothing that you have done to receive the trials and challenges in your life today, but do you see the blessings? Can you count the many blessings that you receive each day? Shift your focus for a little while and see what God has done and is doing for you. In everything, give thanks.

Gloria Barnes-Gregory

I Got Someone

"For I know the plans I have for you."
—Jeremiah 29:11, NIV

A note was pushed under my front door to the effect that I had to send my driver's license, car insurance, and car registration to the management office of my apartment. Why? It had become necessary to change the chips hanging in our cars that allow us to enter our parking lot. I quickly got my papers and went to the office. The manager rejected my license because it did not have the address of the building. I reminded her that it was valid until 2022 and that we were still in March 2021. She insisted that it was required to get a new one showing the new address one month after moving in. She gave me a few days to get a new one; otherwise, my car would not be able to enter the parking lot and could be towed away from the premises.

At the motor vehicle office, I was told to apply online. Unfortunately, some of us who were not born yesterday have problems with technology, and the website directed me to a different motor vehicle agency. Again, I was told to solve my problem online. A yo-yo now. Right? Disappointed, with tears and prayers, I called our daughter, Abby, who lives in another state. Within a few minutes, the same website sent me an interim license to print, sign, and add to the old one while I waited for a new license to be mailed to me. I then rushed to the management office only to realize that the new chip project was completed. What was I expected to do? Park on the roadside? Really?

But as the day's message goes, "I got Someone." Yes, I do; and He is looking out for me. He never stops.

Friends, I called the officer in charge of the building, and he explained, "Your car will be OK in the parking lot because management will set a new date for those who did not get the new chip." Unbelievable!

That is how He works. God has His own ways, and He always has our backs. God has the best plans for every one of His own. He knows our voices and hears when we call. Just as Jesus said, "I am the good Shepherd; I know my sheep and my sheep know me" (John 10:14, NIV). Do you know Him?

Mable Kwei

November 6

The One True Thing

For I am persuaded, that neither death, nor life, nor angels, nor principalities, nor powers, nor things present, nor things to come, nor height, nor depth, nor any other creature, shall be able to separate us from the love of God, which is in Christ Jesus our Lord.
—Romans 8:38, 39, KJV

In the pandemic of 2020, a virus roamed the earth like a curse and pushed people into hiding. As a captive in my home, my life consisted of online meetings, phone conversations, and email deliberations. I missed my children, family, friends, and colleagues. I yearned for the things I took for granted: dinners with family, walks in the park, and hugs from my grandchild. My heart hurt for my aunt struggling with the disease, my mind meditated on the threat to my sister living with cancer, and my soul supplicated for the curse to vacate our planet.

To fight fears, I counted my blessings often: The smile of my son, Samuel. The laughter of my daughter, Crystal. The sweet voice of my grandchild, Adrian, calling me Nana. The love of my friends and family. The peaceful home with my husband, Walden, and my sister, Nathalie. And the joy of my educational ministry.

One particularly dark day, I caught a glimpse of a picture of Samuel, and my heart overflowed with a swell of gratitude and love that startled me! While the whole world stopped and the globe froze, in the corner of my couch, looking at my son's picture, I had a revelation, and it is simply this: God loves me. The veracity and the grandeur of God's love sat me down and settled me into an unquestionable certainty that if I, being a sinner, can love my son so intensely, God's love for me must be immeasurable and incomprehensible. I imagined that even a quick look or a fleeting thought of me must overwhelm God's heart with love and mercy and pity for me even now.

In my darkest moment, God drew close and reached into the deepest part where the Holy Spirit shone the light of the truth that He loves me! Much more than head knowledge, it was a deep conviction that even the possibility of death or the promise of disease couldn't extinguish the brilliance of God's love for me. When life is at its hardest, God will use anything to draw us to Him so we can trust and believe, beyond all doubt, that His love for us is the one true thing.

Rose Joseph Thomas

The Strength of Failure

But he said to me, "My grace is sufficient for you, for my power is made perfect in weakness." Therefore I will boast all the more gladly about my weaknesses, so that Christ's power may rest on me. That is why, for Christ's sake, I delight in weaknesses, in insults, in hardships, in persecutions, in difficulties. For when I am weak, then I am strong.
—2 Corinthians 12:9, 10, NIV

I don't like to fail. When I do, it's easy for the enemy to move me from failing to feeling like a failure. And then, it can be a downward spiral into shame and feeling that I am not enough and ready to quit.

But what if God redeems and uses even our failures?

I was reading the story of Peter, Jesus' disciple, walking on water. It's often been told, and typically Peter gets a bit beat up for taking his eyes off Jesus and sinking in the raging, stormy waves. (Personally, I think we need to give him a shout-out for having the courage to even step out of the boat in the first place—he may have sunk, but he is the only one besides Jesus who walked on water!) But what if he hadn't taken his eyes off Jesus and had walked all the way to Jesus and then walked with Jesus back to the boat? How would that change the story? What would have happened next?

I imagine that the disciples would be high-fiving Peter and cheering for him, slapping him on the back. The story would easily become all about Peter and what he had just done. Because Peter failed, the story is about Jesus and what He does. It tells us that God is a God who reaches down and grabs us when we go under—even when it's our fault. Through Peter's failure, the disciples, and now those of us who read his story all these years later, find encouragement in knowing that Jesus loves us that much. We see a glimpse of God's power and strength and His powerful love.

In Peter's weakness, we see God's strength. And it brings us hope and courage.

So while the enemy desires to use our failures as a way to discourage us and take out our hearts, God desires to use our failures as a way to encourage us and others in knowing and trusting that He is a God who reaches down, lifts us up, and gets us back on our feet.

Grateful.

Tamyra Horst

November 8

A Measureless Shore

This is how we know what love is:
Jesus Christ laid down his life for us.
—1 John 3:16, NIV

This particular year would be a milestone June birthday for my twin sister, Kathy, and me. We lived many states apart from one another and were rarely able to spend our birthday together. We determined that we would spend our sixtieth with each other. The trip to the beach was planned. Kathy and her family went there each summer; however, the place was new to me. I flew to the Charlotte airport, where Kathy picked me up. We then headed by car to Sunset Beach, North Carolina.

Being from Nebraska, where an ocean is nonexistent, I find the beach to be a very magical and majestic place. We went to the beach early in the morning and walked along the deserted shoreline. It seemed endless as we looked toward the horizon. I was amazed by the large mansions that were built so close to the water's edge. We were near the North Carolina Bird Island Reserve. The sight of the hundreds of pelicans on the shoreline, the taste of the saltwater, the sound and power of the waves, and the sand in my toes elevated me to new heights. We walked for miles that day, singing hymns and soaking in the glory of God's creation. We found a lone mailbox along the way with "Kindred Spirits" written on it. Inside was a notebook where we left a message of love for those who came next on the trail.

One of my favorite writers states: "In the contemplation of Christ we linger on the shore of a love that is measureless. We endeavor to tell of this love, and language fails us."* As I lingered on the beach shore, I thought about God's great love for us and the messages He has left for us in His Word. He came to earth to walk as one of us. He sacrificed His life for us. He now works as our Advocate (Kindred Spirit) in the heavenly realm. He is preparing a mansion for those who love Him.

Remember today that God's love enables our characters to be renewed and elevated, just as I was inspired and changed walking along the beach that day.

Karen M. Phillips

* Ellen G. White, *The Acts of the Apostles* (Nampa, ID: Pacific Press®, 2005), 333.

When Fear Complicates Our Lives

"Say you are my sister, that it may go well with me because of you, and that my life may be spared for your sake."
—Genesis 12:13, ESV

We have all at some time felt fear for not only real threats but also for those that we believe exist. This fear drives us to decide for ourselves and make mistakes instead of trusting God. That's what Abram did. "When he was about to enter Egypt, he said to Sarai his wife, 'I know that you are a woman beautiful in appearance, and when the Egyptians see you, they will say, "This is his wife." Then they will kill me, but they will let you live' " (Genesis 12:11, 12, ESV).

The Bible tells us that Sarai was beautiful. But what if Abram had told the truth and said that she was his wife? Would they have killed him? Or would they have respected him? Would God have protected Abram if he had told the truth and trusted Him?

Things can go badly when we make decisions based on our fears instead of trusting God. Let's look at Abram's case:

He lied because he was afraid.

He made his wife lie, and that lie caused Pharaoh to take Sarai as his wife.

Pharaoh and his house suffered different plagues because of this lie.

When we analyze the facts, we realize that this decision affected Abram and everyone around him. This wrong decision caused the people he loved the most to suffer. Abram had listened to God before. What would have happened if he had placed his faith in God and followed what He asked of him? What example could Abram have set for Pharaoh and the Egyptians if he had told the truth?

Surely everything would have ended differently because God would have taken care of Abram, and he wouldn't have needed to lie.

I don't know what fears you have today, but place your trust in God to help you make good decisions. He will take care of you.

Cecilia Nanni

November 10

What Will They Say About Me?

His lord said to him, "Well done, good and faithful servant; you have been faithful over a few things, I will make you ruler over many things. Enter into the joy of your lord."
—Matthew 25:23, NKJV

If I should die today, what will they say about me? This has been a recurring question at different stages of my journey. The thought is more overwhelming when I attend funerals and memorial services. I have heard the tearful comments of loved ones and friends relating the impactful stories of the deceased on their lives. But I have also heard stories of regret, shame, and anger. Deep regret is often expressed with the words, "I wish I had one more moment, one more day, to make things right!"

All of us have lost loved ones and acquaintances and have experienced varying emotions. Some of us wish we had taken the time to say that last kind word. We wish we could take back that last look of disdain. We wish we had reached out that loving hand to give a gentle touch, given that warm smile, or had just been there to support, to comfort, and to cheer. We wish we had said that last "I love you!"

The Bible tells us that Enoch walked with God. Scripture calls David a man after God's own heart and identifies Abraham as a friend of God. In Hebrews 11, many names are mentioned, including Rahab, Sarah, Jephthah, Samson, and Gideon. "And all these, having obtained a good testimony through faith" (Hebrews 11:39, NKJV). If we had been giving the tributes and eulogy about them, what would we have said?

So, when the time comes, what will they say about me? Would I be included in that faith chapter? Is my life currently reflecting the beauty of Christ's presence? Are the nine segments of the fruit of the spirit reflected in my everyday life?

The most important question to ask is this: what will He say about me in the final analysis? What will He say about each of us? Will it be "Well done," or "I know you not"?

In the end, it is what God says that really counts!

Sonia Kennedy-Brown

The Ultimate Sacrifice

For God so loved the world that he gave his one and only Son.
—John 3:16, NIV

We had just fastened our seat belts and were awaiting the departure of our flight when the captain exited the cockpit and stood at the front. He welcomed passengers on board and thanked us for choosing to fly on this airline. Then something happened that was unusual; he requested our attention. Immediately my ears perked up, and I listened intently. His tone changed when he announced that underneath where passengers were sitting was the body of a fallen soldier and that when our flight landed at its destination, he wanted us to show our respect by remaining in our seats to allow the soldier escorting the body to exit the plane first. Waves of sadness washed over me.

Approximately five hours later, the plane arrived safely. The pilot again appeared and reminded us of his earlier announcement. From my seat, I watched a tall, well-built soldier with a somber countenance exit the plane. Looking out the window, my eyes captured a picture that I will remember for a long time. A distance away from the airplane, green fire trucks and police vehicles with flashing lights were parked. Standing not too far away were family members, including children, waiting to receive the body of their loved one. Also near the family were uniformed soldiers and a hearse.

We disembarked, and with deep sadness, I continued to watch from inside the airport. Tears rolled down my cheeks, as well as the cheeks of the passenger standing next to me. She turned and said that she'd read that the fallen soldier was a young mother. The solemnity of the moment impacted me more deeply. Never will she hug her children again. How fragile life is! This young mother had paid the ultimate sacrifice in service to her country. I pondered what was going on in the thoughts of her family members as they watched the soldiers remove her lifeless body from the plane.

My husband and I continued to the baggage claim area with heavy hearts. Somehow, I couldn't help thinking of this young soldier and her family. My thoughts drifted to centuries ago when Jesus, the beloved Son of God, also paid the ultimate sacrifice not just for His country but for the entire world. And that includes you and me. What unfathomable love!

Shirley C. Iheanacho

November 12

Somebody's Prayin'

Therefore I exhort first of all that supplications, prayers, intercessions, and giving of thanks be made for all men.
—1 Timothy 2:1, NKJV

In 2007, my son joined the United States Marine Corps. At the end of each boot camp, there is a three-day final challenge, called The Crucible, which tests the recruits physically, mentally, and morally. As a worried mother, I petitioned my prayer warrior friends to help cover my son in prayer twenty-four hours a day, with each lady signing up for a specific hour. Afterward, I mailed the schedule to my son. The recruits were allowed to take only certain items with them (neither a prayer schedule nor a watch was on that list). However, one recruit in their group could estimate time fairly accurately, and my son managed to hide the prayer schedule during his crucible. When he encountered tough times, my son would ask his fellow recruit what time it was and secretly look at the schedule to see who was praying for him.

At the end of The Crucible, they hike back to the base, where all recruits end up at the Iwo Jima Memorial, and their drill instructors call them marines for the first time. They then receive an EGA medallion (a medallion with an eagle, globe, and anchor on it).

This reminds me of another three-day physical, mental, and moral crucible—the one that our Savior faced during the last hours of His life, which consisted of a betrayal, trial, and crucifixion.

As we go through this life with all its trials and difficulties, let us remember to look at our prayer list and see that every hour has Jesus' name written beside it. Hebrews 7:25 tells us, "He ever liveth to make intercession for [us]" (KJV).

At the end of our crucible, when we reach those gates of pearl, our Instructor will give us a new name. Instead of an EGA medallion, we will be given a crown, robe, and harp. How I long for that day. "Even so, come, Lord Jesus" (Revelation 22:20, KJV).

Listen to the words of the song "Somebody's Prayin'," by Ricky Skaggs, and picture a young man at boot camp and later doing two tours of duty in Afghanistan. That is my son's story—and it's yours as well. Thank you to all faithful prayer warriors and our Great Prayer Warrior!

Kathy Hull

The Power in Jesus' Name!

"The Lord is my strength and song,
and He has become my salvation;
He is my God, and I will praise Him;
My father's God, and I will exalt Him.
The Lord is a man of war;
The Lord is His name."
—Exodus 15:2, 3, NKJV

November 18, 2013. A date branded into my mind and spiritual fabric. I awoke wondering what to wear to the university that afternoon. Considering my options, I was prompted to wear navy blue. Deciding on beige, I took the outfit from the closet. A "nag" began about the blue suit, but I argued internally that it didn't match my upbeat mood. However, I departed in navy blue, trying to make sense of the persistent "nag."

Journeying home later that day was uneventful until my car started sputtering on a dark, lonely, dangerous road. Losing power, it finally stopped and refused to restart. A few SOS calls found no one readily available. I then remembered having the number for a tire shop about a minute away. The operator said that he would come immediately. Seven minutes into waiting, I heard a rustle. It was not the breeze. I quickly put my keys into the door pocket, stuffed my purse under my seat, and hid my mobile phone on the seat under my leg. My heart palpitated, and I could only whisper, "Jesus!" as one intruder went to the back seat, and the other sat beside me, making demands and threats, weapon aimed toward my head. I convinced them of my occupation with the manila exam packages on the back seat. But I could only be seen properly with headlights from the very few passing vehicles. Color me navy blue!

The intruders almost hurt themselves trying to escape unnoticed when my help arrived. His apology didn't matter, but his timely presence certainly did—I was unharmed! Then without hesitation, my car engine started when he told me to try! Two days later, my testimony at church about the experience inspired the congregation to encircle me, clapping, dancing, and singing this truth, "What a mighty God we serve!"*

Cloreth S. Greene

* Anonymous, "What a Mighty God We Serve," public domain.

November 14

Unseen Hands

"Are not two sparrows sold for a copper coin? And not one of them falls to the ground apart from your Father's will. But the very hairs of your head are all numbered. Do not fear therefore; you are of more value than many sparrows."
—Matthew 10:29–31, NKJV

What favorite thing do you enjoy with your family? Mine is to enjoy tea with my two sisters, brother, Mum, and Dad around the kitchen table. This is when we have the best conversations, laugh uncontrollably over something funny, listen avidly to stories of Mum and Dad's childhood, and reminisce about the good old days. One day, Mum and I were enjoying our tea when the conversation turned to my childhood. My family was living in Sydney, New South Wales, Australia, when I was born, and six months later, Dad accepted the call to study ministry, so we moved to Avondale College in Cooranbong, North New South Wales.

I was about nine months old when Mum placed me in a baby walker with wheels to encourage me to walk and keep me entertained while she went about the household duties. Our house wasn't large—three bedrooms—and had wooden floors. The ground behind the house sloped, so there was a long staircase from the back door to the backyard. Mum said that she had to go down the back stairs to hang the laundry on the clothesline that was in the backyard. She thought I was in another part of the house, but unbeknownst to her, I was right behind her and made it to the landing of the stairs before the door shut. Mum had made it down the steps when she thought she heard a noise. As she turned to see what it was, she watched horrified as I started falling down the stairs in my baby walker. Mum said that the incident occurred in slow motion. Somehow, I was thrown from the baby walker, and while the walker fell to the ground, she saw me being gently placed on a step halfway down the stairs. While I did not sustain any injuries, I did cry out of shock. Mum is certain that hands caught me midair, cradled me, and placed me safely, gently on the step. There is no other explanation except that God protected me that day with unseen hands.

I always think of that story with awe, overwhelmed by the knowledge that God cares about me—that He protected me and saved my life at nine months. What can I do to repay Him for His loving care? Honor Him, serve Him, and fulfill His purpose in my life!

Jenny Rivera

Revealed

Teach me knowledge and good judgment,
for I trust your commands.
—Psalm 119:66, NIV

Some time ago, I agreed to take on a challenge someone asked me to help them with. As time went by, I did not receive any further details, so eventually, I inquired into how we were going to proceed. I was told that the original plan was canceled. I was confused but accepted the change of heart.

Life soon became very hectic, and my devotional time suffered as a result. There were meetings, projects, home duties, and a little child to care for. Mornings quickly rolled into evenings. I would spend time in prayer and a brief reflection, but I knew that I needed more spiritual nourishment. So one day I decided to change things. I awoke earlier than usual and sneaked to a section of the house to pray and meditate. As I began to do so, the solution to the matter that perplexed me revealed itself.

The revelation was sparked by a remark I had heard the previous day in addition to a series of events that happened a few weeks before. It was as though God opened my eyes and unveiled everything to me. The pieces in the puzzle all began to fit together neatly. As I reflected on the insight I received during my prayer time, it was as though God spoke to me in three ways. The first was that He gave me a clear understanding of a situation. Second, and most important, He taught me that it is important to spend time in prayer and meditation because He can reveal more things to me. Third, God reminded me that He is in control of my life and is arranging things for my benefit. You see, unbeknownst to me, God was working on an employment opportunity that would have been impossible to do had I gone ahead and completed the project I described earlier. This was a very strong reminder that I should not be disappointed by doors that seem to close in my life because God is working everything together for my benefit.

So, my dear sister in Christ, if you are facing a difficult decision or situation, I challenge you to look to God for help. He has all the answers you will ever need, and He is willing to reveal His will to you according to His divine wisdom. Remember to spend time each day in communion with God and rely on Him to show you what you ought to do.

Taniesha K. Robertson-Brown

Do Not Fear All Year

Here is the patience of the saints: here are they that keep the commandments of God, and the faith of Jesus.
—Revelation 14:12, KJV

We won't soon forget the year 2020. As the pandemic continued, people found ways to cope, like reaching out to those in need. For others, staying cooped up inside was difficult. They complained about doing virtual school at home with their children. Some people took their own lives. Many young people became paranoid, depressed, discouraged, and weary.

If only we had that one ounce of faith, trusted God, and focused our lives on Jesus' return. Like the Bible says, "Therefore be ye also ready" (Matthew 24:44, KJV). We don't know the time or the hour. We just need to be ready for the second coming of Jesus, have faith, and claim God's promises.

Many say the pandemic pushed us into a new normal. We should continue to trust God and draw closer to Him whether we are in a new normal or not. Be content with change and accept life for what it is. Focus on our Creator; He is still in control. Some are questioning, "Where is God in this?" He is still here. We've just turned our backs on Him by not praying. God doesn't want anyone to perish; if He did, He wouldn't have sent Jesus to earth.

Whether we are consumed with fear or filled with hope, all depends on where we are looking. If you are looking at natural disasters, if you are consumed with bad news, if pestilences and disease occupy your thoughts—if that's where you are focused, your heart is going to be filled with fear. Jesus says, "Look up!" Why? When we look to heaven's sanctuary, we see Jesus and discover strength in His promises.

In Christ we find confidence. At times, we may experience the emotion of fear, but we will not be paralyzed by fear because our confidence in God triumphs over our fear.

The Bible says "do not fear" or "fear not" repeatedly. Many have suggested that there are 365 times that an expression like "fear not" is used throughout the Bible—that is one for every day of the year. God has the entire calendar year covered. He invites us to rest in His love, trust in His grace, and rejoice in His power.

Camilla E. Cassell

Let's Party!

All of us should be encouraging one another as true brothers and sisters do, building up each other's faith.
—Romans 15:2, *The Clear Word**

My husband, Johnny, and I celebrated our seventieth wedding anniversary during the early throes of COVID-19. However, most of the world was in lockdown. Life as we knew it was at a standstill. No cards of congratulations were expected because very few people we knew went close to a post office. Who knew where the uninvited virus lurked?

However, to our surprise, we heard a knock at our door. There stood years-long friends, Virginia and Steve, with a card and a cake that they handed through the door with socially distanced outstretched arms and loving words. Then off they drove with waves.

A couple of hours later, another knock at our door and two more friends stood there: our masked-friend Fred with another cake as his dear Gladys waved cheerfully from a distance at their car. Again a few dear words were exchanged, and then they were on their way. We like cake, but how could we use all this cake and no one with whom to party? After pondering on those two scrumptious cakes, I said to Johnny, "Let's party!"

I emailed some of our closest neighbors (we live in an Adventist retirement community of apartments), inviting them to come and get some of our gifted anniversary cake. All accepted the invitation, and we happily chatted through the door. Dear words from these brothers and sisters encouraged us when we might have felt a bit blue otherwise. After all, seventy years of marriage is quite a blessing. It isn't always a sermon we humans need, but we all do need loving words and actions. Our anniversary wasn't lonely at all. We don't feel that we missed out on anything because the most wonderful celebration in earth's history is coming up when Jesus comes to take His redeemed to heaven.

Betty Kossick

* Jack Blanco, *The Clear Word* (Hagerstown, MD: Review and Herald®, 2003), 1182.

November 18

Remembering Friends

He hath put my brethren far from me,
and mine acquaintance are verily estranged from me.
My kinsfolk have failed, and my familiar friends have forgotten me.
—Job 19:13, 14, KJV

When COVID-19 invaded the United States, I immediately thought of family and friends and wondered how they were doing. Required social distancing kept us from being physically together; however, we could still connect by phone and social media. I decided to check on some long-lost friends. I called one friend in a nearby city. She was doing fine. I logged on to Facebook and connected with several people whom I had not talked to in a while. They were all doing well.

The next day, I found my college alumni directory and looked up a friend who was in the same major as I was in college. I found her phone number and nervously pushed each digit. When she came to the phone, I identified myself and she said, "Who is this?"

"Sylvia, we went to college together and had the same major. Do you remember me?" I asked.

"No!" she replied.

"OK, I'm sorry to bother you. Have a good day," I answered quickly as I hung up the phone. I was crushed.

Perhaps my idea to connect with old friends was a huge mistake! About thirty minutes later, my phone rang. The husband of my college friend was calling to let me know that his wife was having some medical problems that accounted for her responses when I called. They found their yearbook and were now looking at my picture. He attended the same college but was a year behind us. He asked me some questions, and I let him know how I met his wife and shared a little about our time together in college. I admitted that we had not connected in years, and I was checking on people I had not talked to in a while.

Throughout my life, I have met tons of people and made many friends. I do not remember everyone, but I do hope that I have made a difference in someone's life. Whatever illnesses, afflictions, or maladies we experience here on earth, I pray that we can say like Job, "I know that my redeemer liveth, and that he shall stand at the latter day upon the earth" (Job 19:25, KJV).

Sylvia A. Franklin

Pandemic Praises

Whoever dwells in the shelter of the Most High
will rest in the shadow of the Almighty.
—Psalm 91:1, NIV

The COVID-19 pandemic was the worst event that I have experienced in my lifetime, yet I could still praise God during it. One day, I went out for my allowed "essential chores." I returned home but sat for a while in the car before going indoors. Later that evening, I heard on the news that at that exact time, parts of Jamaica, including the place where I was sitting, were rocking to a 7.3 earthquake, which I did not feel! The word *earthquake* terrifies me. *But God*, who knows that, kept me from experiencing it.

I always choreograph my "essential chores" expeditiously the night before I hit the road. My plan one night was to visit a bank south of an intersection near my home, but in the morning, I somehow woke with a different plan—to go north instead to another bank. That day, there was a shooting incident south of the intersection I would have traveled through that could have affected me in various ways, *but God* gave me a change of plans during the night.

Another day, I was heading home when I stopped behind a huge front-end loader at a red light. The light turned green, and initially it didn't move, then it began moving—in reverse! I started blowing my horn, and he waved me to pass him, but I could not because he had rolled too close. I tried to reverse but had to stop as the motorist behind started blowing. I wish I could say I prayed then, but I just froze as this huge mass pushed me back, then stopped! I calmly exited my car, without any injury, and I heard the driver explain that his vehicle had shut down. I completed all the legal requirements like a robot and then drove the car away. Someone told me later that when those vehicles shut down, they don't stop rolling back, so by logic I should have been crushed, *but God* . . . , and my morning prayers before I left home.

Thanks to God, my family has not been infected by COVID-19, but stay-at-home orders have affected me emotionally. However, I choose to praise an awesome God for His goodness during an awful time. I wish to express my sincere condolences to all who have been negatively affected by this pandemic.

Cecelia Grant

November 20

Give Thanks to God Always

And always be thankful.
Let the message of Christ, in all its richness, fill your lives. Teach and counsel each other with all the wisdom he gives. Sing psalms and hymns and spiritual songs to God with thankful hearts. And whatever you do or say, do it as a representative of the Lord Jesus, giving thanks through him to God the Father.
—Colossians 3:15–17, NLT

Maybe you will agree with me that 2020 and 2021 will probably go down in history as two horrific years because of the invasion of the COVID-19 pandemic into people's lives worldwide. This pandemic filled us with fear, stress, anxiety, pain, and worry. Millions became ill, and millions succumbed to death, including some of my dear friends. No one was left unscathed. I was unhappy because it had also interrupted plans my husband and I had to travel. We were stuck at home. No way in my heart did I feel any gratitude. I pondered whether anything good could come from this awful and painful experience. But God! Yes, only He could do it.

Early one morning during my devotion, I rattled off to God my long list of things I wanted Him to do. Quietly, my conscience began to gnaw at me; guilt overwhelmed me. I was impressed to change my prayer, and instead of my regular prayer asking Him to do this and that, why not spend some time just thanking Him. As I reflected on my incredible journey, my eyes welled up with tears. God had done so much for my family and me, yet I was drowning in the sea of ingratitude.

I recalled how God had provided the opportunity for me to speak more than eleven times on seven prayer lines and health ministries' calls over the past year. That was the first in my lifetime. I also received texts, emails, and phone calls from individuals who were blessed and inspired by my messages and articles published in recent devotional books. God had also protected us from the coronavirus and spared my life to reach eighty-one years. I had so much for which to be thankful.

Dear reader, today, amid your busyness and pressures of life, take time to consider what God has done and continues to do for you and offer Him your thankful heart. May you be inspired by these powerful words in 1 Thessalonians 5:16–18, "Rejoice always, pray continually, give thanks in all circumstances; for this is God's will for you in Christ Jesus" (NIV).

Shirley C. Iheanacho

Two Little Words

I will praise the name of God with a song,
And will magnify Him with thanksgiving.
—Psalm 69:30, NKJV

Among the lovely words in our English vocabulary, I think my two favorites are "thank you." I can always count on receiving a warm smile whenever I say these words to someone or they are said to me. Sometimes, the words are said in the midst of tears, yet the heart is smiling.

Many years ago, when I first moved to Orlando, Florida, United States of America, I was enthralled with the beautiful weather and year-round greenery. I'll never forget the first night I spent in my new house because I was awakened around four in the morning by a chorus of birds chirping! I could hear at least seven or eight different birds just chattering away. I smiled to myself, thinking, *Well, how nice! Every bird in the neighborhood is out on my front lawn to welcome me!* Then I went back to sleep with a prayer of thanks to God for giving me such a wonderful experience.

When I arose later that morning, I heard the cheerful chorus of sounds once again, and I could not wait to see the lawn covered with my new feathered friends. So I opened the front door, but there was not one bird there! As I heard the sound once again, it caused me to look up, and there, sitting high on a light pole, was my one-bird choir! You guessed it. It was a mockingbird. I had never heard a mockingbird before and had no idea they could make the exact sounds of perhaps a dozen other birds!

As I settled into the neighborhood, I discovered there were very wide, smooth sidewalks to walk on. Each time I took a walk, I was compelled to say, "Thank You, God, for these wonderful sidewalks and especially for the mockingbirds!" Just two little words, *thank you*, are very sweet to hear and also very sweet to say.

In every aspect of our lives—no matter what is going on—let us be on the lookout for even the smallest thing for which we can say thank you to our spouses, children, grandchildren, friends, neighbors, or coworkers.

Father God, I want to thank You for loving us all and especially for sending our dear Jesus to this world so that we can know what true love really is.

Terry Wilson Robinson

November 22

Grateful

In everything give thanks; for this is the will of God in Christ Jesus for you.
—1 Thessalonians 5:18, NKJV

Undoubtedly 2020 will be a year hard to forget, though many of us will want to try to forget it. As I write this, it is May 2, 2020, and so many things have happened in the four months that have passed already since the pandemic descended on us. I saw a meme on social media asking if we could go back to 2019 and do a reset. The technologically savvy who read this will know exactly to what I refer. For those not so savvy, it just means a do-over. Unfortunately for us mortals, there is no reset or do-over in this life. It is onward ever and backward never, regardless of what we are facing ahead. The most we can hope for is to change course if life allows us that option.

It is sometimes difficult to be thankful when times are hard as they have been recently. People have lost their jobs. They have had to stay inside for weeks on end. Food has been in noticeably short supply in many households. Why could we possibly be thankful? Yet I challenge you today to list at least five things for which to be thankful. Here's my list:

First, I am thankful for life. I am still here above the ground despite the risks and exposure I face daily. Parts of my body hurt, but I can still move.

Second, I have a loving and supportive family. Even though we are apart as I write this and the future is uncertain, I still feel their love and support from across the miles.

Next, I am thankful for PPE (personal protective equipment) to do my job as a nurse. So many workers on the front lines both here in my country and elsewhere are put at great risk because they do not have the protective gear they need to do their work during this pandemic.

Fourth, I am thankful for work and the ability to still earn a living, despite my job being an area of great anxiety and stress.

Finally, I am thankful that my son completed high school last year instead of this year, although I know God would have helped us through as He is doing for many students and their families. I must admit compiling this list was a bit of a challenge, but the more we dwell on the positive things in our lives, the more we will be able to be grateful to God for even the things that don't seem to be so wonderful.

Raylene McKenzie Ross

Gift Giver

Every good and perfect gift is from above, coming down from the Father of the heavenly lights, who does not change like shifting shadows.
—James 1:17, NIV

Thanksgiving! What a wonderful holiday, a day to be thankful for all the wonderful things that our heavenly Father has provided for us and the promises we have that make even our trials things for which to be thankful. When we stop for a moment or two to think about our lives, past and present, it is true: "Not one of all the good promises the Lord your God gave you has failed. Every promise has been fulfilled" (Joshua 23:14, NIV).

By now, people have been bustling around for some time getting ready for Christmas, buying gifts and hoping they will be the "right" present for the receiver. Our Jesus is a gift giver too. I am not thinking of material things; I am thinking about how lavishly He bestows the gifts of nature upon us: rainbows and waterfalls, flowers and plants whose beauty defies description, and friendships that uplift and comfort us. He gives us little children whose innocence and enthusiasm fill us with joy and the trials that make us stronger and more able to help those who come to us in need. God is so good!

This is the time of year that Hebrews 13:5, 6 talks to us about. "Keep your lives free from the love of money and be content with what you have, because God has said,

'Never will I leave you;
never will I forsake you.'
So we say with confidence,
'The Lord is my helper; I will not be afraid.
What can mere mortals do to me?' " (NIV).

This past week, my granddaughter emailed me pictures of a trip she took to the Smokey Mountains. She was on a hike to Laurel Falls, and the pictures were gorgeous. Nature has a way of showing us the beauty and power of the love that God has for each of us. The greatest show nature has to offer is free. Doesn't cost you anything. We just can't lose sight of these good things because they are intended for us to experience, share, and draw closer to the God who created them.

Grace A. Keene

November 24

Close Calls

The eyes of the LORD are upon the righteous,
and his ears are open unto their cry.
—Psalm 34:15, KJV

Shortly after I moved from Jamaica to Canada, I was living in British Columbia in a town named Kitimat. It was a very small town, and there was no Seventh-day Adventist church there. The closest bigger town was Terrace, which was about forty minutes away by a winding highway through the mountains. I traveled to Terrace very often for church and also for shopping.

One day, on my return trip from Terrace to Kitimat, I was very tired and fell asleep at the wheel. My car rolled onto the rumble strips lining the side of the highway, which woke me up. As I opened my eyes, I realized that I was heading off the road as my car was approaching a bridge and quickly righted the steering wheel to get back on the road. My guardian angel was working overtime. I thanked the Lord for His watch care over me and the rush of adrenaline that enabled me to get home safely after that.

There was another time that I had stayed in Terrace after church on Sabbath and went to someone's house for lunch and fellowship. The sun had set very early, and it quickly became dark. There are no lights on the highway heading back to Kitimat. Whenever I drive, I ask the Lord for journeying mercies on the road to keep us safe from harm and danger. After a while of driving, I saw a pair of yellow eyes glowing up through the top of my windshield. I quickly applied my foot to the brake pedal as I saw the eyes moving across my line of sight and the outline of a huge moose walking across the road in front of my car. I can only imagine how devastating it would have been had I hit that moose. Another close call!

A few years ago, when we were still living in Leduc and working on the north side of Edmonton, I picked up Alyssa from school and was heading home on the highway. Traffic had been very heavy, and I was exhausted. I fell asleep at the wheel and woke up hearing the sirens of emergency vehicles. There were no emergency vehicles whatsoever anywhere at all. The Lord had again protected us.

Thank You, Lord, for keeping us safe from all harm and danger.

Noella (Jumpp) Baird

God Is a Gentleman

But Daniel resolved not to defile himself with the royal food and wine, and he asked the chief official for permission not to defile himself this way.
—Daniel 1:8, NIV

God is a gentleman who will not force any of His children to obey His laws. He is not a *bully*! He allows us to decide which force we will obey—will it be God or Satan?

We must learn to practice self-control in all areas of our lives, especially in eating. Like Daniel and his three Hebrew friends, we must purpose in our hearts not to ruin our health by making poor choices of food, drink, and activities. We must follow biblical principles that will bring a blessing to body, soul, and mind.

The fruit of the Spirit is not only love, joy, peace, forbearance (patience), kindness, goodness, faithfulness, and gentleness, but also self-control. I am sure the Hebrew captives had similar passions as we have today, yet they managed to rise above the influences of the courts of Babylon. We must do the same in our time and rise above the world's influences. Faithful people will have greater physical stamina and increased power of endurance. Yes, we all need stamina and endurance. The right physical habits will promote mental advantage, intellectual power, physical stamina, and a longer length of living. God does not step in, bully, or save us from the consequences of our choices but encourages us to be moderate in all matters.

We must make wise decisions. Daniel's quick thinking, firmness of purpose, and quickness in acquiring knowledge and resisting temptation were due to the plainness of his diet and the connection he had with God in his prayer life. The history of Daniel and his youthful companions was recorded in the inspired Word for our benefit and for future generations. Through the book of Daniel, we learn the principles of temperance and how those values favor us. God is speaking the same truth to us today, especially, during the pandemic. He desires that we place ourselves in the right place to follow the laws of health. Take the time to plan healthy meals and commit to exercising daily. Your body will thank you! Remember, God will never bully you into obedience; He is too much of a Gentleman.

Yvonne E. Ealey

November 26

Challenge on the Zambezi River

"When you pass through the waters,
I will be with you;
and when you pass through the rivers,
they will not sweep over you."
—Isaiah 43:2, NIV

Yuka Adventist Hospital (Kalabo, Zambia) owns an eighty-horsepower small speedboat and a twenty-five-horsepower longboat that can accommodate thirty passengers. During the rainy season, the usual travel time for the longboat is eight hours downstream and twelve hours upstream.

One day Harville, who was the hospital's maintenance manager, together with Dr. Conception, a volunteer medical intern from Argentina, and Harrington, the longboat's cockswain, left for Mongu, forty-eight miles (seventy-eight kilometers) away, to purchase some needed materials.

Early the next day, the heavily loaded boat started the slow journey upstream expecting to be back in Yuka late in the afternoon. After smooth sailing for the first ten hours, suddenly the propeller quit. They managed to fix the propeller shaft and continued on their way. Three more times the engine quit before finally stopping for good. They had to cling to the grasses along the crocodile-infested riverbank to keep the boat from being carried downstream by the strong current.

It was getting late, so they decided that Harrington would take a passenger boat back to the hospital while Harville and Dr. Conception waited in a village along the river. Finally, Harrington returned with a speedboat to tow the longboat back to Yuka. Unfortunately, the longboat with its cargo was too heavy for the small speedboat to drag against the strong current of the Zambezi River. Harville prayed, "Lord, please help us. I know You are in control."

After several attempts, someone suggested, "Let us tie the speedboat to the side of the longboat." The brilliant idea worked! Slowly, the small speedboat and the longboat traveled upstream together . . . side-by-side. After twenty-four hours on the river, they finally made it back home. Serving at Yuka Adventist Hospital was challenging yet filled with evidence of God's guidance and protection.

Ellen Porteza Valenciano

Gaining From the Tempest and Storms

The Lord is good, a strong hold in the day of trouble; and he knoweth them that trust in him.
—Nahum 1:7, KJV

Tempest can be likened to or used interchangeably with *blast, gale, hurricane, tornado, squall, excitement, violent commotion*, or *disturbance/violent windstorm*. Seasons of grief and despair are usually represented by storms in the Bible; they are moments to exercise endurance until the storms pass. The Bible provides wisdom and guidance to overcome and get through the storms of our lives while following the path of God through hard and gloomy times.

Isaiah says to God,

> You have been a refuge for the poor,
> a refuge for the needy in their distress,
> a shelter from the storm
> and a shade from the heat (Isaiah 25:4, NIV).

Recounting times when storms threatened the peace of my home, I could say, "Thank You God, for Your mercies endure forever." In 2018, my family was thrown into a hopeless situation because we couldn't find a solution for my husband's illness. God miraculously healed him just as the tempest was at its peak and all hope was lost.

During those days, I found solace in Psalm 91:1–4, which says,

> Whoever dwells in the shelter of the Most High
> will rest in the shadow of the Almighty.
> I will say of the Lord, "He is my refuge and my fortress,
> my God, in whom I trust."
> Surely he will save you. . . .
> He will cover you with his feathers,
> and under his wings you will find refuge (NIV).

May God help us to gain from our storms and tempest by putting our trust in Him!

Joy Bakaba Igwe

November 28

Our Investment Project

Delight yourself also in the Lord,
And He shall give you the desires of your heart.
—Psalm 37:4, NKJV

Evelyn was two years old when she started gasping for breath from what we thought was a simple cold. After calling her doctor, we were told to take her immediately to the hospital. The nurses scurried around as they connected her to an IV tube, put her under an oxygen tent in the ICU, and placed her on the critical list. Asthma attack! Who knew? We were clueless and felt like terrible parents!

After being told that she might not live through the night, all we could do was pray, cry, and call everybody we knew. Telling her brothers, ages seven and nine, that their little sister might not live through the night was one of the hardest things we had done in our marriage. By morning she was still hanging on—thank You, Jesus! By day six, she was taken off the critical list. After two weeks, we left the hospital with a very thin little bundle and a bag filled with medicine and instructions. We were told to strip Evelyn's room of anything that might collect dust: books, pillows, wool blankets, rugs, curtains, stuffed animals, and pictures on the wall.

Her life was filled with medicine, allergy shots, and breathing treatments. We learned to watch for signs of the beginning of an asthma attack. Frequently, she was too sick to attend church, so one of us stayed home with her. I talked to many parents with asthmatic children and read health books that suggested eliminating dairy and sugar from her diet.

One particular Sabbath we were impressed to make Evelyn our investment project for the year. We promised the Lord that we would give a certain amount of money for a mission offering every Sabbath that Evelyn felt well enough so that that all five of us could attend church together. We kept our commitment all year and the Lord blessed. It was the best investment project we ever made.

Evelyn is grown now with children of her own. We praise the Lord that she has not been in the hospital from asthma since that time. When she sings, people often mention how powerful her voice is for such a small frame. My heartfelt response is, "Thank You, Jesus, for healing her lungs!" She knows that her life was spared that night for a purpose—"to God be the glory, great things He has done."* Don't be afraid to invest and watch the Lord work.

Shirley Sain Fordham

* Fanny Crosby, "To God Be the Glory," 1875, public domain.

A Boundless God

And it shall come to pass, that before they call, I will answer;
and while they are yet speaking, I will hear.
—Isaiah 65:24, KJV

Transitioning from a third-world nursing practice to a Western culture requires adaptation, learning, and unlearning. A paradigm shift in ways of thinking and clinical reasoning quickly happened with learning and unlearning.

Working as a critical care nurse brought meaning and reality to my nursing career. Intensive care unit (ICU) nursing requires quick clinical decision-making. Patient safety and quality of life are the core of nursing. I loved it and enjoyed the fast-paced nursing practice, but my heart's desire was to teach. The Lord knew that I needed to be well rooted in the dynamics of nursing practice and management to be equipped to teach. He led my path to a management position at a step-down pediatric unit. The responsibilities were extensive but challenging. The knowledge learned grew in relation to managing safe patient care, strict compliance to regulations, and staying on budget, yet maintaining excellent outcomes.

The global economic depression affected hospital operations in 1993 and led to hospital layoffs. I was laid off as middle-management positions were removed. Losing a job caused feelings of uncertainty. I still had my part-time teaching at the community college. In faith, I placed my case in God's hands. "If the door closes, the Lord opens the window," we assured our children during family worship.

"We heard that before! Yes, from *The Sound of Music*!" our children replied.

Our oldest daughter was going to college. Just as I had asked my husband to get a second job, the telephone rang. It was the dean of the community college. She explained that I had been recommended by the dean of another college to teach. "Edna, we need you badly. Can you come now?" I was awed by God's opening of this window!

Yes, God answers even before we call! We experience crucibles in our lives, but God's promise in Isaiah 65:24 is sure, "Before they call, I will answer; and while they are yet speaking, I will hear" (KJV). The God of heaven always proves that He is a boundless God. He is faithful, and His mercy endures forever!

Edna Bacate Domingo

What's in a Name?

"But I will reveal my name to my people, and they will come to know its power. Then at last they will recognize that I am the one who speaks to them."
—Isaiah 52:6, NLT

I never liked my name as a child. My parents named me "Linda" because of a popular song that was recorded by a well-known crooner. In those days, my folks had a vinyl record with the song on it, and they played it all the time on the record player at home. It was a sappy love song, and I endured a fair amount of teasing by the boys in grade school. Apparently, in the United States, many little girls born in the mid-1940s were also named Linda. I say this because of the thirty boys and girls in my first-grade classroom, five of us girls were named Linda. I went by "Linda N." for many years so that my teachers would know which papers and reports were mine. And for the longest time, I wished I could change my name.

In Bible times, parents often gave children names with a particular meaning or symbolism. Rebekah named the second of her twin boys Jacob, which means "heel-grasper." The name, according to *Strong's Concordance*, means "heel-catcher," "heel holder," or "supplanter." The root word of the name means "to supplant, circumvent, take by the heel, follow at the heel, assail insidiously, overreach." I guess, by comparison, Linda doesn't seem so bad.

As it came to pass, Jacob eventually deceived his father and his brother, which had life-changing implications for him. But after his true conversion, God gave him a new name, "Your name will no longer be Jacob. . . . From now on you will be called Israel, because you have fought with God and with men and have won" (Genesis 32:28, NLT). Jacob—now, Israel—may never have been a perfect man, but that day, his life turned a corner.

The Bible describes the book of life where the names of Jesus' followers are written (Revelation 13:8; 17:8; 20:12; 21:27). In fact, when speaking to a group of disciples who were going out to preach, Jesus said, "Rejoice because your names are registered in heaven" (Luke 10:20, NLT). That's good news indeed! It means I won't have to explain who I am in heaven. Not only does Jesus know my name, but also in God's blessing to all nations, He says, "For the name I will give them is an everlasting one. It will never disappear!" (Isaiah 56:5, NLT). Let's all look forward to the day when Jesus will welcome us home by our own name!

Linda Nottingham

God's Master Plan

"For I know the plans I have for you," declares the LORD, *"plans to prosper you and not to harm you, plans to give you hope and a future."*
—Jeremiah 29:11, NIV

Every time I drive by a certain Taco Bell in Bowie, Maryland, I think, *I remember when that building was just a plan.*

When I worked as a newspaper reporter, I covered Bowie City Hall regularly as one of my assignments. I remember the meeting when that new Taco Bell was just an idea being proposed by planners to the city council members. I still have memories of the planning team stating their case and then skillfully persuading the councilmen and councilwomen that building and opening a new Taco Bell in Bowie was a good idea.

It took about two years for that building to be established, but once the doors of Taco Bell were open, customers flocked. I know this because I see cars in the parking lot every time I drive by. It amazes me how an idea on paper grew into a reality that makes so many people who love to eat happy!

All of this makes me think of a spiritual lesson. God knew us before we were even an idea in our parents' minds; God knows who we are (see Psalm 139 and Jeremiah 1:5). He sees the full potential for the story of our lives, and He has a master plan for us to follow as He establishes our steps.

God's plans for us are good, and no matter how much we work to make our plans come true, God's plan for our lives always prevails (Proverbs 16:9). We make plans, but God establishes our steps.

One of my favorite features of being a journalist is seeing how a story I covered about a plan for a restaurant, park, or another place where people gather starts as an idea on paper and, if approved, is built and opened to the public.

There's something special about seeing something in its beginning stages and then watching it develop into an establishment that makes people happy. It helps me imagine how God feels when He thinks of us and allows us to be created, and then we enter this world and grow up into all He's called us to be in this life.

Alexis A. Goring

December 2

Connected to the Root

For this reason I bow my knees to the Father of our Lord Jesus Christ, . . . that Christ may dwell in your hearts through faith; that you, being rooted and grounded in love, may be able to comprehend with all the saints what is the width and length and depth and height—to know the love of Christ which passes knowledge; that you may be filled with all the fullness of God.
—Ephesians 3:14–19, NKJV

With the coming of spring, it was time to do some yard work at the church. It was decided to pull up some of the old landscaping and put in some new plants. In the flower bed next to the stairs was a bush they wanted to take out. They got shovels and a long metal pry bar. The guys worked and worked at this bush, but it was very root-bound, and the ground was hard. After a good half hour, they finally got a little piece of it out, but it was obvious that the roots were deep and went under the cement stairs. It was hard, hot work, and it looked as though it would take another hour or better to get the roots chopped through. Finally, we got a truck and wrapped a strap around the bush, and with one good yank, the truck pulled, and the bush was out. Hurrah!

In the parable of the sower (Matthew 13:1–23), we are encouraged to let our roots grow deep so that we are not easily uprooted. Jesus wants more than anything for us to be attached to Him because He never fails and will never lead us the wrong way. We can grow and bear fruit in Him, even when we have been wild, headstrong people.

I think the analogy of the stubborn bush has two meanings for me.

First, I want all the sin in my life uprooted. To do this job by myself is labor-intensive because sin's roots are deep and stubborn—just like that old bush. To get rid of sin, I need to allow Jesus to yank it out of my life. Sometimes, this process takes some time because the roots of sin hold on with tenacity. But holding on to Jesus, I know He will be successful.

Second, I want more than anything to be grafted into Jesus and bear fruit because He is the root and the supplier of every good thing in my life. Don't you want the same things? It's exciting that our God, who made us and everything in the universe, wants us to be attached to Him, and by being attached, we can learn every day about His wonderful love for us!

Mona Fellers

What's in a Name?

"Fear not, for I have redeemed you;
I have called you by name, you are mine."
—Isaiah 43:1, ESV

I was delighted that we were having our first grandson. My son and his girlfriend were considering names. As I sat in church one Sabbath, a name popped into my head. It was not a familiar name to me, so I smiled and sent Tremayne a text saying "Bryson." His response was, "Who is that?" And I said it was the baby's name that God gave me. Bryson arrived several months later, in August 2017.

I began thinking about how some of the Bible characters came by their names. The Gospel of Luke states that while Zechariah ministered at the altar of incense, an angel of the Lord appeared and announced to him that his wife, Elisabeth, would give birth to a son, whom he was to name John (Luke 1:12–17).

In Genesis, we read the story of Creation and the fall of man. Genesis 3:20 states that Adam "called his wife's name Eve, because she was the mother of all living" (ESV).

Mary was a young woman who was engaged to marry Joseph. An angel appeared to her and said, "Fear not Mary: for thou hast found favour with God. And, behold, thou shalt conceive in thy womb, and bring forth a son, and shalt call his name JESUS" (Luke 1:30, 31, KJV).

There is power in the name of Jesus; it's the sweetest name I know. Some other names used when referring to Jesus are God with us, our Rock, Savior, Messiah, Immanuel, Lamb of God, King of kings, Lord of lords, Alpha and Omega, Prince of Peace, Light of the world, the Word, the Door, the Good Shepherd, Chief Cornerstone, Master, Teacher, Lion of the tribe of Judah, the I Am, Great High Priest, the Great Physician, Wonderful Counselor, Redeemer, Bridegroom, Deliverer, Friend, Brother, the Way, the Truth, and the Life.

Jesus, name above all names. No matter what situation you find yourself in, in this life, Jesus is the answer to all our questions. As I write this, we are nine months into COVID-19 and in the midst of uncertainty. God has not left us alone, so cry out to Him today. If you are sick, cry out to the Great Physician; if you are sad, call on the Comforter. Whatever you need, He will supply if you ask in accordance with His will.

Sharon Long

December 4

Consciously Fashionable

I love them that love me;
and those that seek me early shall find me.
—Proverbs 8:17, KJV

I wake up each morning and do a daily regimen of personal care of my body. It features a habit of facial care that is very important to me. Whenever I travel or visit friends and family, I am known to carry the products essential for this skin-care habit. I believe that whenever I take care of my body, the temple of God, I am doing what God asked of me.

The same principles apply to our hearts and minds. When we wake up each morning, we need to care for our spiritual lives even more than our physical bodies. I begin my day with prayer and giving God thanks for all He has done and provided. I spend time praising Him through songs and feasting on scriptures. Meditating on His Word throughout the day heightens my faith and trust. I set aside time to petition the throne of mercy for my family, friends, church leaders, world leaders, and people. This daily routine ignites something in me. I feel more connected to God because the Holy Spirit guides and comforts me along my journey. It deepens and energizes my walk with God.

Praising God is a spiritual tradition that I treasure dearly. It was passed down to my siblings and me from my mother, who always made sure that we learned to give homage and reverence to our heavenly Father. It is a privilege to glorify Him. Praising Him makes my day easier and my heart stronger. My burdens lighter, I walk in His confidence and wisdom, and my spirit becomes more pleasant. While I still have my bouts of persecution that discourage me, I am reminded that Jesus is always on my side, so I press on.

Although the body He gave us is important, caring for our spiritual lives is even more important. God's Words are spirit and truth (John 6:63). As we memorize His Word, God promises to write it on our hearts (Hebrews 10:16). As we study to show ourselves approved unto God, we can serve Him without shame or beating ourselves up (2 Timothy 2:15). Our faces will glow and be radiant, not from a skin-care regime but from the time we spend with God. "They looked to Him and were radiant, and their faces were not ashamed" (Psalm 34:5, NKJV).

Corletta Aretha Barbar

Travel Safety Tips

In spite of this, you did not trust in the L*ORD your God, who went ahead of you on your journey, in fire by night and in a cloud by day, to search out places for you to camp and to show you the way you should go.*
—Deuteronomy 1:32, 33, NIV

I know my love for my children causes me to put their needs before my own, but this is not always wise. Consider the flight safety instructions that we receive as plane passengers before taking off. In the event of an emergency, we are advised to place our oxygen masks on first before assisting minors or anyone else. These are practical instructions because we can provide the best help when we are performing optimally. Our life on earth is oftentimes described as a journey, or we may be referred to as pilgrims in a foreign land. If these figurative expressions must be sustained, it is only fitting that we observe travel safety instructions. Selfishness is sometimes good. We must learn to set aside personal time for ourselves and not put others' needs ahead of our own all the time. We must find time for rest, recreation, and spiritual rejuvenation and practice healthy lifestyle choices that will promote quality of life. When we are at our best, we can offer the best care to our loved ones.

The same principle can be applied to our spiritual lives. God has commissioned us to preach and teach the good news of salvation. This job can be done more effectively when we are healthy. Therefore, effective missionary work is intrinsically tied to healthy habits. Returning to my analogy with the oxygen mask, just as it is critical to put one's oxygen mask on first, it is also vital that we feast on the bread of life daily. "Anxiety in a man's heart weighs him down, but a good word makes him glad" (Proverbs 12:25, ESV). When we are filled with God's words, we become less anxious and will naturally have more to share. Daily Bible study is the beginning of the development of a relationship with God. Finally, do not allow your anxieties about your long to-do list to deprive you of a good night's rest. "And which of you by being anxious can add a single hour to his span of life? If then you are not able to do as small a thing as that, why are you anxious about the rest?" (Luke 12:25, 26, ESV). Rather than worry, pray and allow God's perfect peace to abide with you. God wants us to succeed, and He has an eternal goal in mind. Allow the Holy Spirit to lead you. Allow Him to equip you.

Jodian Scott-Banton

December 6

The Hardest Job I Ever Had

"Inasmuch as you did it to one of the least of these My brethren, you did it to Me."
—Matthew 25:40, NKJV

I was watching 3ABN and seeing graphic pictures of the damages from Hurricane Katrina. Andrews University (Berrien Springs, Michigan, United States of America) students had been volunteering, but they had to go back to school. There was a need for older folks to volunteer. I said right out loud to my computer, "I could do that."

I called my son, and he encouraged me to volunteer. I was given a two-week assignment. When I looked at the ten-passenger van I was assigned to drive, I thought, *I could never drive it.* But I did. I spent twenty-three hours in that vehicle.

Our schedule was worship at 7:00 A.M. followed by breakfast and a brief meeting, and on the floor by 8:00 A.M. Standing on a concrete floor for eight hours was not easy. We had two breaks and an hour-long lunch. We were served three meals a day. I opened boxes, sorted items, coded them, re-boxed them, and put them on pallets. The warehouse received shipments all day. We processed them and got them ready to ship to distribution centers where people came to receive items. One by one, my nails broke, so I just cut them all off. Along with forty other volunteers, I used the makeshift shower facilities in the warehouse. The hot water tank held only six gallons, so I learned how to take cold showers.

On Sunday, we went to Pecan Island with supplies. Keep in mind, I was there ten weeks after the hurricane. Picture this—trailers up in trees, houses upside down, and areas where just the roof of a house rested on the ground. All the ruined furniture and appliances rested in huge mountains along the side of the road. I witnessed a man lighting a match and watching his house go up in smoke. People lost their homes and jobs, and their deceased loved ones resting in graves were washed away.

The people were so thankful for whatever I gave them. They often cried as they spoke to me, and I held them in my arms to comfort them. I prayed with folks after they introduced God into our conversation. The experience changed my life and allowed me to serve Him by helping His children who were in need.

Patricia Hook Phyndress Bodi

They That Go Down to the Sea in Ships

They that go down to the sea in ships,
That do business in great waters;
These see the works of the LORD,
And his wonders in the deep.
—Psalm 107:23, 24, KJV

There is a great story in Psalm 107. The psalmist recounts the storms that sailors experience out on the sea and how they see the wonders and power of God save them in the storms (of life). The sailors are often overcome by the waves. Their "soul is melted because of trouble" (verse 26, KJV). They are often at their "wit's end" (verse 27, KJV). They are being tossed about on the sea. The waves are crashing over them. They have no control and no power. They are sinking. They are helpless in the storm. But then they cry unto the Lord in their trouble, and He calms the winds and the waves. The psalm repeats this promise, "Then they cried unto the LORD in their trouble, and he delivered them out of their distresses" (verses 6, 13, KJV; compare verses 19, 28).

Apparently, we as humans stay in trouble. We continually need God to deliver us out of our troubles. I can remember several times in recent months that I felt like I was under water and sinking with no help in sight. The winds and the storm were blowing over me, and I felt myself sinking beneath the waves. I knew it was the end for me. I knew I had gone too far this time, but when I cried out to God, He provided a way out of my situation. He provided an escape and brought me safely to shore.

The chapter begins with the reminder, "O give thanks unto the LORD, for He is good: for his mercy endureth for ever" (verse 1, KJV). The psalmist repeats this thought of giving thanks for God's mercy: "Oh that men would praise the LORD for his goodness, and for his wonderful works to the children of men!" (verses 8, 21, 31, KJV). Amen! God's mercy and goodness are everlasting. He is available to show us mercy even when we are in storms of our own making. The last verse of this chapter gives us the final admonition, "Whoso is wise, and will observe these things, even they shall understand the lovingkindness of the LORD" (verse 43, KJV). Let us remember to cry out to God when we are in stormy weather. He hears us, and He will bring us safely to shore.

Eva M. Starner

December 8

What I Learned About Empathy

Rejoice with those who rejoice, and weep with those who weep.
—Romans 12:15, NKJV

One of the most poignant songs I've ever heard is called "Walk a Mile in My Shoes." The ability to mentally put oneself in another's shoes is a very desirable character trait. But it often seems to be in short supply when it comes to trying to understand how someone else really feels, given what they are going through.

Can we rejoice when someone has good fortune? Or do we turn green with envy?

Unfortunate circumstances are definitely harder to deal with. Many people are genuinely uncomfortable when a friend or acquaintance suffers a tragic loss. They can be heard saying, "I have no idea what to do or say. I don't know how to comfort them."

I had an important learning experience when our second child, Julie, was a few months old. Bindi, a friend of mine, was expecting her first child. When the due date came, the child was stillborn. The navel cord had wrapped itself around her little neck. Bindi and her husband, Perry, were devastated!

I went and viewed the baby privately. A small card attached to the inside of the casket top gave her personal information. Little Sandra Jean was beautiful! She looked exactly as our little Julie had at birth: similar hair, skin tones, and facial features. She was six pounds, thirteen-and-a-half ounces, and twenty-and-a-half inches long—the same size as Julie. It was almost as if that were my baby lying there. I teared up as I left.

My husband, Carl, and I attended the regular viewing and the burial the next day. Bindi and I cried together.

"Too bad what happened to Bindi," whispered an older member of Perry's family. "She'll probably never have a child that lives!" she added.

"I hope that's not true. It's not Bindi's fault," I said. How I hoped this person had not said that to Bindi and Perry.

I learned that it's OK to cry. And that a hug, handclasp, or simple "I'm so sorry for your loss" speaks volumes to a grieving heart. May we always treat the sad as we'd like to be treated if a misfortune happens to us.

Bonnie Moyers

December 9

Slave or Free?

"Therefore if the Son makes you free, you shall be free indeed."
—John 8:36, NKJV

Slavery—what picture does this bring to your mind? I read recently of a beloved twelve-year-old African girl who was kidnapped, put onto a slave ship with over one hundred strangers, subjected to starvation and untold hardship for two or more months, put off the ship under the cover of darkness, had to hide in a dangerous and scary swamp for several nights and days, then was separated from all the other slaves, given in marriage to an older slave who spoke a different language, and then put with him on the auction block to be sold to the highest bidder. Can you imagine the anguish if this had been your little girl?

This child was one of the final survivors of the *Clotilda*, the last ship to carry slaves, more than fifty years after the transporting of slaves had been ruled illegal. From 1525 to 1866, more than twelve and a half million had been sold into slavery, almost two million of whom did not survive the trip. The dead and the dying were dumped into the Atlantic like trash. The conditions on the ships were so bad, up to 20 percent of the crew never made it to shore, having succumbed to illness or disease.

How fortunate that we are not slaves, sold into bondage to a living death! But wait—could there be another kind of slavery? Could you and I be lulled into a false security? Satan is determined to do everything possible to rob us of eternal life. He is cruel and calculating. His deceptions are sly; his net, entangling. Without Jesus and the Word of God, what defense do we have? When temptations come that are questionable, He is our refuge and strength. We are told, "Therefore submit to God. Resist the devil and he will flee from you" (James 4:7, NKJV). There is a fine line between legalism and obedience born of love. One is slavery; the other is freedom.

We have an opportunity each morning to make a commitment to live for Jesus and not for self. Hard things are not accomplished without a struggle; the pull of habits is strong. Yet the power of the Holy Spirit is stronger still. We can avail ourselves of that power and claim victory in the name of the One who is "not willing that any should perish but that all should come to repentance" (2 Peter 3:9, NKJV). We were not meant to be slaves but daughters of a loving heavenly Father. Freedom can be ours, and for that, we can rejoice!

Lila Farrell Morgan

December 10

Abundant Mercy, Peace, and Love

Mercy, peace and love be yours in abundance.
—Jude 2, NIV

I have always found the book of Jude a very interesting admonition letter. Written by Jude, it seems very appropriate for our days and for the situations we face in our lives.

Jude's greeting includes the desire that we would experience an overflowing amount of mercy, peace, and love. To fight false teaching and adversities, we would need to experience God's mercy—His compassionate help. We would also need a strong sense of wellness (peace) and supernatural love—specifically a love for God and for others. We would need God's compassionate help while under attack from Satan.

In verse two, Jude prays for three gifts for all of us:

- God's mercy
- God's peace
- God's love

Christians cannot earn any of these qualities. They are free gifts from God.

Mercy that we receive from God can best be expressed as His kindness and compassion in action, not only to save but also as His intervention in our everyday lives.

Peace is that quiet confidence and boldness that allows us to face life's difficulties with resilience and security that produces well-being and joy.

Love is God's love for us revealed in Jesus Christ and is His generosity in bestowing His favor upon us and meeting all our needs.

I pray that His mercy, His peace, and His love be your everyday experience as a never-ending and all-sufficient supply. May it be yours in abundance.

God bestows upon us His mercy, peace, and love to share with all mankind. May God bless each one of us to avail of these free gifts and be a blessing to others. Amen!

Premila Pedapudi

Silent Defense

Do not be overcome by evil, but overcome evil with good.
—Romans 12:21, NKJV

One evening after I got off from work, I decided to make a quick stop at the grocery store. The store was remarkably busy. I hurriedly picked up my items and found a spot in the checkout line. I stood behind a woman and her two young children. I inquired whether she was the last person in the line. She assured me that she was the last person before I arrived. As we waited for our turn, two other people seemed to join the line but did not stand behind me. They formed a new line in another direction but intended for the same registers. As the line began moving, we positioned ourselves to get to the next available registers. At that moment, I heard someone behind me say, "Excuse me!" My new friend and I turned around to see who was speaking. The call came from a woman standing behind me. She pointed directly at me and said, "Hey you! The line's back there!" She pointed to the very back of the new line where three or four persons had gathered since I joined the line.

Before I could reply, my new friend spoke out in my defense, "She has been standing in the line before you got here."

That night I read,

> Under a storm of stinging faultfinding words, keep the mind stayed upon the word of God. Let mind and heart be stored with God's promises. If you are ill-treated or wrongfully accused, instead of returning an angry answer, repeat to yourself the precious promises:
>
> "Be not overcome by evil, but overcome evil with good." Romans 12:21.*

What a contrast to how our world operates today! Many arguments, quarrels, and fights would be prevented if people would follow Paul's advice.

This also reminded me of our great archenemy, Satan. I reflected upon how he accused Job of serving God only because God had bestowed blessings upon him and his family. Jesus promises to be at our side in every situation. However, we must trust Him in every difficulty. Psalm 34:19 reminds us, "Many are the afflictions of the righteous, but the Lord delivers him out of them all" (NKJV). Won't you let the Lord fight your battles today and always? You can never go wrong.

Sacha Clarke

* Ellen G. White, *The Ministry of Healing* (Mountain View, CA: Pacific Press®, 1942), 486.

December 12

The Lost Horse

We love Him because He first loved us.
—1 John 4:19, NKJV

Our neighbor, Richard, lost a horse last night. He finally found her at the bottom of a small ravine. Somehow, she had stumbled in the dark iciness of the early winter evening and slipped over the edge. And there she lay, legs folded beneath her, unable to get up.

This situation reminds me of the story Jesus told about the good shepherd who went looking for his lost sheep, then returned, rejoicing, carrying it on his shoulders. But the ending of this story is different. Another difference is that the horse doesn't even belong to Richard. Pacer belongs to his wife, Diana, but that really doesn't matter because Richard loves Diana. And Diana loves this horse. Deeply. She's had her since she was a newborn filly. Pacer is more than twenty years old now. But she has another problem. The vet says that cancer spreading throughout her innards will take her before spring. So she's been spending her days in her warm stall, only venturing out of the barn each evening for a slow ramble around the pasture.

It's dark now—and cold. Below zero. Richard has found the horse, but he can't rescue her. Richard and Diana's ranch lies in a remote piece of country in southeast Montana, at the end of a road that is equally remote and completely innocent of gravel or scoria or any such improvement. These conditions preclude most kinds of travel in anything but dry, sunny weather. And the ravine in which the horse lay is inaccessible to his tractor, which he would need to help lift the nine-hundred-pound animal to her feet.

So Richard did the only thing his love could think to do. He went back to the barn and got her heavy padded blanket. Tucking it carefully around her, Richard then lay down beside her, hoping that his closeness and his own body heat would somehow lessen her coldness and comfort her through the night. She died the next morning.

Yes, I thought that the ending of this story was different from the story of the Good Shepherd, but maybe it's not. Sometimes the sheep suffers. Maybe even dies. But it is never alone. Always it is covered with the Shepherd's warm blanket of love. And the even warmer sense of His lovely presence never leaves. One day He will come, rejoicing, carrying His beloved sheep on His shoulders.

Jeannette Busby Johnson

I Will Help You!

Fear not, for I am with you;
be not dismayed, for I am your God;
I will strengthen you, I will help you,
I will uphold you with my righteous right hand.
—Isaiah 41:10, ESV

My best friend called me one day, expressing gratitude for God's everlasting love. One evening, as she drove home from work, she discovered that one of her tires had low pressure. *Not a problem*, she thought. She drove to the nearest gas station and put air in the tire and drove home. The next day, as she drove her son to school, she noticed the tire pressure was lower than the night before. "Not a problem," she said to herself. She rationalized that the change in climate and environment had affected her tire. She thought about taking her car to the mechanic on her lunch break. However, wrapped up in the day's chaos, she never got a chance to get her car checked.

That evening, as she walked to her car, the tire was visibly deflated. She looked at the time. The mechanic was closed, and she had to go get her son from school. She did not have an alternative. She drove herself to a gas station, added air to her tire, and went to get her son. The next morning, the tire was completely flat. What was she going to do? She said a quick prayer, drove to the nearest gas station, added air, and drove her son to school. She then drove forty-five minutes to the mechanic that was across the street from her job. She constantly checked the digital indicator and realized that the tire was deflating quickly. She was concerned but not afraid. She believed God's promise to help. God allowed the tire to remain inflated until she got there.

The mechanic provided her with an estimate to replace the tire. The cost seemed high, but what was she going to do? Her car had to be fixed. After work, she went to get her car. The mechanic gave the bill. It was 85 percent less than the estimate! The mechanic was able to repair the tire without replacing it. What an amazing God! God had it all worked out. He was there with her all along the way. He was a present help in her time of need. God's promise is very clear: "For I am your God; I will strengthen you, I will help you" (Isaiah 41:10, ESV).

Diantha Hall-Smith

December 14

But Wait . . . I Feel Good!

"For God so loved the world that He gave His only begotten Son."
—John 3:16, NKJV

I grew up attending the Seventh-day Adventist church. My dad was an Anglican, and my mom was a Seventh-day Adventist, but they decided before they had children that the girls would go with mom and the boys with dad. And guess what? They had four girls! So, from birth, we were taught the song about Sabbath being a happy day.

As I entered my teenage years, the part of the song that proclaimed a love for Sabbath resonated with me because my mom did everything possible to make Sabbath special. She baked and cooked special dishes. She rearranged our home and brought in special plants. She told us that we celebrated Christmas once a week.

At the end of 2019, I began experiencing health challenges. Doctors were unable to diagnose the problem. With all that was going on, I realized that I would feel unwell all week, but as soon as Friday evening came, I began to feel good. In fact, I would feel much better. At first, I thought it was just a coincidence, but as I checked on it closely, I realized that it happened every week.

This took me back to my childhood days and the love and joy I felt each Sabbath. The Sabbath became more special to me as an adult. It truly was a happy day, and I loved every Sabbath. God reminded me weekly that He loved me and had created a special day with a special blessing just for me. When everything is going well with us, we overlook the blessings that God has in place for us. We take life for granted and overlook the mercies of God.

Sisters, we serve a loving God. Because of His love for us, He sent His only Son to die for us. He has special plans and blessings for us. From the beginning of creation, He gave us a special day to commune, reflect, and rejuvenate. Yet often, we get so caught up in our daily chores that we don't stop and appreciate what God has done and is doing for us. I encourage you, sisters, to take time to enjoy the love and rest your God has prepared for you—not only on Sabbath but every day of the week. As you fall in love again with Jesus, may you realize that it is the best thing that you have ever done, and each day walking with Him is the best day of your week.

Jill Springer-Cato

Overnight Success

Good planning and hard work lead to prosperity,
but hasty shortcuts lead to poverty.
—Proverbs 21:5, NLT

I was speaking with my daughter's dentist. Over the years, I've had the opportunity to talk with her about various topics ranging from family and vacations to religion and work. In the last year, she had moved from renting office space to owning her office space that better caters to her young clients—even down to the rooms with different happy colors. Her move was similar to one I was to make a few months later. So I used the opportunity to ask her a lot of questions.

When we had last seen each other, I filled her in on all the things that I would be doing. I would be speaking on faith and obedience in a morning program, then speaking about finance and retirement in the afternoon. A few days after that, I would share my faith journey at a conference and then discuss financial planning at a women's retreat. She was amazed to hear all the things that seemed to be happening so quickly for me since I left my previous corporate role.

I chuckled a bit and told her that I had been writing for a number of years, and I'd been in the financial profession for nearly twenty. Of course, this got me thinking, *How often do we see "overnight success" and wonder how we can attain that too?*

I was recently on a Zoom call, and as the other financial advisors introduced themselves, it was clear that they were well established. I had just ended year one as an independent advisor. Many of them were much older. I had to keep reminding myself that I could not compare year one of my journey to their fifteen or twenty years in business.

Many of these overnight successes that we see are built on years of failure, tears, and a decision to keep persevering no matter how it may seem to others. In those trying and discouraging times, we are being prepared to do what God has called us to do.

Dear heavenly Father, please stop me in my tracks when I start complaining about things not happening quickly enough. Please remind me that there are fundamental processes that You need to take us through to get us to where You want us to be.

Kaysian C. Gordon

December 16

Sweet Peppers and Faith

Now faith is confidence in what we hope for and assurance about what we do not see.
—Hebrews 11:1, NIV

One December, I finally started a project that I had intended to get to for several months: backyard gardening. I had my dirt, my containers, and my sweet pepper seeds. I was so excited to finally get started!

I got to work filling my containers with dirt and planting my sweet pepper seeds. I was excited yet apprehensive because I didn't know how they'd turn out. As I went out some mornings to water them, I began to wonder when they'd start growing, whether they would actually grow, and when I'd see the first plant. In my mind, I could already see myself picking sweet peppers. Maybe big ones or small ones. I wasn't too fussy. I just didn't enjoy the anxiety during the waiting period. I wanted to see some growth very soon. I started to do some research to determine how long it should take before any seedlings would appear.

This is how I sometimes feel and act when I ask God for something. I have planted a spiritual seed of faith in something, and I want to see it fulfilled—quickly. I sometimes feel anxious and am frustrated and impatient waiting for the results. I just want to see it happen! *Why is it taking so long?* I wonder. *Doesn't God know that I need this thing or that I need to get to this place or attain this goal to feel more fulfilled and happy?*

Of course, God knows everything. He knows things that I don't know, and He definitely knows what is best for me. Sometimes, waiting is what is best. I imagine that just as my anxiety to get to picking sweet peppers from my garden would not make them grow any faster, my anxiety for God to fulfill my requests will not let them happen any faster either. It might only make the wait frustrating and strenuous. Instead, I can make the wait productive by doing all I can to facilitate the growth of my peppers. I can ensure they have a conducive environment for growth and leave the rest to God.

Now that sounds like a good recipe not just for sweet peppers but for whatever we might be waiting for from God.

Mirian Taylor

December 17

Never Alone

"I will not leave you."
—Genesis 28:15, NIV

Late one night, my husband, who was in the gas station business at the time, was nearly robbed by someone he thought to be a lone assailant. After the man's arrest, Jim learned from the local sheriff that the stranger was a member of a dangerous gang that had wreaked havoc on the neighborhood overnight. Referencing this experience later, Jim told me, "I thought I was all alone during that midnight hour, but now I know God was a lot closer to me than I realized."

A long time ago, another man thought he was all alone. Jacob had deceived his father Isaac and stolen his brother Esau's inheritance, and now he was fleeing—still empty-handed.

Appearances told Jacob he was a goner. At dusk on the second day of his flight, he collapsed onto the desert sand, his head on a rock pillow, and fell into an exhausted sleep. Sometime during the night, Jacob dreamed he saw God at the top of a stairway being used as a ladder, of sorts, by angels. "I am the LORD. . . . I am with you and will watch over you wherever you go. . . . I will not leave you until I have done what I have promised you" (Genesis 28:13–15, NIV). What an infusion of hope! God was *with* him. God cared. Jacob arose, anointed his rock pillow as an altar, and consecrated his future to God: "The LORD will be my God" (verse 21, NIV).

As you face life right now, appearances may be telling you you're all alone in these uncertain times. If so, do what Jacob did. Trust that God knows your circumstances and your location even if you have not been "aware" of His presence (verse 16). Admit your inability to save yourself. Even Jesus, the Son of God, said, "I can do nothing on my own" (John 5:30, NLT). Submit your situation to God in prayer. Then declare, as did Paul, that "I can do all this through him who gives me strength" (Philippians 4:13, NIV). When Jacob surrendered his circumstances to the One at the top of the staircase, he experienced the promises, provisions, and purposes of God for his life—and for the rest of his life. God wants to reveal Himself to you too. Not necessarily in a dream at the top of a shining staircase, yet in ways you might never expect.

When needed most, Jesus will remind you that you're never alone (John 14:27). He will meet your needs and fulfill the longings of your heart (Psalms 34:4; 37:4). So today, face life's challenges by trusting the One who is closer to you than you ever thought possible.

Carolyn Rathbun Sutton

December 18

Nothing Is Impossible

"For nothing will be impossible with God."
—Luke 1:37, NASB

This is Monday morning, Lord! You've reached my heart today through Your Word. As I ponder how God's miracles work with the women and men of the Bible, I stand in wonder and awe again how Your timing is so pertinent—so always on time!

I am reminded of the story in Luke about Elizabeth becoming pregnant at a very old age—a humanly impossible thing and yet the timing was perfect. You respected her as she honored You in life. Then You not only did the impossible for a very old woman but also went to a virgin, Mary (at a very young age), and the Holy Spirit impregnated her—unheard of! You work with impossible situations! That is where You shine!

Lord, teach me how to bring those impossible circumstances to You and wait on You while you bring a God-solution to the messy spiritual lives with whom I come in contact and as I walk beside my people with love, care, and concern. Teach me to bring these God-growing situations to You sooner and receive the peace that passes all understanding. I pray that You will never give up on me as in my daily life I slip into being a human fixer instead of leaning on and learning from You.

Keep distractions away from my life today. I must stay focused on You.

We wander, we have our own agendas, and we suffer from self-gratification in ways that keep us from being God-centered and God-filled. I need to allow You to push me out of my way because I'm too selfish to know how. It is in the valleys and the crises of life that we see You in Your glory at work—yet it is in the mundane where You are doing Your grunt work in my own spiritual, ordinary life.

Prepare my heart, O Lord. Prepare my mind, my soul, my thoughts, my desires to be constantly in the center of Your will. It feels impossible to even do this, yet You promised that without You, I can do nothing. Keep that in the forefront of my mind, dear Lord.

Your Word is a precious reminder that with You all things are possible! That is Your promise for me today. Hold on to me for dear life, in Jesus' precious and holy name. Amen.

Mary H. Maxson

Light Your World

"You are the light of the world. A city that is set on a hill cannot be hidden. Nor do they light a lamp and put it under a basket, but on a lampstand, and it gives light to all who are in the house. Let your light so shine before men, that they may see your good works and glorify your Father in heaven."
—Matthew 5:14–16, NKJV

Light your world. About a week before Christmas, I went to the assisted living home to visit an elderly church member named Alice. I found her in the lunchroom. Two other ladies were sitting at her table. One lady told me that her family was going to pick her up for Christmas and shared what they were going to do. I asked the other lady, Kathleen, what was she going to do on Christmas. Instead of answering the question, she unexpectedly became very angry. I didn't say anything. I understood why. I knew that her son would not be there for Christmas.

On Christmas day, my husband and I picked up Alice from her room to have lunch in the cafeteria. There sat Kathleen alone. We joined her, and I presented her with a Christmas gift.

Light your world. I was at a crowded deli near the holidays. As I stood there waiting for my turn to be served, I watched one of the ladies serving the people who had a slight mental disability. She was very stressed and frustrated. When she served me, I was determined to be as kind as I could be to her. I received my purchase and proceeded to the checkout counter with my groceries. I was in luck; I found a line where I would be next. A man came up next to me and asked, "Are you holy?"

"I am definitely not holy," I assured him. "Why do you ask?"

He told me that he saw how I had treated the lady at the deli counter and asked me to pray for his relative who was having surgery for cancer. We prayed together as the cashier rang up my purchases.

There is a song sung by the group Newsong that encourages us to light our world and allow God's love to shine through us. The words remind us that lighting our world takes only a little time—and yet God may use us to answer someone's prayer. There are many lonely people around you this holiday season. Please light up their world with God's love.

Ruth Cantrell

December 20

No Room

There was no room for them in the inn.
—Luke 2:7, NKJV

"Are you ready for Christmas?" people ask when they greet each other during December. I always ask for a definition of what it means to be ready for Christmas. If it means shopping for everyone on my list, baking lots of desserts, decorating my home, wrapping presents, hosting or attending a Christmas party, then I'm never ready!

If preparing for Christmas simply means Jesus is coming to stay with me, then oh yes, I am ready and overjoyed to see Him! I certainly would find time to clean the house, cook a special meal, buy a lovely present, and transform space into a beautiful, comfortable guest room.

When Jesus was born, Middle Eastern hospitality meant washing dusty feet, providing water to drink, sharing a meal, and giving shelter to weary travelers—in your home.

In Luke 2:7, the Greek word *katalyma* is translated as *inn.* It appears again in Luke 22:11, when Jesus needs a "guest chamber" for the Passover meal. The *katalyma* was an upper room that could be a locked storeroom, space for large gatherings, or room for visitors. Being an innkeeper might have meant that neighbors directed travelers to your *katalyma.*

With King David's descendants returning to their hometown for the census, did the village of Bethlehem have adequate space? What accommodation did Mary and Joseph need? Probably they wanted just enough space to lie down. Mostly likely, the innkeeper's urgent dilemma was finding enough floor space to squeeze in two more sleeping mats.

I ponder the innkeeper's refusal to find room for the Son of David about to make His entrance into the world. I want to believe I would have given up my own bed for the Son of God. But to be honest, I would have wearily waved them on and barred the door before they could ask for a meal.

Today, Jesus knocks on the door of my heart, asking me to open it and let Him perform the miracle of my rebirth. How do I respond? Do I make space in my life for the Savior? Is He the guest of honor in my daily routine? Do I invite Him into the intimate chamber of my heart? The critical question is, am I part of the "Inn Crowd" or one of the "Stable Few"?

Rebecca Turner

Splendiferous Christmas

"But there's only one thing you need. Mary has chosen what is better."
—Luke 10:42, ISV

Isn't life just splendiferous?" Melissa jumped from the picnic-table bench and whirled around and around on the grass. (Four of us were enjoying lunch in the park.)

"I love that word, *splendiferous*," her friend Angelina said, laughing. "There's a library book called *Splendiferous Christmas*!" Angelina also started whirling around and around.

"Splendiferous and year-end celebrations do not go together," Angelina's mother sighed. "It's only September, but there's so much to do, I have to start now. Then it's February before everything is put away. It's hectic and frenetic—oh my, I'm exhausted just thinking about it!"

"Whatever do you do that you have to start now?" Melissa asked. "We put up our tree December 15. And we draw names, so we give and get one present each. Each of us gives a present to a less-fortunate person too. Sometimes several of us go together and pack a big food basket for a needy family. That's 'splendiferous simplicity.' And we aren't exhausted. We love it!"

Angelina's mother looked at me questioningly. "The holidays have turned into a complicated commercial frenzy for many," I said. "A couple of years ago, after reading Luke's telling of the Mary and Martha story, our family decided 'enough is enough.' We still exchange gifts, but now we emphasize music, relationships with family and friends, eating a special dinner together, and helping the less fortunate. It's been great. And, I might add, a relief."

"Yes," said Melissa, quickly. "It's really about celebrating God's greatest gift to us—His Son. If people forget that, they tend to celebrate the gifts Saint Nicholas used to give instead. Which has gotten completely out of hand!" Melissa exclaimed, finding a way to insert another favorite phrase. "And splendiferous simplicity goes right out the window."

"Splendiferous simplicity," Angelina's mother mused. "I've been so wrapped up in preparations that I forgot about the Mary and Martha story. Mary chose what is better, didn't she?" We nodded encouragingly. "I'm choosing that too. Starting now," she said firmly.

Could you use some splendiferous simplicity? Choose what is better. Starting now.

Arlene R. Taylor

Going Home

"In my Father's house there's plenty of room for everyone. If that weren't so, I would have told you. I'm going home to prepare a place for you. And if I go to prepare a place for you, you can be sure that I'll come back to take you home with me, so you can be with me forever."
—John 14:2, 3, *The Clear Word**

One day, I went shopping for a picture frame for a cross-stitch picture I had made. It was an unusual size, and I was having trouble finding a frame. Finally, after searching in several stores, I decided to look at pictures that were already framed, and then I found one. I purchased it, took it home, and was just ready to remove the picture and put my cross-stitch in when I read the saying in the picture. It said, "Life takes you to unexpected places; love brings you home." Suddenly I knew I had to hang the picture just the way it was and continue searching for another frame.

I was born and raised in Topeka, Kansas. It was home, but life had taken me to some unexpected places. I had married a pastor, and we had spent time in a number of places in different states, but love always took me back to Topeka, back home, every summer, every Christmas.

Our children have grown, married, and are raising families far from Colorado where my husband and I now live. But every summer and some holidays, they make their way to Colorado. Love brings them home.

There's a story in the Bible about a young man who thought he wanted something his home didn't offer, so he left. But after experiencing what the world had to offer, he knew he wanted to go back home. He made his way back home into the waiting, loving arms of his father.

Because of love, Jesus *left* His home and came to this sin-ravaged world so we can one day go to a heavenly, forever home with Him. When we spend time with Jesus, contemplating His love for us, our response will be a loving "I want to go home" response. As the Bible says, "Christ's love compels us" (2 Corinthians 5:14, NIV). Spend time with Jesus every day, and that love relationship will take you home—your heavenly home.

Sharon Oster

* Jack Blanco, *The Clear Word* (Hagerstown, MD: Review and Herald®, 2003), 1106.

Deliverance

For he shall give his angels charge over thee,
to keep thee in all thy ways.
—Psalm 91:11, KJV

I woke up and went to the Christmas tree, and there was my bike. I was ten years old, and I got a beautiful green bike with a white basket attached. It was cold outside, but I wanted to ride my new bicycle. That's when I looked at the back tire. It was flat. I asked my uncle (who was my guardian at the time), "When are you going to the store?"

"Later," he replied.

I decided I would take my bicycle to the Junior Market four blocks over myself and see if I could get air in the tire. I was hoping there wasn't a hole in the inner tube. I dressed in my coat, shoes, hat, and scarf and went out the door. I told my aunt I was going to the store to get my tire inflated. She asked if I had told my uncle. "He's not going anywhere for a while," I responded.

It was cold, but I persevered and made it to the store. My hands were frozen because I had no gloves. I could see the tire gauge in front of me, but my hands were no use. I parked the bicycle and went and looked through the glass window, but I did not see anyone.

Now I was faced with the decision to either go home without getting air in my tire or continue to the boulevard, where there were two service stations across from each other. Something made me look at the front door. To my surprise, a man came outside wearing a service shirt and a hat. He came to where I was standing and seemed to know what was wrong. He was very nice and put air in my tire.

I thanked him and went back home. Later that day, my sister asked me, "Where did you go to get my tire inflated?"

"Junior Market," I told her.

She looked at me in disbelief. "It was closed, and no one was there when I went."

I won't know until I get to heaven, but I just might meet an angel who knows how to put air in the tires of little girls' bikes and one day helped a determined little girl at the Junior Market. I will give him a big hug.

Sharon Denise Smith

December 24

A COVID-19 Christmas

After this I heard what sounded like the roar of a great multitude in heaven shouting: "Hallelujah! Salvation and glory and power belong to our God."
—Revelation 19:1, NIV

December 2020 was the worst holiday season of my life. Because of the COVID-19 pandemic, most activities were canceled. No extended family party. No school parties. No church parties. No in-person Christmas programs. One of the biggest disappointments was that there would not be a sing-along Handel's *Messiah*. I looked forward to this each year. Around November, I would get out my score and start practicing my alto part. I would listen to alto soloists sing the popular choruses on YouTube in anticipation of that glorious evening when I would join fellow choristers and sing excerpts from Handel's *Messiah*, especially the "Hallelujah Chorus." Some years, I would even get to go to two of these special programs.

But not this year. This year, my immediate family was recovering from having COVID-19. My mom had it really bad. She usually enjoyed going Christmas shopping with me. But not this year. My brother, who usually has a big appetite and enjoys my special Christmas meals, could barely get out of bed, let alone eat anything. I was feeling quite blue, especially because I was the one who had the virus first and gave it to them.

Then, when I was driving one day, I heard the "Hallelujah Chorus" on the radio. I started to sing along. I started feebly and then boldly began to belt out the notes. Tears began to stream down my face as I thought of what the words really meant. "And He shall reign forever and ever . . . Hallelujah." Wow, that sunk in more than ever this time! That means that one glorious day, there will be no more COVID-19, no more death, no more masks, no more canceled events. All the saints will sing together in harmony on that great and beautiful day. It helped to put things into perspective. I reflected on the year 2020 and what I had missed out on as a result of the pandemic—mission trips, camp meetings, attending meetings, prayer retreats, and women's retreats. However, I sure don't want to miss out on the biggest event ever and on singing that hallelujah chorus in the sky! Won't you join me on that day? I pray that I will meet you there.

Mary C. D. Johnson

Immanuel, God With Us

Therefore, the Lord himself shall give you a sign; Behold a virgin shall conceive, and bear a son, and shall call his name Immanuel.
—Isaiah 7:14, KJV

In the book of Isaiah, God gave His people a sign. He said that a virgin would get pregnant without the help of any man. This same virgin would have a Son, and His name would be Immanuel, "which being interpreted is, God with us" (Matthew 1:23, KJV). This is in fulfillment of a promise back in the book of Genesis. God speaking to the serpent told him that He would put enmity between the woman and the serpent; her Seed would bruise the serpent's head, or in other words, destroy him (Genesis 3:15).

In the Garden of Eden before Adam sinned, God used to walk in the garden in the cool of the day and talk with His people. Adam and Eve were able to talk face-to-face with God. They were able to sit with Him and discover the secrets of creation and the universe. Just like little children running to their father to hear the latest story, Adam and Eve would run to God to be with Him—until sin happened. Then humans were no longer able to sit and talk with God openly, face-to-face.

The loss of communication between God and man was difficult not only for man but also for God. He missed the communion with His creatures. So God gave His people a sign. This communication loss wouldn't go on forever. A virgin would get pregnant and have a Son, and that Son would be God, who would dwell among the people. He would walk with them, and talk with them, and tell them wonderful stories, just like in the Garden of Eden. The difference this time was that His special people didn't accept Him as God. The ones whom He had ordained to be the keepers of His Word and to spread the good news about Him hated Him. They beat Him. They tried to stone Him. They spat on Him. Finally, out of rage, they nailed Him to a cross and killed Him. His people.

He was born so He could die. He knew in His childhood what His responsibility was. He readily accepted the challenge just so He could be with us and talk with us and walk with us. He was born. He grew up. He lived. He loved. He died. He lives again. All so He can be with us for eternity. I want to spend eternity with someone who loves me that much.

Eva M. Starner

December 26

Feeding a Multitude

"For I was hungry and you gave Me food; I was thirsty and you gave Me drink; I was a stranger and you took Me in."
—Matthew 25:35, NKJV

Dozens of people had come to Kukkia School Hall from all over the neighboring villages for the Sabbath service with the visiting education students from Pacific Adventist University (PAU), who were there for their annual curriculum Bible class retreat.

The meetings went well, and the message during the church service led many to recommit their lives to the Lord. Many had not attended any worship service for over three years since the missionaries from Adventist Frontier Missions were there to bring light and Christian lifestyle to them.

After the service, everyone was invited to have lunch with the PAU students. They had prepared a pot of rice, a pot of sweet potatoes, two pots of soup, and a pot of greens. This was enough for the forty-eight PAU students on retreat—but not for a multitude. Many of those visiting had not brought lunch with them even though asked to in the invitation.

The students knew that without God's intervention, the food would run out. Before serving, they stood around the pots of food and prayed that the Lord would bless every morsel to feed this modern multitude. As they served, the containers from which they served never ran out. As people helped themselves to the food, there were always plates of food on the serving table. God worked a miracle right before their eyes.

The girls counted the number of visitors—two hundred were fed that day! The forty-eight PAU students also ate lunch, and everyone was satisfied. God had worked a miracle that Sabbath to honor the faith of these students who surrendered their lunch to feed the multitude.

The Lord reminds us to be considerate of others and to feed those who are hungry. By doing this, we are rendering that act of kindness to Jesus Himself. Let us open our hearts to people and invite them to share whatever little we may have to benefit in the blessings and miracles that Jesus wants to work in our lives. May we be blessed as we engage in service for others.

Fulori Sususewa Bola

My Eternal Home

But as it is written,
Eye hath not seen, nor ear heard,
Neither have entered into the heart of man,
The things which God has prepared for them that love him.
—1 Corinthians 2:9, KJV

Monday, December 27, 2020, was a cold morning. I got out of bed, walked over to the windows, pulled back the curtains, and was greeted by a most spectacular display of beauty.

I saw the golden sun shining brightly on the land and trees and even bouncing some rays of warmth on the windowpane. I touched the window and felt the warmth despite the cold temperature on the outside. I looked up and saw a most beautiful blue sky garnished with puffs of silky white clouds, interspersed with larger patches moving ever so slightly across the sky. The large pine trees in the neighbor's yard provided a good backdrop for the panorama. It seemed as if God the Creator were smiling at me and saying, "I made this for you to enjoy."

I took a deep breath and exclaimed, "Thank You, Lord, for creating all these things for me to enjoy." My mind then drifted back to God's original and perfect creation. Even though His creation has been marred by the ravages of sin for over six thousand years, there is still so much beauty all around.

As I contemplated what I had just experienced, I envisioned heaven and all the beautiful things that await me there. Eden will be restored. This will be my eternal home. It will be a place of perpetual beauty. All of God's children will reside there in peace and love.

Mrs. A. S. Bridgewater captures the scene in the song "How Beautiful Heaven Must Be":*

> We read of a place that's called heaven,
> It's made for the pure and the free;
> These truths in God's words He hath given,
> How beautiful heaven must be.

It is my prayer, dear sisters, that we all will be there. I look forward to seeing you.

Kollis Salmon-Fairweather

* Mrs. A. S. Bridgewater, "How Beautiful Heaven Must Be," 1920, public domain.

December 28

How Do We Show Our Love?

"If you love Me, keep My commandments."
—John 14:15, NKJV

Because her mom, a teacher, was still on Christmas break, Sarai had not seen her babysitter for two weeks. A curious and happy one-year-old, Sarai now reveled in the attention from her four older siblings, who were also enjoying their little vacation. Though tiny for her fourteen months, Sarai was mentally a little giant. She emphatically spoke exactly what she did or did not want.

When the break was almost over, Marguerite, Sarai's babysitter, came by for a New Year's visit. Seeing her, Sarai abandoned her toys, bypassed her beloved mother, and rushed to Marguerite, who joyfully picked her up. Then in an action that spoke volumes, Sarai nestled her head on Marguerite's shoulder and would not be moved. It was a silent, yet vocal, "I love you, Marguerite. I am overjoyed to see you again." Sarai had shown her love.

We have so many options for expressing our love. We can vocalize, or like Sarai, we can demonstrate our love by our actions. Yet, some children and adults lament about never hearing their parents say "I love you" or even expressing it in their actions. Many husbands and wives live a loveless marriage, longing—no pining—for the least token, the slightest utterance of the fact that they are loved and cherished.

How much does it cost to speak and demonstrate that love? How life-changing could it be in a family where such expression is missing!

But could the same be true for expressing our love for our Savior?

He demonstrated His love for us with the ultimate sacrifice—His death on the cross. Then He clearly said, "If you love Me, keep My commandments." As we demonstrate our love, are we spending time in His house of worship, or are we worshiping other gods? Are we reaching out to Him early in the morning and throughout the day, or are we reaching for the remote control? Are we enjoying the gifts He has prepared for us—the lakes, the forest, the fragrant flowers—or are we giving all our time to electronic gadgets and shopping malls? How do we show our love?

Every day God demonstrates His love for us—He awakens us. He has given us eyes to read and minds to think. He has promised to protect and guide us. Now, how do we show our love?

Annette Walwyn Michael

Speck and Plank Problems

"Do not judge others, and you will not be judged. For you will be treated as you treat others. The standard you use in judging is the standard by which you will be judged. And why worry about the speck in your friend's eye when you have a log in your own?"
—Matthew 7:1–3, NLT

Being the old people my husband and I have become, we retired around ten o'clock last night, which was the same time the neighborhood fireworks began. I have never heard such a celebration for New Year's in all my years of living here. The local effects of a pandemic the year before seemed to create an extra desire for a change of any sort in our community. But what annoyed me was their music playing till two o'clock in the morning.

Usually, my next-door neighbors are super respectful, and I don't mind the Tejano music they play during celebrations; it makes me crave tacos, which I also don't mind. But this was no Tejano music. It was some obnoxious, modern party stuff. I crankily rolled over and shook my fist at them. However, my complaints changed nothing. Sleep eluded me.

As I struggled for conscious alertness, my ears strained for the source of my frustrated slumber. Where should I confront them? Should I politely tap on the front door or barge into their backyard to get their attention? How would I admonish them? Then a greater wave of annoyance threatened to drown me in a flood of ultimate irritation.

My husband rolled over in bed, sensing my exasperation, and I gripped his arm with one hand and exclaimed, "It's our radio!"

He ripped the cord of that contraption out of the wall as if it had been more than the cause of a few hours' annoyance. It seemed to be the release of frustrations from the entire previous year. Indeed, I believe it was the defining move that ushered us into the New Year, not the ball dropping (or the potato if you happen to live out here in Idaho), nor the flip of a calendar page. No, my friends, it was the extraction of our alarm clock radio!

As for my New Year's resolution?

I'm going to pay more attention to the plank in my eye instead of the speck in my neighbor's.

Wendy Williams

December 30

My Prayer

"When these things begin to take place, stand up and lift up your heads, because your redemption is drawing near."
—Luke 21:28, NIV

Dear Father, how sweet is Your name to my ears. You bring me to this hour of a brand-new day. You wake me in my right mind, able to put words together to express my gratitude and appreciation for how deep Your love is for me. You are my Creator and my Guide. Today, help me to be ready to accept Your Holy Spirit. Lord, thank You that You are in control of my total existence.

As I come to Your throne, please forgive my sins. Humbly, I petition You for strength, help, and a song in my heart to rally through this day and the coming days according to Your will. Whatever concerns and desires my children and grandchildren may have, help them understand this journey that we are on—that we live in unprecedented times and that changes are occurring rapidly. Lord, I know that we are in the time of probation now, and I ask for Your help to make it known to my family what we must do to be ready. Lord, I understand that probation comes first, then judgment from the Most High God. It is during judgment that You will decide where we will spend eternity: heaven or hell. As Your servant, help me to do all that I can to bring awareness of the seriousness of this waging war of good and evil that bombards us. May we all be ready to meet You in peace.

Lord, another opportunity presents itself today to grow a deeper relationship with You. Fill me now with the knowledge that You want me to have concerning my purpose for being here. You are a Mighty God, and words cannot express my deep gratitude and dependence on You. Whatever lies before me, may it glorify You in every way. Father, I just want to do Your perfect will.

As we approach the unknown future, Lord, come near to us and help us realize that time grows shorter each day and that the coming of Your Son is near. The social unrest, global pandemics, and other calamities testify of Your Scriptures daily.

Father, blessed be the name of Jesus, who warns us of the coming calamities and gives us hope through the promises and salvation of Jesus Christ. Amen.

Debra Slack

Change

Jesus Christ the same yesterday, and to day, and for ever.
—Hebrews 13:8, KJV

As the clock was about to strike midnight, marking the end of the twentieth century and bringing us into the twenty-first century, there was concern that all the computers running our world would crash because they wouldn't know which century they were operating in.

When we awakened on January 1, 2000, our world was relatively normal, but it didn't take long for things to change. On September 11, 2001, the twin towers in New York City came tumbling down, all air travel was stopped for two days, and airport security changed forever. The year 2008 saw a big dip in our economic well-being, and 2020 began the life-changing worldwide pandemic.

We find dramatic life-changing events in the Bible too. First, Adam and Eve's expulsion from their perfect garden home into a world of thistles and weeds; then, a worldwide flood changed life for Noah and family.

Job, the greatest man in the east, loved and obeyed God and avoided evil. In the short amount of time it took to tell his story, he went from being the richest servant of God to a broken man with a distraught wife and three judgmental friends (Job 1:14–22).

Joseph, the indulged son of the favorite wife of Jacob, was used to being favored. He had the nicest coat of all the brothers. He stayed home while the brothers pastured the animals. He thought his dreams about family members bowing to him would delight the rest. But suddenly, while on a mission for his father to take supplies to his brothers and get a report of the flocks, his brothers seized him, threw him in a pit, and sold him to traders going to Egypt (Genesis 37).

Daniel, of the king's seed and of the princes, was suddenly taken captive and marched from Judah to Babylon. There, he and his friends were put into the palace and served royal food. They asked for simple food and promised to prove that it would make them healthier. Their experiences varied from being sentenced to death with the other wise men to his friends being thrown into the fiery furnace and then Daniel being cast into the lions' den (Daniel 2; 3; 6).

As we face future monumental change, let us ponder the strength of those before us who depended on God to get them through life-shattering experiences and follow their examples.

Elizabeth Versteegh Odiyar

2023 Author Biographies

Betty J. Adams is a retired teacher. She was born and lived in California, United States of America, for most of her life until the death of her husband of sixty-six years. Then she moved to Camden, Maine, United States of America, to live with her youngest daughter. She has been writing for the women's devotional books since the third edition in 1995. She also helps with her daughter's Creative Memories home business, which keeps her occupied when not keeping up with many grandchildren, great-grandchildren, and great-great-grandchildren. **July 26, Aug. 25**

Anysia Alexander-Archibald lives in Richmond, Texas, United States of America. She's the president of Najja Hope, Inc., a nonprofit family services organization. She serves as the Women's Ministries coordinator of the Southwest Region Conference of Seventh-day Adventists, a wife, and mother of twin sons. **Aug. 13**

Isabel Cristina de Almeida is a retired mother of three children. Living in Brazil, she loves to read and walk in nature. **Mar. 17, May 23**

Lydia D. Andrews, CNM, is a retired university professor of nursing. She and her husband, Newton, worked as missionaries in Kenya and Ghana in Africa. She is the mother of three adult children and four delightful grandsons. They live in Huntsville, Alabama, United States of America, and she enjoys cooking, traveling, reading, music, prayer ministry, encouraging young people, and spending time with family. **Feb. 27**

Jean Arthur lives in Silver Spring, Maryland, United States of America. She is an attorney by training but recently retired from thirty-three years of service with the local government. She now works as a substitute teacher in the local public school system. She is active in her local church and volunteers with the church and in her community. She spends her free time gardening, traveling, bicycling, running, baking, and reading. **Mar. 5, Aug. 26**

Flore Aubry-Hamilton loves the Lord and wants her light to shine for Him. She and her husband, George, live in Huntsville, Alabama, United States of America. They enjoy working with disabilities ministries. **Mar. 16, July 2**

Noella (Jumpp) Baird, born in Jamaica, is a registered nurse living in Edmonton, Alberta, Canada, with her husband, Alan, and three children: Alyssa, Natalia, and Eric. She loves reading, singing, diamond painting, adult coloring, and meeting new people. **May 12, Nov. 24**

Jennifer M. Baldwin writes from Australia, where she works in risk management at Sydney Adventist Hospital. She enjoys family time, church involvement, and relaxing with crossword or sudoku puzzles. She has been contributing to the devotional book series for more than twenty-five years. **July 29, Sept. 21**

Corletta Aretha Barbar, a native of the island of Jamaica, West Indies, currently resides in Sacramento, California, United States of America, with her husband, Michael Barbar. She has a passion for writing. Her involvement within the church varies from serving as head of the music ministry to being a hospitality team player. Her hobbies are writing, traveling with Michael, crocheting, walking, sightseeing, and singing. **June 22, Sept. 25, Dec. 4**

Jenetta Barker lives in Bedfordshire, England, United Kingdom, with her husband and daughter. She attends Luton Central Seventh-day Adventist Church. She enjoys spending time with her family, reading, walking, writing, and traveling. **Apr. 18**

Gloria Barnes-Gregory, PhD, MA, BSc, CM, is inspired by everyday experiences and especially interactions with her granddaughters. She and her husband, Milton, continue to serve others in health, family life, and leadership ministries, enabling others to make positive lifelong changes for themselves and to honor God. **Jan. 10, Mar. 24, Nov. 4**

Dottie Barnett is retired and lives in a beautiful country setting in southeast Tennessee, United States of America. For more than fifty years, she has been involved in children's and adults' Sabbath School leadership. She has written a devotional blog for the past several years called *Whispers of His Wisdom*. She loves working with plants and flowers, mowing her large lawn, photography, and camping with her family. **Sept. 27, Oct. 23**

Gyl Moon Bateman lives in Niles, Michigan, United States of America, and has three grown sons. She is recently retired from working as a behavioral medicine nurse at a local hospital. She enjoys pursuing her hobbies, being active in the local community and her church, and helping her sons at their nearby store. **Sept. 29, Oct. 21**

Dana M. Bean is an educator from a small, beautiful island in the middle of the Atlantic Ocean—Bermuda. She loves the arts of writing, reading, and capturing moments through photography. **Nov. 1**

Raquel Bendita Larico is from Peru. She is studying for a master's in geology at Loma Linda University, California, United States of America. She likes church involvement and writing and loves geology, igneous rock, and minerals. Her dream is to do geochemistry research. At the same time, she wants to preach about the message of God's creation and spread the three angels' messages (Revelation 14:6–12). **May 22, Sept. 4**

Sylvia Giles Bennett recently retired and enjoys the privilege of taking care of others and spending time with her grandchildren. She is celebrating almost forty years of marriage with Richard. She enjoys reading and writing. A member of Windsor Seventh-day Adventist Church, Windsor, Virginia, United States of America, she frequently visits Calvary Seventh-day Adventist Church in Newport News, Virginia. **Oct. 22**

Cynthia Best-Goring lives in Glenn Dale, Maryland, United States of America. She is a wife, the mother of two adult children, a first-time mother-in-law, and a Sabbath School teacher. She enjoys being retired from her position as a school principal. **Feb. 26**

Moselle Slaten Blackwell is a widow, and she has two adult children and one granddaughter. She is retired and enjoys serving as a deaconess, Sabbath School teacher, and choir member in her church. Her favorite interests are working in the yard, listening to religious music, watching beautiful sunsets, and enjoying a clear, moonlit night sky—all of which speak of God's sovereignty. **Apr. 17**

Patricia Hook Rhyndress Bodi enjoys life in Vista, California, United States of America. She is an active senior, walking five miles each day. Her goal is to make a difference in this world as she looks for opportunities to share her faith with everybody. **June 16, Aug. 19, Dec. 6**

Fulori Sususewa Bola, a retired schoolteacher, is serving as a volunteer with Hope Channel Fiji. She enjoys working with women, being involved in prayer ministry, and working with young people to share God's love through media and television. **Dec. 26**

R. Bowen is a Canadian woman, teaching English and living for Christ in Northeast Asia. She enjoys traveling, meeting new people, and watching God work to draw others closer to Him. She is supported by her family living in Toronto, Canada, and her international family of prayer across the world. **June 17**

Althea Y. Boxx, MPH, is a registered nurse with backgrounds in critical care and emergency nursing. She has authored a motivational devotional entitled *Fuel for The Journey*. She enjoys writing, photography, and traveling. **Mar. 18, Apr. 10**

DeeAnn Bragaw joyfully serves as the director of Women's Ministries for the North American Division of Seventh-day Adventists. She's passionate about connecting women to Jesus, each other, and their communities and thrives on creating space for those connections to happen. A native of Colorado, United States of America, DeeAnn loves to be outside hiking, biking, paddle boarding, snowshoeing, and camping with her husband, Paul. They also love spending time with their two young adult sons. **Jan. 1**

Mary Head Brooks, a retired psychiatric nurse, lives in Georgia, United States of America, with her husband, Marshall. She is a member of the Oakwood University Nursing Advisory Council (OUNAC) and enjoys gardening, traveling, and spending time with her grandson, Mason. **Mar. 30**

Brenda Browne-Ashe is from the island of Antigua in the Caribbean and is the Women's Ministries island coordinator. She has great passion for this ministry to which God has called her and is grateful to be working for and with women. **June 9**

Elinor Harvin Burks lives with her husband and soulmate, Winfield, a lay pastor, in Birmingham, Alabama, United States of America. For fun, they demonstrate God's hand in nature with "Science for Kids" programs at libraries, churches, schools, and health fairs. A church treasurer, she loves giving Bible studies and making soap. A journalism graduate of Detroit's Wayne State University, she retired from the City of Birmingham in 2010. **July 25, Aug. 27**

Jayne Byrd-Moody resides in Belleville, Illinois, United States of America. She is a retired educator who enjoys a variety of hobbies and sharing the good news of our Savior's love and His soon return. She has served in the New Jerusalem Seventh-day Adventist Church of East Saint Louis, Illinois, as clerk, Sabbath School superintendent, and the leader of the communication, health ministries, and women's ministries departments. **May 21**

Elizabeth Ida Cain is an educator by profession, working in human resources and administration, where she finds fulfillment in caring for employees in the workplace as

Jesus would. She is a professional florist who enjoys teaching the art and cheering others with beautiful floral arrangements. One of her spiritual blessings is writing devotionals for the women's devotional books. She lives in Jamaica, West Indies. **May 19, Oct. 3**

Hyacinth V. Caleb, born and raised in Antigua, presently resides in Saint Croix, United States Virgin Islands. She is a mother of two and a grandmother of six. She is a retired educator who loves reading, writing, and working outside in her garden. **Sept. 15**

Florence E. Callender is an educational and wellness consultant who lives in New York, United States of America. Her passion is helping mothers of children who learn differently work with them at home so they can be propelled from struggle to success in school and life. She also enjoys going on mission trips with her daughter. **Jan. 19, Aug. 8**

Laura A. Canning focuses most of her energy these days on writing children's books—but it still gives her a real thrill to see how God inspires her to write for the women's devotional books. She loves her family and pets and enjoys gardening and home projects where she lives near Windsor in the United Kingdom. **Apr. 1, June 2, Nov. 3**

Ruth Cantrell, a retired Detroit school teacher and counselor, lives with her husband in Belleville, Michigan, United States of America. Her family is the joy of her life. She has two sons, two daughters-in-law, and three grandchildren. She enjoys women's ministries, prayer ministry, reading, flowers, music, and organizing programs. **Aug. 28, Dec. 19**

Camilla E. Cassell, a retired postal employee, attends Berea Temple Seventh-day Adventist Church, in Baltimore, Maryland, United States of America. She has two children and treasures her grandson, Amari. She has compassion for families and feels they should spend quality time with each other. She enjoys reading God's Word, doing crafts, designing greeting cards, encouraging others in the Lord (especially young people), and making music. **Aug. 20, Nov. 16**

Suhana Chikatla, PhD, born in India, has two master's degrees in addition to her doctorate. She volunteers in children's and youth leadership positions and is currently the Adventurers Club director at her Hanceville, Alabama, church in the United States of America. She is an executive council member for the Gulf States Conference Women's Ministries Department. She and her husband, Royce Sutton, have a beautiful daughter, Rehana. **Feb. 6, Mar. 28, May 25**

Rosemarie Clardy enjoys nature and is truly blessed to live in the country with her husband and her household of pets. She is currently involved in leading a small group and coordinating a Bible school for her local church. **Apr. 15, Sept. 16**

Sharon Clark is a retired educator who still loves learning. Widowed in 2021, she enjoys spending time in nature, hiking, camping, being with family, serving God, and writing. She is homesick for heaven and prays for the soon return of Jesus. **Jan. 9, May 29, Aug. 11**

Sacha Clarke resides in Baytown, Texas, United States of America, with her husband, Kelvin, and two sons: Chalum and Chasiah. She is originally from the small Caribbean island of Saint Lucia. She is a social worker by profession and currently works at the local hospital in Baytown. She enjoys crafting and spending time with her family. **Dec. 11**

Sherma Webbe Clarke writes from Bermuda, where she serves in women's ministries and a variety of administrative roles in her church. Her interests include sewing, photography, and travel. She has contributed to previous devotional books and enjoys writing plays, short stories, and poetry. **Apr. 13**

Valerie Knowles Combie, PhD, is a professor at the University of the Virgin Islands. She is a career educator and author in various genres—poetry, creative nonfiction, personalized essay, and memoir. She is the director of the Virgin Islands Writing Project (VIWP). **Jan. 4, Feb. 10**

Aminata Coote lives in Montego Bay, Jamaica, with her husband and son. She is the author of the book *Royal: Life Lessons From the Book of Esther*. She's also the creator of the website Hebrews12Endurance.com, where she encourages women to "know God, know themselves, run their race." **Feb. 18, June 26**

Raquel Queiroz da Costa Arrais is a minister's wife who served as an educator for twenty years. At the time of this writing, she worked as the associate director of the General Conference Women's Ministries Department. She has two adult sons, two daughters-in-law, and four adored grandchildren. Her greatest pleasures are being with people, singing, playing the piano, and traveling. **Jan. 11**

Patricia Cove, married to George for over sixty years, is a semiretired teacher. She is active in her church and community. She spends as much time as possible in her flower gardens. She enjoys many other hobbies, including hiking, baking, sailing, and freelance writing. Her five children are all very busy with the many grandchildren and great-grandchildren that continue the Cove generations. **Feb. 2, Mar. 31, Sept. 20**

Lee Lee Dart is a pastor living in Kansas City, Missouri, United States of America. This wife and mother of two is passionate about being a conduit of God's love to others. **Jan. 23, July 28**

Jean Dozier Davey and her husband, Steven, live in the beautiful mountains of North Carolina, United States of America. A retired computer programmer, she enjoys family, cooking, walking in the Pisgah National Forest, reading, sewing, photography, and encouraging others. **May 24, Oct. 2**

Edna Bacate Domingo, PhD, MSN, RN, lives with her husband in Grand Terrace, California, United States of America. A retired nursing professor, she still actively runs her nursing school. She serves as one of the Sabbath School superintendents at Loma Linda University Church. She has three grown-up children and two grandchildren. She loves nature and being with her grandchildren. **Nov. 29**

Dagmar Dorn is the Women's Ministries director for the Inter-European Division of Seventh-day Adventists and lives in Switzerland. She is a nurse-midwife who has worked in different countries. She enjoys traveling and meeting people and is impressed over and over again with God's love. **Apr. 9**

Gail Dotski was born and raised in northern Michigan, United States of America, and has lived there ever since. She has five beautiful children and three gorgeous grandchildren. In her spare time, she enjoys playing her trumpet, doing cross-stitch projects, and coloring in adult spiritual coloring books. Her current project is to crochet her five-year-old granddaughter an afghan. **June 23, Oct. 9**

Louise Driver is retired and living in Idaho, United States of America, where her three sons and their families live. Her husband, a retired pastor, is still preaching, and they are involved with various churches. Reading, gardening, traveling, putting together puzzles, and helping with a church community thrift store keep her busy. **May 7**

Pauline A. Dwyer-Kerr holds two doctorate degrees. She is an advanced practice nurse and a professor of nursing. She is a life member of the Cambridge Honors Who's Who. She has received numerous awards, including Childhood Amblyopia Prevention Screening. She is an ordained elder in her church in Florida, United States of America. She loves her children and grandchildren and enjoys the outdoors. **Sept. 10**

Shylet Chabata Dzvene, a freelance writer residing in Zimbabwe, is a wife and a mother of one sweet boy. Her favorite book is *The Desire of Ages*. **Jan. 20**

Yvonne E. Ealey, MEd, is in a multiple relationship with God and man, is an active member of Dupont Park Seventh-day Adventist Church, Washington, DC, United States of America, and is a retired teacher who substitutes, writes, and shares her thoughts. She enjoys stories that reflect the beauty and complexity of the Christian life. She is looking toward the next adventure in our world. **Feb. 25, Nov. 25**

Haley Enochs was a student at Campion Academy, Colorado, United States of America, at the time of this writing. She graduated in 2021. **Aug. 12**

Mona Fellers is a retired paramedic living in the beautiful prairie of Wyoming, United States of America. She along with her husband and another couple bought an old schoolhouse they are renovating into a home. She enjoys time with her daughters, grandchildren, and critters. Most of all, she loves to share the love of Jesus. **May 6, Oct. 19, Dec. 2**

Sharon Follett writes from the beautiful Sequatchie Valley in Dunlap, Tennessee, United States of America, where she and her husband, Ron, pastor three churches. She enjoys taking walks in the woods with Ron and their pets as well as singing, leading church choirs, teaching children to play the piano, and spending time with her granddaughter, Savannah. **June 27, June 28, Sept. 19**

Shirley Sain Fordham is a retired educator, wife, mother of three married children, and grandmother of eight. She enjoys family and friends, technology, crocheting, and scrapbooking. She also loves befriending transfer members at her home church in Atlanta, Georgia, United States of America. She has learned to occupy well—living, loving, laughing, and learning until Jesus comes again. **Nov. 28**

Sylvia A. Franklin lives with her husband, Joe, in Rocklin, California, United States of America, and currently works as a human resources analyst for Sacramento Public Library. She is the administrative assistant to the Women's Ministries director in the Pacific Union Conference of Seventh-day Adventists. She enjoys planning community events, playing games, and singing. **Feb. 19, Oct. 1, Nov. 18**

Edith C. Fraser, PhD, has been married for more than fifty-two years. During much of her ministry, she has been a family life facilitator, leader, and presenter. She and her husband, Trevor, have published the book *Saving Marriages by Applying Biblical Wisdom*. She is committed to helping families using her personal, professional, and spiritual insights. **Jan. 17, June 3**

Forsythia Catane Galgao, originally from the Philippines, taught English in Ethiopia for eighteen years, Madagascar for seven years, and Thailand for fourteen years. Currently, she serves as an adjunct lecturer at Asia-Pacific International University, Thailand. Some of her hobbies include singing, reading, and playing with two grandchildren. **Oct. 11**

Cherryl A. Galley, PhD, teaches part-time and operates a counseling practice. She has served God as first elder, Sabbath School superintendent, and musician. She enjoys writing, reading, photography, traveling, and praying and is looking forward to Christ's return. **Oct. 4**

Claudette Garbutt-Harding, originally from Belize, retired after more than forty years as a Seventh-day Adventist educator from kindergarten to college. She recently published a manual, *Ten Helpful Hints for Principals*. She continues to share in ministry with her husband of forty-three plus years, Keith. She enjoys swimming, sailing, writing, and traveling, especially on cruises. They live in Orlando, Florida, United States of America. **May 14, July 10, Oct. 25**

Diane McLean Gaspard is a retired community college professor living in southern New Hampshire, United States of America. She serves as the church clerk and a member of the communication team for her church across the river in Vermont. She and her husband of forty-one years have two daughters and two granddaughters. She loves to travel, read, and do handicrafts of all sorts. **Sept. 23**

Cheri Gatton lives in Idaho, United States of America, and holds an MA in pastoral ministry from Andrews University. She has been a keynote speaker for many events across North America with a special passion for ministry to women, youth, and young adults. Cheri and her husband, Dave, live close to their two married children and are "Gigi" and "Papa" to five precious grandchildren! **Jan. 14**

Lindsey Gendke is a writer, wife, teacher, and mom who lives in Texas, United States of America, while pursuing her PhD in English, with an emphasis in composition pedagogy. The author of numerous books and articles on mental health, she continues to write both personally to manage stress and publicly to raise mental health awareness. Connect with her at LindseyGendke.com. **Aug. 1**

Marybeth Gessele lives in Gaston, Oregon, United States of America, with her husband, Glen. She is a retired hospice caregiver. Donating various sewing projects to charitable organizations is her favorite hobby. **Feb. 13**

Ana Maria de Souza Gonçalves is a member of the Orlando Brazilian Central Seventh-day Adventist Church in Florida, United States of America. She is the mother of two young adult women who are her most precious gift. She likes to work with youth and be with her family. **June 29, Aug. 24**

Kaysian C. Gordon is a mother, financial advisor, author, speaker, and Bible teacher. She has published two devotionals and a children's book coauthored with her daughter. She is her church's director of finance and stewardship and is passionate about stewarding God's resources in all areas of our lives. She is also a Sabbath School superintendent and speaks to various women's groups. **Feb. 23, Oct. 24, Dec. 15**

Alexis A. Goring is an author of inspirational books, founder of the *God Is Love* blog, a devotional writer, a trained journalist, an editor, and a photographer. She loves God, family, friends, church, music, movies, and good food. She enjoys sharing the gospel of Jesus Christ with everyone she meets. **Apr. 22, Sept. 8, Dec. 1**

Raquel Gosling-George is an elder at Baltimore White Marsh Seventh-day Adventist Church. She lives in Maryland, United States of America, with her husband, Errol, and two cats, Eclipse and Ashes. She enjoys all aspects of church ministry, especially the Pathfinders and working with the youth. She loves nature, photography, puzzles, and helping others and lives by the motto "one day at a time." **July 11**

Cecelia Grant is a medical doctor retired from government service and living in Kingston, Jamaica. Her hobbies are traveling, gardening, and listening to good music. She has a passion for young people, to whom she is always giving advice. **Mar. 2, Nov. 19**

Jasmine E. Grant, a retiree, mother, and grandmother, resides in New York City, United States of America. She enjoys sharing the Scriptures and testimonies with folks in general, but she has a special place in her heart for young people. She enjoys teaching them about the Savior and encouraging them to excel in whatever they do. **Mar. 13, Oct. 10**

Winsome Joy Grant, a Jamaican-born mother and grandmother, writes from Valley Stream, New York, United States of America. She has served as the church clerk and Adventurer director in her local church. She is an avid reader and has had a lifelong passion for writing. She is honored to contribute to this devotional and, ultimately, to glorify God. **Sept. 11**

Mary Jane Graves is a long-time contributor to the devotional books from her home in North Carolina, United States of America. She has worked as a secretary, school registrar, and school and church librarian but is now retired. She enjoys reading, table games, and gardening. **July 12**

Cloreth S. Greene, MEd, MA, ABC, is an education and communications consultant from Jamaica who currently resides in Canada. She appreciates the outdoors, enjoys music and cooking, and is passionate about prayer, youth, and children's ministries. **Nov. 13**

Glenda-mae Greene, PhD, writes from her wheelchair in the Western Canadian prairies. A retired educator, she delights in working with anyone who needs her assistance. Crafting is her testimony to the Savior's abiding love. **Apr. 25, Oct. 26**

Zandra LaMar Griffin-Willingham is a retired captain from the New York City Department of Correction. She resides in Alabama, United States of America, with her husband, Stanley, and two dogs, Alpha and Atlas. She ministers to the hungry and needy on the third Sabbath of each month. **May 5**

Galina Gritsuk writes from Grants Pass, Oregon, United States of America. From the 1980s through the 1990s, Galina was a translator for speakers and evangelists visiting the Soviet Union from the General Conference of Seventh-day Adventists. She has recently retired from substitute teaching and lives with Vitaly, her husband of forty-plus years. They have two adult sons and one daughter. She longs for Jesus' return. **May 11**

Diantha Hall-Smith is a daughter of God. She is wife to a devoted Christian husband who serves in the United States Air Force, and she is the mother of two beautiful children. She was born in New York City, United States of America, and has had the honor and privilege to have lived and visited interesting places, domestically and globally. She enjoys writing, traveling, and spending time with her family. **Aug. 18, Dec. 13**

Diana Halverson lives with her husband in East Tennessee, United States of America, where she is also a mother of four and grandmother of nine. She is a licensed building contractor who retired from McKee Baking Company as a mechanic. She is currently a state prison chaplain and was a missionary for over twenty years in the jungles of Nicaragua. At her home church in Dayton, Tennessee, she directs women's ministries and Vacation Bible School. **Oct. 14, Oct. 15**

Marsha Hammond-Brummel is a math teacher who lives in Claremont, New Hampshire, United States of America. From May through October, she can often be found at the historical Washington, New Hampshire, Seventh-day Adventist Church and Sabbath Trail, where she and her husband, Ken, tell the stories of the early Adventist pioneers to visitors. **Jan. 6, Mar. 1**

Myrna L. Hanna is the assistant vice president for administrative affairs and alumni and donor relations at Loma Linda University Health, California, United States of America. Her favorite things include traveling, spending time with family, and encouraging others to make the most of the talents God has given them. **Oct. 16, Oct. 17, Oct. 31**

Marian M. Hart-Gay lives in Florida, United States of America, with her husband, David. She is a mother, grandmother, and great-grandmother. She is also a former elementary teacher and nursing home administrator. She enjoys being active in her church, time with family, knitting, and living near a lake and the Gulf of Mexico. Her greatest desire is to see her entire family ready for Jesus to come. **Aug. 3, Sept. 9**

Bessie Russell Haynes is a retired teacher who served as a missionary teacher in South Korea for more than twelve years. She has relocated to the Pacific Northwest in the northern part of Washington, United States of America, to be near her precious grandchildren—two live in Vancouver, British Columbia, Canada, and the other two near Seattle, Washington. Traveling, reading, writing, and gardening are still her hobbies. She awaits Jesus' soon return! **Apr. 27, June 24**

Beverly D. Hazzard is retired from health-care administration and is an active volunteer with her local church and school in Kelowna, British Columbia, Canada. She enjoys time with family, her dogs and cats, travel, sailing, and mission trips. **Mar. 15**

Denise Dick Herr, an emeritus professor of English at Burman University in Alberta, Canada, loved teaching but relishes retirement: she has more time to see family, travel, count animals, and identify birds. **Feb. 5, Apr. 5, Nov. 2**

Andrea D. Hicks is the founder of FOCUS Ministries, women's ministries director, motivational speaker, and product manager for intraoral imaging for an innovative company for dental professionals and lives in New York, United States of America. **July 15**

Patricia Hines is originally from the Caribbean island of Jamaica. She is now retired and lives in Sebring, Florida, United States of America. She likes to write, enjoys music, and spends much of her days gardening. **May 31, July 23, Oct. 18**

Tamyra Horst, an international author and speaker, serves as the director of Communication, Women's Ministries, and Family Ministries for the Pennsylvania Conference of Seventh-day Adventists, United States of America, and also serves as the Women's Ministries director for the Columbia Union Conference of Seventh-day Adventists. Her passion is to "encourage, equip, and challenge people to grow deeply and serve uniquely." She loves being a mom to her two young-adult sons and their beautiful wives, enjoying her back-porch swing with a great book and a cup of chai, and sharing adventures with her husband of forty years. **Jan. 27, Nov. 7**

Jacqueline Hope HoShing-Clarke has been a Christian educator for over forty years and has a PhD in education administration. She serves as the chairperson for the Teacher Education department at Northern Caribbean University in Jamaica and is an ordained elder at her church. She is the mother of two adult children, Deidre Clarke-Jumpp and Deneil Clarke. She is further blessed with three grandchildren, Demetrio, Alayna, and Jude. **Mar. 14, Apr. 21, May 10**

Charmaine Houston is a health-care professional who lives in Pennsylvania, United States of America, with her two children. She enjoys reading and running—recently completing a half-marathon. **Aug. 14**

Sigrid Hruby works as an x-ray assistant and lives with her cat in Vienna, Austria. A favorite story in her self-published book, *Zartbitter, Edelherb, Süb* (written in Austrian German and available from Amazon Kindle books), is the account of how God miraculously brought this cat into her life. She supports others in achieving their goals through her role as a certified life coach. This passion for helping others is an outcome of her experience as a pastor's daughter. **Sept. 2**

Kathy Hull lives in Maiden, North Carolina, United States of America, with Johnny, her husband of forty-one years. They have two sons, John and Justin. Justin and his wife, Katie, are the parents of their precious grandson, Hunter. Spending quality time with God, family, and friends are her favorite activities. **Nov. 12**

Joy Bakaba Igwe is the associate director of Women's Ministries of the Port Harcourt Conference, Rivers State, Nigeria. She is an accountant and educator by profession. She is married to Dr. Martin Igwe, and their marriage has been blessed with four children. Her hobbies are singing, making disciples for Christ, and nurturing young women. **Sept. 24, Nov. 27**

Shirley C. Iheanacho is a wife, mother, grandmother, international speaker, and writer. One of her passions is encouraging women to write devotional articles. Since 2011, more than sixty-five articles written by thirty-four women have been published in devotional books. She is the author of the book *God's Incredible Plans for Me: A Memoir of an Amazing Journey*, available on Amazon.com. At the age of eighty-one, God continues to use her to share His love through sermons, songs, and ministries. **Feb. 9, Nov. 11, Nov. 20**

Jonsaba C. Jabbi is a writer, storyteller, and emerging archivist, born and raised in Toronto, Ontario, Canada. Her passions include reading, scrapbooking, blogging, black histories, and women's issues. She currently works at a local community arts nonprofit as a communication specialist. She desires to be more involved in ministry—especially in women's interests and the black community. **June 6**

Avis Floyd Jackson lives in Pleasantville, New Jersey, United States of America, and is a mother of five. She does business out of her home and is a party planner. She is active in her local church and is an Adventist by calling. **Jan. 3, Aug. 17**

Unathi Jiya is a legal manager, leader, mediator, wife, and mother of three sons, who lives with her family in Johannesburg, South Africa. She was a deaconess in East London Seventh-day Adventist Church before moving to Johannesburg. Her hobbies are listening to worship songs, reading, and coaching young women. **May 2, May 3**

Greta Michelle Joachim-Fox-Dyett is a potter, writer, blogger, and educator from Trinidad and Tobago. She is married to her love, Arnold, and the proud mama of an adult daughter. **Feb. 16, Feb. 17, July 16**

Elaine J. Johnson enjoys sharing testimonies about the goodness of God. She has been blessed to be married for over fifty years to her best friend. She enjoys reading and writing and has been published in several of these devotional books. She is retired after working for thirty-five years with children. **June 21, Aug. 5**

Jeannette Busby Johnson lives in Miles City, Montana, United States of America, not far from the homestead her Norwegian grandparents settled on in the late 1800s, where their thirteen children were born. She thinks that it's likely she's related to almost anyone she meets on the streets of Miles City. **Mar. 7, Dec. 12**

Mary C. D. Johnson is an enthusiastic high school Spanish teacher in California, United States of America. She travels the world on mission trips whenever she gets a school break. When not on a mission trip, she enjoys scrapbooking, writing, and being outdoors. When she is at her home church, she enjoys telling the children's story, serving as a deaconess, and teaching the Spanish adult Sabbath School lesson. **Feb. 14, July 14, Dec. 24**

Simone E. Johnson is an educator who resides in Goshen, Saint Elizabeth, Jamaica, and cherishes God's promise recorded in Jeremiah 29:1. She embraces Benjamin Franklin's quote "Well done is better than well said!" as a guiding principle. **Mar. 9, June 20**

Deidre A. Jones and her husband recently moved to Mineral, Virginia, United States of America. She assists her new church with its graphic design needs. Previously, she ministered in various roles including communications, treasurer, and children's ministries coordinator. Since 2017, she has written a blog called *Sabbath Thoughts*. Her hobbies include cooking and playing with her little Yorkie, Tuff. **Mar. 29, May 1, Aug. 4**

Gerene I. Joseph is married to Pastor Sylvester Joseph. They have two adult children. She served as the director of Women and Children's Ministries of the North Caribbean Conference for six years. Presently, she is the director of Education in the same conference. She enjoys writing poems and playing the piano in her spare time. She is also a certified lay preacher and has conducted three crusades. **Aug. 29**

Grace A. Keene was born on December 31, 1935. For twenty years she lived in New Rochelle, New York, before moving to Florida, both in the United States of America. There she raised her family (and some other people too), whom she still points to the lovely Lord Jesus and His joy and comfort. She resides in a Tennessee retirement center and remains intensely interested in doing what Jesus asks all of us to do: "Go and tell." **Apr. 7, Nov. 23**

Sonia Kennedy-Brown lives in Ontario, Canada, and is a retired nurse. She loves to read, write, and witness to others. Since the publication of her autobiography, *Silent Tears: Growing Up Albino*, she has become a motivational speaker for people with albinism and those with other disabilities. To support the book project, contact her at Soniab47@msn.com. **Mar. 3, May 26, May 27**

Sandy Kolb lives in Lincoln, Nebraska, United States of America. She is happily married with lovely daughters, wonderful sons-in-law, two adorable grandchildren, and a lovable goldendoodle. She thoroughly enjoys working as an office manager at Union College. She also serves as a College View Church Pathfinder Trailblazers counselor. She enjoys reading, writing, camping, and continuing her education. **June 10**

Kênia Kopitar, born in Brazil, now lives in Kissimmee, Florida, United States of America. She volunteers, teaching children in her community to play bells. She loves traveling, reading, and finding a home for stray animals. **July 5**

Betty Kossick continues as a freelance writer of varied genres and as a journalist, author, and poet for both religious and secular publications. She developed and edits *Front Porch Visits*, the newsletter for Florida Living Retirement Community. Much of her work appears on Google. Contact her at onwingsofthedove@gmail.com. **Feb. 20, Feb. 21, Nov. 17**

Mabel Kwei, a retired university and college lecturer, did missionary work in Africa for many years with her pastor husband and their three children. Now living in New Jersey, United States of America, she reads a lot and loves to paint, write, and spend time with little children. **June 4, June 5, Nov. 5**

Juliet L. Lucas Languedoc has been teaching for more than fourteen years. Presently, she serves as the Bible teacher for the junior and secondary levels at the Saint Thomas/ Saint John Seventh-day Adventist School in the United States Virgin Islands. She is married to Pastor Jerry Languedoc. She holds a master's in educational psychology from the University of the Southern Caribbean. She is a certified and commissioned teacher who enjoys praying for others, meeting people, singing, witnessing, decorating, crocheting, sharing, and planting and grooming flowers. **July 21**

Maite Lavado lives in Madrid, Spain, with her American husband. In addition to working full-time, she also enjoys studying psychology, in which she has specialized in abuse, gender violence, child abuse, and violent behavior in childhood and youth. She actively works with women's ministries in Spain, presenting workshops around the country, and creating a series of videos focused on gender violence and different aspects of child abuse. She serves in her local congregation and in the past has been the director of her church's Pathfinder club, completing all the requirements for Master Guide. **July 24, Sept. 6**

Judie Lewis is a registered nurse living in Houston, Texas, United States of America. She was born into the Seventh-day Adventist faith and has continued to serve God throughout her life. She loves writing poems, crocheting, sewing, and reading. On her days off, she visits craft stores looking for yarn and material to do her projects. She donates the items she makes to family and friends. She has two daughters and two adorable grandchildren. **Sept. 22**

Sharon Long was born in Trinidad but lived most of her life in Canada. In 2015, she retired from the government of Alberta after thirty-four years in child welfare. She does contract work for the Alberta College of Social Workers and is active at the West Edmonton Seventh-day Adventist Church. She is the mother of four, grandmother of six, and great-grandmother of two. She is passionate about people and is happiest when serving others. She sees every day above ground as a good day and a new opportunity. **Apr. 11, Sept. 3, Dec. 3**

Rosemary Kasandra Lucien hails from the beautiful West Indian island of Saint Lucia. She is presently employed as the bookstore assistant with the Inter-American Division Publishing Association bookstore. Her passion is to serve the Lord as she intercedes on behalf of His people. Currently, she is doing a course in budgets and managing money. Her interests are reading, writing, and beach hopping. **Apr. 23**

Nancy A. Mack is a blonde American born in India to a missionary family. She attended college in the United States of America. She is married to Bill (also a missionary kid) and has raised their family in Maryland, United States of America. When they relocated to India to direct Adventist Child India, a donor-funded program for educating needy children, she became the third generation of Mattison missionaries who have served India for more than half a century. **Apr. 4**

Rhona Grace Magpayo enjoys going on mission trips with her husband, Jun. A photography enthusiast, she loves traveling the world and capturing sunsets with her camera. She always returns home to Maryland, United States of America. **June 15**

Carolyn Venice Marcus lives in North Carolina, United States of America. She and her husband are the proud parents of two adult children. She is retired and was blessed to work for several years as a physician assistant. She enjoys walking, traveling, singing, listening to spiritual music, and the company of family and friends in her faith community. **Aug. 6**

Beverley Martin currently lives in California, United States of America, with her husband of thirty-five years. Together, they have four adult children and one grandson.

She attends the Lancaster Seventh-day Adventist Church and is currently serving as the Women's Ministries director for the Southern California Conference of Seventh-day Adventists. She is a school principal and also a college professor. She loves the outdoors, cooking, and entertaining. Education is her passion, and she believes every child can learn if educators decipher how they learn and teach to their uniqueness. **Sept. 26**

Melissa Martinez lives on the beautiful island of Grand Cayman but needs frequent trips to see mountains, the one wonder of creation Cayman is not blessed with. She is blessed with not only an amazing twin sister but also twin daughters. **Apr. 6**

Mary H. Maxson, daughter of the King, is a retired associate pastor who resides with her husband, Ben, in Calhoun, Georgia, United States of America. For forty-seven years, she has faithfully served God as an administrative church assistant, in women's ministries (Argentina and Uruguay), as Women's Ministries director in two conferences, as director of ministry spouses, and as an editorial and administrative assistant with *Adventist Review* and Adventist World Radio. Mary served for more than seven years as the director of Women's Ministries for the North American Division of Seventh-day Adventists. Her passion is to daily follow Jesus and disciple people. **May 30, July 17, Dec. 18**

Lynn Mazarin is a secondary teacher and personal coach living in France. She is a Christian blogger at mysunnyposts.com. Grateful to be the Lord's servant, she is involved in the women's and youth ministries at Nuilly Seventh-day Adventist Church in Paris, France. **May 20, Aug. 15**

Raschelle Mclean-Jones is a fifth-grade teacher at Oakwood Academy in Huntsville, Alabama, United States of America. She is a mother of three sons and one daughter: Aaron, Josiah, Malachi, and Sarah. She enjoys cooking, singing in the choir, and spending time with loved ones. **Feb. 7**

Gertrude Mfune, originally from Malawi but living in Maryland, United States of America, works in the meeting planning section of the Treasury department at the General Conference of Seventh-day Adventists. She is the mother of four grown children and grandmother to three girls and one boy. She loves gardening, learning new things, mentoring young women, and making a positive change in others. **June 8**

Annette Walwyn Michael writes from Saint Croix in the United States Virgin Islands. In her retirement, she enjoys spending time with her husband, a retired pastor, her adult children and grandchildren, and her Central Seventh-day Adventist Church family. **Apr. 16, June 19, Dec. 28**

Judi Mmari lives in Acton, Massachusetts, United States of America, with her husband, John, and their two sons. She works as a language instructor at a nearby college. She thoroughly enjoys listening to gospel music and taking nature walks. **July 4**

D. Renee' Mobley-Neal, PhD, is trained in clinical pastoral education and counseling and is a master certified life coach and a relationship counselor. She has written six workbooks on singleness and a devotional for women about women of the Bible, *Ambitious Faith*. She is the mother of two adult women and the best son-in-law God could give a mother. She is blessed with the perfect husband for her, Willie James, and a beautiful family of in-laws. She is proud to say she lives in Wrens, Georgia, United States of America (her Mayberry). **Mar. 6, Apr. 19, Oct. 30**

Susen Mattison Molé is a missionary child and preacher's kid. She enjoyed attending high school in Singapore at Far Eastern Academy and loves the culture and food of all places where she has lived. She's married to a retired US Navy doctor, and they have two very special and wonderful daughters. Presently, she and her husband are working in the small country of Nepal at a hospital that helps the poor and those in need of healing spiritually and medically. **July 19**

Marcia Mollenkopf, a retired teacher, lives in Klamath Falls, Oregon, United States of America. She likes to read, write, and share Jesus. She has been blessed with a postcard ministry. **July 9, July 31**

Maureen H. Moncrieffe, EdD, resides in the sunshine state of Florida, United States of America, with her husband, who retired from pastoral ministry. She is a retired reading specialist and kindergarten teacher but has traded jobs to be her ninety-five-year-old mom's full-time caretaker. When she has the time, tending to her flower and vegetable gardens gives her enormous pleasure and fulfillment. She and her husband of fifty-one years are blessed with five adult children and seven grandchildren. **June 7, July 30**

Jane Wiggins Moore lives in Coalfield, Tennessee, United States of America, where she is the Community Services leader for her church and is active in their food ministry program, Hope for the Hungry. A retired registered nurse, she has two grown sons and delights in her granddaughter, Micah, and grandson, Andrew. She still mourns her beloved husband, John, who went to sleep in Jesus in 2001. **June 30**

Lila Farrell Morgan, a widow, lives in a small town in the foothills of western North Carolina, United States of America. She loves her four adult children, five grandchildren, and three great-grandchildren. Her favorite pastimes are reading, contemplating the Creator's handiwork in nature, researching different topics on the internet, baking, and table games. She looks for the positive in life and enjoys a good laugh. **July 6, Dec. 9**

Valerie Hamel Morikone is the wife of a retired pastor. She works at the Mountain View Conference of Seventh-day Adventists, United States of America, as the Communication director and conference clerk. She enjoys her granddaughter, Emma, and her two children, Greg and Janelle and their spouses, and she adores her husband, Daniel. She also loves Jesus with all her heart. **Feb. 3**

Bonnie Moyers lives with her husband, Carl, and Milo, a ragdoll kitty, in Staunton, Virginia, United States of America. This freelance writer is a mother of two, a grandmother of three, and a musician for several area churches. **July 8, Aug. 30, Dec. 8**

Esther Synthia Murali works as honorary director for Women's Ministries in South Karnataka Section, Mysore, India. She is a physiotherapist by profession, but her passion is ministering with her pastor husband. She has a son, Ted, and enjoys playing guitar, painting, gardening, and photography. **Jan. 18**

Jannett Maurine Myrie, MSN, RN, is a medical missionary who finds joy and fulfillment in sharing the love of Jesus with everyone! She is the proud mother of

Delroy Anthony Jr. She enjoys traveling, especially cruises; entertaining; reading; and just being still. She is ever so thankful to Jesus for loving her unconditionally and blessing her to trust the plans He has for her. **Jan. 12**

Cecilia Nanni earned a postgraduate degree in coaching, NLP, and team leadership, a degree in psychology, a master's degree in mediation and conflict resolution, and a master's degree in education, management mode. She has received an international diploma in volunteer management from UNESCO. Currently, she works as a volunteer coordinator in Central Asia. **Feb. 4, Feb. 24, Nov. 9**

Bienvisa Ladion Nebres, from the Philippines, teaches at Asia-Pacific International University in Thailand. She treasures the experience of having been able to work in Africa for two decades. A mother of three and grandmother of two, she likes poetry, church activities, traveling, and writing. **Mar. 22, Mar. 23**

Barbara Burris Neequaye, PhD, is a semiretired community college professor living in Charlotte, North Carolina, United States of America. She is the mother of one grown son and enjoys reading, writing, and going on cruises with her sisters. She is active in her church in various ministries. **May 18, June 18**

Christine B. Nelson is an avid reader and glad for the extra time to read since retiring from Stetson University in 2013. She's inspired by the writings and life stories of Amy Carmichael, Oswald Chambers, Corrie ten Boom, Abraham Lincoln, and Ellen G. White, among others. Old Testament Joseph is her favorite Bible character. She and her husband, Len, celebrated their fiftieth anniversary in 2021 and live in DeLand, Florida, United States of America. **Jan. 29, Feb. 1**

Samantha Nelson is a pastor's wife who loves serving alongside her husband, Steve. She is also the CEO of The Hope of Survivors, a nonprofit organization dedicated to assisting victims of clergy sexual abuse and providing educational seminars to clergy members of all faiths. She and Steve live in Wyoming, United States of America, and love traveling, hiking in the mountains, and enjoying the beauty of God's creation. **Mar. 25**

Maureen Nembhard is a retired administrator from the Bernard Fineson Developmental Disabilities Service Office. She lives with her husband of nearly forty-six years in New York, United States of America. She enjoys spending time with her grandchildren and seeks every opportunity to do so. She is an emergency response volunteer and loves to inform others, especially in her church, about disaster preparedness. Her hobbies include scrapbooking, reading, writing, and nature walks. **Oct. 7**

Linda Nottingham lives in Florida, United States of America, and teaches an adult Bible study class at her church. She is semi-retired but serves as a mentor to women business owners. She can be reached at lNottingham34@gmail.com. **Feb. 22, Nov. 30**

Elizabeth Versteegh Odiyar of Kelowna, British Columbia, Canada, has served God through church, Pathfinders, and mission trips. She has retired from thirty-three years of managing the family chimney sweep business. She is married to Hector, and they have twin sons and a daughter—all married, all serving God—and four delightful grandchildren. **Dec. 31**

Pauline Gesare Okemwa is married to a pastor, and they have three grown children. She lives in Kisii, Kenya. She is a professional counselor and lecturer at Kisii University. She enjoys guiding and counseling young people, reading, gospel music, gardening, and traveling. **Oct. 12**

Monique Lombart De Oliveira is retired and lives in the United Kingdom. She is busy adapting *The Desire of Ages* into stories for children. She makes laminated religious bookmarks to insert in *Steps to Christ* books to give away. **Oct. 20**

Michelle Vanessa O'Reilly is a teacher at Forest Lake Education Center in Orlando, Florida, United States of America. She enjoys writing and recently published a book with Westbow Press, a division of Thomas Nelson/Zondervan. **Sept. 18**

Sharon Oster is a retired teacher assistant living in Evans, Colorado, United States of America, with her retired pastor husband. She enjoys automobile day trips in the nearby Rocky Mountains. She and her husband have three children and eight grandchildren. **July 27, Sept. 1, Dec. 22**

Hannele Ottschofski lives in southern Germany, where she has been active in many facets of women's ministries. She has written two books in German, *Das Hemd meines Vaters* (My father's shirt) and *Mit am Tisch* (Together at the table), and one in English, *Tired of Waiting—Women in Church and Society*. **Mar. 4, July 22**

Ofelia A. Pangan and her husband just came back from Hawaii, United States of America, where they ministered to the members of the Molokai and Lanai churches for a year and a half. They recently returned to California to be near their children and minister again to their grandchildren. **July 20**

Grace Paulson is working as a project manager for the South Pacific Division and lives in Cooranbong, Australia, with her family. She is interested in the agency (and voices) of the biblical women, and her master of philosophy thesis on Esther reflects this interest. **Apr. 26**

Premila Pedapudi is the administrative assistant for the department of Women's Ministries at the General Conference of Seventh-day Adventists in Maryland, United States of America. She is married to Joseph Kelley and is mother to a son, Praveen, and twin daughters, Serena and Selena (who are married to Samuel and Ebenesar)—all are a great support to her in her ministry. Her first grandson arrived in July 2019. She is passionate about women's ministries and loves to sing, read, teach, and preach. **Dec. 10**

Sueli da Silva Pereira lives in Patos de Minas, Brazil, and works in the local city hall. She has been married for twenty-nine years and has three children: Arthur, Eric, and Samuel. She likes music, writing, and working with teenagers. She currently participates in the instrumental praise group of the Central Seventh-day Adventist Church of Patos de Minas. **Feb. 11, Apr. 3**

Diane Pestes, the author of *Prayer That Moves Mountains*, served for ten years in Women's Ministries at the Oregon Conference of Seventh-day Adventists in the United States of America. Her priority is being a servant and friend of God whenever she speaks at evangelistic series, prayer conferences, retreats, or prisons. She loves reciting

Scripture in nature and putting it on YouTube. **Sept. 17**

Dawn M. Phillips lives in Orlando, Florida, United States of America. She is happily married to Daniel Phillips, the love of her life for thirty-one years. They have three young adult sons. She currently works as secretary and office manager of the Beryl Wisdom Adventist School. She loves to work with the school family's and family life ministry. **Mar. 26**

Karen M. Phillips lives in Nebraska, United States of America, and is happily married to her husband, John. Together they conduct an international ministry, which includes publishing efforts, health ministry, missionary support, and more. Check it out at HeReturns.org. With four adult children and three grandchildren, she praises God every day for His amazing love. **May 17, Oct. 8, Nov. 8**

Merian Richardson lives in Orange, New South Wales, Australia, where her husband is a retired pastor, and she works part-time as a nurse in an aged care facility. She has three adult sons, with two married. At church, she is a musician and leads the primary and junior Sabbath School. She is also involved in the City of Orange brass band as treasurer and plays the tenor horn. Other interests are sewing and gardening. She has also transposed hymns from the *Seventh-day Adventist Hymnal* for different pitched musical instruments, which can be found at transposedhymns.com. **Aug. 10**

Jenny Rivera works as a registered nurse at the local regional hospital and lives on the north side of Brisbane, Australia. She is an active member at her church, playing her flute, being part of praise and worship, and serving as an adult Sabbath School leader. She enjoys reading and traveling, baking to share with others, playing the flute, and spending time with family and friends. **May 15, June 1, Nov. 14**

Delina Ashley Roberts-James, a qualified attorney in the republic of Trinidad and Tobago, is married to Pastor Kirt James of the South Caribbean Conference of Seventh-day Adventists. They have two sons. Apart from her official role as a legal advisor, she enjoys a good story since her young days of listening to Uncle Arthur's Bedtime Stories. As such, she has cultivated the art of scripting experiences where God's lessons have been learned in her life. **Aug. 9**

Taniesha K. Robertson-Brown, a contributor since 2013, is a teacher and author who writes from Pennsylvania, United States of America. She enjoys inspiring others through the written word and appreciates the support of her husband, Courtney, and the love of her children, Preston and Prescott. **Apr. 30, May 16, Nov. 15**

Charlotte A. Robinson has spent most of her life working and helping her husband raise three children. She has been published in *Our Little Friend*, *Primary Treasure*, *Guide*, and *Insight*. After living seventeen years with her parents near Ozark Academy, she moved to nearby Decatur, Arkansas, United States of America, when she married. She now lives on her late mother's property, where she grew up. **Nov. 10**

Terry Wilson Robinson lives in Hendersonville, North Carolina, United States of America, with her husband, Harry, who is an ordained minister. She enjoys working side by side with him teaching Revelation Seminars. **Apr. 29, Nov. 21**

Avis Mae Rodney writes from Guelph, Ontario, Canada, where she lives with Leon, her dear friend and husband of over fifty years. She is a retired justice of the peace and also a retired leader of women's ministries for the Guelph Seventh-day Adventist Church. She enjoys the extraordinary blessings of being a mother and grandmother. **Feb. 8, Apr. 14, May 9**

Terry Roselmond-Moore lives in Dayton, Ohio, United States of America. She is a registered nurse and enjoys traveling, reading, and gardening. She is the mother of one daughter, Taryn. **Apr. 12**

Raylene McKenzie Ross is a labor and delivery nurse who lives in Jamaica and commutes to New Jersey, United States of America, for work. She is wife to Leroy Ross and mother to Zachary and Ricardo. As she writes this devotional, the world is in the middle of the COVID-19 pandemic, but she is able to work and is praying every day to be reunited with her family as soon as possible. **Nov. 22**

Robin Widmayer Sagel lives in Choctaw, Oklahoma, United States of America, with David, her husband of thirty-six years. They have a daughter and three granddaughters. She works part-time at the Midwest City Library and volunteers at the Parkview Adventist Academy library. She loves books! Along with reading, she also enjoys writing, public speaking, and baking. She has been published in *Primary Treasure*, *Our Little Friend*, *Insight*, and the women's devotional book series. **Oct. 5**

Kollis Salmon-Fairweather resides in beautiful Central Florida, United States of America. She continues to enjoy Bible studies and witnessing. She plans on spending her remaining days working for the Master through outreach ministry. **Dec. 27**

Danijela Schubert lives in Sydney, Australia, where she works in the South Pacific Division, caring for women's ministries and women in pastoral ministry. Originally from Croatia, she has lived, studied, and worked in France, the Philippines, Pakistan, Papua New Guinea, and Australia. She is happily married to Branimir. Together, they have two grown sons. **Jan. 2**

Shirley P. Scott lives in Huntsville, Alabama, United States of America, with her husband of fifty-six years. She currently serves as the Southern Union Conference Women's Ministries director. **Mar. 11**

Jodian Scott-Banton is a Jamaican currently residing in the Turks and Caicos Islands. She teaches at the Maranatha Academy. She is married to a very loving and supportive husband, David, and God has blessed them with two lovely daughters named Johanna and J'Lissa. **Dec. 5**

Khametova Mariia Sergeevna was born in Kyrgyzstan into a pastor's family, where participating in church activities and services was a way of life. Recently married, she met her husband while both were students at Zaoksky University in Russia. They are currently serving God together as a pastor's family in Kazakhstan. **Sept. 7**

Sherry Taujale Shrestha and her husband, Prakash, live on run-down acreage near Berrien Springs, Michigan, United States of America. They enjoy the farm critters and challenges their woodland home brings to them. Three grandsons are the light of their lives. **Mar. 12**

Rose Neff Sikora and her husband, Norman, live happily on their hobby farm in the beautiful mountains of North Carolina, United States of America. She is retired from a forty-five-year career as a registered nurse, and she volunteers at Park Ridge Health. She enjoys walking, writing, and helping others. She has one adult daughter, Julie, and three lovely grandchildren. She desires that her writing will bless others. **Feb. 15.**

Ella Louise Smith Simmons is a vice president at the General Conference of Seventh-day Adventist headquarters in Silver Spring, Maryland, United States of America. She is the first female to hold this position. A veteran educator, she has served as provost, academic vice president, and professor in church and public sector universities. She is married to Nord, and they have two children, three grandchildren, and one great-grandson. **Feb. 28**

Debra Slack writes from Alabama, United States of America, and is a graduate of Oakwood University. She is a retired educator with interest in reading and gardening. Her involvement in the church includes four ministries. She has received awards from the Alabama State Board of Education, a Resolution and City Housing Initiative. She has adult children, grandchildren, and great-grandchildren. **Dec. 30**

Heather-Dawn Small is director of Women's Ministries at the General Conference of Seventh-day Adventists in Maryland, United States of America. She has been Children's Ministries and Women's Ministries director for the Caribbean Union Conference of Seventh-day Adventists, located in Trinidad and Tobago. She is the wife of Pastor Joseph Small and the mother of Dalonne and Jerard. She loves air travel, reading, and scrapbooking. **Jan. 24, Aug. 7**

Yvonne Curry Smallwood enjoys spending time with God, family, and friends along with reading, writing, and crocheting. When she is not writing, you can find her in a craft store purchasing yarn for the many crocheted items she creates and donates to local charities. Her articles and stories have appeared in several publications. **June 25**

Ann Hickman Smith, a retired RN at age fifty-four, returned to Oakwood University, receiving a master's degree in pastoral ministry. She lives in North Carolina, United States of America and has been married for forty-six years. She has two married sons and five grandchildren (and one on the way). She is an ordained elder and enjoys serving in women's ministries. Her hobbies are cooking, reading, gardening, and spending quality time with her grandchildren. **Sept. 28**

Sharon Denise Smith lives in Orlando, Florida, United States of America. She enjoys reading, traveling, and bicycling on the nature trails where she lives. **Apr. 20, Dec. 23**

Debra Snyder was born and raised in Massachusetts, United States of America, but God led her to Nebraska and her husband Kevin in 2012. She is the mother of three wonderful children, Jacob, Samantha, and Steven. She is active in her church and enjoys writing, especially spiritual poetry. She loves connecting with others and sharing what God places on her heart about her life experience and how He has led in her life. If you would like to know more about her poetry, you can contact her at dlSnyder70@gmail.com. **July 18, Oct. 6**

Candy Monique Springer-Blackman is from the twin-island Republic of Trinidad and Tobago. She attended the University of the Southern Caribbean, class of 1999.

Currently, she and her husband of seventeen years reside in his home country of Barbados and attend the King Street Seventh-day Adventist Church. She is an administrative assistant by profession, but her passion is doing décor and design for church services, events, and displays. **Aug. 23**

Jill Springer-Cato lives with her husband in the lovely Caribbean twin-island Republic of Trinidad and Tobago. She is the mother of two young adult sons. A music minister, she enjoys listening to local gospel ministers. She is involved in all aspects of church life, especially treasury, women's ministries, and communications. **Dec. 14**

Summer Stahl now lives in Northeast Washington, United States of America, with a husband who planted more fruit trees than she can keep up with. She is grateful that she now knows the goodness of God for herself and tastes His blessings daily. **Aug. 22**

Sylvia Sioux Stark is an artist living in East Tennessee, United States of America, who specializes in local scenes, landscapes, and flowers. She also tutors a special needs individual and loves feeding the wild critters that come to her door each evening for handouts. She has also been published in *Guide*. **Jan. 13**

Eva M. Starner, PhD, LPC, is an educator and counselor. She has worked with families for more than thirty years. She is divorced and has facilitated her church's Divorce Care (divorcecare.org) sessions since 2013. Her greatest accomplishment is her children. She has three adult daughters and is very thankful for the lives that they are leading. She also has grandchildren whom she spoils as often as she can while she waits for the soon return of our Lord and Savior, Jesus Christ. **Apr. 24, Dec. 7, Dec. 25**

Ardis Dick Stenbakken served as editor of this women's devotional book for years after her retirement as director of Women's Ministries at the General Conference of Seventh-day Adventists. She and her husband, Dick, love their two children and their spouses and four grandchildren. She is still hoping to find time to pursue some hobbies once again. **Jan. 28**

Rita Kay Stevens is a church administrator's wife whose family recently moved to Olympia, Washington, United States of America. She has been working as a medical technologist in a hospital. Until their recent move from New Mexico, United States of America, she was a liaison for Women's Ministries and sponsor for the minister's wives in the Texico Conference for Seventh-day Adventists. She is the mother of two grown sons and is thankful for a daughter-in-law, grandson, and granddaughter. **Apr. 2**

Barbara Stovall, DBA, MAEd., MBA, raised in the city of Myrtle Beach, South Carolina, presently lives in Huntsville, Alabama, both in the United States of America. She is the archivist for Oakwood University. Her travels to a myriad of places at home and abroad (via military dependent) afforded a deep appreciation for different cultures and people from diverse backgrounds. She loves to read, take long walks on the beach, and travel and is a firm believer in and follower of Jesus Christ. **May 4**

Carolyn Rathbun Sutton and her husband, Jim, are volunteer field representatives for Adventist World Radio who live in Alabama, United States of America. She served as editor of this devotional book for several years before retiring to spend more time caring for her husband and enjoying her children and grandchildren. **July 1, Aug. 21, Dec. 17**

Evelyn Porteza Tabingo is a retired cardiac nurse living in Oceanside, California, United States of America. She and her husband, Henry, are from the Philippines and have served as missionaries to East Africa. She enjoys reading, writing, gardening, music, traveling, and spending time with family and her grandchildren. **June 12**

Arlene R. Taylor recently retired from health care after decades of working with Adventist Health facilities. Still living in the Napa Valley of northern California, United States of America, she devotes her time and energy to brain-function research, writing, and speaking. **Aug. 16, Oct. 29, Dec. 21**

Edna Thomas Taylor is a conference Women's Ministries coordinator, former church women's ministry leader, and entrepreneur. She is the mother of Junia, Jamila, and Jamaal and the grandmother of Ammi, Najja, and Tyra. She writes from Tampa, Florida, United States of America. A musician, she enjoys reading, writing, and working with our "legacies"—young women. **July 13**

Mirian Taylor is a registered midwife living on the beautiful island of Jamaica. She is single and enjoys writing, spending time in nature, and sewing. She has had the privilege of serving in different departments of the church such as Sabbath School, Adventist youth, and health ministries. **Dec. 16**

Maureen Thomas lives in Waynesboro, Tennessee, United States of America. She is a retired teacher who enjoys gardening, the outdoors, decorating, and writing poetry. Reading the Bible and finding interesting nuggets from God's Word are also of great delight to her. **May 8**

Rose Joseph Thomas, PhD, is the associate director for Elementary Education for the Southern Union of Seventh-day Adventists. She lives in the United States and is married to her best friend, Walden. She has two adult children: Samuel Joseph and Crystal Rose. She has a precious grandchild, Adrian, and her daughter-in-law, Rebekah, will give her a second grandchild soon. **Nov. 6**

Sharon M. Thomas is a retired public-school teacher who has enjoyed working various jobs in retirement. Other interests include quilting, card making, word games, biking, walking, and piano. She is always grateful for our omnipotent, omnipresent, and omniscient heavenly Father. **Mar. 10, Aug. 2**

Stella Thomas is retired and enjoys her peaceful life in Maryland, United States of America. She is blessed with and loves her three wonderful grandchildren. Her passion is to share God's love with the world so that many will be saved when Jesus comes. **Jan. 15, Sept. 12, Oct. 27**

Bula Rose Haughton Thompson is a member of the Goshen Seventh-day Adventist Church in the West Jamaica Conference of Seventh-day Adventists. She has been married to Norman for twenty-one years. **Apr. 8, Apr. 28**

Joey Norwood Tolbert lives in Chattanooga, Tennessee, United States of America, with her husband, Matthew; their children, Lela and Charlie; and Smoky, their large dog. She is active in music ministry and loves to read books about the Bible that dig into scripture. She currently works part-time at Southern Adventist University. She graduated from Southern Adventist University in 2007 with an MA in religious studies and her secondary education certification. **Jan. 8**

Ann Trout and her husband, Steve, enjoy spending time with their two adult children, their spouses, and especially their grandchildren. She teaches at a local community college and has published two devotional books. **Jan. 7**

Rebecca Turner belongs to several small groups and studies the Bible deeply. Her mission in life is encouraging her friends and family, particularly three tiny grandsons, to fall in love with Jesus. She is an editorial assistant at the General Conference Women's Ministries Department and lives with her husband, Charles, in Maryland, United States of America. **Jan. 22, Sept. 5, Dec. 20**

Ekele P. Ukegbu-Nwankwo, DMin, BCC, ND, is a Nigerian-born mother of four and a board-certified chaplain with a doctor of ministry degree in health care chaplaincy (Andrews University) and doctor of naturopathy (International Institute of Original Medicine in Virginia). She is trained in the counseling of singles, groups, and families. Her passion is to empower others for holistic, sustainable life transformation through the power of the Holy Spirit. Her published book, *Simple Solutions: A Trip Into Sustainable Well-Care*, is available on Amazon.com. She lives in Columbus, Ohio, United States of America. **Mar. 8, July 7**

Olga Valdivia is a published author and passionate gardener living among the trees and birds surrounding a little house located in Idaho, United States of America. This is where she lives and makes a living with her husband. **Jan. 25, Jan. 26**

Ellen Porteza Valenciano writes from Mugonero Adventist Hospital in Rwanda, where she works as a physician. She and her husband, Harville, have been missionaries to Zambia, South Sudan, and Kenya. She is actively involved in the health and music ministry. She enjoys playing the piano and organ, traveling, and collecting coins and stamps. **Nov. 26**

Olivia D. Valentine is a medical student at Montemorelos University, Mexico. She enjoys socializing, listening to good music, lively debates, and making her parents proud. **May 28, Aug. 31**

Yvita Antonette Villalona Bacchus, graphic designer, works in the music department of her local church in the Dominican Republic. She is grateful for the opportunity to bless and be blessed through devotionals. **Jan. 5**

Cora A. Walker resides in Atlanta, Georgia, United States of America. She is a retired nurse, editor, and freelance writer. She enjoys reading, writing, sewing, swimming, classical music, traveling, and spending quality time with her family. **June 14**

Anna May Radke Waters is a retired administrative secretary at Columbia Adventist Academy. She and her husband of sixty-nine years are now living in College Place, Washington, United States of America, where they enjoy their family, near and far away. **Mar. 21, June 11, Oct. 28**

Noni Weidemann is a wife, mother, grandmother, banjo player, and nurse practitioner living in Central California, United States of America. She and her husband, Russ, have a large, blended family. They enjoy landscaping, gardening, sharing healthy lifestyle pointers and products, and serving others wherever they can help and bring comfort. **Jan. 30, Jan. 31**

Lyn Welk-Sandy lives in Adelaide, South Australia. She has worked as a grief counselor and spent many years as a pipe organist. She loves church music, choir work, and playing the hand chimes. She enjoys nature, photography, and caravaning around outback Australia with her husband, Keith, serving where needed. She is mother of four, grandmother of nine, and great-grandmother of five. **Feb. 12, Mar. 27**

Avonda White-Krause is a wife, mother, grandmother, and great-grandmother to fifteen children. She loves family, friends, going to church, reading, computers, gardening, and traveling. She is a retired special education teacher. **May 13**

Kimasha P. Williams is currently working as a communication professional in London, England, and is involved in youth ministries at church. She loves sharing her personal testimonies with family and friends and really enjoys writing. **Mar. 19, Sept. 13**

LaKeisha Williams resides in Huntsville, Alabama, United States of America, with her husband, Toussaint, and two teenage sons. They enjoy spending time together, including taking long walks with their dog, playing games on a quiet evening, or joining in an impromptu singing concert. She and Toussaint share a personal ministry called 90 Degree Ministries. More information is available at 90degreeministries.com. **Jan. 21**

Wendy Williams lives in Idaho, United States of America. Her favorite pastimes are writing, photography, traveling, hiking with her husband, and eating the world's supply of chocolate. **Sept. 14, Dec. 29**

Rachel Williams-Smith, PhD, EdD, is a wife, mother, writer, and speaker. She has a bachelor's degree in language arts, a master's degree in professional writing, and a doctorate in communication. She is a dean at Southern Adventist University, in Collegedale, Tennessee, United States of America. Her devotional is adapted from her biography, *Born Yesterday*. **Oct. 13**

Dalores Broome Winget is a retired elementary teacher living in Warwick, Pennsylvania, United States of America, with her husband of fifty-one years, Richard. This much-published writer has two married children and two grandchildren. She is a Sabbath School Kindergarten teacher. She enjoys being with family, reading, and traveling. **Jan. 16**

Melanie Carter Winkler is married to a wonderful man; they are both involved in Pathfinders. She uses most of her spare time writing and has self-published a novel, *Rosewood* (available at https://www.smashwords.com/books/view/181138). **July 3**

Cyndi Woods is a mom of two and wife to a wonderful, God-fearing man for twenty years. She is a blogger and writer and has written articles for the Disability Network for over a year. Her heart is in ministry and leading others to know Jesus. She is also blind. Visit her on her blog Around the Table at CyndiWoods.com. **Mar. 20, June 13**

Yan Siew Ghiang lives in Singapore. She has been helping to care for her mother for more than six years. She loves to read, write, and do indoor exercises. **Sept. 30**